MW01154229

Theology and Tolkien

Theology and Tolkien

Constructive Theology

Edited by
Douglas Estes

LEXINGTON BOOKS/FORTRESS ACADEMIC
Lanham • Boulder • New York • London

Published by Lexington Books/Fortress Academic
Lexington Books is an imprint of The Rowman & Littlefield Publishing Group, Inc.
4501 Forbes Boulevard, Suite 200, Lanham, Maryland 20706
www.rowman.com

86-90 Paul Street, London EC2A 4NE, United Kingdom

British Library Cataloguing in Publication Information Available

Library of Congress Cataloging-in-Publication Data

Names: Estes, Douglas, editor.
Title: Theology and Tolkien: constructive theology / edited by Douglas Estes.
Description: Lanham: Lexington Books/Fortress Academic, 2024. | Includes
  bibliographical references and index. | Summary: "J.R.R. Tolkien's fantasy epics are
  imbued with a deep sense of the spiritual from which readers discern aspects of his
  beliefs about God, life, good, and evil. In this book, an international group of scholars
  explore and build on numerous theological ideas that percolate through Tolkien's
  works"—Provided by publisher.
Identifiers: LCCN 2024022866 (print) | LCCN 2024022867 (ebook) | ISBN
  9781978712638 (cloth) | ISBN 9781978712645 (epub)
Subjects: LCSH: Tolkien, J. R. R. (John Ronald Reuel), 1892–1973—Criticism and
  interpretation. | Theology in literature. | LCGFT: Literary criticism.
Classification: LCC PR6039.O32 Z8348 2024 (print) | LCC PR6039.O32 (ebook) | DDC
  823/.912—dc23/eng/20240520
LC record available at https://lccn.loc.gov/2024022866
LC ebook record available at https://lccn.loc.gov/2024022867

Contents

Figures and Tables

FIGURES

TABLES

Abbreviations

ACW	Ancient Christian Writers
AJEC	Ancient Judaism and Early Christianity
ANE	Ancient Near East
APCT	Aris & Phillips Classical Texts
BBR	*Bulletin for Biblical Research*
BCLC	Blackwell Companions to Literature and Culture
BMCI	Bloom's Modern Critical Interpretations
BMCV	Bloom's Modern Critical Views
BSac	*Bibliotheca Sacra*
BZAW	Beihefte zur Zeitschrift für die alttestamentliche Wissenschaft
CD	*Church Dogmatics*
CESFF	Critical Explorations in Science Fiction and Fantasy
CSCD	Cambridge Studies in Christian Doctrine
CSEL	Corpus Scriptorum Ecclesiasticorum Latinorum
CSSFF	Contributions to the Study of Science Fiction and Fantasy
CWS	Classics of Western Spirituality
DSD	*Dead Sea Discoveries*
EGS	The Étienne Gilson Series
EvQ	*Evangelical Quarterly*
FAT	Forschungen zum Alten Testament
FC	Fathers of the Church
FR	*The Fellowship of the Ring*
FTL	Figurative Thought and Language
HeyJ	*Heythrop Journal*
HME	The History of Middle-earth
HTR	*Harvard Theological Review*
IJPT	*International Journal of Philosophy and Theology*
IJST	*International Journal of Systematic Theology*

JFA	*Journal of the Fantastic in the Arts*
JRS	*Journal of Religion and Society*
JSCE	*Journal of the Society of Christian Ethics*
JSP	*Journal for the Study of the Pseudepigrapha*
JTR	*Journal of Tolkien Research*
JTS	*Journal of Theological Studies*
Lays	*The Lays of Beleriand*
LBS	Linguistic Biblical Studies
LCL	Loeb Classical Library
LCS	Literary Companion Series
Letters	*The Letters of J.R.R. Tolkien*
LHBOTS	The Library of Hebrew Bible/Old Testament Studies
LNTS	Library of New Testament Studies
Lost Road	*The Lost Road and Other Writings*
LOTR	*The Lord of the Rings*
LSFTS	Liverpool Science Fiction Texts and Studies
LT 1	*The Book of Lost Tales, Part One*
LT 2	*The Book of Lost Tales, Part Two*
LXX	Septuagint
MFS	*Modern Fiction Studies*
Monsters	*The Monsters and the Critics and Other Essays*
Morgoth	*Morgoth's Ring*
Nature	*The Nature of Middle-earth*
NICOT	New International Commentary on the Old Testament
NMA	The New Middle Ages
OECS	Oxford Early Christian Studies
OFS	*Tolkien On Fairy-stories*
OTE	*Old Testament Essays*
PCP	Pop Culture and Philosophy
Peoples	*The Peoples of Middle-earth*
PTMS	Princeton Theological Monograph Series
RIPL	Routledge Interdisciplinary Perspectives on Literature
RK	*Return of the King*
RO	Radical Orthodoxy
RSMRC	Routledge Studies in Medieval Religion and Culture
Sauron	*Sauron Defeated*
Silmarillion	*The Silmarillion*
TL	*Tree and Leaf*
TS	*Tolkien Studies*
TT	*The Two Towers*

TynBul	*Tyndale Bulletin*
UT	*Unfinished Tales of Númenor and Middle-earth*
VC	*Vigiliae Christianae*
VTSup	Supplements to Vetus Testamentum
WSA	Works of Saint Augustine
WSCL	*Wisconsin Studies in Contemporary Literature*

Introduction

Douglas Estes

Plato famously remarked that "fantasy novels are not to be taken seriously or treated as a serious undertaking with some kind of hold on the truth, but that anyone who is anxious about the constitution within him must be careful when he reads them."[1] Of course, Plato never mentioned fantasy novels *per se*; the word he used is ποίησις ("*poiēsis*"), a hard-to-translate concept that we often gloss as *poetry* because "it pertains not only to the content of the discourse, but also to its form."[2] From this Plato linked ποιητής ("*poiētes*"), the teller and sometimes maker of *poiēsis*, with μῦθολογος ("*mȳthologos*"), the teller and sometimes maker of myth, μῦθολογία ("*mȳthologia*").[3] Although Plato wasn't the first philosopher to question the epistemological qualities of poetry and myth, he is the first Greek writer to use the word *mȳthologia* (and related), and also the first to liken most myths and much poetry to what we today call "fiction" in English.[4]

One could say that poetry and myth have never recovered from Plato's dismissal. "Nonfiction poetry" and "nonfiction myth" are not genres one would expect to find in a literary anthology or bookshop. Nor for that matter, "nonfiction fantasy" nor "nonfiction science fiction." But Tolkien's works *are* fantasy, at least as we use the term today. It is also true that Tolkien's works are a kind of *poiēsis*, if for no other reason than they are created stories and betray a sense of melody and rhythm in their Westron and Elvish. His works are certainly also *mȳthologia*, in that they purport to tell tales of a mythical past. Yet, when we read them, they feel true, unfeigned. Part of this is undoubtedly Tolkien's skill as a writer—or better, a creator of a world, a Middle-earth, with people, languages, and history. Part of it, though, is Tolkien's unique view and application of *mythopoeia*—"myth-making,"[5] but in Tolkien's mind, the word indicates "a process of *retelling* the world," as "only through stories can we recover the cosmological sense of this world,"

1

where we come from and why we are here.[6] It is through this process that people can find truth, not as a flood of unadulterated light, but as "refracted Light," derived from a singular source, white and pure, and from this singular source it diffuses its message:

> to many hues, and endlessly combined
> in living shapes that move from mind to mind. (*OFS*, 65)

Readers of *The Lord of the Rings* and Tolkien's other works understand intuitively that his fairy-stories contain truth, even if it is a splintered hue. Unlike most, Tolkien believed that fairy-stories, myths, and poetry often contain truth, even if that truth was not readily accepted (or acceptable) (*Letters*, 147). The most obvious example of this is the Christian Gospels, which are truth yet "contain a fairy-story" (*TL*, 71). We could say that *The Lord of the Rings* is the inverse of this, as it is a fairy-story that contains truth. Even though Tolkien only makes this implicit for his readers, *The Lord of the Rings* is a fairy-story whose theme is "Death and Immortality" (*Letters*, 186), and whose central conflict is "about God, and His sole right to divine Honour" (*Letters*, 183). This, on the face of it, seems an incredible claim—God is never mentioned in *The Hobbit* or *The Lord of the Rings*, and only fleetingly in the appendices, *The Silmarillion*, and the legendarium. No mention of God in Jackson's films, either.

This was on purpose, as Tolkien wrote and rewrote every part many times over, and he considered every factor (*Letters*, 131). With purpose and precision, God is at the center of the story, but also, nowhere to be seen, hidden from view.

The Lord of the Rings is the Esther of the Inklings—but even the story of Esther can teach us a great deal about God. Esther *has* a theology, even if it is not always explicit, nor easy to understand, nor universally accepted. If there is one thing learned from the history of the interpretation of Esther, it is that "unreflective" interpretations are common and try to discover the missing God within the story.[7] This is also true of the history of Tolkien interpretation—a temptation by readers to find God in all sorts of places, some heavy handed, some nuanced. Yet, like Esther, truth about God *is* present in Tolkien's works, and as we read Tolkien, we are able to discern his theology of the divine, even as it is set in a "fantasy" mode. We can very much accomplish this because "to think theologically is not to think of [the Incarnation], but to think by means of [the Incarnation]."[8] Thus, we can absorb God and divine truth through our reading of *The Lord of the Rings* by means of God's work of revelation in the Primary World. Not only this, but Tolkien's work is also highly applicable to the working out of theology, not only in our thoughts but also our lives.[9]

In this book, we have set out to explore currents in Tolkien's theology, as well as ancillary works, endeavoring to add to a preliminary framework for understanding his theology: essays on areas such as theology proper, creation, angelology, sin and evil, virtue and love, theological ethics, and eschatology. It is for these reasons that we consider this work to be one of *constructive theology*. In employing this concept, "constructive theology is a reminder that all of our theological ideas are also constructed—none of them fell straight from heaven without passing through the sieves of human interpretation, languages, wonderment."[10] This seems especially important with the study of Tolkien; there really are no explicit theological statements within his oeuvre that one can simply take and run with. Therefore, we must build the scaffolding to peer over the edge of the wall between our world and Middle-earth and into the truth that Tolkien has so carefully embedded within his fairy-story, intently using "a distinctive form of Christian theology that does not separate heavenly concerns from worldly ones."[11]

In this volume, the fifteen international contributors engage Tolkien's (and Jackson's) works in a way that tries to build on the elements of Tolkien's theological thoughts. We did not limit the scope of this project only to Tolkien's works, but included his popular interpreters in art and film. This is because so many people read Tolkien through Peter Jackson's eyes (among others, such as John Howe and Alan Lee). In part one, *Aman*, the five essays by Broadhead, Milbank, Freeman, Estes, and Trimm explore the blessed realm of God and his creation. In part two, *Erebor*, the five essays by Coutras, Stovell, Novaes, Torres, and Barboza, Shaeffer, and Rios dig into the depths of theological meaning that color readings. In part three, *Ithilien*, the five essays by Brown, Loveland Swanstrom, Juričková, McDowell, and Williams sit uneasily between the good of the divine and the world that we occupy. Two key motivations animate these essays: faithfulness to Christian theology and faithfulness to Tolkien's works. For the latter, this even includes areas of spelling (e.g., Ring instead of ring) and style (e.g., Men instead of people).[12]

***

In chapter 1, *Bradley K. Broadhead* reflects on what musical improvisation can reveal to us about Tolkien's creation myth in the *Ainulindalë*, especially in the type of relationship Ilúvatar has with the Ainur. Broadhead notes the differences between improvisation and composition, and emphasizes the freedom of will that the Ainur enjoy as a result of Ilúvatar's improvising creativity. Even as Melkor introduces discord into the Great Music, Ilúvatar reacts at first with benevolence and improvises further, hoping to bring Melkor's dissonance into harmony; when Melkor refuses Ilúvatar's overture, Ilúvatar brings creation to completion in his own sovereign way. This speaks to Tolkien's own theology, one where God works with the dissonance of his creation, turns evil into good, yet maintains his provident authority.

In chapter 2, *Alison Milbank* argues that since there are discontinuities between the creation accounts in the legendarium and the biblical texts, these discontinuities reverberate through any correlation with Christian theology, especially as relates to the origin of evil and the atonement. Middle-earth is a world marred, and—as a result of the actions of Melkor—this marring is universal in nature, and thus, any atonement must also be universal in nature. Milbank notes that 'to mar' is to damage a creation, such as a work of art, or the natural world. Thus, redemption occurs through the restoration of Middle-earth, and Elves and Men take on priestly, rather than lordship, roles in the world. When this occurs, the Great Music is reharmonized and restored, and Arda remade.

In chapter 3, *Austin M. Freeman* examines three points of concern in Tolkien's theology that revolve around Tolkien's understanding of evil, human agency, and divine Providence. Freeman cautions that readers cannot approach Tolkien's theology directly through his fiction, as if these were always representative of what he *really* believed about these issues; instead, readers must discern views that are instantiated within his fictional world—a fictional world that stands in the place of a mythic past to our own world. The first concern is whether Tolkien's reimagining of the fall in the "Tale of Adanel" is unfair to Men. The second concern is whether readers can truly conclude that death can be a gift from a benevolent God. The third concern is whether readers can and should view Ilúvatar as lacking in omniscience and immutability. Together these point to potential discontinuities between biblical and Tolkienian theology, and suggest areas for future dialogue.

In chapter 4, *Douglas Estes* suggests the reason so many readers experience the divine when reading *The Lord of the Rings*—even though God is never mentioned—is because Tolkien's theological tendencies are apophatic. Apophatic, or negative theology, is an approach to God that emphasizes what one cannot say about God, due to his incredible transcendence, thereby clearing away the limits of reason and language to experience God directly. Tolkien's philological studies as well as his familial, literary, and theological background steered him toward an apophatic orientation to theology. Estes marshals examples of Tolkien's apophatic tendencies from Tolkien's letters, Faramir's doxology in the *LOTR*, and his creation accounts in the *Silmarillion* and legendarium. He discovers that Tolkien hides God from his readers to avoid inadvertent theological error and to heighten God's magnificence.

In chapter 5, *Charlie Trimm* investigates the angelology of Middle-earth, with primary emphasis on the Maiar (including the Istari and the Balrogs), and with an eye to how readers can reimagine their own understanding of angels in the contemporary world. Trimm shows there are several continuities (such as their ability to fall into evil and their great power to help people) and several discontinuities (such as their connection to a bodily form and their ability to die) that readers must consider between the biblical concept of angels and the Maiar in the legendarium. These continuities and discontinuities, when applied to biblical angels, can spur the reader to think about angels—their nature and mission—in innovative ways.

In chapter 6, *Lisa Coutras* explores the richness of the dual influences of Germanic mythological imagery and Catholic devotion on Tolkien's female characters. Focusing on Galadriel, Coutras examines the ways in which this character reflects both a Marian archetype and a Valkyrie motif. She finds that Tolkien's prime characterization of Galadriel was as a warrior with ambition, but that with the character's growth from the *Silmarillion* to *The Lord of the Rings*, Galadriel renounces her ambition in order to embrace a deeper Marian humility. Thus, the reader encounters glimpses of Tolkien's deeply-held theology in the life of one of his greatest characters, Galadriel.

In chapter 7, *Beth M. Stovell* studies the metaphors of light and darkness in Tolkien's work using modern theories of conceptual metaphor. As a case study, Stovell scrutinizes the phial of Galadriel—which contains the light of Eärendil's star—in the story of the attack of Shelob on Frodo and Sam. To do this she teases out the significance of Eärendil and his star in both the legendarium and Tolkien's personal life. This she contrasts with the imagery of darkness that Sam and Frodo encounter in Shelob's lair. With Tolkien's conceptual metaphors of light and darkness in mind, Stovell then compares these with biblical metaphors for light and darkness, finding that Tolkien's metaphors mesh closely with biblical metaphors, especially those found in Genesis and echoed in the Gospel of John. Tolkien's use of light and darkness metaphors reflect not merely a deep theology, but Christology, as light overcomes the darkness.

In chapter 8, *Allan M. de Novaes, Milton L. Torres*, and *João Fernando O. Barboza* apply the typology of H. Richard Niebuhr to assess Tolkien's use of both Northern European (pagan) and biblical symbolism in his creation story. To do this, Novaes, Torres and Barboza distill the theological binomials that underlie Niebuhr's typology rather than attempting to apply Niebuhr's categories directly. From this they identify three different attitudes of Tolkien scholars toward Tolkien's symbolism: more pagan than Christian, Christian but also pagan, and inherently Christian. Their analysis reveals that Tolkien scholars' view of Tolkien's symbolism often originates from their prior philosophical and literary commitments.

In chapter 9, *Adam B. Shaeffer* considers how Tolkien depicts the growth of spiritual perception within his characters, a perception that illuminates the material and immaterial aspects of Middle-earth. With a nod to the work of Hans Urs von Balthasar, Shaeffer demonstrates that as characters grow in virtue, and are ennobled in their endeavors, that they are able to perceive greater spiritual realities such as the movement of Providence as well as truths about the workings of the world and the motives of others. With a primary focus on the development of the Hobbits, especially Sam, Shaeffer recognizes Tolkien's spiritual-corporeal theological commitments and suggests *The Lord of the Rings* may stimulate readers into their own growth in spiritual perception.

In chapter 10, *Jeremy M. Rios* looks at the metanarrative backgrounds of Tolkien's *The Lord of the Rings* and Jackson's film trilogy. He argues that while Tolkien's works contain a consciously sub-created metanarrative that innately criticizes modern culture, Jackson's film versions shift toward a metanarrative that reflects culture. After detailing recent philosophical discussion of metanarrative, Rios points out that one of the most compelling features for contemporary readers of the *LOTR* is its metanarrative—a surprising situation, since the *LOTR*'s metanarrative has displaced other metanarratives within Western cultural conscious, including the Christian faith. The cultural shifts in metanarrative are displayed in how the *LOTR* is presented to modern audiences, and these cultural accommodations of Middle-earth stories weaken the force of Tolkien's original critical-of-culture metanarrative.

In chapter 11, *Devin Brown* critiques the tendency by critics to perceive the plot of *The Hobbit* and *The Lord of the Rings* as too contrived, too lucky for the protagonists. Against these critics, Brown examines Tolkien's narrativity for instances and evidences of divine Providence at work behind the scenes of the story. As the superb storyteller that he is, Tolkien's skill is such that Providence is not found in anomalous occurrences but woven into the fabric of the greater story. Brown suggests that this prompts the reader to consider the role of free will in both Middle-earth as well as our own world.

In chapter 12, *Julie Loveland Swanstrom* encourages viewers of Jackson's films to see the elevated love story of Arwen and Aragorn as the highest example of the redemptive power of love in these films. Loveland Swanstrom notes that while readers often remark on the importance of platonic love in Tolkien's works, Jackson's films flesh out the importance of romantic love that is implicit in Tolkien. Looking to Augustine's theology of love, she explains how Arwen inverts the Augustinian Edenic fall with Arwen's salvific love for Aragorn. At the heart of Augustine's theology is his belief about the love of Father and Son through the Spirit; similarly, this love draws people to God, having the power to redeem them and unify them with God. Loveland Swanstrom discovers that Arwen is an anti-Eve, in that Arwen's labor for Aragorn, and her emptying herself for him, redeems him and inspires him to fulfill his providential destiny.

In chapter 13, *Martina Juričková* analyzes diligence (virtue) and sloth (vice) in the lives of Tolkien's characters as a way to unpack the contemporary debate on whether the moral distinctions of Tolkien's characters are two-dimensional, black and white, or not. To assist in this analysis, Juričková reviews the theologies of virtue and vice in several medieval fathers, including Thomas Aquinas and Evagrius of Pontus. She begins with the vice of sloth, noting examples of it throughout Tolkien's primary works in its physical manifestation, in *acedia*, in disbelief, in superstition, and in fear, depression, and despair. Next, she turns to the virtue of diligence, searching for examples of it in curiosity, in hope, in Providence, and in joy. Juričková observes how Tolkien's rich theology undergirds the moral sensibilities of his characters—sensibilities that are three-dimensional and often pass unnoticed in black and white treatments of good and evil in Tolkien's work.

In chapter 14, *John C. McDowell* considers how evil functions in Tolkien's *LOTR* as well as Jackson's films. He observes five ways that Tolkien's view of evil is essentially Augustinian: evil is not eternal, it is not something, it misshapes when it occurs, it is against the wellness of people, and it precludes a clean resolution. Tolkien's works do not try to make sense of evil, or justify it; instead, they challenge the reader to consider practices for resisting evil. McDowell also considers the role of violence in Tolkien and Jackson, especially as it relates to trivializing the death of orcs—something that Jackson furthers for cinematic effect. This challenges us theologically to consider how we should resist evil in the world while remaining faithful to our divine calling.

In chapter 15, *Donald T. Williams* turns to a relatively unexplored area of Tolkien's theology—his eschatology, or his view on how the story of the world ends. Tolkien wrote feigned history, with a celebrated beginning, much like the biblical history of our own world. Since the ending of our world's story is found in its beginning, Williams postulates that readers also find Tolkien's ending in his beginning. Starting with a contrast of Hebraic and polytheistic Ancient Near Eastern creation stories, he observes that Hebraic (and later Christian) senses of time are driven by *telos*, Providence, purpose. Williams argues that we find this same *telos*, Providence, and purpose in Tolkien's narrative, and that experiencing it there can rejuvenate our own hope in the Final Chord of the Great Music in the Primary World.

***

Finally, we express our appreciation to all of those involved in making this book a reality. Much thanks and gratefulness go especially to Gayla Freeman, former associate editor, Megan White, acquisitions editor, as well as Neil Elliott, the former senior acquisitions editor at Lexington Books/Fortress Press who believed in the vision for this project. We also thank the rest of the team at Lexington/Fortress who had a hand in producing this book. We also are very gratified for permission to use the amazing artwork of Matthew Stewart, who inspired us with his visuals of the world of Tolkien, and whose work *The Scroll of Isildur* graces the cover of this volume. Each of us as contributors express thanks to our families and friends who encouraged us during the writing, editing, and production of this volume. As editor, I would like to thank all of the contributors who participated, all for a love of Middle-earth. I dedicate my part of the effort to my wife, Noël; my children, Wyatt, Bridget, Violet, Everett; and my mom and patron, Nadine. As Tolkien himself read and believed, "we þæs þonc magon secgan sige-dryhtne symle bi gewyrhtum þæs þe he hine sylfne us sendan wolde."[13]

NOTES

1. Plato, *Republic*, 608a (Grube).

2. Luc Brisson, *Plato the Mythmaker*, trans. Gerard Naddaf (Chicago: University of Chicago Press, 1998), 148.

3. Brisson, *Plato the Mythmaker*, 35, 148.

4. Jan N. Bremmer, "Myth, Mythology, and Mythography," in *The Oxford Handbook of Hellenic Studies*, ed. George Boys-Stones, Barbara Graziosi, and Phiroze Vasunia (Oxford: Oxford University Press, 2009), 684.

5. Laurence Coupe, *Myth*, New Critical Idiom (London: Routledge, 1997), 18.

6. Eduardo Segura and Guillermo Peris, "Tolkien as Philo-Logist," in *Reconsidering Tolkien*, ed. Thomas Honegger, Cormarë 8 (Zurich: Walking Tree, 2005), 36; for further discussion, see Kirstin Johnson, "Tolkien's Mythopoesis," in *Tree of Tales: Tolkien, Literature, and Theology*, ed. Trevor Hart and Ivan Khovacs (Waco: Baylor University Press, 2007), 26–31.

7. Jo Carruthers, *Esther: Through the Centuries*, Blackwell Bible Commentaries (Malden: Blackwell, 2008), 22.

8. Vladimir Lossky, *Orthodox Theology: An Introduction*, trans. Ian and Ihita Kesarcodi-Watson (Crestwood, NY: St. Vladimir's Seminary Press, 1978), 18.

9. Douglas Estes, introduction to *Theology and Tolkien: Practical Theology* (Lanham: Lexington / Fortress, 2023), 1–4.

10. Laurel C. Schneider and Stephen G. Ray, Jr., eds., *Awake to the Moment: An Introduction to Theology* (Louisville: WJK, 2016), 38.

11. Schneider and Ray, *Awake to the Moment*, 12.

12. In style, spelling, and citation, we followed Tolkien wherever possible and, for later works, relied on the *Tolkien Society Stylesheet*.

13. From the poem "Christ" by Cynewulf that sparked Tolkien's 'Ēarendel moment'—"Wherefore we must ever, dutifully, say thanks unto the Lord triumphant that He was willing to send to us Himself," Cynewulf, "Christ," 127–29 (Gollancz).

BIBLIOGRAPHY

Bremmer, Jan N. "Myth, Mythology, and Mythography." Pages 678–86 in *The Oxford Handbook of Hellenic Studies*. Edited by George Boys-Stones, Barbara Graziosi, and Phiroze Vasunia. Oxford: Oxford University Press, 2009.

Brisson, Luc. *Plato the Mythmaker*. Translated by Gerard Naddaf. Chicago: University of Chicago Press, 1998.

Carruthers, Jo. *Esther: Through the Centuries*. Blackwell Bible Commentaries. Malden: Blackwell, 2008.

Coupe, Laurence. *Myth*. New Critical Idiom. London: Routledge, 1997.

Estes, Douglas, ed. *Theology and Tolkien: Practical Theology*. Lanham: Lexington / Fortress, 2023.

Gollancz, Israel, ed. *The Exeter Book: An Anthology of Anglo-Saxon Poetry*. Part I. London: Early English Text Society, 1895.

Johnson, Kirstin. "Tolkien's Mythopoesis." Pages 25–38 in *Tree of Tales: Tolkien, Literature, and Theology*. Edited by Trevor Hart and Ivan Khovacs. Waco: Baylor University Press, 2007.

Lossky, Vladimir. *Orthodox Theology: An Introduction*. Translated by Ian and Ihita Kesarcodi-Watson. Crestwood, NY: St. Vladimir's Seminary Press, 1978.

Schneider, Laurel C., and Stephen G. Ray, Jr., eds. *Awake to the Moment: An Introduction to Theology*. Louisville: WJK, 2016.

Segura, Eduardo, and Guillermo Peris. "Tolkien as Philo-Logist." Pages 31–44 in *Reconsidering Tolkien*. Edited by Thomas Honegger. Cormarë 8. Zurich: Walking Tree, 2005.

Tolley, Clive. "Tolkien's 'Essay on Man': A Look at *Mythopoeia*." Pages 43–60 in *A Hidden Presence: The Catholic Imagination of J.R.R. Tolkien*. Edited by Ian Boyd and Stratford Caldecott. South Orange, NJ: Chesterton Press, 2003.

PART I

Aman

Chapter 1

Freedom and Fidelity

Improvisation in the Ainulindalë

Bradley K. Broadhead

Tolkien aficionados periodically return (or, at least, ought to return) to the *Ainulindalë* for insight into J.R.R. Tolkien's legendarium. To know and understand the creation story of a given culture is to know and understand much of what that culture values and how it perceives itself. Similarly, the *Ainulindalë* provides us with insights into the values and perceptions of its author. My objective is not to use the *Ainulindalë* to delve into Tolkien's psychology (something he would undoubtedly have frowned upon),[1] but rather to examine the theology of his creation narrative (something he may have tolerated).[2]

Rather than setting out yet another summary or exposition of the *Ainulindalë*,[3] I focus on the role of musical improvisation in it.[4] Musical improvisation is central to Tolkien's creation myth: it sets up the relationship between Ilúvatar and the Ainur, it describes how Ilúvatar himself responds to the insubordination of one of the Ainur, and it sets the parameters for how the Ainur interact with one another. These relationships and interactions touch on agency, freedom within constraints, and the problem of evil. A closer look at musical improvisation will yield a deeper understanding of the theological themes of the *Ainulindalë* and, indeed, the whole of Tolkien's corpus relating to Middle-earth.

IMPROVISATION

Before embarking on this quest, I must acknowledge that the word 'improvisation' is completely absent from the *Ainulindalë*. Is it then an accurate term for describing what is going on in the text or would another word better describe the music-making taking place? According to Bruce Ellis Benson, "The problem with improvisation is that it does not fit very neatly into the schema that we normally use to think about music making—that is, the binary opposition of composition and performance."[5] He goes on to helpfully disambiguate improvisation from performance by suggesting that we do not "think of performance as being *wholly* repetitive"—that is, a performer is free to take limited liberties with a musical composition—"yet we do take it as being *essentially* a kind of repetition in a way that improvisation is not."[6]

Even though in the *Ainulindalë* Tolkien compares "the voices of the Ainur" to "harps and lutes, and pipes and trumpets, and viols and organs, and like unto countless choirs singing with words" (*Silmarillion*, 15), which sounds much like a full orchestra with a choir, the Ainur are not analogous to musicians and singers performing an orchestral work. Ilúvatar does not hand out sheet music for a grand composition and then conduct it himself. Melkor's rebellion and Ilúvatar's response are not *performed* according to a script. The music described in the *Ainulindalë* also fails to meet the criteria of a *composition*, at least in the Western tradition. If the Ainur are not simply performers of Ilúvatar's composition, neither do they carefully compose and notate their own parts in advance of the Great Music. Igor Stravinsky writes of composed work, "the work offered to the public, whatever its value may be, is always the fruit of study, reasoning, and calculation that imply exactly the converse of improvisation."[7] So what exactly is improvisation?

Musical improvisation involves more than performance because the person improvising is not tied down to a written score. Yet it also differs from composition because it must occur in 'real time.' In fact, improvisation lies on a spectrum between performance and composition. Jeremy Begbie writes, "in improvisation, conception and performance are interwoven to a very high degree, certainly to a greater extent than in music which involves an extended period of shaping material prior to performance."[8] The result is that "the stress will be on process rather than product, activity rather than result."[9] To illustrate this principle from another domain, it is one thing to read a carefully polished book or journal article and another to feel the frisson of a live debate between two Tolkien experts with differing opinions on whether or not Balrogs have wings.

The nature of musical improvisation is shaped by constraints. According to Begbie, "Constraints relevant to improvisation may be divided into three broad and overlapping types: 'occasional,' 'cultural' and 'continuous.'"[10] Begbie defines occasional constraints as "the unique circumstances which are specific to a social, spatial or temporal situation."[11] The occasional constraints that bind the participants in the Great Music include the Void—the setting for the music, Ilúvatar and the Ainur, and their dispositions—their mood and outlook toward the music.[12] "Cultural constraints," in Begbie's taxonomy, "are frameworks and patterns of action brought to an improvisation by the improvisers and listeners, constraints which have developed from interaction with others."[13] Before the "mighty theme" that becomes the precursor to the Great Music, Ilúvatar propounds "to them themes of music" (*Silmarillion*, 15). The Ainur sing in response to these themes, but only as soloists or in small ensembles while the rest listen. It appears that they are learning the "frameworks and patterns" that will enable them to participate in the Great Music. Then, of course, there is the "mighty theme" itself, which forms the basis for the Great Music, perhaps in a way analogous to the role of a cantus firmus in counterpoint or a chord progression in jazz.[14] Finally, continuous constraints encompass the mediums that allow persons to be in relation to one another. In the case of Ilúvatar and the Ainur, this involves a logical sequence if not a literal passage of time.[15] It also entails some sort of sonic order, which is necessary for tones to relate to one another in different ways.

We now have enough for a working definition of musical improvisation: *To enact the freedom to alter and elaborate upon given musical materials in relation to various constraints in the moment the music is being played.* The improviser is not limited to re-presenting a series of interlocking pitches and rhythms determined in advance but is able to alter and elaborate upon given materials in relation to his or her internal disposition, what other improvisers are doing, and cultural conventions that have been worked out over time. The constraints necessary for musical improvisation are present in the *Ainulindalë*, but what of the freedom to alter the music in relation to these constraints?

Drawing on Hans-Georg Gadamer, Benson writes, "In order for a genuine dialogue to take place, the outcome cannot be settled in advance. Without at least some 'loose-play' or uncertainty, true conversation is impossible."[16] In order for the Ainur to be truly improvising with one another and with Ilúvatar, the direction of the musical dialogue or interplay must be left open rather than predetermined. As we have already seen, the Great Music certainly does involve preparation beforehand, but this preparation does not entail Ilúvatar as a solitary composer meticulously determining everything in advance. Rather, the Ainur sing and listen to one another in order to come "to deeper understanding" and to increase "in unison and harmony" (*Silmarillion*, 15). They create "frameworks and patterns" for future interaction, the cultural constraints necessary for musical improvisation. As the narrative of the *Ainulindalë* progresses, the Ainur involved in the Great Music exercise their freedom to adorn, or even attempt to counter, the theme Ilúvatar has given them.

Secondary literature on the *Ainulindalë* seems to take it for granted that the Great Music is improvised,[17] so perhaps I have been a bit Hobbit-like up to this point, filling a book with things already known by my readers, and "set out fair and square with no contradictions" (*FR*, Prologue, 1). I hope to justify this excursion with the theological yield it will produce when applied to exercising creaturely freedom in relation to divine intention, to Ilúvatar as a responsive/improvising character, and to navigating the constraint of others.

CREATURELY FREEDOM AND DIVINE INTENTION

To understand the nature of the freedom Ilúvatar grants to the Ainur as well as its abuse by Melkor, we need to understand something of his directions to them and his relationship with them. We need to understand Ilúvatar's intentions as a composer. Ilúvatar's relationship with the Ainur bears some similarities to a composer's relationship with the one performing or improvising on their work. First, there is a clear distinction between Ilúvatar and the Ainur and between Ilúvatar and the Great Music. Even though the Ainur are said to be "the offspring of his thought," they are nonetheless "made" by him (*Silmarillion*, 15).[18] Tolkien does not adopt a Platonic emanationist model of creation,[19] nor does he liken the Ainur to Athena springing from the head of Zeus. Like the God of biblical Christianity, Ilúvatar possesses aseity;[20] his existence is not dependent on creation or any other external factor.[21] He does not create the Ainur and allow them to participate in further creation (what Tolkien terms 'sub-creation') out of necessity, but freely. Unlike Ilúvatar, the existence of the Ainur is contingent and their music is possible only within the bounds of the abilities and constraints given by Ilúvatar. With this sketch of Ilúvatar's relationship with the Ainur in place, we can move on to his directions to them.

Randall Dipert helpfully divides a composer's intentions into "*low-level intentions*," dealing with matters such as instrumentation, special fingerings for certain notes and the like, "*middle-level intentions*," which "concern the intended *sound*, such as temperament, timbre, attack, pitch, and vibrato," and "*high-level intentions* which are the effects that the composer intends to produce in the listener."[22] Ilúvatar gives a summary of his intentions for the Great Music in the opening paragraphs of the *Ainulindalë*: "'Of the theme that I have declared to you, I will now that ye make in harmony together a Great Music. . . . ye shall show forth your powers in adorning this theme, each with his own thoughts and devices, if he will. But I will sit and hearken, and be glad that through you great beauty has been wakened into song'" (*Silmarillion*, 15). Ilúvatar sets out something analogous to instrumentation in his decision to create individual Ainur, reflecting his low-level intentions.

The theme he propounds to them is a sketch of his middle-level intentions. As a musical theme, Ainur may presumably elaborate upon it, transpose it, use it in retrograde, harmonize it, or develop it in any other number of ways, but should not set it aside or ignore it. Tolkien gives no indication that details such as timbre, attack, or vibrato are laid out, leaving a great deal of space for interpretation. Ilúvatar's high-level intention is that the music be beautiful. The harmony between the Ainur combined with the particular contributions of each individual should create this beauty. Harmony in the musical sense has to do with different notes sounding simultaneously to produce chords and chord progressions; applied to interactions between beings, it means that the actions they take accord with one another. The "powers" and unique "thoughts and devices" of each point to how Ilúvatar values the distinct contribution of each. They have the freedom to be what they have been uniquely created to be, much like the various body parts in Paul's metaphor of the Body of Christ (1 Cor 12). But improvisation delighting in cacophony lies outside of Ilúvatar's intentions. If we view Ilúvatar as a composer, he has much more in common with George Gershwin than Stravinsky.[23]

Before proceeding any further, we should note that Tolkien claims to "have little musical knowledge." He writes, "Music gives me great pleasure and sometimes inspiration, but I remain in the position in reverse of one who likes to read or hear poetry but knows little of its technique or tradition, or of linguistic structure" (*Letters*, 260). It would be unwise, then, to press the musical terms he uses too far. But then again, other selections from his letters suggest we need not consider him entirely musically illiterate.[24] If we take the musical terms he uses in their commonly understood, rather than technical senses, we should stay true to his authorial intentions. That caveat out of the way, we can now turn to how the Ainur respond to Ilúvatar's constraints.

In spite of the considerable freedom Ilúvatar grants to the Ainur, one of them in particular chafes against the given constraints. The fall of Melkor is the founding tragedy of *The Silmarillion*; all the suffering in Middle-earth can be traced back, at least in part, to his rebellion.[25] The seeds of his rebellion are found in his attitude toward the constraints of the Great Music. Tracing his journey from the preparation for the Great Music to the Music itself offers an opportunity to explore the boundary between rightful and wrongful use of creaturely freedom.

The *Ainulindalë* introduces us to Melkor after the Great Music has already begun. For a while, his participation—along with that of the other Ainur—pleases Ilúvatar, but then, "it came into the heart of Melkor to interweave matters of his own imagining that were not in accord with the theme of Ilúvatar; for he sought therein to increase the power and glory of the part assigned to himself" (*Silmarillion*, 16). The narrative also reveals Melkor's impatience with Ilúvatar's process of creation and his isolation from his fellows as, prior to the Great Music, he seeks for the Imperishable Flame that he believes will allow him to create in the same way Ilúvatar does. When his imaginings come to fruition in the Great Music, the result is that some of those close to him flounder because of the discord between his music and the music his fellows are improvising in keeping with Ilúvatar's theme. Others "attune their music to his rather than to the thought which they had at first" (*Silmarillion*, 16). It is telling that when his music attains to a unity, it is monophonic rather than polyphonic: "it had little harmony, but rather a clamorous unison as of many trumpets braying upon a few notes" (*Silmarillion*, 17).[26] Furthermore, it does not develop its theme, but repeats its notes "endlessly." Instead of being able to integrate the contributions of others, it demands strict conformity. Instead of seeking to complement the Great Music, "it essayed to drown [it] by the violence of its voice" (*Silmarillion*, 17).

Melkor refuses the constraints of Ilúvatar's theme, refuses the constraints of the contributions of his fellows (harmony), and tries to refuse the underlying constraint of being a created, contingent being. The only constraint he does abide by is asserting his own personality (though even this is at the expense of the expression of others). At the root of his refusals is his pride; like Esau, he despises the gifts he has been given (Gen 25:29–34). It is not enough that he was created with "the greatest gifts of power and knowledge, and he had a share in all the gifts of his brethren"; he wants to write his own 'great theme' (*Silmarillion*, 16). But unlike Ilúvatar, Melkor does not seek to give others freedom and agency; rather, he seeks to impose his own vision on others. This is why his music is repetitive, monophonic, and tries to drown out other voices by force. In fact, one might say that he tries to seize the power of a composer in the Western sense of the word, the power they have to insist that the notes they write be the notes that are performed. As Stravinsky writes in *The Poetics of Music*, "Conductors, singers, pianists, all virtuosos should know or recall that the first condition that must be fulfilled by anyone who aspires to the imposing title of interpreter, is that he be first of all a flawless executant."[27] Similarly, those who follow Melkor do not harmonize with or embellish his theme, but simply play it in unison, over and over again. I am not saying that composed music in the Western tradition is inherently wrong or tyrannical in and of itself. Certainly, great composers have enriched the Western musical tradition and Western culture in general. I simply wish to point out that Ilúvatar's Great Music has space for improvisation, for creaturely agency and creativity, while Melkor's does not.

Melkor's rejection of the creative agency of his fellows is reflected in his solitary musings that set him apart from his fellows, who listen attentively to one another while forming the traditions and conventions necessary to successfully improvise upon Ilúvatar's theme. An inward approach to composition is not foreign to certain Western composers. Chelle Stearns offers a

critique of the philosophy of unity championed and put into practice by twentieth century composer Arnold Schoenberg in her book, *Handling Dissonance*.
Likening Schoenberg to Melkor seems perhaps unduly harsh (and I certainly
would not wish to analogously lay all the ills of contemporary music on
his doorstep), but I do wish to draw upon her insight into the problematic
nature of Schoenberg's philosophy with respect to composition.[28] According
to Stearns, "In Schoenberg's philosophy, the primary purpose of all music is
to express the interior self, which is the expression of the composer's idea.
No other goal exists. Nothing is outside of that vision."[29] Stearns shows how
Schoenberg's idea of unity negates particularity. From such a vantage point,
nothing is really gained by listening to the particularity of other voices since
music is an expression of the final, undifferentiated unity that underlies reality. Melkor's music is similarly drawn from interior reflection rather than in
dialogue with his peers. Like Schoenberg, he wishes to make a contribution
of his own apart from and independent of the contributions of others.[30]

Although it appears in the *Quenta Silmarillion*, the story of Aulë's attempt
at forming creatures of his own has significant similarities and differences to
Melkor's desire to create music of his own. Aulë, another prominent Ainur,
forms creatures in imitation of what he understands of the coming children of
Ilúvatar. These creatures are the Dwarves. He undertakes this project alone,
notably apart from his spouse, Yavanna, because he is afraid that she and the
other Valar might disagree with his undertaking. Ilúvatar upbraids him, pointing out that Aulë has overreached in trying to create creatures with their own
being; that is Ilúvatar's provenance alone. Yet unlike Melkor, Aulë responds
with humility, acknowledging his error. Ilúvatar graciously gives the Dwarves
agency of their own and makes a place for them in his plans, even though he
knows the strife that will eventually rise between the Dwarves and the Elves.
Aulë's actions are born in part from fear and impatience, but also in part from
a desire to imitate Ilúvatar's work. Even though he does not fulfill Ilúvatar's
intentions perfectly, Ilúvatar accepts his contribution and gives it an independent existence. If he had responded with humility, Melkor could have been
redeemed and blessed as Aulë was, but alas, it was not to be. We turn next to
the question of whether and how Ilúvatar improvises with the Ainur.

ILÚVATAR GIVES GIFTS

The initial "mighty theme" Ilúvatar propounds to the Ainur is not the only
theme of the Great Music. When Melkor introduces music that does not
accord with Ilúvatar's theme, Ilúvatar responds to the resulting musical war
by introducing a second theme, "like and yet unlike to the former theme, and

it gathered power and had new beauty" (*Silmarillion*, 16). The curious thing is that Ilúvatar smiles when he introduces his second theme. Cami Agan writes,

> Eru reminds Melkor gently of the value of process, integration, and moving towards the other; his smile and his left hand suggest a willingness to reconsider, to offer a new theme, a new potentiality for Melkor and the Ainur. Eru humbles himself, as it were, to accommodate Melkor's will into the choric harmony, or he allows for the possibility that from this challenge (margin) might come further creation (harmony).[31]

The fact that Ilúvatar raises his left hand when he smiles and his right hand when he appears stern supports her reading. One's right hand is typically the dominant hand, representing strength and assertiveness; it seems plausible that, for Tolkien, the left hand combined with a smile might symbolize openness and acceptance.

As Keith Jensen observes, "In itself, Ilúvatar's patience and his willingness to incorporate Melkor's dissonance into the Divine Theme seems oddly discomfiting."[32] Given the disruptive effects of Melkor's music, which include silencing some and dominating others, one almost expects divine judgment on the spot. Jensen goes on to show how Ilúvatar's sovereignty is maintained throughout, but before we explore Eru's sovereignty, it may be instructive to delve deeper into his willingness to uphold the free agency of his creatures, even when it results in dissonance. Begbie's work on gift giving in the context of musical improvisation provides a promising way of analyzing how and why Ilúvatar responds to Melkor in the Great Music as he does.

Drawing on John Milbank and others, Begbie notes that giving, receiving, and returning are essential aspects of the human condition. In fact, "a good gift usually is aimed at receiving something back, even if only the pleasure that we have sought to benefit another."[33] In his reading of Milbank, "*gratuity* can characterize gift, provided, first, that there is a *delay* of return, a delay of unpredictable, indeterminate duration—to give a return gift straightaway implies the discharge of some kind of debt—and second, that there is a relation of '*non-identical repetition*' between gift and counter-gift—the counter-gift cannot be the same object (without insult)."[34] Applied to the *Ainulindalë*, Ilúvatar provides the 'givens'—the gifts of the constraints he gives to the Ainur. Melkor has perhaps fallen short of what Ilúvatar might hope for in a return, but Ilúvatar nonetheless accepts Melkor's music as a return gift and gives back a new theme. Note that he delays in his return gift and that his gift does not mimic Melkor's nor does it merely repeat his initial gift. Drawing insights from improvisatory theatre, Begbie writes of 'overaccepting' a gift, that is, making the most of what another has given to you rather than an overemphasis on what you are giving.[35] Note how even in providing constraints for the Ainur, Ilúvatar humbly asks for the unique contribution of each and anticipates the beauty of their 'return.' Yet, as Begbie cautions,

> The gift to be received is not necessarily regarded as totally good, or wholly to be affirmed. (And there may be rare cases when the gift does need to be rejected outright for the sake of good improvisation; although even this is only after it has been considered carefully.) Neither does 'overacceptance' imply total passivity, dissolving the initiative entirely on to others. Rather it means being willing to treat the gift as fundamentally something from which fruit can come, as an inherently valuable constraint ('as interesting as possible') from which a novelty (a counter-gift) can be generated which is consistent with the 'story' of the drama, and which in turn will provoke further novelty, and so on.[36]

Using the terminology of improvised theatre, Melkor 'blocks' Ilúvatar's gifts by refusing to engage with them. If Ilúvatar benevolently gave Melkor the benefit of the doubt when Melkor first introduced "matters of his own imagining" into the music, his refusal of Ilúvatar's gift and ongoing hostility toward it lays bare his insolent rebellion for all to see. Ilúvatar's "stern countenance" and uplifted right hand at his introduction of the third theme are certainly justified. However, instead of drowning out Melkor's contribution, as offensive as it is, Ilúvatar chooses instead to subvert it, weaving Melkor's music into something deeper.

The way jazz musicians reharmonize popular tunes provides an illustration of how harmony can subvert the way a listener hears a given melody. For example, if a given melody contains the notes C, E, and G, the obvious chord to play under it is a C major triad. However, depending on the harmonic context, one could also play an A minor seventh. Changing the harmony supporting the melody from major to minor alters the effect of the melody on the listener. C, E, and G sound consonant and stable on top of a C major triad, but they have a different relationship to an A minor seventh. Something like this effect is perhaps what Tolkien has in mind when he writes of Melkor's music in relation to Ilúvatar's third theme, "it seemed that its most triumphant notes were taken by the other and woven into its own solemn pattern" (*Silmarillion*, 17). As Trevor Hart observes, "it is by a superior artistry that is, as it were, able to redeem disharmony rather than overwhelm it that Ilúvatar triumphs."[37]

Evidently, Ilúvatar changes in his initial orientation to the music. At first, he was content with the way his theme was unfolding in the capable hands of the Ainur. He was in a similar relation to his music as Gershwin listening to pianist Art Tatum improvise on his work.[38] However, when Melkor transgresses Ilúvatar's intentions as a composer, Ilúvatar does not remain aloof, but actively works to ensure his purposes are not thwarted. Far from being a composer sitting back and evaluating a performance of his music—theologically, one might call such a view of God deistic,[39] Ilúvatar steps into the fray and improvises a response to the discord that does not (yet) bring it to a definitive end. If this were his only response to Melkor's transgression, one might be tempted to think Tolkien's vision of God (as represented by Ilúvatar) might be compatible with the God of process thought or certain varieties of openness theology.[40] Such theological perspectives attempt to resolve the problem of evil by placing limitations on God's power. Yet Tolkien refuses to take the easy way out of limiting God's sovereignty. The Great Music ends on Ilúvatar's terms. While Melkor still struggles for ascendency against Ilúvatar's third theme, "Ilúvatar arose a third time, and his face was terrible to behold. Then he raised up both his hands, and in one chord, deeper than the Abyss, higher than the Firmament, piercing as the light of the eye of Ilúvatar, the Music ceased" (*Silmarillion*, 17). Ilúvatar demonstrates remarkable patience with Melkor's continued rebellion, but it ends here. The Great Music does not founder or simply peter out, nor does Melkor's music have the final word; Ilúvatar takes it upon himself to resolve it. His upraised hands and terrible look signify that this resolution is not merely a conclusion, but a judgment. In other words, while Ilúvatar demonstrates patience and forbearance for a time, he is willing and able to forcefully and decisively resolve discord—to judge evil.[41]

Ilúvatar, then, in accord with God as he is depicted in the Bible, is responsive to the agency of his creatures (e.g., Jas 5:13–18). Not only is he the ultimate origin of all themes and all musics, but he enters into the music himself, as an improviser. Yet he is not among equals. What distinguishes him in terms of his role from the Ainur is his unique powers of originating a theme and bringing the music to a conclusion. Returning to Benson's notion (via Gadamer) that, "In order for a genuine dialogue to take place, the outcome cannot be settled in advance," one might wonder if Ilúvatar has cut off the possibility of such a dialogue by taking its resolution into his own hands. Yet this is not the case. As per Begbie, the emphasis in musical improvisation is by nature on the process rather than the result. The Great Music (as far as the text is concerned) is not thoroughly composed in advance; there is space for the unique contributions of each participant. Furthermore, Ilúvatar's disposition at the final chord is not inevitable; in the event that Melkor had been willing to accept Ilúvatar's gifts instead of blocking them, another form of resolution may have been possible. In other words, to use Tolkien's own terminology, the response of creatures always involves sub-creation; only God can create *ex nihilo*. And God reserves to himself the final resolution of dissonance and the judgment of evil.

CREATURELY INTERACTIONS

We touched on Melkor's attitude toward his fellow Ainur in passing when we contrasted his domineering approach to making music with others to the way Ilúvatar encourages others to express their particularity as they engage with the constraints he gives them. Beyond this observation, Tolkien's account of the Great Music does not dwell much on how the Ainur interact with one another; it is after Ilúvatar shows them the vision of the world that will be that Tolkien names some of the chief Valar—the great among the Ainur who descend into Arda to work out the implications of the Great Music. As the rest of *The Silmarillion* records, they seek to work together to carry out the vision of the music in the world Ilúvatar has brought into being. In the process, the particularities among each of the Valar result in predictable friction between them that must be worked out. Furthermore, Ilúvatar's subversion of Melkor's theme turns up in unexpected places that end up enhancing the ways the Valar interact with one another. Although they are not set forth as a description of music, these interactions among the Valar can also be seen through the light of improvised music.

Ilúvatar's speech to Ulmo provides something of a justification of Ilúvatar's decision to incorporate the music of Melkor rather than overthrowing it:

> Seest thou not how here in this little realm in the Deeps of Time Melkor hath made war upon thy province? He hath bethought him of bitter cold immoderate, and yet hath not destroyed the beauty of thy fountains, nor of thy clear pools. Behold the snow, and the cunning work of frost! Melkor hath devised heat and fire without restraint, and hath not dried up thy desire nor utterly quelled the music of the sea. Behold rather the height and glory of the clouds, and the everchanging mists; and listen to the fall of rain upon the Earth! And in these clouds thou art drawn nearer to Manwë, thy friend, whom thou lovest. (*Silmarillion*, 19)

Melkor's brash, noisy music parallels his excesses in cold and heat. Yet Ilúvatar's subversion of this music ends up enhancing the domains of Ulmo and Manwë, mingling them in unforeseen ways. Joseph's summation of God's Providence working through the treacherous acts of his brothers is apropos here: "Even though you intended to do harm to me, God intended it for good" (Gen 50:20a NRSV).

Above I briefly mentioned the similarities and differences between Melkor's rebellion and Aulë's impatient making of the Dwarves. Returning to Aulë, his solitary effort in making the Dwarves also has repercussions for his relationship with his spouse Yavanna. It spurs Yavanna to bring quieter voices in the Great Music to the attention of Manwë. When Aulë finally confesses what he has done to Yavanna, she tells him, "Yet because thou hiddest this thought from me until its achievement, thy children will have little love for the things of my love" (*Silmarillion*, 45). Aulë points out that the children of Ilúvatar (Elves and Men) will also use the things that grow upon the earth for various purposes. He expresses hope that, according to the purpose of Ilúvatar, they will use these things with respect and gratefulness. However, this does not placate Yavanna and she goes to inquire of Manwë, the king of the Valar. She believes the trees in particular should have someone to speak on their behalf, pointing out that, "it was in the Song" (*Silmarillion*, 45). After listening to Yavanna, Manwë recalls the song in a vision, "and he heeded now many things therein that though he had heard them he had not heeded before" (*Silmarillion*, 46). He then speaks a word from Ilúvatar to Yavanna, "Do then any of the Valar suppose that I did not hear the Song, even the least sound of the least voice?" (*Silmarillion*, 46). Yavanna is assured that growing things will have some defense; the Shepherds of the Trees (also known as the Ents) will speak and act on their behalf.

Much can be drawn from the story of Aulë and Yavanna, but I wish to focus in on two related ideas: the first is the limitations of individual understanding and creativity, the second is the value in attending to less prominent voices. Aulë's decision to hide his making of the Dwarves from the Valar and Yavanna, his own spouse, in particular, has consequences. Tolkien writes, "Aulë made the Dwarves even as they still are, because the forms of the Children who were to come were unclear to his mind" (*Silmarillion*, 43). Combined with the insight from the appendices of *The Return of the King* that dwarf-women "are in voice and appearance . . . so like to the dwarf-men that the eyes and ears of other peoples cannot tell them apart" (*RK*, Appendix A, III), it appears that one of the effects of Aulë's impatience and unwillingness to let others share in his making is that dwarf-women lack the feminine beauty of the natural children of Ilúvatar. This is as instructive as it is entertaining. Alone, without the aid of others to enhance or correct it, Aulë's vision of the Children of Ilúvatar is incomplete. In other words, his biases, preunderstandings, and personality cloud his perception and understanding. Without the input of others, his making is limited to the range of his own strengths and hindered by his own weaknesses.

By contrast, Yavanna's encounter with Manwë shows the value of attending to quieter voices. Although Manwë had heard the Great Music he (unlike Ilúvatar) had not given all of it his full attention. As a result, he misses the role of the Ents in the music until Yavanna points it out to him. In *The Lord of the Rings*, the Ents play a key role in the demise of the traitor Saruman, freeing up the Rohirrim to prevent the fall of Gondor, and helping to hold the gaze of the Dark Lord Sauron so that he fails to notice two small hobbits. In the history of Middle-earth, it is those who seem of little account who change the course of history. As Paul writes to the church in Corinth, "But God chose what is foolish in the world to shame the wise; God chose what is weak in the world to shame the strong" (1 Cor 1:27). Theologically, Tolkien shows us that God often works through those the world overlooks.

Because Ilúvatar does not override the making of Aulë and because Manwë heeded Yavanna, the tension resulting from Aulë's willfulness is resolved (at least in part). In *The Lord of the Rings* Gimli the Dwarf encounters Treebeard the Ent. Treebeard is suspicious, showing that the tension between Dwarves and trees prophesied by Yavanna has been woven into the history of Middle-earth, but through Legolas's advocacy, they are reconciled. In the denouement of the destruction of the Ring, Treebeard permits Gimli and Legolas to "visit the deep places of the Entwood" (*RK*, 6, vi).

THEOLOGICAL YIELD

Tolkien intended Middle-earth as a fictive ancient history of our own world.[42] As such, what he says about God, good, and evil should resonate with the real world. Yet, as Verlyn Flieger points out, "Tolkien was writing fiction, not theology."[43] Readers attempting to work out Tolkien's underlying theology must keep in mind that Tolkien's writings are not intended to mirror the real world in every respect. Furthermore, if they are not careful, they may end up simply reading into his work what they wish to see, emphasizing certain elements while downplaying others. I trust that I have not done violence to Tolkien's authorial intent in my reading of his work. If I have erred, I trust I have done it in the spirit of Aulë rather than Melkor.

If Ilúvatar does in fact reflect of Tolkien's view of God, then we can draw some tentative conclusions on Tolkien's view of Providence on the basis of how he governs and interacts with the beings he creates. As we have seen, Ilúvatar simultaneously upholds the freedom of created beings and asserts his own sovereignty. Created beings like Melkor are free (for a time) to rebel.[44] Ilúvatar knowingly allows Melkor to reject his intended role in the Great Music and to coerce some into joining his cause and to silence others. This is not because Ilúvatar is impotent or unable to stop Melkor but because through Melkor he will work a greater good. Nonetheless, he does not simply stand aside and let Melkor have his own way. Instead, he works through those who listen to him to subvert Melkor's rebellion without destroying or negating Melkor's music. As the author of *The Epistle to Diognetus* writes, reflecting on God's nature and incarnation, "compulsion is no attribute of God."[45] In Tolkien's view, for the most part, God actively works through the agency of his creatures to realize his creation and the course of history. Yet as Ilúvatar determines the point of resolution for the Great Music, so God

reserves to himself the completion of history and the final judgment on what
his creatures have accomplished through their agency.[46] In short, Tolkien's
view of Providence is neither meticulous, nor wholly open. God has and
exercises the right to intervene directly (e.g., *Akallabêth*),[47] to work through
those who align themselves with him, and reserves to himself the conclusion
and judgment of all things.

Tied up in Tolkien's view of Providence is his view of the origin and
nature of evil and his accompanying theodicy.[48] Tolkien is no dualist; evil
does not originate in Ilúvatar, nor is it coeternal with him. Rather, Melkor's
refusal of Ilúvatar's gifts, his rejection of his nature as a created being, and
his domination of others warps and twists the good of Ilúvatar's creation.
And yet Ilúvatar works through his rebellion and in spite of it. The position that free will as an intrinsic good that outweighs its abuse combined
with the ability of God to bring good out of intended evil forms a classic
Christian theodicy that countless theologians have written variations on or
have rejected for one reason or another.[49] It is consistent with the overarching
teaching of the Bible, which insists that God works through sin and suffering
to accomplish his purposes.[50] In addition, a reader encounters the goodness
and beauty of Middle-earth not only in the idyllic situations found in the Shire
and Rivendell, but in the way the undeniable darkness of its history serves
to throw this beauty and goodness into relief. Just as Sam takes comfort in
seeing a star shining in the darkness of night in Mordor (*RK*, VI, ii), so acts
of courage, compassion, and constructive creativity stand out against the
perversion and pollution of the dark powers and the treachery of those who
collude with them.

Although Tolkien has no obvious parallel to the Church or to ecclesiol-
ogy in Middle-earth, the interaction of the Ainur before and during the Great
Music and the story of Aulë and Yavanna carried down through to Gimli's
encounter with Treebeard carry with them ecclesiological applicability. Here
we find Tolkien's acknowledgment of the limitations of individuals (something he also works out beautifully outside of Middle-earth in his short story,
Leaf by Niggle). Pride, impatience, and an unwillingness to allow others
to enter into our work have consequences, even if they can be redeemed.
On the other hand, attuning carefully to quieter voices can result in a fuller
appreciation of God's gifts to others and a fuller understanding of his will and
purpose, just as Manwë discovered by listening to Yavanna. Just as the great
and the small alike play essential roles in the history of Middle-earth, so the
great and small play essential roles in God's Church.

Musical improvisation runs through and ties together the themes of
Providence, theodicy, and the right use of creaturely freedom in Middle-earth.
This gives us some (tentative) insight into Tolkien's theology, but its useful-
ness does not end here. If we find these themes and their interconnectedness

via the Great Music to be at all compelling, we have good reason to re-imagine these themes and their interconnectedness in Christian theology and practice.

NOTES

1. Tolkien writes, "I object to the contemporary trend in criticism, with its excessive interest in the details of the lives of authors and artists. They only distract attention from an author's works (if the works are in fact worthy of attention), and end, as one now often sees, in becoming the main interest" (*Letters*, 213).

2. Tolkien writes concerning *The Lord of the Rings* it "is of course a fundamentally religious and Catholic work" (*Letters*, 142).

3. See for example, John Carswell, *Tolkien's Overture: Concerning the Music of the Ainur* (Franklin, TN: True Myths, 2018), Randel Helms, *Tolkien and the Silmarils* (Boston: Houghton Mifflin, 1981), and Paul H. Kocher, *A Reader's Guide to the Silmarillion* (Boston: Houghton Mifflin, 1980).

4. Chiara Bertoglio also looks at improvisation in the *Ainulindalë*, but she focuses on polyphony in the Middle Ages while I am more concerned with the philosophy of improvisation. See Chiara Bertoglio, "Polyphony, Collective Improvisation, and the Gift of Creation," in *Music in Tolkien's Work and Beyond*, ed. Julian Eilmann and Friedhelm Schneidewind, Cormarë 39 (Zurich: Walking Tree, 2019), 3–28.

5. Bruce Ellis Benson, *The Improvisation of Musical Dialogue: A Phenomenology of Music* (New York: Cambridge University Press, 2003), 24.

6. Benson, *Improvisation*, 24.

7. Igor Stravinsky, *Poetics of Music in the Form of Six Lessons*, trans. Arthur Knodel and Ingolf Dahl (Cambridge: Harvard University Press, 1970), 132; cf. Benson, *Improvisation*, 25.

8. Jeremy S. Begbie, *Theology, Music and Time*, CSCD 4 (Cambridge: Cambridge University Press, 2000), 184.

9. Begbie, *Theology*, 184.

10. Begbie, *Theology*, 200.

11. Begbie, *Theology*, 201.

12. Cf. Begbie, *Theology*, 205.

13. Begbie, *Theology*, 201.

14. See Bertoglio, "Polyphony," 15.

15. As John Carswell notes, "We are ultimately dealing in things of mystery, matters incomprehensible according to normal sensory and intellectual perception," in *Tolkien's Overture: Concerning the Music of the Ainur* (Franklin, TN: True Myths, 2018), 11.

16. Benson, *Improvisation*, 15.

17. For example, Cami Agan writes of an "improvisatory concert of the Ainur," in "Hearkening to the Other: A Certeauvian Reading of the *Ainulindalë*," *Mythlore* 34.1 (2015): 124; Robert A. Collins describes Ilúvatar as a "composer/director" who "allows each musician room to improvise," in "'Ainulindalë': Tolkien's Commitment

to an Aesthetic Ontology," *JFA* 11 (2001): 257; and Stratford Caldecott similarly describes the Great Music as "an improvisation" in "A New Light: Tolkien's Philosophy of Creation in *The Silmarillion*," *Journal of Inklings Studies* 4.2 (2014): 78.

18. In the earlier version of the *Ainulindalë* found in *The Book of Lost Tales, Part One* ("The Music of the Ainur"), Ilúvatar actually sings the Ainur into existence (52).

19. See Michael John Halsall, *Creation and Beauty in Tolkien's Catholic Vision: A Study in the Influence of Neoplatonism in J.R.R. Tolkien's Philosophy of Life as "Being and Gift"* (Eugene: Pickwick, 2020), 54–55.

20. For a defense of biblical aseity, see William Lane Craig, *God Over All: Divine Aseity and the Challenge of Platonism* (Oxford: Oxford University Press, 2016); plus cf. Ps 90; Isa 40:21–28, 43:10–13; John 1:1–2; Acts 17:24–28; and Col 1:15–17. For a challenge to divine aseity, see Sallie McFague, *Models of God: Theology for an Ecological, Nuclear Age* (Philadelphia: Fortress Press, 1987).

21. In a related vein, Tolkien makes it clear that Ilúvatar is not "bound by the Theme, nor by the *Ainulindalë* (as made by the Ainur), [so] it would be rash to assert that He is or will be bound by Eä realized; since he is outside Eä but holds the whole of Eä in thought (by which it coheres)" (*Nature*, 289).

22. Randall R. Dipert, "The Composer's Intentions: An Examination of Their Relevance for Performance," *Musical Quarterly* 66.2 (1980): 206–7.

23. See below for a contrast between the feelings of each composer toward improvisation.

24. For examples of Tolkien's familiarity with, and appreciation for, music, see *Letters*, 167 and his passing reference to Beethoven in *Letters*, 213.

25. In the abandoned story, *A New Shadow*, the character Borlas says, "The evils of the world were not at first in the great Theme, but entered with the discords of Melkor" (*Peoples*, 413).

26. Cf. Chiara Bertoglio, *Musical Scores and the Eternal Present: Theology, Time, and Tolkien* (Eugene: Pickwick, 2021). She writes concerning Melkor, "his willingness to adjust his tune to those of the others decreases progressively as he starts to weave an accompanied monody, a soloistic melody to which the others play a musical background" (121).

27. Stravinsky, *Poetics*, 127.

28. For another comparison between Schoenberg and Melkor, see Reuven Naveh, "Tonality, Atonality and the *Ainulindalë*" in *Music in Middle-earth*, ed. Heidi Steimel and Friedhelm Schneidewind, Cormarë 20 (Zurich: Walking Tree, 2010), 36–43. Naveh is interested in the parallels between dissonance and evil. He writes, "Whereas Ilúvatar represents the traditional conception of tonality, Melkor himself probably represents the challenge to this conception in the early twentieth century, when some composers abandoned tonality in favor of its diametric opposite, atonality" (40).

29. Chelle L. Stearns, *Handling Dissonance: A Musical Theological Aesthetic of Unity*, PTMS 239 (Eugene: Pickwick, 2019), 171.

30. See Stearns, *Dissonance*, 152–53.

31. Agan, "Hearkening," 126. It is interesting to note that "The Music of the Ainur" in *LT* says that Ilúvatar "smiles sadly" at the beginning of the second theme and

weeps at the beginning of the third (54). However, since Ilúvatar's disposition at the beginning of the third theme differs markedly between "The Music of the Ainur" and the *Ainulindalë* (weeping versus a stern countenance), it seems unlikely the former version can be used as a reliable guide to what Tolkien intends to convey regarding the second theme in the latter.

32. Keith W. Jensen, "Dissonance in the Divine Theme: The Issue of Free Will in Tolkien's *Silmarillion*," in *Middle-earth Minstrel: Essays on Music in Tolkien*, ed. Bradford Lee Eden (Jefferson, NC: McFarland, 2010), 105.

33. Begbie, *Theology*, 248.

34. Begbie, *Theology*, 248.

35. Begbie, *Theology*, 250–51.

36. Begbie, *Theology*, 250–51.

37. Trevor Hart, "Tolkien, Creation, and Creativity," in *Tree of Tales: Tolkien, Literature, and Theology*, ed. Trevor Hart and Ivan Khovacs (Waco: Baylor University Press, 2007), 47.

38. Oscar Levant recalls that George Gershwin was delighted by jazz pianist Art Tatum's improvisation on his song "Liza." Oscar Levant, *A Smattering of Ignorance* (Garden City, NY: Doubleday, 1942), 196.

39. Thomas Paine, *The Age of Reason* (London: Eaton, 1794), is a classic work on deism.

40. See for example, Ann Pederson, *God, Creation, and all that Jazz: A Process of Composition and Improvisation* (St. Louis: Chalice, 2001) for a creative combination of insights from improvised music and process theology and Thomas Jay Oord, *The Uncontrolling Love of God: An Open and Relational Account of Providence* (Downers Grove: InterVarsity, 2015) for a take on openness theology in which God is incapable of acting independently of cooperative agents in his creation due to his loving nature. In my view, Oord's limits on God's ability to intervene in his creation contradict what the Bible teaches about God's sovereignty (e.g., Ps 115:3) and makes biblical eschatology implausible.

41. Bertoglio is less sure of the meaning of this chord, which she suggests is "probably left purposefully open by the author" ("Polyphony," 5). She takes the view that this chord "demonstrates Ilúvatar's omnipotence" but suggests that "it does not entirely conclude the music, leaving a space open for a future revelation, a new music which will be sung by all creation at the end of times" (6). If we consider the first music, the realization of that music, and then the second music and its realization as movements in an overarching work, I agree with Bertoglio. However, I still maintain that this chord and the judgment it symbolizes are necessary in order for the second music—which is true to the intentions of Ilúvatar—to take place. Cf. Carswell, *Overture*, 32. Caldecott suggests that, "The final great Chord represents the bringing of the world to Judgement through the Incarnation and Passion of Christ," in Caldecott, "A New Light," 72.

42. In *Letters*, 165, Tolkien writes, "'Middle-earth,' by the way, is not a name of a never-never land without relation to the world we live in (like the Mercury of Eddison). It is just a use of Middle English *middle-erde* (or *erthe*), altered from Old English *Middangeard*: the name for the inhabited lands of Men 'between the seas.' And

though I have not attempted to relate the shape of the mountains and land-masses to what geologists may say or surmise about the nearer past, imaginatively this 'history' is supposed to take place in a period of the actual Old World of this planet."

43. Verlyn Flieger, "The Music and the Task: Fate and Free Will in Middle-earth," *TS* 6 (2009): 175.

44. The nature of this freedom, as Flieger points out, is different for Elves and Men. Elves are bound by fate in a way that Men are not. Yet Elves appear to have a degree of freedom with respect to their dispositions even if they cannot escape what is fated to happen to them. See Flieger's discussion in "Music and the Task."

45. Diogn. 7:4; cf. Irenaeus, *Haer.* 4:37,1.

46. Incidentally, the author of *The Epistle to Diognetus* also keeps the final judgment in view (7:6).

47. In a later version of the *Quenta Silmarillion*, Manwë says, "For these 'new things,' manifesting the finger of Ilúvatar, as we say: they may have no past in Arda and be unpredictable before they appear, yet they have thereafter future operations which may be predicted, according to wisdom and knowledge, since they become at once part of Eä, and part of the past of all that followeth" (*Morgoth*, 244).

48. According to John Garth, the *Ainulindalë* "is nothing less than an attempt to justify God's creation of an imperfect world filled with suffering, loss, and grief." John Garth, *Tolkien and the Great War: The Threshold of Middle-earth* (Boston: Harcourt, 2003), 255. Cf. Flieger, "Music and the Task," 176–77.

49. For a contemporary defense of the Christian belief in an omnipotent and perfectly good God, see Alvin Plantinga, *God, Freedom, and Evil* (Grand Rapids: Eerdmans, 1977).

50. See, for example, Gen 50:20, Rom 8:28.

BIBLIOGRAPHY

Agan, Cami. "Hearkening to the Other: A Certeauvian Reading of the *Ainulindalë*." *Mythlore* 34.1 (2015): 117–38.

Begbie, Jeremy S. *Theology, Music and Time*. CSCD 4. Cambridge: Cambridge University Press, 2000.

Benson, Bruce Ellis. *The Improvisation of Musical Dialogue: A Phenomenology of Music*. New York: Cambridge University Press, 2003.

Bertoglio, Chiara. *Musical Scores and the Eternal Present: Theology, Time, and Tolkien*. Eugene: Pickwick, 2021.

———. "Polyphony, Collective Improvisation, and the Gift of Creation." Pages 3–28 in *Music in Tolkien's Work and Beyond*. Edited by Julian Eilmann and Friedhelm Schneidewind. Cormarë 39. Zurich: Walking Tree, 2019.

Caldecott, Stratford. "A New Light: Tolkien's Philosophy of Creation in The Silmarillion." *Journal of Inklings Studies* 4.2 (2014): 67–85.

Carswell, John. *Tolkien's Overture: Concerning the Music of the Ainur*. Franklin, TN: True Myths, 2018.

Collins, Robert A. "'Ainulindalë': Tolkien's Commitment to an Aesthetic Ontology." *JFA* 11 (2001): 257–65.

Craig, William Lane. *God Over All: Divine Aseity and the Challenge of Platonism.* Oxford: Oxford University Press, 2016.

Dipert, Randall R. "The Composer's Intentions: An Examination of Their Relevance for Performance." *Musical Quarterly* 66.2 (1980): 205–18.

Flieger, Verlyn. "The Music and the Task: Fate and Free Will in Middle-earth." *TS* 6 (2009): 151–81.

Garth, John. *Tolkien and the Great War: The Threshold of Middle-earth.* Boston: Harcourt, 2003.

Halsall, Michael John. *Creation and Beauty in Tolkien's Catholic Vision: A Study in the Influence of Neoplatonism in J.R.R. Tolkien's Philosophy of Life as "Being and Gift."* Eugene: Pickwick, 2020.

Hart, Trevor. "Tolkien, Creation, and Creativity." Pages 39–53 in *Tree of Tales: Tolkien, Literature, and Theology.* Edited by Trevor Hart and Ivan Khovacs. Waco: Baylor University Press, 2007.

Helms, Randel. *Tolkien and the Silmarils.* Boston: Houghton Mifflin, 1981.

Jensen, Keith W. "Dissonance in the Divine Theme: The Issue of Free Will in Tolkien's Silmarillion." Pages 102–113 in *Middle-earth Minstrel: Essays on Music in Tolkien.* Edited by Bradford Lee Eden. Jefferson, NC: McFarland, 2010.

Kocher, Paul H. *A Reader's Guide to the Silmarillion.* Boston: Houghton Mifflin, 1980.

Levant, Oscar. *A Smattering of Ignorance.* Garden City, NY: Doubleday, 1942.

McFague, Sallie. *Models of God: Theology for an Ecological, Nuclear Age.* Philadelphia: Fortress Press, 1987.

Naveh, Reuven. "Tonality, Atonality and the *Ainulindalë*." Pages 29–51 in *Music in Middle-earth.* Edited by Heidi Steimel and Friedhelm Schneidewind. Cormarë 20. Zurich: Walking Tree, 2010.

Oord, Thomas Jay. *The Uncontrolling Love of God: An Open and Relational Account of Providence.* Downers Grove: InterVarsity, 2015.

Paine, Thomas. *The Age of Reason.* London: Eaton, 1794.

Pederson, Ann. *God, Creation, and all that Jazz: A Process of Composition and Improvisation.* St. Louis: Chalice, 2001.

Plantinga, Alvin. *God, Freedom, and Evil.* Grand Rapids: Eerdmans, 1977.

Stearns, Chelle L. *Handling Dissonance: A Musical Theological Aesthetic of Unity.* PTMS 239. Eugene: Pickwick, 2019.

Stravinsky, Igor. *Poetics of Music in the Form of Six Lessons. Translated by Arthur Knodel and Ingolf Dahl.* Cambridge: Harvard University Press, 1970.

Chapter 2

"When Things Are in Danger, Someone Must Give Them Up"

Redemption and Ecology in Tolkien's Legendarium

Alison Milbank

Theological accounts of Tolkien's legendarium tend to focus on the *Silmarillion* account of the creation by Ilúvatar and the Ainur, because it allies in interesting ways with a Christian worldview, filling in the pre-story to Genesis rather in the manner of Jewish Midrashic commentary on the Torah, where gaps are supplied with new stories. Even the less obviously biblical co-creative role of the Ainur has antecedents in Dionysius the Areopagite's (ca. 6th century) understanding of the angelic orders and in the creative role of the angels in the poet Dante's (1265–1321) cosmology.[1] Tolkien's understanding of sin and its redemption in his invented world, however, is quite distinct and has been less easily assimilable into a Christian frame of reference, although as long ago as 1967, Barry Gordon discerned a tripartite taxonomy of atoning action in Christ's roles of prophet, priest, and king, which also shaped Philip Ryken's Hansen lectures in 2017.[2] Such accounts pick up undeniable echoes of Christological salvific actions, but they fail to take account of the difference in the relation of creation and fall in the legendarium. For Tolkien parts company with a Judaeo-Christian understanding of the original creation in the role of Melkor, the fallen angelic being akin to Lucifer. His attempt to mar the music of Ilúvatar is taken up into the song that imagines creation, making of it music 'deep and wide and beautiful, but slow and blended with an immeasurable sorrow, from which its beauty chiefly came' (*Silmarillion,* 16–17). His secret thoughts which seek to spoil and dominate are included and transformed to serve the whole vision from the very beginning.[3] As Tolkien wrote in an unsent letter: "in this Myth the rebellion of created free-will precedes the creation of the world (Eä); and Eä has in it, sub-creatively introduced, evil, rebellions, discordant elements of its own nature already when the *Let it Be* was spoken" (*Letters,* 286).

This has significant consequences for an understanding of how far the concept of atonement has a place in the theology of Middle-earth. Although a Christian writer such as Mark Eddy Smith can devote a whole chapter of his *Tolkien's Ordinary Virtues* to atonement, Ralph Wood is far less happy with such language applied to the virtuous actions of Tolkien's protagonists, and Michael Halsall argues that "his mythology reveals no developed messianic theology of atonement."[4] Atonement may be beyond any of the creatures in Middle-earth, but it is properly the action of God, and in that sense, it is fully a part of Tolkien's legendarium. Redemption, in the sense of reconciliation and restoration of a broken relationship, is already built into the original creative act and is not a later response to human sinfulness as in the Incarnation in Christian theology (even if one wants to emphasize that in Christianity, redemption is all a part of God's creative activity). Secondly, this original fallenness and its redemption concerns everything that is made: plants, minerals and creatures, as well as Men and Elves. It is all 'things' which are in danger thus, Tolkien's theology has a potentially ecological dimension.

There are, indeed, suggestions of a universal restoration in the Pauline epistles, especially Colossians 1:19–20: "For in him all the fullness of God was pleased to dwell, and through him God was pleased to reconcile to himself *all things,* whether on earth or in heaven, by making peace through the blood of his cross" (ESV, my italics). "All things" here suggests a universal restitution or *apokatastasis panton* as also does Acts 3:21. There is also a strong awareness of the way in which nature is implicated in our sinfulness and redemption in Romans 8:20–21: "the creation itself will be set free from its bondage to decay and will obtain the freedom of the glory of the children of God. We know that the whole creation has been groaning in labor pains until now" (NIV).

While I agree with those who see no easy messianism in Tolkien's fiction, yet because of the union of creation and redemption, there is a participation in the life or God or Eru for all things, and for those with free will in his creative/ redemptive activity. This essay will argue that Tolkien's legendarium develops this Pauline theology of restoration further, in that he includes rational, free beings among beasts and plants, among those who act in priestly and redemptive fashion on behalf of their genus and species. "Would that trees might speak on behalf of all things that have roots, and punish those that wrong them!" Yavanna the angelic consort of Aulë prays (*Silmarillion,* 45), and this comes to pass, for the trees will so act in *The Lord of the Rings* in their march on Isengard, moved by their shepherds, the Ents. She also refers to the trees singing to Ilúvatar within his original song, so that their active liturgical role is part of the original creation (*Silmarillion, 46*). Tolkien's vision, as with the Ainur, is that of the mystical hierarchy of Dionysius the Areopagite, the sixth-century Christian Platonist, who envisions the created order as a vast pleroma of reciprocity and theurgic raising of the lower by the higher into participation in the Divine life, whether trees or angels. It is also what we would now perceive as ecological, in that each part relies on the others and is affected by them. "All have their worth," urges Yavanna, "and each contributes to the worth of the others" (*Silmarillion, 45*).

Ideas of redemption then, must necessarily be conceived in universal terms in Tolkien and not confined to Elves or Men. Universal also, however, is the marring of this creation from almost the beginning, through Melkor's spite and destruction: "nothing . . . wholly avoids the Shadow upon Arda or is wholly unmarred so as to proceed unhindered on its right courses" (*Morgoth,* 217). Sin is not understood as a single transformative trespass by Adam and Eve, so much as a potential to do wrong, be weakened or put off course by the wrong of others. The etymology of "mar" leads back to a Germanic root and includes ideas of hindering, confusing and troubling as well as disfiguring.

In particular, "marring," the preferred word for evil action in the legendarium, is conceived in relation to making through the idea of spoiling or defacing. Melkor wants to assert his own musical composition and spoil the polyphony or harmony of the other Ainur. His later temptation is a longing "to bring into Being things of his own" (*Silmarillion, 16*), which is also Aulë's desire, leading to the creation of the Dwarves. The difference between them is that Aulë delights in making for its own sake and "the thing made and neither in possession nor in his own mastery" (*Silmarillion, 19*), whereas Melkor wants to make out of envy and hate and to dominate and literally de-face. Ironically, this affects his creativity, so that his negativity produces only mockeries of the ideas of others. In this way, Tolkien intensifies the Augustinian privation theory of evil as parasitic on the good, as he had done, as we have seen, in his original song of creation in which the evil only made the music more beautiful.[5]

Any redemptive activity discernible in the fiction, therefore, will focus aesthetically on the restoration of a marred artwork, which is what the natural world is, seen from its Creator's perspective, and in a renewed attitude to the things that we make. If, as Miklós Vassányi suggests, *The Lord of the Rings* is essentially a narrative of the Fall, this is equally true of *The Silmarillion*, which centers round an artwork; the jewels crafted by Fëanor are so prized by him that he refuses to break them open to obtain the light of Laurelion and Telperion within, which is all that is left after Ungoliant and Melkor have destroyed these trees that lit the world.[6] His refusal leads to war against

Morgoth, who steals the jewels and thereafter to a sundering of elvish relations that has catastrophic consequences.

The actions of Elwing and Eärendil to plead for Elves and Men before the Valar involve their offering of one of the Silmarils to them, and it is decided that Eärendil will bear the jewel in his forehead as he sails the skies bringing light to the world. This is a redemptive act and one which anticipates the quest of the Fellowship of the Ring to restore Sauron's own jewel to its place or origin. The return of the Silmaril, containing the unmarred light of the Two Trees is effectual, in that it is freely restored to the Valar, the original kindlers of the stars. There is restitution and reconciliation of the relationship with the Valar. Sauron's jewel is a more transgressive creation, forged in deception, and its restoration is not up to the heavens but down into the abyss of Sammath Naur, where it was created. Gandalf at the gates of Gondor, similarly sends Sauron's creature, the Black Rider, "back to the abyss prepared for you . . . the nothingness that awaits you" (*RK*, V, iv). Both made thing and corrupted human are unmade.

In this example, we can see how created as well as natural things are central to atonement in Tolkien, for whom as Tom Shippey pointed out, his own vocation as a writer and creator remained at the heart of all his writing: it always has a self-referential element.[7] Indeed, the subject of everything that Tolkien makes, from "Leaf by Niggle" to *Smith of Wootton Major*, including even his drawings of Father Christmas's workshop for his children, is about the theology and ethics of human making and his own sub-creative art of fantasy as a particularly intense form of sub-creation.

It is noticeable how carefully in his essay, *On Fairy-stories*, Tolkien seeks to avoid the taint of idolatry, which the art of fantasy might suggest, being the creation of one's own fictional world. In the King James Bible, "the imagination of their hearts" (Luke 1:51) is the capacity to make conceptions as rivals to the divine creation: it is always presented as idolatrous. This is not only because the maker sets up a rival to God but because he fails, as it remains only a lifeless object:

> Their idols are silver and gold, the work of men's hands.
> They have mouths, but they speak not: eyes have they, but they see not:
> They have ears, but they hear not: noses have they, but they smell not:
> They have hands, but they handle not: feet have they, but they walk not: neither speak they through their throat.
> They that make them are like unto them; so is every one that trusteth in them. (Psalm 115:4–8 KJV)

From early on Melkor seeks to create and "interweave matters of his own imagining" (*Silmarillion*, 16) but can only pervert, although in *Morgoth's Ring* Tolkien suggests that Melkor puts some of his own power into the monsters he breeds, so that they have the capacity for seemingly independent action: "One of the reasons for his self-weakening is that he has given to his 'creatures,' Orcs, Balrogs, etc. *power of recuperation and multiplication.* So that they will gather again without further specific orders" (*Morgoth,* 391). Yet as he makes clear later, any freedom is illusory. In the case of orcs, for example, "their 'talking' was really reeling off 'records' set them by Melkor. Even their rebellious critical words—he knew about them" (*Morgoth,* 410–11). And as verse 8 of the Psalm indicates, those who create such idols become like them, and Sauron, who puts his power into the idolatrous Ring, is brought to nothing with its destruction.

In *On Fairy-stories* Tolkien is anxious to suggest that his own making is the opposite of this self-replication. It is described as an act of liberation:

> Creative fantasy, because it is mainly trying to do something else (make something new), may open your hoard and let all the locked things fly away like cage-birds. The gems all turn into flowers or flames, and you will be warned that all you had (or knew) was dangerous and potent, not really effectively chained, free and wild; no more yours than they were you. (*OFS,* 68)

The mind gives up its imaginings for their transformation into something beyond the self. The use of the word "hoard" suggests a collection of items, like the medieval concept of the memory palace, which can also become the dragon hoard of objects of worth kept for the lust of possession, or like Morgoth's crown, to which he attached the Silmarils. The true sub-creative artist gives things up in a manner that has analogies with Lurianic Kabbalah, where the Creator withdraws to allow things to be. This revision of Kabbalistic mysticism was made in order to better understand the relation of finite and infinite. God, the "Ein Sof" voluntarily limits himself and withdraws (*tzim-tzum*) to make a void into which the light of creation can shine, just as Eru sends the flame imperishable into the void in the *Silmarillion.*[8] Ilúvatar himself seems to behave in this withdrawn fashion, and it appears to be an idea central to Tolkien's purposes in allowing freedom to the words and ideas in one's mind by expressing them.

Tolkien is also faithful here to George MacDonald's highly hedged-about theory of the fantastic imagination, where all invention is a finding, not a creating: "For what are the forms by means of which a man may reveal his thoughts? Are they not those of nature? But although he is created in the closest sympathy with these forms, yet even these forms are not born in his mind."[9] Similarly, in Kabbalah the human adherent seeks for the lost shards of the divine, the shekinah, within the natural world and then reunites them, repairing the world (*tikkun olam*). It is interesting that in the popularizing of kabbalistic ideas among the Hassidim, this repairing and reuniting can be effected directly through the imagination, as the inspired zaddik reclothes the lost sparks in stories, which then have great theurgic power.[10] And this is a redemptive action in Judaism, so that when everyone fully completes the law (including storytelling as a mitzvah) the world will be fully holy and restored to its Creator.[11]

What I am seeking to argue here is that the most central concept of redemption in Tolkien's world is at the meta level, by which his work of writing fantasy is one which frees the world to be itself, revealing its divine source, as the storytelling zaddik does through *tikkun olam*. And as the examples from *On Fairy-stories* make plain, this liberation is primarily of things which we have appropriated and among them leaves of oak, ash and thorn, seeds, sheep, iron, horses, stone, bread and wine (*OFS*, 69). In his insightful study of Tolkien's ecological vision, Liam Campbell denies it any precisely Christian character because "his environmentalism is not consistent with an understanding that humanity has some pre-eminence over nature."[12] One can contest the interpretation of Genesis 1:26 as humankind having pre-eminence in favor of a stewardship model. Yet this list of objects to be set free is significant in its ending with bread and wine, the elements of the Eucharist, and suggests that Tolkien's understanding of the human relation to nature is priestly rather than one of dominance.

I would contend that Tolkien regards the act of storytelling itself in priestly terms, as an offering back of objects to their source in God who created them, anticipating David Jones's essay, "Art and Sacrament," which argues for the sacred nature of all sign-making; for Jones all art is a "re-presenting," a "making over" in the manner of the Mass.[13] In the Eucharist, according to a broadly Catholic understanding, the world is made over and restored to God that he may divinize it, so that reconnected, it lives from him, which is one way of thinking of the Catholic doctrine of transubstantiation, outside its Aristotelian terminology. The bread and wine "remain eschatologically alongside God" attaining to "pure createdness as pure transparency, as pure mediation of the divine" as John Milbank and Catherine Pickstock put it.[14] Jones demonstrates that this sacramental quality adheres to all human actions of meaning, from bowling at cricket to cake-making—and Tolkien has much to say about the latter activity as art in *Smith of Wootton Major*, published in 1967 and therefore capable of having been influenced by Jones's essay. Indeed, in Tolkien's explanation of its symbolism, he gives the story an ecclesial interpretation; the hall is the village church and the cook the priest, so that the feast already has a eucharistic significance.[15] The child who imbibes the fairy star learns a desire for "otherness": the faërie, which is an image itself of the imagination as a divine gift. The star, in fact, stands for that excessiveness that lies in human art and in human desire, which Jones terms gratuitousness. For in another sense the cook is artist as much as priest, who decorates his cake gratuitously with wonderful snowy scenes.

The letting-go, which is such an important feature in *Smith of Wootton Major,* is a sacramental action, part of the action of thanksgiving. For only the Holy Spirit can effect the sanctification of the elements, not the priest. Indeed, priest and people are part of what is offered, which is Christ himself, who called himself "the bread of life" in John 6—In the same way the writer of fantasy offers his imaginative hoard of images to be transformed into "gems or flowers." In Catholic theology, the eucharistic action of presentation of the bread and wine is a sharing in Christ's sacrificial action as in the early church fathers such as Irenaeus: "He took from among creation that which is bread, and gave thanks, saying, 'This is my body.' The cup likewise, which is from among the creation to which we belong, he confessed to be his blood. He taught the new sacrifice of the new covenant."[16] It is interesting that Irenaeus writes: "he took from the creation," which emphasizes the offering of the whole created order through Christ, its Logos or shaper, and in this offering humanity and nature are one. As Christ shapes the world—medieval representations of God with compasses are showing Christ as creator in this sense—so the writer shapes a world, although for him, as Mary Shelley writes in relation to *Frankenstein*, "the materials must, in the first place, be afforded."[17]

Tolkien wrote most movingly in a letter to his son Michael about the Eucharist as at the center of his life:

> Out of the darkness of my life, so much frustrated, I put before you the one great thing to love on earth: the Blessed Sacrament . . . There you will find romance, glory, honour, fidelity, and the true way of all your loves on earth, and more than that: Death: By the divine paradox, that which ends life, and demands the surrender of all, and yet by the taste—or foretaste—of which alone can what you seek in your earthly relationships (love, faithfulness, joy) be maintained, or take on that complexion of reality, of eternal endurance, which every man's heart desires. (*Letters,* 53–4)

The context of the letter is Christian marriage but Tolkien's words about death introduce an idea of sacrifice. It is through offering Christ's death, and by sharing in its self-giving, that we can live and taste eternity in our relationships. There is a necessary ascesis in our human loves just as in our relationship to the natural world.

The Elves in *The Lord of the Rings* represent that artistic sub-creation and those that we encounter, most notably Galadriel, have the ability to give up,

Figure 2.1.   God as Creator of the World.
By unknown, Paris, 2nd quarter of the 13th century

which the earlier Fëanor, creator of the Silmarils, most certainly lacked. It is
the great temptation that haunts the Elves: the wish to fix, to stay the passage
of time and the transience of beauty. When Frodo offers Galadriel the Ring,
awed by her prophetic power and beauty, she can resist: "'I will diminish,
and go into the West'" (*FR*, II, vii), echoing the words of John the Baptist in
John 3:30: "I must decrease." Galadriel follows this act of renunciation by

gift-giving, including light from Eärendil's star, one of the original Silmarils, whose own light came from the Two Trees and her own hair.

Giving up, therefore, is the activity which is most closely allied to artistic making and to eucharistic sacrifice in Tolkien. It is redemptive, although in a manner quite different from substitutionary and penal models that describe the sacrifice of Christ. I have allied it to Jewish Kabbalistic models of redemption as a healing activity and a repairing of relationships with nature as well as with God and each other. This has a Christian iteration in the early Christian *Christus Medicus* idea, which is most famously expressed in the interpretation of the parable of the Good Samaritan, where fallen man is rescued by Christ and healed by the oil and wine of Baptism and the Eucharist.[18] Augustine also addresses God as his 'Physician' in the *Confessions*.[19]

There are, of course, sacrificial actions within *The Lord of the Rings* that we might more nearly compare to Christ's self-offering. Gandalf's sacrifice of himself in battle with the Balrog to allow the Fellowship to escape is one clear example. He breaks the bridge of Khazad-dûm on which he stands to save his companions from destruction and in doing so dies in his incarnate form. He saves the fate of the Fellowship and without his action they would all have been destroyed by the fiery spirit. Moreover, he is then raised, encountered in a wonderfully ambiguous scene in Fangorn Forest, which combines biblical resonances of Mary Magdalene's encounter with Christ in John 21 with the scene of the transfiguration of Christ in the synoptic gospels. Yet Gandalf's sacrifice is a limited action, which allows a further stage of the journey of the Ring to Mordor: it has none of the cosmic significance of Christ's passion, as Tolkien explicitly states (*Letters,* 181). It is part of a text that is not Christian but wishes to be consonant with it, which as we know is why Tolkien removed traces of religious practices. Like the authors of *Beowulf* and the Icelandic *Edda*, both Christians describing a pagan past, Tolkien casts his fictional culture somewhat in the role of a pagan Old Testament ("a monotheistic world of 'natural theology'" (*Letters*, 165)); and therefore he presents antetypes of redemptive activity, which look forward to the Incarnation, and shadow and point to Christ's action.

For if Christ's coming redeems the whole of history as the Creator comes to his world, then all time has the capacity to share in his sacrificial self-offering. As C.S. Lewis writes in the final chapter of *The Great Divorce*, "there is no spirit in prison to whom he did not preach," meaning that Christ's descent into Hell is for all times and people.[20] Similarly, through the priestly sub-creation of Tolkien's art, he can reveal redemptive action operative at all times, rather in the manner of David Jones's poetry in which soldiers in the trenches of World War I participate also as guards at the crucifixion in his war epic, *In Parenthesis* (1937). And Tolkien is careful often to stress that *The Lord of the Rings* is set in our world, although very long ago. So various members of the Fellowship exhibit individual aspects of redemptive activity. This is particularly true of Aragorn, who functions as a type of Christ in the way he anticipates the Advent antiphons, which are sung during the last seven days of the season leading up to Christmas Eve, and which call for the coming of Christ according to various titles and roles.

Aragorn is wisdom, *Sapientia* ("mightily and sweetly ordering all things") in his strategic leadership and *Adonaï* ("Lord") in his rescue of Gondor: "Come and deliver us with outstretched arm," entreats the antiphon, as God rescued the Israelites.[21] Aragorn's descent from the lost line of Isildur enacts the *Radix Jesse,* in which Christ is branch from the root of Jesse, while he is *Oriens* in his name of Elessar: as the one who bears the elf-stone, he represents a star of hope, like Christ the morning star. The sixth antiphon refers to Christ as *Rex Gentium*, which Aragorn will become at the end of the novel, although only an earthly king, albeit one associated with imagery from the book of Revelation, such as the white tree of life in the garden city of Gondor. The final antiphon, *Emmanuel*, God with us, is not realized, since the Incarnation lies far ahead in the history of Middle-earth, although it is antici-pated in the words of Andreth in her debate with the Elf, Finrod in Tolkien's later *Athrabeth Finrod Ah Andreth*: "they say that the One will himself enter into Arda, and heal Men and all the Marring from the beginning to the end" (*Morgoth*, 321). The Advent hope of these words is echoed in the text of *Cryst*, the Anglo-Saxon poem from which Tolkien drew early inspiration for the invention of another world, and which contains some of the Advent "O" antiphons. It was through the image of the morning star, "*O Oriens*," apply-ing primarily to Christ, that Tolkien imagined a Christological type, Earendil, belonging to a different world (*Letters,* 385).[22] It seems very likely, therefore, that Tolkien should reach to typology, and Advent typology in particular, to imagine redemptive activity in *The Lord of the Rings.*

The above list omitted the fourth antiphon, naming Christ as "*Clavis David*," in his lordship over the dead. The full antiphon is as follows:

> O Key of David and sceptre of the House of Israel;
> That openest and no man shutteth;
> And shutest and no man openest:
> Come and bring the prisoner out of the prison house,
> And him that sitteth in darkness and the shadow of death.[23]

Aragorn fulfills this title fully as he descends to the "prison house" of the dead in an anticipation of the harrowing of Hell, when he takes the "Paths of the Dead" to Dunhallow, to call the dead to their oath. Like Hell Dunhallow has a gate like a mouth, a "Dark Door," which "gaped before them like the mouth of night" and "fear flowed from it like a grey vapour" (*RK*, V, ii).

Éowyn plays the role here of Lazarus's sister Mary in John 11 who cannot believe in life beyond the grave, and Aragorn's suicidal choice of the Paths of the Dead, as she sees it, precipitates her own despairing search for death in battle. Christ's descent into the underworld is referred to in 1 Peter 3:19–20: "in which also he went and made a proclamation to the spirits in prison, who in former times did not obey, when God waited patiently in the days of Noah, during the building of the ark" (NRSV). There is the same idea of preaching to the disobedient in Aragorn's calling of the oath-breakers to the black stone of Erech but there the story diverges, as these dead are called to join Aragorn's forces in the coming battle (*RK*, V, ii). There is, however, a suggestion of liberation, both for the oath-breakers, now released from their shadowy half-existence and for Aragorn and the grey company who ride with him, who face the fear of death and overcome it.

I emphasize this incident because overcoming death is so central to the Christian *evangelium*, but in Tolkien's world, death is to be regarded as a gift of the Creator to humankind and not an effect of the Fall, and therefore removing its shadow and fearfulness is the redemptive act. The debate between Andreth and Finrod about death is poignant in that the wise woman believes death to be the effect of Melkor's malice and will not be convinced by Finrod's claims to the contrary. The effect of this belief, however, is terror: "the fear of it is with us always and we flee from it for ever as the hart from the hunter" (*Morgoth,* 309). Andreth even talks of despair because she believes "the Nameless is Lord of this world, and your valour, and ours too, is fruitless" (*Morgoth*, 313). The importance of so many of the redemption scenes in *The Lord of the Rings* lies in the defeat of evil, indeed, but equally in the overcoming of fear of its power and with that, the power of fear itself.

One of the most redemptive scenes, in this sense, is the moment when Sam ascends the tower of Cirith Ungol, seeking for Frodo. He looks on death as he witnesses the cruel murder of one orc by another as he climbs higher and higher into this nest of enemy troops. His climb leads to a dead end: he feels "weary and finally defeated." And yet in the fear and darkness of defeat, he begins to sing:

> His voice sounded thin and quavering in the cold, dark tower: the voice of a forlorn and weary hobbit that no listening orc could possibly mistake for the clear song of an Elven-lord. He murmured old childish tunes out of the Shire, and snatches of Mr Bilbo's rhymes that came into his mind like fleeting glimpses of the country of his home. (*RK*, VI, i)

Before long he finds his own voice and a new song of his own invention. He describes his imprisoned situation "in darkness buried deep" but takes heart from the constant presence outside of the stars and sun, and concludes:

I will not say the Day is done,
Nor bid the stars good-bye. (*RK*, VI, i)

Sam gains hope, the quality missing from Andreth's vision, and he does so through creative imagination and through the art of his song. Yet the hope comes from the physical existence of natural forms: the sun and stars. Sam, if you like, is saved by things, the common stars we share as we look in the sky, which mediate this hope. He has given them up to enter the shadow of Mordor, but the reality of their existence enables him to see beyond the darkness and take hope. Soon he believes he hears a voice respond and is bearing down in rage on the orc guarding Frodo, shocking him into falling through an open trapdoor and thus rescuing his master.

This scene is paralleled and inverted by the events at the top of Mount Doom. Frodo is so affected by his long bearing of the Ring that his redemptive giving-up fails and instead of feeling defeated and forlorn like Sam, he surges with a Nietzschean will-to-power and puts on the Ring, whereas Sam, who had borne it less long, often forgets it when he carries it, protected by his humility and by his intense local loyalties, like a lesser Tom Bombadil. Frodo becomes like Sauron or Morgoth in that moment of possession, and where Sam is defeated, he is triumphant, and where Sam looked up, he gazes down pitilessly on Gollum, for whom he had previously felt compassion, and calls him "creeping thing" (*RK*, VI, iii). Soon the Ring becomes an idol to be fought over and destroys its possessor. As the thing cannot be given up eucharistically, it destroys its possessor.

Although the day this occurs is the equivalent of March 25th in the Shire calendar, and thus the traditional day of the Annunciation and the Crucifixion, it is not a type of Christ's sacrifice on Calvary, although it does announce the end of Sauron's power in Middle-earth, and in that sense has something of the Annunciation about it. In terms of the atonement, this event leads to a liberation from the power of evil, but only through the self-destruction wrought by evil, which can be thought of providentially. Like the sinners in Dante's *Inferno*, the words and actions of Frodo and Gollum show the good by a depiction of what has been perverted. Art, nature, and hobbit-ness are all marred by the Ring and cannot save themselves.

We have already seen how Sam acted redemptively in his use of song to rescue Frodo, an imitation of the original creation of the world by song in the legendarium. If we view redemption as unmarring, reconciling and liberating, this is an activity shared by in the novel by creatures: the eagles, who rescue Sam and Frodo from the dissolving mountain, the trees, who march on Isengard and defeat Saruman, and the plant *athelas*, which heals the wounded. As the free peoples ready themselves to beard Sauron's messenger at the Black Gate, to deflect his attention from Frodo, Aragorn talks of making themselves into things: bait in a trap: "we must make ourselves the bait, though his jaws should close on us" (*RK*, V, ix). The language casts them as cheese in a mousetrap, or worms on a fishhook, both venerable images for the atonement in early Christian writers, such as Augustine:

> The Devil exulted when Christ died, and by that very death of Christ the Devil was overcome: he took food, as it were, from a trap. He gloated over the death as if he were appointed a deputy of death; that in which he rejoiced became a prison for him. The cross of the Lord became a trap for the Devil; the death of the Lord was the food by which he was ensnared. And behold, our Lord Jesus Christ rose again.[24]

The devil takes that to which he is not entitled—Christ's sinless person—and thus loses his power. Aragorn and his companions, of course, expect no resurrection, but they act in hope, trusting that their act will help the liberation of Middle-earth.

Earlier in this essay I suggested that redemption in Tolkien always has something of artistry about it: it is acting creatively, which is enacted in the making free of words and things. It is an activity that calls the whole cosmos into cooperation from wizards to wild-men, trees to eagles. So far, I have said little about the Elves' contribution, which is primarily that of wisdom and conservation. Their magic—or art, since it is a part of them—however, should also be thought of in redemptive terms, especially given the kabbalistic aspects of Tolkien's thought. In the tradition of mystical Judaism, art can be thought of as uniting the sephirot, the structures of reality, and in so doing, repairing the world and releasing the divine sparks hidden in creation.[25] In contrast to the tyrannical magic of a Sauron, the enchanted art of the Elves reveals a divine spark in ordinary things. They unite with the object that they create: "we put the thought of all that we love into all that we make" (*FR*, II, viii) and it reflects their land. Their way-bread lasts many days and their rope unties itself. Jonathan McIntosh argues that "the powerful Elvish soul, or *fëa*, that exerts so formative an influence over the Elvish body, or *hröa*, making it immortal or at least undying, is also what gives their art its heightened spiritual command over matter—in short, its 'magic.'"[26]

Above all they are gift-givers and thus eucharistic, in offering their best and even themselves, with Galadriel as we saw cutting off hairs from her own head to give her former enemy. Everything Elves make signifies and has a radiant and communicative quality because it is not hoarded, as is Fëanor's temptation, but given freely to aid others. And ironically, it is an elf, Finrod, one of a race bound to the mortal fortunes of Middle-earth and sure to fade, who has the most cosmic redemptive vision of all, which has a place for nature in Arda remade and expresses the liturgical fulfillment of art:

Of all the children of Eru, I was thinking that by the Second Children we might have been delivered from death. For ever as we spoke of death being a division of the united [body and spirit], I thought in my heart of a death that was not so. . . . I beheld in a vision Arda Remade; and there the Eldar, completed but not ended could abide in the present for ever, and there walk, maybe, with the Children of Men, their deliverers, and sing to them such songs as, even in the Bliss beyond bliss, should make the green valleys ring and the everlasting mountain-tops to throb like harps. (*Morgoth*, 319)

In Finrod's vision, the Children of Men bring redemption and the Elves creation, and the natural world too has its part, echoing and responding to the songs in an eternal present in which 'giving up' is now transformed into the exchanges of antiphonal music, like a choir alternating the chanting of a psalm across a cathedral, beyond the walls of this world.

NOTES

1. See *The Celestial Hierarchy* in *Pseudo-Dionysius: The Complete Works,* trans. Colm Luibheid, ed. Paul Rorem (London: SPCK, 1987) and Dante Alighieri, *Paradiso* 28 and 9:61–3.

2. Barry Gordon, "Kingship, Priesthood, and Prophecy in *The Lord of the Rings*," unpublished paper, University of Newcastle Australia, ca. 1967; Philip Ryken, *The Messiah Comes to Middle-earth: Images of Christ's Threefold Office in* The Lord of the Rings, Hansen Lecture Series (Downers Grove: IVP, 2017), 45, 56–57.

3. On the importance of dissonance in polyphonic music and its theological significance, see Chiara Bertoglio, "Dissonant Harmonies: Tolkien's Musical Theodicy," *TS* 15 (2018): 93–114.

4. Mark Eddy Smith, *Tolkien's Ordinary Virtues: Exploring the Spiritual Themes of* The Lord of the Rings (Seattle: CreateSpace, 2021), 54; Ralph C. Wood, *The Gospel According to Tolkien: Visions of the Kingdom in Middle-earth* (Louisville: Westminster John Knox, 2003), 6; and Michael John Halsall, *Creation and Beauty in Tolkien's Catholic Vision: A Study in the Influence of Neoplatonism in J.R.R. Tolkien's Philosophy of Life as Being and Gift* (Eugene: Pickwick, 2020), 152.

5. Augustine of Hippo, *City of God,* trans. Henry Bettenson, intro. David Knowles (Harmondsworth: Penguin, 1972), Book XXII, 2, 1023–24. For scholars who ally Tolkien with the privation theory, see Scott A. Davison, "Tolkien and the Nature of Evil," in The Lord of the Rings *and Philosophy: One Book to Rule Them All*, ed. Gregory Bassham and Eric Bronson, PCP 5 (Chicago: Open Court, 2003), 99–109; and Colin Gunton, "A Far-Off Gleam of the Gospel: Salvation in Tolkien's *The Lord of the Rings*," in *Tolkien: A Celebration*, ed. Joseph Pearce (London: Fount, 1999), 124–40. For the most sophisticated account of his flirtation with more dualistic conceptions, see Jonathan S. McIntosh, *The Flame Imperishable: Tolkien, St. Thomas and the Metaphysics of Faërie* (Kettering, OH: Angelico Press, 2017), Chapter 9. Austin

Freeman, "The World, the Flesh and the Devil: The Nature of Evil in J.R.R. Tolkien," *Journal of Inklings Studies* 10.2 (2020): 139–71 proposes a tripartite taxonomy within an Augustinian framework.

6. Miklós Vassányi, "'At Journey's End, in Darkness': A Reticent Redemption in *The Lord of the Rings*," *IJPT* 76.3 (2015): 232–40.

7. Tom Shippey, *J.R.R. Tolkien: Author of the Century* (Boston: Houghton Mifflin, 2002), 120.

8. See Eliahu Klein, *Kabbalah of Creation: The Mysticism of Isaac Luria, Founder of Modern Kabbalah* (Berkeley: North Atlantic Books, 2005).

9. George MacDonald, "The Imagination: Its Functions and Its Culture," in *A Dish of Orts* (London: Sampson, Low, Marston and Co., 1893), 5.

10. See Arnold J. Band, "The Bratslav Theory of the Sacred Tale," in *The Tales*, by Nahman of Bratslav, trans. Arnold J. Band, CWS (New York: Paulist, 1978), 28–39.

11. For the view of Rabbinic Judaism, see Sanhedrin 98a in *Everyone's Talmud: The Major Teachings of the Rabbinic Sages*, ed. Abraham Cohen (New York: Schocken, 1995), 351–2. For the Hasidic application to storytelling as a theurgic act, see Moshe Idel, *Hasidism: Between Ecstasy and Magic* (Albany: SUNY, 1995), 180–88.

12. Liam Campbell, *The Ecological Augury in the Works of J.R.R. Tolkien*, Cormarë 21 (Zurich: Walking Tree, 2011), 21.

13. David Jones, "Art and Sacrament," in *Epoch and Artist* (London: Faber, 1959), 173.

14. On this manner of considering transubstantiation, see John Milbank and Catherine Pickstock, *Truth in Aquinas* (London: Routledge, 2001), 105–9, esp. 107.

15. J.R.R. Tolkien, *Smith of Wootton Major*, ext. ed., ed. Verlyn Flieger (London: HarperCollins, 2005), 101.

16. Irenaeus, *Haer.* 4.17.5.

17. Mary Wollstonecraft Shelley, "Introduction to the 1831 Edition," in *Frankenstein; or, The Modern Prometheus*, ed. D. L. Macdonald and Kathleen Scherf (Peterborough, ON: Broadview, 2001), 354.

18. See Riemer Roukema, "The Good Samaritan in Ancient Christianity," *Vigiliae Christianae* 58.1 (2004): 56–74.

19. Augustine of Hippo, *Confessions,* trans. Henry Chadwick (Oxford: Oxford University Press, 2008), Book II, vii (15), 33.

20. C.S. Lewis, *The Great Divorce* (London: Collins, 1946), 124.

21. *The New English Hymnal* (Norwich: Canterbury Press, 1990), 735–36.

22. Kristine Larsen, "'Following the Star': Eärendil, Númenor, and the Star of Bethlehem," *JTR* 16.2 (2023), article 9 argues that Tolkien deliberately aligns this Morning/Evening star with the star over Christ's stable.

23. *New English Hymnal*, 737.

24. Augustine of Hippo, *Tractates on the Gospel of John 1–10*, ed. Thomas P. Halton, trans. John W. Rettig, FC 78 (Washington, D.C.: Catholic University of America Press, 1988), 53.

25. Gershom Scholem, *Kabbalah: A Definitive History* (New York: Meridian, 1974), 142–44.

26. McIntosh, *Flame Imperishable*, 242.

BIBLIOGRAPHY

Augustine of Hippo. *Tractates on the Gospel of John 1–10*. Edited by Thomas P. Halton. Translated by John W. Rettig. FC 78. Washington, D.C.: Catholic University of America Press, 1988.

Band, Arnold J. "The Bratslav Theory of the Sacred Tale." Pages 28–39 in *The Tales*. By Nahman of Bratslav. Translated by Arnold J. Band. CWS. New York: Paulist, 1978. https://hasidicstories.com/Articles/Hasidic_Theories/bratslav.html.

Bertoglio, Chiara. "Dissonant Harmonies: Tolkien's Musical Theodicy." *TS* 15 (2018): 93–114.

Campbell, Liam. *The Ecological Augury in the Works of J.R.R. Tolkien*. Cormarë 21. Zurich: Walking Tree, 2011.

Cohen, Abraham, ed. *Everyone's Talmud: The Major Teachings of the Rabbinic Sages*. New York: Schocken, 1995.

Dionysius the Areopagite. *The Celestial Hierarchy* in *Pseudo-Dionysius: The Complete Works*. Translated by Colm Luibheid. Edited by Paul Rorem. London: SPCK, 1987.

Davison, Scott A. "Tolkien and the Nature of Evil." Pages 99–109 in The Lord of the Rings *and Philosophy: One Book to Rule Them All*. Edited by Gregory Bassham and Eric Bronson. PCP 5. Chicago: Open Court, 2003.

Freeman, Austin. "The World, the Flesh and the Devil: The Nature of Evil in J.R.R. Tolkien." *Journal of Inklings Studies* 10.2 (2020): 139–71.

Gordon, Barry. "Kingship, Priesthood, and Prophecy in *The Lord of the Rings*." Unpublished paper, University of Newcastle Australia, ca. 1967. https://downloads.newcastle.edu.au/library/cultural%20collections/pdf/Kingship_priesthood_prophecy_in_the_LOTR.pdf.

Gunton, Colin. "A Far-Off Gleam of the Gospel: Salvation in Tolkien's *The Lord of the Rings*." Pages 124–40 in *Tolkien: A Celebration*. Edited by Joseph Pearce. London: Fount, 1999.

Halsall, Michael John. *Creation and Beauty in Tolkien's Catholic Vision: A Study in the Influence of Neoplatonism in J.R.R. Tolkien's Philosophy of Life as Being and Gift*. Eugene: Pickwick, 2020.

Idel, Moshe. *Hasidism: Between Ecstasy and Magic*. Albany: SUNY, 1995.

Jones, David. *Epoch and Artist*. London: Faber, 1959.

Klein, Eliahu. *Kabbalah of Creation: The Mysticism of Isaac Luria, Founder of Modern Kabbalah*. Berkeley: North Atlantic Books, 2005.

Larsen, Kristine. "'Following the Star': Eärendil, Númenor, and the Star of Bethlehem." *JTR* 16.2 (2023): article 9.

Lewis, C.S. *The Great Divorce*. London: Collins, 1946.

MacDonald, George. *A Dish of Orts: Chiefly Papers on the Imagination, and on Shakespeare*. London: Sampson, Low, Marston and Co., 1893.

McIntosh, Jonathan S. *The Flame Imperishable: Tolkien, St. Thomas and the Metaphysics of Faërie*. Kettering, OH: Angelico Press, 2017.

Milbank, John, and Catherine Pickstock. *Truth in Aquinas*. RO. London: Routledge, 2001.

The New English Hymnal. Norwich: Canterbury Press, 1990.

Roukema, Riemer. "The Good Samaritan in Ancient Christianity." *Vigiliae Christianae* 58.1 (2004): 56–74.

Ryken, Philip. *The Messiah Comes to Middle-earth: Images of Christ's Threefold Office in* The Lord of the Rings. Hansen Lecture Series. Downers Grove: IVP, 2017.

Scholem, Gershom. *Kabbalah: A Definitive History.* New York: Meridian, 1974.

Shelley, Mary Wollstonecraft. "Introduction to the 1831 Edition." Pages 353–59 in *Frankenstein; or, The Modern Prometheus.* Edited by D. L. Macdonald and Kathleen Scherf. 2nd ed. Peterborough, ON: Broadview, 2001.

Shippey, Tom. *J.R.R. Tolkien: Author of the Century.* Boston: Houghton Mifflin, 2002.

Smith, Mark Eddy. *Tolkien's Ordinary Virtues: Exploring the Spiritual Themes of* The Lord of the Rings. Seattle: CreateSpace, 2021.

Tolkien, J.R.R. *Smith of Wootton Major.* Extended ed. Edited by Verlyn Flieger. London: HarperCollins, 2005.

Vassányi, Miklós. "'At Journey's End, in Darkness': A Reticent Redemption in *The Lord of the Rings.*" *IJPT* 76.3 (2015): 232–40.

Wood, Ralph C. *The Gospel According to Tolkien: Visions of the Kingdom in Middle-earth.* Louisville: Westminster John Knox, 2003.

Chapter 3

Critiquing Tolkien's Theology

Austin M. Freeman

J.R.R. Tolkien participated in the culture of academic critique throughout his entire life. He and his boyhood club the T.C.B.S. (Tea Club, Barrovian Society) read and commented on each other's poetry and art. Later in Tolkien's life, the Inklings also offered constructive criticism and not mere praise. For instance, Tolkien takes C.S. Lewis to task for his treatment of divorce in *Mere Christianity* (*Letters*, 49).[1] This criticism did not in any way detract from their deep admiration for each other. In the spirit of this collaboration, I offer my own fond and constructive critique of Tolkien's theology.

In my previous work, *Tolkien Dogmatics*, I attempted as far as possible merely to present Tolkien's own thoughts on Christian truth. This does not mean simply reading *The Lord of the Rings* as a "Christian story," in the same style of apologetic narrative as Narnia. Tolkien's project was too sophisticated for that. Many have erred in trying to "decode" Tolkien's fiction, unearthing what he must have meant beneath the story. My approach is the opposite: beginning with Tolkien's nonfictional statements—letters, essays, articles—and then looking to the Middle-earth writings (the "legendarium") for ways in which he creatively instantiates his expressed theological thoughts.[2] But whereas in *Tolkien Dogmatics* I refrained from offering my own views on Tolkien's theological decisions, in this chapter I want to discuss three points at which I believe Tolkien's theology needs fine-tuning.

First, I argue that Tolkien's reimagining of the fall in the "Tale of Adanel" unjustly condemns Men due to their lack of knowledge. Second, I take issue with the *Silmarillion*'s perspective on death as a gift of God. Finally, I disagree with Tolkien's views on the relationship of divine Providence and freedom. All three of these issues, dealing as they do with the interplay between evil and human agency, may fruitfully be discussed together. The essay therefore moves from the event of the fall to its result (death), and then on to a larger picture of God's relationship to evil and human decisions.

But first, an objection: all three of these issues arise from Tolkien's fictional writings. We cannot be *certain* that Tolkien would have held to these perspectives in the real world. And did Tolkien himself not say he felt no restrictions on his sub-creative activity, barring a violation of the law of non-contradiction (*Letters*, 153)? How then is it legitimate to speak of these as critiques of Tolkien's *theology* rather than his *mythology*?

First, it is not true that Tolkien felt no restrictions whatsoever on his sub-creative work. He bound himself fictionally to portray Middle-earth as the mythic past of our own world, and as such felt the need to make it metaphysically consistent with revealed religion, to the extent that he considered scrapping any version of a "Flat Earth" before the fall of Númenor (*Morgoth* 367ff).[3] The origin of humanity, the fall, and death as outlined in Genesis are supposed to be those of Middle-earth as well, so Tolkien's fictional theology ought to remain consistent with it. And (by *modus tollens*) if Tolkien's mythology is misaligned with Genesis, his theology may be as well.

Second, Tolkien also believed that the moral law must remain the same in any sub-created world. The moral law is rooted in God's own being, and thus a necessary and not a contingent truth. Since God's being is the same in all possible worlds, the moral law must also be the same.[4] Any part of his mythology that impinges upon the character of God or the nature of right or wrong is therefore also a theological claim and should be brought into line with the theology of the primary world. For example, if Tolkien himself did not view death as a gift, then given his working methodology, he is theologically obligated not to portray death as a gift in a fictional sense.

MIDDLE-EARTH'S FALL IS UNFAIR

Tolkien's unpublished "Tale of Adanel," appended to the very important text *Athrabeth Finrod ah Andreth* ("The Debate of Finrod and Andreth") has received virtually no scholarly attention on its own, despite its overt reimagining of the Eden narrative in Genesis.[5] Tolkien himself does not present the story as an authoritative account of the fall of Man in Middle-earth, only as a piece of oral tradition handed down through the ages, and itself subsidiary to the (for him) more authoritative *Athrabeth* (*Morgoth*, 303).[6] As Verlyn Flieger points out, Tolkien is at pains to deny the authoritativeness of "Adanel."[7] As such, we cannot hold the piece to the same standard as completed works such as *The Lord of the Rings*. But given Tolkien's position on the historicity of Genesis, such an account is likely close to his own view of what happened "behind the text."[8] So, in the spirit of the Inklings, we might offer some constructive critical comments on Tolkien's work in progress.

The tale begins with the first humans being addressed within their hearts by "the Voice," here clearly referring to Eru (*Morgoth*, 346). He tells them "Ye are my children. I have sent you to dwell here. In time ye will inherit all this Earth, but first ye must be children and learn. Call on me and I shall hear; for I am watching over you." The humans struggle to express themselves in language, and while the Voice answers them when they call upon it, it does not often answer their questions about the world. Instead, echoing an Irenaean account of the garden, it replies, "First seek to find the answer for yourselves. For ye will have joy in the finding, and so grow from childhood and become wise. Do not seek to leave childhood before your time." The humans instead become impatient and pull away from the Voice.

At this time, they encounter another being, not an inner voice but an embodied and glorious person who says he has come to them in pity. "Ye should not have been left alone and uninstructed . . . The world is full of marvellous riches which knowledge can unlock. Ye could have food more abundant and more delicious than the poor things that ye now eat. Ye could have dwellings of ease, in which ye could keep light and shut out the night. Ye could be clad even as I." They accept him as a teacher when he claims they could be as he is. This figure is, of course, Melkor, the Satanic tempter.

He maintains their loyalty through satisfying their impatient desires, claiming, "I am the Giver of Gifts . . . the gifts shall never fail as long as ye trust me." So, says Adanel, they "revered" him and were "enthralled" by him (here playing on the ambiguous meaning of the word). Slowly, he begins to sow false teachings in among the rest of his instruction: "Greatest of all is the Dark . . . for It has no bounds. I came out of the Dark, but I am Its master. For I have made Light. I made the Sun and the Moon and the countless stars. I will protect you from the Dark, which else would devour you." He angrily claims that the Voice is "the Voice of the Dark. It wishes to keep you from me; for It is hungry for you."

After an eclipse (manufactured no doubt by Melkor himself), he brings them to a crisis: "'There are some among you who are still listening to the Voice of the Dark,' he said, 'and therefore It is drawing nearer. Choose now! Ye may have the Dark as Lord, or ye may have Me. But unless ye take Me for Lord and swear to serve Me, I shall depart and leave you; for I have other realms and dwelling places, and I do not need the Earth, nor you.'" The humans swear allegiance to him out of fear, crying, "Thou art the Lord; Thee only we will serve. The Voice we abjure and will not hearken to it again . . . Thou art the One Great, and we are Thine." Melkor institutes a temple with a sacrificial system and becomes increasingly tyrannical. His true nature is exposed. This is the non-negotiable element for Tolkien. Whether in *Andreth* or elsewhere, Men fell because they took Melkor as king and god.

They only hear the voice of Eru once more, in the quiet of the night, saying "Ye have abjured Me, but ye remain Mine. I gave you life. Now it shall be shortened, and each of you in a little while shall come to Me, to learn who is your Lord: the one ye worship, or I who made him."[9] The Men are still in error, however, and believe the voice is that of the evil one. They run to Melkor for aid, and he dismisses them cruelly. Some, seeing the truth, declare, "Now we know at last who lied, and who desired to devour us. Not the first Voice. It is the Master that we have taken who is the Darkness; and he did not come forth from it, as he said, but he dwells in it. We will serve him no longer! He is our Enemy." These leave and eventually enter the tale of the Elves as the Edain.

But the troubling point here is that the Men in such a situation are in no real position to know beforehand who is telling the truth, Eru or Melkor. We have only two reported addresses by Eru, and none after Melkor appears, either to correct or instruct. Neither of these addresses provide proof that the Voice's claims are true, nor that Melkor lies. When a shining supernatural being appears and aids you, you have no reason not to believe him. He claims to be the bearer of light against the darkness, and he displays proof that this may well be so. Melkor only discloses his true character after the humans have already sworn allegiance to him.

There are only two reasonable suspicions a well-intentioned human being may have had. First, the Voice speaks internally while Melkor speaks externally. Second, Melkor claims the Voice has violent purposes, of which the humans have no evidence. Then again, the same could be said of Melkor at this point. Perhaps more evidence of the Voice's claims comes off-stage, in the instructional remarks it offers at the beginning of the story, but we as an audience are left unsatisfied. Tolkien's Eru demands not blind obedience but trust, which is only established on the basis of proven faithfulness and character. Both in this tale seem somewhat lacking.

In the Genesis account, on the other hand, Adam has quite a lot more direct experience with God before the arrival of the serpent (Gen 2:7–9, 15–25). He has already seen God's rulership over every animal. He has seen God create another soul (Eve). He has seen God's goodness in the provisions of the garden. And when the tempter makes its debut, it is in the form of a mere animal, one which seems to violate the natural order already established (no other animals are recorded as speaking). Satan's lie is much less elaborate, and his questioning of God's goodness goes much more clearly against the evidence than the divine reticence of Eru and the extended relationship-building of Melkor. Most importantly, there is no explicit ban or prohibition in Tolkien's version of the story. Eru gives no command which the first Men consciously break. They swear allegiance to another, true, but that other has at that stage seemed more beneficent than Eru, who frequently denies their prayers. Nor is there a warning of the consequences should they depart from obedience. Men have not been told, as in Genesis, that death is the penalty for their disloyalty. This brings us to the next area of critique.

DEATH IS NOT A GIFT

We ought secondly to push against Tolkien's concept of the "gift of death," and his attempts to construe death as somehow less than the final enemy.[10] Tolkien is from the beginning well aware that, according to credal Christianity, "'death' is not part of human nature, but a punishment for sin (rebellion), a result of the 'Fall,'" (*Letters*, 212). The Scriptures speak of death as the last enemy of God (1 Cor 15:26), something that will be destroyed and judged at the end of all things. But according to Tolkien's Death-as-Gift view, "certainly Death is not an Enemy!" (*Letters*, 208).

The reason for this rather shocking statement lies in Tolkien's assertion that death is the exit point from the spatio-temporal world. It is the avenue by which the human being returns to the presence of God outside creation. We can detect a certain sort of defensiveness when he writes, "It might or might not be 'heretical,' if these myths were regarded as statements about the actual nature of Man in the real world: I do not know. But the view of the myth is that Death—the mere shortness of human life-span—is not a punishment for the Fall," (*Letters*, 156).

In this we have to acknowledge that Tolkien himself changed his views on the matter, and in his most mature writings adopts a basically ortho-dox approach to the problem of death in the *Athrabeth Finrod ah Andreth*, discussed above. However, Christopher Tolkien's decision to exclude the *Athrabeth* from the published *Silmarillion* leaves most readers familiar only with the most heterodox version of Tolkien's views on human mortality. The salient passage reads:

> It is one with this gift of freedom that the children of Men dwell only a short space in the world alive, and are not bound to it. . . . the sons of Men die indeed, and leave the world; wherefore they are called the Guests, or the Strangers. Death is their fate, the gift of Ilúvatar, which as Time wears even the Powers shall envy. But Melkor has cast his shadow upon it, and confounded it with dark-ness, and brought forth evil out of good, and fear out of hope. (*Silmarillion*, 42)

The passage remains virtually unchanged through the many subsequent revisions.[11] In the earliest formulations, the idea that Men leave the world entirely was not present. But already by the time of *Lost Road*, we see an early shift in the mythology in which Men do not simply flee to Mandos but leave the world for eternity (cf. *LT 1*, 90). Tolkien must at least gesture toward the immortality of the soul and its union with God. The short work "The Statute of Finwë and Míriel" in fact includes a debate among the Valar as to whether Death can be considered a good twisted by Melkor or an evil that God is able to use for His own purposes. We can view this as a transitional intermediate stage in the development of Tolkien's views.

By the time of the *Athrabeth* above (1958–60), the human view is that death is indeed a consequence of sin, and God's curse for human worship of Melkor as God-King. Were it not for this violation, Andreth insists, humans would be truly immortal, lasting beyond even the ending of the world which marks the termination of Elvish longevity. Tolkien remarks in a 1958 letter draft that the Death-as-Gift view "does not necessarily have anything to say for or against such beliefs as the Christian that [death is a punishment.] It should be regarded as an Elvish perception of what death—not being tied to the 'circles of the world'—*should now become* for Men, however it arose," (*Letters*, 212, emphasis added; cf. *Silmarillion*, 264–65). By this stage of composition, the consideration that death is a "good" and a source of "hope," present in the published *Silmarillion*, ought not to be considered theologically correct even within Middle-earth.

Of course, in one sense there is a biblical warrant for such a view. In Genesis 3:22, God prevents Adam and Eve from eating also of the Tree of Life and being trapped in their corrupted forms forever. We might consider this a gift in the sense of an undeserved mercy. The text of the *Ainulindalë* specifically notes that only the Gift of Freedom was given pre-creationally, while the discussion of the Gift of Death takes place in a context that makes it clear this is an Elvish perspective, and there is no direct speech of Ilúvatar assigning the Gift of Death to Men.

Perhaps Tolkien's Gift is nothing but a literary approach crafted to address the fact of human mortality in a mythico-emotive register. Thus, he writes, "You may call that 'bad theology.' So it may be, in the primary world, but it is an imagination capable of elucidating truth, and a legitimate basis of legends" (*Letters*, 153). I have my purposes for it, he seems to say, and they are not those of real-world theodicy. What then *is* the purpose of such a view, we might wonder? Likely it exists to emphasize the eternal destiny of the human soul as enjoying the beatific vision of God. For Tolkien, human destiny lies not within creation but outside of it in God Himself. As such, the created world is something to be passed through and left behind, while we seek beyond the circles of the world for our true home.

Christian doctrine holds that the *telos* of redeemed humanity is the beatific vision, yes, but not in a disembodied or timeless existence. We shall indeed be with God, but in a new creation—what Tolkien calls Arda Healed or Arda Remade (*Morgoth*, 319–20, 351). Of this neither his Elves nor his pre-Abrahamic Men have any surety, however, and so we are left with a Middle-earth almost Platonic in its understanding of death as a beneficial escape from creation. The proper placement of the *Athrabeth* would have done much to correct this overemphasis on a sort of flight from materiality and creatureliness, but regardless we could wish that Tolkien had drawn stronger lines around his Elvish spin on Death as Gift.

GOD IS NOT OUR DUNGEON MASTER

Finally, and most extensively, Tolkien's views on Providence are somewhat difficult to untangle.[12] It is very clear that Tolkien has a strong emphasis on human freedom, but the relation between this freedom and the divine government is less clear. Here, I pose some concerns about a few unpublished comments where Tolkien seems to portray God more as a strategist or dungeon master, constantly adjusting his plan in response to human freedom, than as the great Author of all things.

Before we begin, we shall likely require some terminological clarity. When we speak of Providence, we mean the way in which God rules the world and brings about his purposes within it.[13] Depending on one's theological view of human freedom, Providence may take one of several different shapes. They can be broadly categorized as *incompatibilist* (in which God's sovereignty and human free will mutually limit one another) or *compatibilist* (in which the two exist simultaneously). An incompatibilist account presumes a sort of zero-sum game in which God and human wills operate on the same plane. If God causes something, then the human being does not; and vice versa. A compatibilist account sees divine and human action as existing on two planes.

In a universe of strong libertarian freedom, God never *causes* a human choice. He may influence choices through the arrangement of events, through motions of the Holy Spirit, through the strengthening of the moral will, and so forth; but this is always persuasion rather than causation. Human free will is never overridden.

The Molinist or middle-knowledge view also accepts this assumption but attempts to give a greater role to God's Providence than mere influence.[14] Molinism begins from the axiom that God knows the outcome of every possible choice. This view states that instead of influencing or causing human free actions all along the way, God in his infinite knowledge at the beginning of time looks into every possible world of free choices and chooses to create the one whose initial conditions best match his desired outcome. Molinism is not deism, as God still intervenes directly in history (speaking to Moses or becoming incarnate, for example). Rather than operating upon the choices themselves, God orchestrates the states of affairs in which those choices come about.

More recent openness or kenotic models of God have asserted that God does not know the future.[15] He radically limits himself in order to establish a genuine relationship of equality with his creatures. His Providence therefore exists as a response to their free choices, a sort of dialogic give-and-take. God may have a desired goal in mind, but may be forced to change his plans. The prime objection to this model is that it seems unable to secure God's ultimate victory over evil. If God is a risk-taker, then it must be the case that his risk can fail, and that God will 'lose.'

In contrast to these three models, theologians like Thomas Aquinas and John Calvin articulate a compatibilist view in which God actually sustains and empowers human freedom.[16] There are two levels of causation here. For example, Frodo can be said freely to choose to take the Ring to Mordor: his decision aligns with his character and results from an unbroken chain of cause and effect; nobody is forcing him to do it; he actively does what he wants. But Frodo also chooses to take the Ring because the author of the story decides he will do so. Indeed, in a sense Frodo *only* makes this choice because, outside and above the text, on a completely different level of agency, Tolkien decides that he will do so.

Tolkien's views on Providence receive more extended treatment in my *Tolkien Dogmatics*. I have elsewhere drawn out the way in which I think Tolkien can ultimately be parsed underneath the Thomist or Calvinist schema.[17] Thus he can write, "in every world on every plane all must ultimately be under the Will of God," (*Letters*, 153) and "the will of Eru . . . may not be gainsaid" (*Sauron*, 382). Tolkien's stress on the two levels of existence, ours and God's, places him more in this camp than in any incompatibilist one. But this requires downplaying certain statements in his most extensive treatment of the subject: a document titled "Fate and Free Will," published most recently in *The Nature of Middle-earth*.

In this document, Tolkien experiments with his authorial analogy to a degree in which God ceases to be an author and instead becomes a sort of dungeon master. For those unfamiliar with the mechanics of *Dungeons & Dragons* or other tabletop role-playing games, the dungeon master is responsible for deciding upon the adventure's 'setting.' She selects the nature of the world the players will explore, from its geography to its metaphysics and even its gods. She populates this world with creatures and non-player characters (NPCs) which she controls. She outlines scenarios into which the players may choose to enter. For example, the thieves' guild in the capital city has recently kidnapped the duke's daughter. Will the players choose to aid the duke in rescuing her, or will they instead choose to leave the city and investigate the ancient ruins on the mountainside? Or more radically still, will the players choose to join the thieves' guild in extorting money from the duke? This is the highlight of such a system. No other games have such a robust sense of player freedom.

The dungeon master may have a plan of how she wants the adventure to proceed–who the players will meet, where they will go, what they will want to choose–but any experienced dungeon master knows that these plans frequently do not survive for very long. The barbarian player may hastily kill the mercenary with crucial plot information. The art of dungeon-mastering involves choosing how and to what extent to continue leading players down a predetermined outline, or instead to adapt fully to the desires and choices of the party.

Players generally do not appreciate being 'railroaded' into a story, as this spoils their sense of openness and freedom in the imagined world. The best dungeon masters therefore either create a tableau of story possibilities into which the players may choose to step, responding extemporaneously to the chains of effects the players set in motion, or instead subtly reroute players' choices back into line with the original plot. Have the players chosen to explore the ruins rather than engage the thieves' guild? Perhaps they simply find the thieves in secret conclave in the ruins rather than in the city sewers as originally planned. Nobody is the wiser that any adjustments have even been necessary.

Such, in large part, is the way Tolkien has Eru operate in "Fate and Free Will." First, Eru creates a world of potentiality, the 'setting.' The ordering of the physical world is "established and pre-ordained" at the moment of creation (*Nature*, 227–28). Personal destiny is not included in the Elvish conception of fate (*Nature*, 229). Eru the dungeon master has set the stage, so to speak. But Tolkien declares, "Until the appearance of Will all is mere preparation, interesting only on a quite different & lower plane: like mathematics or observing the physical events of the world or in a similar way the workings of a machine" (*Nature*, 230). One might take an interest in reading a pre-made adventure guide, but the real fun is in the playing.

Eru therefore sets creatures with libertarian free will (the 'players') loose in the world. He has a plan for the story he wants to tell through them, but that plan is subject to change based on the strong free will of the creatures.[18] It is the dungeon master's assent to player choices that makes them 'exist' within that world, not the players themselves. Just as a dungeon master can choose not to realize some particular choice of a player character, so too Tolkien believes strong freedom can be negated in principle. But Eru binds himself not to do so.[19] A dungeon master who only enacts the player choices he himself would have made strips the delight from the players' experience. As Tolkien writes, "Free Will is derivative, and is only operative within provided circumstances; but in order that it may exist, it is necessary that the Author should guarantee it, whatever betides: [especially] when it is 'against His Will,' as we say, at any rate as it appears on a finite view" (*Letters*, 153). This is to say nothing more than that Eru's sustaining Providence also allows for evil choices to come about.

Tolkien himself, prior to the invention of the tabletop role-playing game, says the closest analogy for Eru's providential relation to the world is that of an author and his story. He explains, "The author is not in the tale in one sense, yet it all proceeds from him (and what was in him), so that he is present all the time. Now while composing the tale he may have certain general designs (the plot for instance), and he may have a clear conception of the character (independent of the particular tale) of each feigned actor. But those are the limits of his 'foreknowledge,'" (*Nature*, 230). Tolkien recalls the common authorial phenomenon in which a character 'comes alive' and does "things that were not foreseen at all at the outset and may modify in a small or even large way the process of the tale thereafter" (*Nature*, 230). Gandalf is essentially a powerful free will—in our analogy, a particularly keen and decisive player character—set loose to cause unpredictable and strange effects in the physical world or adventure setting (*Nature*, 229).

This guaranteed freedom does not mean that we are our own makers in an existentialist sense. Our individual character as given by God can be modified but not essentially changed (*Nature*, 229). Tolkien can speak of a different "plane" of Providence, distinct from that which applies to the material universe. There are thus two relationships between the world and God's sovereignty: the material and the mental. Beings with both bodies and souls blend these two relations (*Nature*, 229–30). No aspect of creation escapes God's ultimate rule. The dungeon master effectively ties all things back to the main plot, as it were. Or as Eru says in Tolkien's creation myth, "no theme may be played that hath not its uttermost source in me, nor can any alter the music in my despite. For he that attempteth this shall prove but mine instrument in the devising of things more wonderful, which he himself hath not imagined" (*Silmarillion*, 17). How does this occur?

Here Tolkien explains that Eru adapts his own planned story to honor and accentuate creatures' choices while also achieving his ultimate goal in the overarching narrative. Bilbo may have been fated to find the Ring, but free to give it up or keep it. If Bilbo did choose to give it up, then Frodo was fated to go on the mission but free to destroy or claim the Ring. And so on and so forth. But since the destruction of the Ring was part of Eru's plan, if either Bilbo or Frodo chose to go against this plan, Eru would adjust the situation to bring his goal about anyway. Tolkien writes, "some other means would have arisen by which Sauron was frustrated: just as when Frodo's will proved in the end inadequate, a means for the Ring's destruction immediately appeared—being kept in reserve by Eru as it were," (*Nature*, 228). Eru's plan is therefore malleable but inevitable. But Tolkien goes further.

In very faint pencil at the end of "Fate and Free Will," Tolkien writes that at the first stage of creation, the Music of the Ainur, "Eru takes up alterations by their created wills ('good' or bad) and adds of His own." In the second stage, the Vision, "the theme now transformed is made into a Tale and presented as visible drama to the Ainur, bounded but great. Eru had not [?complete] foreknowledge, but [?after it His] foreknowledge was complete to the smallest detail—but He did not reveal it all. He veiled the latter part from the eyes of the Valar who were to be actors" (*Nature,* 231).[20] There are some textual uncertainties here, but the above passage in the same document seems to confirm that Tolkien's Eru truly lacks omniscience, at least initially. Tolkien again stresses the real freedom of Eru's creatures to decide things apart from him, but "All such unforeseen actions or events are, however, taken up to become integral parts of the tale when finally concluded. Now when that has been done, then the author's 'foreknowledge' is complete, and nothing can happen, be said, or done, that he does not know of and will or allow to be. Even so, some of the Eldarin philosophers ventured to say, it was with Eru" (*Nature*, 230). To return to our analogy, once the play session is complete, the dungeon master is aware of all that has happened in the imagined world.

There are several theological problems with this dungeon master model. First, it undermines one of Tolkien's great contributions to the doctrine of Providence, the authorial analogy between God and the world which situates human and divine agency on two different planes of action. This is the primary reason why, in other publications, I have attempted to synthesize all of Tolkien's comments as suggesting a Thomistic or Calvinistic two-level scheme in which there remains a hidden Providence of God already aware of and ruling over the free choices of his creatures. Such a position is suggested even within "Fate and Free Will" itself by comments such as the previously quoted "'against His Will,' as we say, at any rate *as it appears on a finite view*" (*Letters*, 153, emphasis added). Unless the evidence is overwhelming, one should favor consistency.

This decision to attempt a synthesis also stems from the alarming suggestion that Tolkien denies to Eru several classical attributes of God. If the suggested readings of the pages above are correct, Eru at one point lacked omniscience, and then gained it later. Would Tolkien say the same of God? Can God be surprised by human freedom? Furthermore, Eru's actually altering his plan in response to human choices ("in a small or even large way,"

Nature, 230) also means denying divine immutability and impassibility. Something outside of God changes God.

Some might welcome a more open and less classical doctrine of God, but it is doubtful Tolkien himself would do so, given his other conservative doctrines. And it really does remain unclear how seriously he took the passages discussed above, or to what extent his hedging about analogies and differences changes the situation theologically. We should remain cautious. His refusal to resolve "the ultimate problem of Free Will in its relation to the Foreknowledge of a Designer," even in a fictional Elvish conception (*Nature*, 229) deserves at least that much.

CONCLUSION

In the spirit of friendly critique, we have here examined three areas in which Tolkien's theology deserves minor correction. First, Tolkien's narrative of the fall, the "Tale of Adanel," seems to place human beings in an unfair position *vis-à-vis* their guilt for trusting Melkor. They do not seem to have sufficient evidence to evaluate whether Melkor's claims are true, or enough of a relationship with Eru to merit absolute trust. Nor is any explicit penalty for disobedience outlined as it is in Genesis. Second, Tolkien's iconic conception of death as a gift of God needs clearer delineation to frame it as a fictionally "partial" perspective rather than an "objective" one. Scripture is unrelenting in its negative portrayal of death, and while death has been conquered in Christ's resurrection, it does not thereby become a good thing in itself. Finally, Tolkien's possible implication that God lacks omniscience and immutability ought also to be denied. Such a motion toward open theism cannot ensure God's ultimate victory over evil and conflicts with the biblical witness.

Now, none of these issues appear in works published while Tolkien was alive. They remain drafts of varying completeness. The first two issues are minor tweaks more than real errors. The third issue is more serious, but also more uncertain. It is doubtful that Tolkien would hold any of them firmly. And of course, they all appear in fictional contexts rather than straightforward theological essays. In conclusion, therefore, none of what is presented here ought in any way to bar appreciative Christians from a deep appreciation for this first-rate interdisciplinary thinker.[21]

NOTES

1. Tolkien in fact gives an extended theological meditation on critique and friendship in *Letters*, 113. Readers interested in the nature of the debates among the Inklings and T.C.B.S may consult John Garth, *Tolkien and the Great War: The Threshold of Middle-earth* (Boston: Houghton Mifflin, 2013) and Diana Pavlac Glyer, *The Company They Keep: C.S. Lewis and J.R.R. Tolkien as Writers in Community* (Kent, OH: Kent State University Press, 2007).

2. Austin M. Freeman, *Tolkien Dogmatics: Theology through Mythology with the Maker of Middle-earth* (Bellingham, WA: Lexham Press, 2022), 1–18.

3. This is much the same distinction on the fictional level as that between God's absolute and ordained power in the late Middle Ages: God binds himself to operate according to certain principles.

4. Cf. Tolkien's various expressions of universal moral law in *Letters*, 310; *Monsters*, 106; *OFS*, 254–55, 257, 270; Christina Scull and Wayne G. Hammond, *J.R.R. Tolkien Companion and Guide: Chronology*, rev. and exp. ed. (London: HarperCollins, 2017), 344–45. This argument is more explicitly formulated by George MacDonald, as noted in Austin M. Freeman, "'The Backs of Trees': Tolkien, the British Theological Romantics, and the Fantastic Imagination," in *Tolkien and the Romantic Spirit*, ed. Julian Eilmann and Will Sherwood (Zollikofen: Walking Tree, 2023), 283–85.

5. For a fuller treatment of Tolkien's doctrine of the fall, including the 'Adanel' narrative, see Freeman, *Tolkien Dogmatics*, 155–81.

6. Tolkien at some point intended the *Athrabeth* to function as the final piece in an appendix to the Silmarillion. Since Adanel's account of human mortality is central to Andreth's presentation, the *fact* of the fall and early Man's blasphemy and angering of Eru, if not the precise details laid out in 'Adanel,' can be considered as much part of the legendarium as any other text appearing in the published *Silmarillion*.

7. Verlyn Flieger, "Whose Myth Is It?" in *Between Faith and Fiction: Tolkien and the Powers of His World*, ed. Nils Ivar Agøy (Uppsala: Arda-Society, 1998), 38–39. Tolkien expresses unease with *Andreth* in a late note, writing "Already it is (if inevitably) too like a parody of Christianity. Any legend of the Fall would make it completely so?" (*Morgoth*, 354). Yet we note that the 'parody' element likely refers to Finrod's musings on the incarnation of Eru, not to the fall. And we see that Tolkien himself resolved this issue in the same note, offering the 'essentials' of the fall account while removing elements such as the snake, the garden, and the fruit of the tree.

8. See Freeman, *Tolkien Dogmatics*, 45–46.

9. There is an alternate version of this second speech, which reads: "If the Darkness be your God, little here shall you have of Light, but shall leave it soon and come before Me, to learn who lieth: [your god] or I Who made him." (*Morgoth*, 351; bracketed text taken from *Morgoth*, 354). Here God speaks in wrath rather than mercy.

10. For a fuller treatment of Tolkien's developing view of death, see Freeman, *Tolkien Dogmatics*, 310–19.

11. These revisions are found in: *LT I*, 59 (1918–1920); *Lost Road* 25, 65, 163, etc. (1930s); the three versions given in *Morgoth* drafted during the 1940s (21, 36–37, 42–43).

12. Not to mention one of the largest targets of secondary scholarly literature. For a few examples, see: Thomas Fornet-Ponse, "Freedom and Providence as Anti-Modern Elements?" in *Tolkien and Modernity 1*, ed. Frank Weinreich and Thomas Honegger, Cormarë 9 (Zollikofen: Walking Tree, 2006), 177–206; Verlyn Flieger, "The Music and the Task: Fate and Free Will in Middle-earth," *TS* 6 (2009): 151–81; Thomas Fornet-Ponse, "'Strange and free'—On Some Aspects of the Nature of Elves and Men," *TS* 7 (2010): 67–89; Helen Lasseter Freeh, "On Fate, Providence, and Free Will in *The Silmarillion*," in *Tolkien among the Moderns*, ed. Ralph C. Wood (Notre Dame: Notre Dame University Press, 2015), 51–78; Freeman, *Tolkien Dogmatics*, 69–83.

13. See, for example, the Catechism of the Catholic Church, 2nd ed. (1997), para. 302–13.

14. Named after Jesuit theologian Luis Molina, whose 1588 work *De liberi arbitrii cum gratiae donis, divina praescientia, praedestinatione et reprobatione concordia* (*On Free Will in Concord with the Gift of Grace, Divine Foreknowledge, Predestination, and Reprobation*) first set forth this idea. More contemporary advocates include Protestant philosopher William Lane Craig and many Wesleyan theologians.

15. See the prominent Clark H. Pinnock et al., *The Openness of God: A Biblical Challenge to the Traditional Understanding of God* (Downers Grove: InterVarsity, 1994). Other theologians such as Jürgen Moltmann, Roger Olson, and Greg Boyd also fall into this camp.

16. E.g., Thomas Aquinas, *Summa Theologiae*, I.22–23; John Calvin, *Institutes*, I.16.

17. Austin M. Freeman, "Tolkien and Calvin: Five Convergences," in *Tolkien among the Theologians*, ed. Austin M. Freeman (Zollikofen: Walking Tree Press, forthcoming).

18. This model is quite similar to an openness view, but differs importantly from open theism in that Eru retains ultimate power. At any moment he may choose to exercise his power to change the world, or even to rewrite history. Thus, unlike an openness eschatology, Eru's plan cannot ultimately be thwarted. As Finrod states, "If we are indeed the Eruhin, the Children of the One, then He will not suffer Himself to be deprived of His own, not by any Enemy, not even by ourselves. This is the last foundation of Estel [hope], which we keep even when we contemplate the End: of all His designs the issue must be for His Children's joy," (*Morgoth*, 320).

19. Returning to the distinction between God's absolute and ordained power: here we should speak not of necessity but of fittingness. God has not bound himself such that by necessity of the consequence he cannot override free decisions. Instead, he operates according to narrative best practice or fittingness. In some cases, it might be most fitting to deny freedom in the interest of other priorities, but this is not generally the case.

20. These are the punctuations as Tolkien wrote them, with proposals for unclear words as supplied by Hostetter.

21. There have been many other theological critiques of Tolkien's work, most of which are ill founded. Classically, see the debate in Paul E. Kerry, ed., *The Ring and the Cross: Christianity and* The Lord of the Rings (Madison: Fairleigh Dickinson University Press, 2011), 57–176 about the extent to which paganism or Christianity predominate in Tolkien's work. Or see, e.g., the debate over Tolkien's "dualism" in Tom Shippey, *The Road to Middle-earth*, 3rd ed. (New York: HarperCollins, 1993); and Tom Shippey, *J.R.R. Tolkien: Author of the Century* (Boston: Houghton Mifflin, 2001), to which I respond in "Flesh, World, Devil: The Nature of Evil in J.R.R. Tolkien," *Journal of Inklings Studies* 10 (2020): 139–71. A more substantial dualism such as proposed by Carrol Fry in "'Two Musics about the Throne of Ilúvatar': Gnostic and Manichaean Dualism in *The Silmarillion*," *TS* 12 (2015): 77–93 can be discarded out of hand. Following Humphrey Carpenter (*J.R.R. Tolkien: A Biography* [Boston: Houghton Mifflin Harcourt, 1977], 31–34), Verlyn Flieger asserts Tolkien has a self-contradictory anthropology (*Splintered Light: Logos and Language in Tolkien's World*, rev. ed. [Kent, OH: Kent State University Press, 2002], 1–4; and "Whose Myth Is It?" in *Between Faith and Fiction: Tolkien and the Powers of His World*, ed. Nils Ivar Agøy [Uppsala: Arda-Society, 1998], 32–39). In response, see Donald T. Williams, "Keystone or Cornerstone? A Rejoinder to Verlyn Flieger on the Alleged 'Conflicting Sides' of Tolkien's Singular Self," *Mythlore* 40.1 (2021): 210–26. More plausibly, Paul Nolan Hyde ("Leaf and Key," *Mythlore* 12.4 [1986]: 27–36), Anita G. Gorman ("J.R.R. Tolkien's 'Leaf by Niggle': Word Pairs and Paradoxes," *Mythlore* 20.4 [1995]: 52–55), Jane Chance (*Tolkien's Art: A Mythology for England*, rev. ed. [Lexington: University of Kentucky Press, 2001], 97), and Austin Freeman (*Tolkien Dogmatics*, 28–29) have noted a deficient role for the Holy Spirit, especially in "Leaf by Niggle."

BIBLIOGRAPHY

Birzer, Bradley J. *J.R.R. Tolkien's Sanctifying Myth: Understanding Middle-earth.* Wilmington: ISI, 2002.

Calvin, John. *Institutes of the Christian Religion.* Translated by Henry Beveridge. Edinburgh: Calvin Translation Society, 1845.

Carpenter, Humphrey. *J.R.R. Tolkien: A Biography.* Boston: Houghton Mifflin Harcourt, 1977.

Chance, Jane. *Tolkien's Art: A Mythology for England.* Rev. ed. Lexington: University of Kentucky Press, 2001.

Coutras, Lisa. *Tolkien's Theology of Beauty: Majesty, Splendor, and Transcendence in Middle-earth.* London: Palgrave Macmillan, 2016.

Davison, Scott A. "Tolkien and the Nature of Evil." Pages 99–109 in The Lord of the Rings *and Philosophy.* Edited by Gregory Bassham and Eric Bronson. PCP 5. Chicago: Open Court, 2003.

Estes, Douglas, ed. *Theology and Tolkien: Practical Theology.* Lanham: Lexington Books/Fortress Academic, 2023.

Flieger, Verlyn. "The Arch and the Keystone." *Mythlore* 38.1 (2019): 7–19.

———. "The Music and the Task: Fate and Free Will in Middle-earth." *TS* 6 (2009): 151–81.

———. *Splintered Light: Logos and Language in Tolkien's World.* Rev. ed. Kent, OH: Kent State University Press, 2002.

———. "Whose Myth Is It?" Pages 32–39 in *Between Faith and Fiction: Tolkien and the Powers of His World.* Edited by Nils Ivar Agøy. Proceedings of the Arda Symposium at the Second Northern Tolkien Festival, Oslo, August 1997. Uppsala: Arda-Society, 1998.

Fornet-Ponse, Thomas. "Freedom and Providence as Anti-Modern Elements?" Pages 177–206 in *Tolkien and Modernity 1.* Edited by Frank Weinreich and Thomas Honegger. Cormarë 9. Zollikofen: Walking Tree Publishers, 2006.

———. "'Strange and Free'—On Some Aspects of the Nature of Elves and Men." *TS* 7 (2010): 67–89.

Freeh, Helen Lasseter. "On Fate, Providence, and Free Will in *The Silmarillion.*" Pages 51–78 in *Tolkien among the Moderns.* Edited by Ralph C. Wood. Notre Dame: University of Notre Dame Press, 2015.

Freeman, Austin M. "'The Backs of Trees': Tolkien, the British Theological Romantics, and the Fantastic Imagination." Pages 275–301 in *The Romantic Spirit in the Works of J.R.R. Tolkien.* Edited by Will Sherwood and Julian Eilmann. Cormarë 51. Zollikofen: Walking Tree Press, 2024.

———. "Flesh, World, Devil: The Nature of Evil in J.R.R. Tolkien." *Journal of Inklings Studies* 10 (2020): 139–71.

———. "Tolkien and Calvin: Five Convergences." In *Tolkien among the Theologians.* Edited by Austin M. Freeman. Zollikofen: Walking Tree Press, forthcoming.

———. *Tolkien Dogmatics: Theology through Mythology with the Maker of Middle-earth.* Bellingham, WA: Lexham Press, 2022.

Fry, Carrol. "'Two Musics about the Throne of Ilúvatar': Gnostic and Manichaean Dualism in *The Silmarillion.*" *TS* 12 (2015): 77–93.

Garth, John. *Tolkien and the Great War: The Threshold of Middle-earth.* Boston: Houghton Mifflin, 2013.

Glyer, Diana Pavlac. *The Company They Keep: C.S. Lewis and J.R.R. Tolkien as Writers in Community.* Kent, OH: Kent State University Press, 2007.

Gorman, Anita G. "J.R.R. Tolkien's 'Leaf by Niggle': Word Pairs and Paradoxes." *Mythlore* 20.4 (1995): 52–55.

Honegger, Thomas. "Tolkien through the Eyes of a Medievalist." Pages 45–66 in *Reconsidering Tolkien.* Edited by Thomas Honegger. Cormarë 8. Zurich: Walking Tree, 2005.

Houghton, John William, and Neal K. Keesee. "Tolkien, King Alfred, and Boethius: Platonist Views of Evil in *The Lord of the Rings.*" *TS* 2 (2005): 131–59.

Hyde, Paul Nolan. "Leaf and Key." *Mythlore* 12.4 (1986): 27–36.

Kerry, Paul E., ed. *The Ring and the Cross: Christianity and* The Lord of the Rings. Madison: Farleigh Dickinson University Press, 2011.

Molina, Luis de. *De liberi arbitrii cum gratiae donis, divina praescientia, praedestinatione et reprobatione concordia.* Rev. ed. Antwerp: Joachim Trognaesius, 1595.

Pinnock, Clark H. et al. *The Openness of God: A Biblical Challenge to the Traditional Understanding of God.* Downers Grove: InterVarsity, 1994.

Purtill, Richard. "Heaven and Other Perilous Realms." *Mythlore* 6.4 (1979): 3–6.

Scull, Christina, and Wayne G. Hammond. *The J.R.R. Tolkien Companion and Guide.* 3 vols. Rev. and exp. ed. London: HarperCollins, 2017.

Shippey, Tom. *The Road to Middle-earth.* 3rd ed. New York: HarperCollins, 1993.

———. *J.R.R. Tolkien: Author of the Century.* Boston: Houghton Mifflin, 2001.

Thomas Aquinas. *Summa Theologica of St. Thomas Aquinas: First Complete American Edition.* 3 vols. Translated by Fathers of the English Dominican Province. New York: Benziger Brothers, 1911.

Timmerman, John H. *Other Worlds: The Fantasy Genre.* Madison: Popular Press, 1983.

Williams, Donald T. "Keystone or Cornerstone? A Rejoinder to Verlyn Flieger on the Alleged 'Conflicting Sides' of Tolkien's Singular Self." *Mythlore* 40.1 (2021): 210–26.

Wood, Ralph C. "Tolkien's Augustinian Understanding of Good and Evil: Why *The Lord of the Rings* is not Manichean." Pages 85–102 in *Tree of Tales: Tolkien, Literature, and Theology.* Edited by Trevor Hart and Ivan Khovacs. Waco: Baylor University Press, 2007.

Chapter 4

In the Brilliant Darkness of a Hidden Silence

J.R.R. Tolkien's Apophatic Tendencies

Douglas Estes

Where *is* God in *The Lord of the Rings*? Why do readers expect God to be *in* Middle-earth? What exactly is Tolkien's theological orientation (or agenda) in his stories, especially *The Lord of the Rings*? These questions are some of the oldest asked by readers—the first known coming a mere two months after *LOTR* appeared in print (*Letters*, 153). Since this time, these types of questions are asked (and answered) perennially in Tolkien scholarship, both popular and academic. As a result, conventional wisdom suggests that Tolkien's world is a theological one, even if readers do not get many overt or explicit glimpses of God. Over the years this has led to many Christian "readings" of Tolkien's works, so many of which have struggled or failed to be persuasive, even as an additional number of works purported to show notable nuances that influenced Tolkien's writing—beyond the inarguable general Roman Catholic/Christian and Northern (Anglo-Saxon, Celtic, Norse, and related) backgrounds. These nuances include Platonic, Neoplatonic, and Thomistic, to name several of the most important.[1] There is no simple or singular theological meaning of Tolkien's works.[2] With some trepidation, the consensus of Tolkien scholarship suggests that Tolkien created a world of faërie that was primarily Northern in style, quietly immersed within a broadly Christian horizon, and one shaped to some lesser degree by quite a few other cultural, literary and philosophical influences—the last not unsurprising, given Tolkien's expertise in languages and literature.[3] As one who read (and debated with friends) as widely as Tolkien did, served in war and in peace, we should expect nothing less than a complex and nuanced world. Yet this does not change the reality that for Tolkien critics, there remains an uneasy inability to figure out what exactly Tolkien does 'under the bonnet.' God is in Tolkien's world, but it is his *absence*, rather than his *presence*, for which readers should search.

Tolkien was not a theologian (*Letters*, 211); but he was an extremely well-read, intelligent and sophisticated Christian who understood much more than his humility permitted him to acknowledge. His intent was that his creation "be consonant with Christian thought and belief," while not feeling constrained for it to "fit with *formalized* Christian theology" (*Letters*, 269, emphasis mine). It is very much this *formalization*—standardized, and in its modern, Roman Catholic vein, boxy—that Tolkien respects but does not wish to engage; not Christian theology itself.[4] This supports Tolkien's plan to eschew the mode of allegory altogether, and to create a fairy-story. With different physics, biologies, and ecologies, a fairy-story will not convey *formalized* Christian theology. This is as true of the world of Jesus' parables as it is Tolkien's Middle-earth. Although Tolkien realizes that some may label this "bad theology," creating fairy-stories and parables invokes "an imagination capable of elucidating truth" (*Letters*, 153). Unlike Jesus' parables, however, fairy-stories orient themselves toward God through the *mystical* (*OFS*, 44, 183). Put it another way, the primary world of human existence is one where people tend to focus on what they *know* about God, but the secondary world of fairy-stories is one where the reader is led by the sub-creator to *experience* things about God.

Here we arrive at the crux of the theological problem in Tolkien. In the primary world, the reasoned work behind *formalized* Christian theology most often focuses on *cataphatic* (or positive) expressions about God, but mystical experiences better lend themselves to *apophatic* (or negative) expressions about God. In short, in this chapter I will argue that the uneasiness with which readers engage Tolkien's theology in his works—especially *The Lord of the Rings*—is largely due to readers' unfamiliarity with mystical aspects of the Christian faith, especially its apophatic theology. Tolkien's apophatic tendencies in his works tie together and explain the various Platonic, Neoplatonic, Thomistic, and mystical nuances that bubble up in his works. These tendencies also fit comfortably well within his "archaic and neo-medieval" theological model.[5] However, awareness of Tolkien's apophaticism does not resolve all theological questions in his works; nor do I believe, can any summary explanation, simply because Tolkien wrote a fairy-story not a theological tract.[6] Still Fleming Rutledge is quite accurate when she describes the "considerable impact" Tolkien's theology makes on readers is due to the "veiled substructure" that has a "*cumulative effect*" over the course of the reading. The theological substructure is not veiled because it is merely backgrounded, as is the case with so many works of literature; in Tolkien it is veiled because it occurs in a mystical and apophatic form.[7] Readers cannot glean Tolkien's theology by reasoning through his works—they must *absorb* the theology of the story from the experience of their reading.[8] Or, to paraphrase the Cappadocian Father Gregory of Nyssa (ca. AD 335–394), to see God in Middle-earth readers must have "penetrated into the luminous darkness."[9]

TOLKIEN ON THE *VIA NEGATIVA*

When people talk about God—who he is, his nature—there are essentially two orientations from which people can approach: the positive (*cataphatic*) and the negative (*apophatic*).[10] The positive approach to God's nature (the *via positiva*) remarks on what people can say about God—God is good, God is holy—whereas the negative approach to God's nature reminds people what they cannot say about God—God is indescribable, God is limitless. An apophatic approach to God often stresses the transcendence of God, and pushes back against a too-cozy cataphatic emphasis on the immanence of God. In Christian theology, apophatic tendencies arise from the close experience of knowing God, and as a result, the realization that creatures—out of reverence and awe—can find no thoughts or words in which to actually talk about the Creator.[11] As a Christian and a philologist, Tolkien was acutely aware of the limitations of language.

Historically, 'formalized' Christian theologians were wary of apophatic theology, fearing its slippery slope into mysticism, agnosticism, or atheism; and there is some validity in this concern, as apophatic philosophies do occur outside of Christian theology.[12] Based on extant writings, scholars suggest that Philo of Alexandria (*fl.* early to mid-first century CE) is the earliest thinker to openly acknowledge the possibility of apophatic theology.[13] It is likely the roots of apophatic thought dig deep into both Hebraic (Moses' interaction with God in Exodus, Elijah's experiences in 1 Kings) and Greek (Plato, possibly the pre-Socratics) histories. Paul does appear to allude to apophaticism in his correspondence (1 Cor 13:12; Col 1:15), and John is perhaps even more explicit (John 6:46). From here, notable church fathers such as Justin Martyr (ca. AD 100–165), Clement of Alexandria (AD 150–211/215) and Gregory of Nyssa contributed, as well as Neoplatonic philosophers such as Plotinus (AD 205–270). The Christian most responsible for bringing negative theology to the fore was Pseudo-Dionysius (*fl.* early 6th century AD), who brought Christian theology into conjunction with Neoplatonic philosophy. From here, negative theology has influenced numerous Christian thinkers—especially those with a bent toward the experiential or mystical—such as Meister Eckhart (ca. 1260–1328), John Henry Newman (1801–1890), and even Hans Urs von Balthasar (1905–1988).[14] The latter two are most important here, as Tolkien was likely influenced by Newman's theology, and his thought is consonant with von Balthasar's.[15] As a professor of Anglo-Saxon, Tolkien also studied and taught from apophatic texts including *The Cloud of Unknowing*, composed in Middle English in the late 14th century. Recent shifts in Western cultural currents have led to a significant increase in interest in apophaticism in the twentieth and twenty-first centuries.[16] This is a positive development for Christian theology, as a robust Christian theology must engage the negative as well as the positive understandings of God's nature, as both approaches complement each other and bring the Christian into closer relationship with God.[17] Negative theology is ultimately the province of all strains and traditions of Christian theology.[18]

Although scholars credit Neoplatonism as the central launching pad for full-blown apophatic philosophy,[19] the God devised by Plotinus is only a shadow of the God of Christian theology. This is due to an approach that eschews a strictly-defined nature of God and turns instead to the revelational and relational overtures of the Creator to his creatures. To put it more clearly, Tolkien is no Neoplatonist in his understanding of God (except as a receiver of Christian tradition that interacted with Neoplatonism). In the first words of the *Ainulindalë* of *The Silmarillion*, Tolkien introduces the God of Middle-earth as "Eru, the One, who in Arda is called Ilúvatar." In comparison, the Nicene Creed opens with "I believe in one God, the Father almighty." In both instances (albeit different genres) there is God, who is one, and whom his creation is to identify as father. In contrast, Plotinus does refer to God as one and father, but more so the Intellect than the One.[20] Though a full argument engaging Plotinus is beyond the scope of this chapter, it is the way God reveals and relates himself to people—especially in the incarnation—that makes Christian theology distinct from Neoplatonic thought (interesting dialogue aside). In this regard, Neoplatonic philosophy is ultimately self-defeating because it begins with intellect (therefore, cataphatically) to try to explain that which is unexplainable, God.[21] The only way for people to explain God is for God to give people those words, as Vladimir Lossky explains:

> Theological procedure is quite different. Since God reveals Himself to us, our whole thought—really, our whole approach, our *conversatio*—should respond and correspond to this fact, should conform to this revelation gathered in faith. Philosophers construct an idea about God. For the theologian, God is someone Who reveals Himself and Who cannot be known outside of revelation. One must open oneself to this personal God, to encounter him in a total involvement: that is the only way to know Him. But this concrete and personal God contains the abstract and impersonal God of philosophers Who is not, most often, a mere mirage, but also a reflection in human thought of the personal God.[22]

And from this, the consequence:

> One must therefore start from faith—and that is the only way to save philoso-
> phy. Philosophy itself, on its summits, demands the renunciation of speculation;
> questing God, it attains the moment of supreme ignorance: a negative way
> where the failure of human thought is acknowledged. Here, philosophy ends in
> a mysticism and dies in becoming the experience of an Unknown God Who can
> no longer even be named. . . . If the summit of philosophy is a question, theology
> must reply by bearing witness that transcendence is revealed in the immanence
> of the Incarnation.[23]

Thus, the philosopher fails to complete their task, as they begin with their
intellect and work backward to God; cataphatically, this is untenable, and apophatically, at best, is incomplete.[24] This seems to be the illusion that readers
of *The Lord of the Rings* often read under; the illusion that Tolkien created an
imaginary world with Elves, Dwarves, and Hobbits, and only later imagined
what kind of God would fit into that world. Instead, Tolkien did not seem to
work backward from creation to Creator; he created a Secondary World that
worked forward from the Creator to his creation. In this Tolkien possibly
felt that he was "given by God the gift of recording 'a sudden glimpse of the
underlying reality or truth'"—revelation, not reason.[25] Middle-earth absorbed
Tolkien's beliefs about God, to such a degree of revelation appropriate for this
world to work (cf. *Letters*, 165, but also, 172). Due to Tolkien's great respect
for God, he would not want to take the chance of "juxtaposing" the God of
his Secondary World against the God of the Primary World.[26] After all, even
in the Primary World, "it is not possible to conceive the one, the unknown,"
so why try to conceive of the One in a Secondary World?[27]

Not every story that omits God is an expression of apophatic theology.
In fact, virtually all stories that omit God are simply agnostic, atheistic, or
non-theistic. But *The Hobbit* and *The Lord of the Rings* do not omit God as
much as they hide God, and "to speak of hiddenness is to indicate presence
and not absence."[28] If nothing else, Providence implicates a hidden God in
Middle-earth. To make the case that Tolkien's intended orientation toward
Eru Ilúvatar in Middle-earth is primarily apophatic—whether he consciously
recognized this or not—we will consider three positive evidences of the negative orientation in his work: (1) Tolkien's personal viewpoint as he expressed
in his letters; (2) Faramir's prayer (the most cited example of religion in
LOTR; cf. *Letters*, 211); and (3) the creation story in the *Ainulindalë* and
Valaquenta.

TOLKIEN AND THE LIMITS OF LANGUAGE

J.R.R. Tolkien occupied the Rawlinson and Bosworth Professorship of Anglo-Saxon at Oxford University for twenty years. Although he specialized in Anglo-Saxon, he "was brought up in the Classics" (*Letters*, 142), and retained a strong commitment to antiquity throughout his life (as evidenced by his collaboration with the Jerusalem Bible project).[29] As a world-class philologist, he was keenly aware of the uses, capacities, and limitations of language, to a degree that most readers of Middle-earth are not. It is his awareness of what language cannot do and cannot say that likely starts Tolkien down the negative path. For example, Tolkien appreciates the difficulties with explaining Faërie to others, explaining that "the Perilous Realm cannot be approached directly."[30] Derek Shank observes this in Tolkien's essay, "On Fairy-stories," writing that "after the opening section where he defines fairy-stories apophatically, by saying what they are not (beast fables, travellers' tales, dream narratives), Tolkien approaches the nature of fairy-stories through a critique of the way in which they have been studied."[31] Similarly, when it comes to talking about God, Tolkien readily admits that people do not know what "God" means:

> Thus we do not know the original meaning of θεός or *deus* or *god*. We can, of course, make some guesses about the formation of these three quite distinct words, and then try to generalize a basic meaning from the senses shown by their relatives—*but* I do not think we shall necessarily by that way get any nearer to the idea 'god' at any actual moment in any language using one of these words. (*Letters*, 209)

Tolkien claims that we cannot grasp the etymology and semantics of "God" in Greek, Latin, or English, but this claim seems more than merely linguistic; it echoes the apophatic claim that people cannot "get any nearer to" the origin and nature of God. Tolkien further observes that no human language can really allow people to draw closer in their understanding of who God is. This truth is at the center of apophatic theology—it is "a form of theology that celebrates how God will always exceed human understanding and language."[32] Pseudo-Dionysius puts it elegantly:

> For the more that we soar upwards the more our language becomes restricted to the compass of purely intellectual conceptions, even as in the present instance plunging into the Darkness which is above the intellect we shall find ourselves reduced not merely to brevity of speech but even to absolute dumbness both of speech and thought.[33]

Literature, as much as language, is a creaturely enterprise from which we can express "a truth that cannot be articulated, only shown."[34] Or, in Tolkien's world, absorbed.

In his depiction of Eru, Tolkien observes that for the people of Middle-earth Eru is "immensely remote" (*Letters*, 156).[35] However, remoteness is not absence; Middle-earth is a theistic world, and Eru Ilúvatar is the One who is known by his children as Father. Eru is remote, and his remoteness is a form of hiddenness. Tolkien addresses this when he notes that "the only criticism that annoyed" him was that Middle-earth "contained no religion" (*Letters*, 165). Instead, Tolkien explains that Middle-earth "is a monotheistic world of 'natural theology.' The *odd* fact that there are no churches, temples, or religious rites and ceremonies, is simply part of the historical climate depicted" (*Letters*, 165, emphasis mine). As someone more at home with Homer than Hardy—Classics than English literature, and who "first discovered the sensation of literary pleasure in Homer" (*Letters*, 142), the monotheistic world Tolkien envisions fits within a sanitized and fantasized Bronze Age of our own world, one with great heroes such as Odysseus and Moses (cf. *Letters*, 165), and one wherein God is still largely hidden from his creation, albeit in a stylized, Northern medieval garb.

Eru may hide from his creation, but so too does the God of the Primary World hide from his creation as well—especially in the ages before the Incarnation. Although YHWH would at times speak to Moses as if face to face (Exod 33:11), he hides himself from the Israelites in a pillar of cloud (Exod 33:9), and is principally unknown to most peoples of the world. When Moses asks to know more about YHWH to the point of looking him in the eye (Exod 33:18), YHWH objects and only allows Moses to see his back (Exod 33:21–23). The God who hides himself can frustrate those who are trying for faithfulness (Job 13:24; Ps 13:1, 44:24, 88:14), but a hidden God is not an inactive God (Isa 45:13).[36] The blessing of the *via negativa* is it "forbids us to follow natural ways of thought and to form concepts which would usurp the place of spiritual realities."[37]

Tolkien observes that while Eru is hidden, he is active in Middle-earth at least two ways. First, while "there is no embodiment of the One, of God, who indeed remains remote, outside the World" (*Letters*, 181), Eru does work through his Powers, agents of his divine will entrusted with oversight of Middle-earth. Although readers may think of these Powers as "gods," they "take the imaginative but not the theological place of 'gods'" (*Letters*, 212). Their oversight is a shepherding role, as they are "appointed to the government of the world" (*Letters*, 286)—as "they cannot by their own will alter any fundamental provision" from Eru (*Letters*, 153). Second, Eru is a Father who "retains all ultimate authority" over his world and his children, and "reserves the right to intrude the finger of God into the story" (*Letters*, 181, 200). As

Father, Eru will not hold back inserting himself when he must. In a later letter, Tolkien makes this explicit: "Sauron was first defeated by a 'miracle': a
direct action of God the Creator" (*Letters*, 211). This "finger of God" that
Tolkien describes is felt by his characters as the guidance of Providence;
Gandalf describes it best when he explains that there is "something else at
work," beyond the power of Sauron, which determined that Bilbo "was *meant*
to find the Ring" and Frodo was "*meant* to have it" (*FR*, I, ii). The "finger
of God" is, of course, most likely a direct reference to the comment by the
mages of Pharaoh on the miracles of YHWH (Exod 8:19), but it also refers to
God's revelatory power (Exod 31:18), especially the power of the Holy Spirit
(Luke 11:20).[38]

Although Eru is hidden from Creation, his engagement with the world creates metaphysical challenges for Tolkien. Notice that Tolkien calls the lack of
religious expression "odd." Is it *odd* because readers would expect some form
of religiosity in a world that is so meticulously articulated as is Middle-earth?
Or is it "odd" because there is a God, one worthy of worship, and readers
would therefore expect some depiction of religious activity, where there is
none? Tolkien does not use words carelessly,[39] so he acknowledges that some
readers will be uneasy with his lack of religion, especially since in Middle-
earth Men are fallen and evil is abundant (*Letters*, 156). In one of the very
few mentions of religious activity, Tolkien explains that when Sauron "got
Ar-Pharazôn's mind under his own control, and in the event corrupted many
of the Númenóreans," that he "*destroyed the conception of Eru*, now represented as a mere figment of the Valar or Lords of the West (a fictitious sanction
to which they appealed if anyone questioned their rulings), and *substituted a
Satanist religion* with a large temple, the worship of the dispossessed eldest
of the Valar (the rebellious Dark Lord of the First Age)" (*Letters*, 156, emphasis mine). This *also* is "odd." Prior to corruption, the Númenóreans seem to
be content with merely "the conception" of God, with a hallowed place on
the summit of the mountain Meneltarma, the Pillar of Heaven (*Silmarillion*,
259; cf. *Sauron*, 400), but when Sauron comes to power, he institutes actual
religious activity with a physical temple consecrated to Morgoth, activity
defined by fire, smoke, and the torment of good people (*Silmarillion*, 272; cf.
Peoples, 182–83). This strikes one as reminiscent—an allusion, not a reference—of the story of the Israelites and the molten calf of gold (Exod 32; also,
the sacrifice to Molech, Lev 18:21, 2 Kgs 23:10). While Moses talks to God
on the mountain, the Israelites grow impatient and create an idol (Exod 32:4).
After creating the calf, Aaron builds an altar for worship, and the Israelites
worship their idol (Exod 32:5–6). Here Moses is out of sight, speaking to
the hidden God, on the mountain, and the Israelites must rely on the conception of God that has carried them into the wilderness (and later, through his
law). Both Sauron and some of the Israelites push people away from Moses'

commitment for his people to know God toward evil religious practices of raging fire and shed blood. Like Tolkien, Gregory of Nyssa uses the metaphor of climbing a high mountain to attain a conception of God.[40]

The source of the oddity is now clearer. Tolkien (like the writer of Exodus) has no inability stating plainly what is evil worship. It is evident that rejecting Eru, ignoring YHWH's prophet Moses, building a temple to Melkor, or creating a golden calf idol, are all erroneous forms of religious activity. But what is good worship? That is much harder to state. Tolkien wrestles with this problem as he *does not want to diminish* the good by making it simpler or easier than it is. Tolkien explains that,

> if you imagine people in such a mythical state, in which Evil is largely incarnate, and in which physical resistance to it is a major act of loyalty to God, I think you would have the 'good people' in just such a state: *concentrated on the negative*: the resistance to the false, while 'truth' remained more historical and philosophical than religious. (*Letters*, 156, emphasis mine)

Tolkien admits that in a world where evil exists as a physical, tangible presences, then simply resisting evil is itself an act of good religiosity. The type of evil that occurs in Middle-earth requires only a *negative* response (cf. *Letters*, 183). In creating Middle-earth in this way, Tolkien avoids the need to imagine positive or cataphatic religious experiences; he only needs his heroes to engage in negative or apophatic religious experiences. In Middle-earth, it is primarily to resist "the false," as the cataphatic knowledge of God can remain hidden and undiscussed, "more historical and philosophical than religious." Men "escaped from 'religion' in a pagan sense, into a pure monotheist world" (*Letters*, 156).

Tolkien was well aware that trying to describe God and his worship on the *via positiva* was impossible. His respect for Christ and the Church was too great. This is the primary reason Tolkien rejects following in the steps of Arthurian legend for his story:

> For one thing its 'faerie' is too lavish, and fantastical, incoherent and repetitive. For another and more important thing: it is involved in, and explicitly contains the Christian religion. For reasons which I will not elaborate, that seems to me *fatal*. Myth and fairy-story must, as all art, reflect and contain in solution elements of moral and religious truth (or error), but not explicit, not in the known form of the primary 'real' world. (I am speaking, of course, of our present situation, not of ancient pagan, pre-Christian days). (*Letters*, 131, emphasis mine)

Tolkien argues that the inclusion of religious activity is "fatal" to the development of faërie. Fairy-stories can and should contain "moral and religious truth," but it cannot be explicit as we know here in the Primary World *lest it cheapen and minimize good worship.* This is true for Tolkien only in the Christian era ("our present situation"), because "ancient pagan" worship is invalid whether in Primary or Secondary Worlds (and thus, potentially could be included in fairy-stories without damage to itself). In a later letter, distancing the return of Gandalf from the resurrection of Jesus, Tolkien is blunter still: "The Incarnation of God is an *infinitely* greater thing than anything I would dare to write" (*Letters*, 181). As a faithful Christian, Tolkien could devise his own fantasy world, but he must take caution not to write anything that could reflect poorly on YHWH, the God of the Primary World.[41] Better to let the one true God of Middle-earth, Eru, remain hidden from his people. Or, as Meister Eckhart put it, better to "be silent and do not chatter about God; for when you chatter about him, you are telling lies and sinning."[42] Tolkien feared being a liar before God.

Given Tolkien's intelligence, wisdom, and faith, how aware was he that he was engaging in apophatic theology? We cannot know for certain, of course, the degree to which he was familiar with the theological concept (especially as it existed in the early twentieth century). We can be reasonably certain that, as a scholar of Anglo-Saxon, he read apophatic texts (at minimum, *The Cloud of Unknowing*). His background, plus his linguistic awareness of the inability to determine the etymology and semantic range of "God," informed his apophatic tendencies about God. In responding by letter to the question of the meaning of life, he admits that we cannot answer the "larger" questions about our world, "because that requires a *complete* knowledge of God, which is unattainable. If we ask why God included us in his Design, we can really say *no more* than because He Did" (*Letters*, 310). Here Tolkien expresses a full-blown apophatic orientation toward the question of the meaning of life. Rather than try to give a positive, and likely flawed (but more comforting!) answer, Tolkien follows his apophatic tendencies and falls back on the foundational acknowledgment that creatures are limited in their understanding of the Creator and his reasons for creating our world.

It is also possible that Tolkien was quite aware of his apophatic theological tendencies. At one point he explains the religious situation in Middle-earth this way:

> While God (Eru) was a datum of good Númenórean philosophy, and a prime fact in their conception of history, He had at the time of the War of the Ring no worship and no hallowed place. And that kind of *negative truth* was characteristic of the West, and all the area under Númenórean influence: the refusal to worship any 'creature,' and above all no 'dark lord' or satanic demon, Sauron, or any other, was almost as far as they got. . . . But there would be no temple of the True God while Númenórean influence lasted. (*Letters*, 156, emphasis mine)

Tolkien's reference to "negative truth" indicates some awareness that the worship of Eru in Middle-earth followed a *via negativa*. In making this claim we remember that a healthy negative theology does not lead to abandoning God, it leads to greater engagement of God.[43] This is why Tolkien, on being asked the meaning of life, stated it "is to *increase* according to our capacity our knowledge of God by all the means we have, and to be *moved* by it to praise and thanks" (*Letters*, 310, emphasis mine).

GRACE AT DINNER AND THE *GLORIA PATRI*

Tolkien famously admits that God reveals himself in *The Lord of the Rings* only rarely and obliquely, and most notably in "Gandalf's conversation with Frodo . . . or in Faramir's Númenórean grace at dinner" (*Letters*, 156). The first example is an acknowledgment of the work of Providence, but the second, something a bit more complex. It is a positive expression of religious faith, and it is the only such occurrence in Tolkien's primary works. It is also a rather curious type of inclusion, as it presents an interesting puzzle for knowledgeable readers. To add to the curiousness, the only character that engages in any overt religious activity—Faramir—is the one character with whom Tolkien personally identifies (*Letters*, 180). In light of Tolkien's own faith commitments, it seems unlikely that this is mere coincidence. In fact, Faramir's expression of faith is the same expression of faith as Tolkien himself encourages.

Tolkien records Faramir's expression of faith as he, his soldiers, and Frodo and Sam prepare to eat a meal together:

> Before they ate, Faramir and all his men turned and faced west in a moment of silence. Faramir signed to Frodo and Sam that they should do likewise.
> 'So we always do,' he said, as they sat down: 'we look towards *Númenor that was*, and beyond to *Elvenhome that is*, and to that which is *beyond Elvenhome and will ever be*.' (*TT*, IV, v, emphasis mine)

There are two parts to Tolkien's description of Faramir's expression of faith—the action and the explanation for the action. The action that Faramir expects of his men and his guests is that they look to the West and remain silent. At first read, it seems that Faramir's expectations are 'more spiritual than religious,' actions meant to simply memorialize a golden age from long ago. This might be a reasonable interpretation if not for Faramir's explanation of the expression to Frodo and Sam. They are blissfully unaware of this tradition, and so Faramir must explain it to them, as this is something "we always do." The "we" pronoun is an indexical, with an unclear reference; it could mean "my men and I" indicating that Faramir, and by extension his men, regularly engage in this moment of silence, but it also could mean "the people of Gondor," either as a nation or as a custom of the children of Númenor. The difficulty with the first reading is that Faramir asks Frodo and Sam if they have "no such custom at meat," implying that most people should have this custom, though "such" is also an indexical that could refer to a custom of varying degrees of similarity. The difficulty with the second reading is that there is no indication that Denethor or Boromir looks West in silence before meals (e.g., *RK,* V, i), and Faramir does not himself do this with Denethor (*RK*, V, iv),[44] though Tolkien may have omitted the practice from these scenes for narrative expediency. The difficulty with the third reading is that Aragorn and the Dúnedain, also children of Númenor, do not seem to practice this, nor for that matter by extension Gandalf or Elrond, nor any of the Elves, partake in this practice. If Tolkien wanted to include an expression of faith of this sort to round out his characters, it would seem that Aragorn would be the most likely character, and that Aragorn would have expressed it earlier in the story (and then it could be omitted for narrative expediency as a regular occurrence at meals). Indeed, the expression comes from Faramir, and perhaps the most likely reference to draw from the "we" is "Faramir and other men of similar faith" (cf. *Letters*, 297, discussed below). We can deduce this from the attitude of the hobbits; although the hobbits have never had contact with the men of Gondor, Frodo, Sam, and Pippin navigate almost all of their customs with little confusion. Yet Sam and Frodo have *no idea* what Faramir intends by his pre-meal expression of faith; they feel "strangely rustic and untutored" (*TT*, IV, v). Although Tolkien uses the word "rustic" seven other times in *LOTR* (including appendices), likely in its primary sense of "rural," Tolkien, as an Oxford philologist, is quite well aware that "rustic" is also a gloss for the Latin word *paganus*, from which English derives the word "pagan."[45] Is it too much a coincidence that Faramir's instance of religious occurrence results in Frodo's admission that they are essentially *pagans*—in the original/historical not pejorative sense—unaware of greater religious truth?[46] Perhaps, but if so it is still clear that Tolkien intends a gentle awakening in the hobbits of a deeper spiritual truth that exists outside their limited cultural knowledge and tribal superstitions—the exact situation for many people in the first centuries of the Common Era in the Roman Empire. Equally notable given Tolkien's philological acumen is that the root of *paganus* is *pagus*, which refers to a district that stands at a distance from central society.[47] In late antiquity, the *pagus* could be a county in England, a rural district at a distance from Rome, but in Middle-earth, the *pagus* is the Shire, the rural district at a distance from Gondor (and therefore, Númenor). The Shire and its people are a place unaware of the greater truth, part of which Faramir is able to continue to awaken in Frodo and Sam through his expression. With virtually any other modern author, this etymological inquiry might be too improbable to suggest; but with Tolkien, it is quite possible if not probable that he was well informed of these semantic shades. In fact, repurposing Tolkien's own words, Frodo and Sam also "escaped from 'religion' in a *pagan* sense, into a pure monotheist world" (*Letters*, 156, emphasis mine). In other words, the experiences of Frodo and Sam convert them from the comfortable, rustic religion of the Shire to pure monotheism where they now begin to call on the name of Elbereth (*FR*, I, xi; *RK*, VI, i).

Faramir's moment of silence before the meal is no mere memorialization but a sincere act of religious faith. We know this in part because Tolkien explains that Eru "is still remembered in (unspoken) prayer by those of Númenórean descent" (*Letters*, 297), a clear reference to Faramir's expression. Thus, Tolkien intends the moment of silence to be a time for unspoken prayer, as "a commemoration of the Departed" (*Letters*, 211), but also out of awe for Eru Ilúvatar (*UT*, 166), not an empty gesture (as it can be in modern, Western cultural rituals in public, secular spaces). Silence is the most apophatic speech the faithful can use to talk about God. We also know this in part due to Faramir's explanation for the practice that he gives to the hobbits. Faramir's explanation is not simply prose exposition; instead, it takes the form of a balanced, poetic liturgy that rather obviously is the Middle-earth version of the *Gloria Patri*, also known as the Lesser Doxology:

> Glory be to the Father, and to the Son, and to the Holy Ghost;
> As it *was in the beginning, is now*, and *ever shall be*: world without end. Amen. (emphasis mine)

The correlation between the two doxologies is unmistakable, as both demarcate the entire extension of God's action in the world—past, present, and future. Doxologies, expressions of faith in the glory of God, bring together both cataphatic and apophatic ideas in their liturgies.[48] In the Númenórean version, Faramir omits the Trinitarian formula, but this is due to Tolkien's belief that Middle-earth in "the 'Third Age' was not a Christian world" (*Letters*, 165), as "the Fall of Man is in the past and off stage; the Redemption of Man in the far future" (*Letters*, 297). Rather than try to have Faramir articulate theologically the pure monotheism of Middle-earth (*Letters*, 156), and risk sounding Neoplatonic or Monarchianist, Tolkien's apophatic tendencies (and good sense) intercede—better to have his characters say *nothing* about God than risk saying something faithless (even if that God is the imaginary God of a Secondary World). What Faramir does instead is remain silent, offering an unspoken prayer to the one true but ineffable God, and then describes this God doxologically, through the *where* and *when* of his glory.

Unlike the Lesser Doxology, which contains only temporal descriptors of God, Faramir's version contains spatial descriptors which supplant the temporal descriptors. On the surface, this is not unexpected due to Tolkien's love and commitment to his world, Middle-earth. Tolkien values place deeply, including over time: "I have, I suppose, constructed an imaginary *time*, but kept my feet on my own mother-earth for *place*" (*Letters*, 211). Even as the Lesser Doxology of the Primary World recognizes the eternal nature of God, from which people may attain eternal life, Faramir's Doxology of the Second World points to the relational nurture of God, from which people may come home to dwell with God in his place. From Númenor, to Elvenhome, to the beyond of the West, the people of God in Middle-earth journey—whether by death or by ship—to dwell with Ilúvatar. Tolkien's emphasis on space is apophatic, wherein the end of theology and belief is a vital "union with God."[49] Tolkien captures this union spatially with the metaphor of the West, which is why when "weary at last of the mortal lands," Frodo and others "could take ship from the Grey Havens and pass into the Uttermost West" (*RK*, Appendix A), even as in the Primary World the people of God go to "dwell in the House of the Lord forever" (Ps 23:6), a spatial synonym of eternal life. References to place help people "speak of the hidden presence of God," in that "these pictures of a 'place' are not literally locations *in which* God is hidden, but which *accord* (like Job 28) with a sense of the hiddenness of God," allowing people to experience the transcendence of God.[50] God's transcendence exceeds human imagination, but the *Gloria Patri* means to help orient people to experience a holy God throughout space and time, as "the glory of God is never only the glory of this world risen to the heights. The glory of God remains the glory beyond, the glory back before back, the glory where nowhere, the glory when noever," world without end.[51] It appears that Faramir, and faithful men of Gondor, took Tolkien's own advice: "If you don't do so already, make a habit of the 'praises.' I use them much (in Latin): the Gloria Patri, the Gloria in Excelsis, the Laudate Dominum," (*Letter*, 54). Tolkien/Faramir's habits of faith are the bright mithril strings that bind the spirituality of the Primary and Secondary Worlds.

SILENCE TO MUSIC, DARKNESS TO LIGHT

The Roman poet Horace (65–8 BC) would not have thought well of Tolkien's works, with his preparatory prose and leisurely pace that launch both *The Hobbit* and *The Lord of the Rings*, and even less of *The Silmarillion* with its *ab ovo* creation story in the *Ainulindalë* and *Valaquenta*.[52] Yet these creation accounts have become one of the most remarked upon stories in the entire Tolkien corpus, as their cosmogonic motifs resonate well with

Western readers—readers who, unlike Horace, have two extra millennia of conditioning to prepare them for *ab ovo* openings that epically unite God and creation. Tolkien opens the *Valaquenta* with the phrase, "in the beginning," an unambiguous reference to the Hebraic creation story (Gen 1:1), as well as the Christian reflection on that creation (John 1:1–2):

> In the beginning Eru, the One, who in the Elvish tongue is named Ilúvatar, made the Ainur of his thought; and they made a great Music before him. In this Music the World was begun; for Ilúvatar made visible the song of the Ainur, and they beheld it as a light in the darkness. (*Silmarillion*, 13)

The *Valaquenta* teaches there is one God, Eru, the Father of All, who spoke into existence the Ainur, who in turn made music, which Ilúvatar transformed into a physical world that became a light in the otherwise darkness. Although there is no doubt that Tolkien is waxing theological, there remain uncertainties over what type of theology Tolkien engages (e.g., Christian or Neoplatonic) and how he mixes his accounts with the Genesis accounts (e.g., allusion, homage, or pastiche). While we cannot venture to solve the latter question here, we can certify a rather definitive answer to the former: The *Valaquenta* and *Ainulindalë* depict a creation story that is strongly consonant with a Christian understanding of creation. Now, "Christian understanding" is a broad phrase spanning two millennia of diverse (if related) thought, to which John William Houghton makes the critical clarification that it is a *medieval theological* Christian understanding of Genesis that overlaps so well with Tolkien's vision.[53] To add to this is Bradford Lee Eden's observation that the music motif is also at home in medieval thought.[54] Other attempts to situate Tolkien's creation story adjacent to, or outside Christian thought completely, fail to appreciate the distinctly Christian paradox of a fully transcendent yet fully immanent God. For example, Verlyn Flieger argues "Father of All he may be, but he has no further role in the action," for Eru Ilúvatar "remains throughout the Unknown God, unknowable and unreachable in his oneness, perceivable and approachable only to the extent by which the part can represent the whole."[55]

Although Tolkien intentionally hides Eru, the reader discerns that Eru is *good*. For example, Yavanna, a High One of Arda, praises him for being "merciful," and later, "bountiful" (*Silmarillion*, 34, 36). This is not the God of Plotinus; this is the God of the Bible; for example, the Psalmist describes God as both "merciful" and "bountiful" (Ps 114:5, 7 DRB).[56] Similarly, the reader learns that "Ilúvatar had compassion upon Aulë" for his humility (*Silmarillion*, 33), even as God has "mercy" on his people who "yield" to him (2 Chr 30:8–9 DRB). Further, in what little direct speech of Eru Tolkien records, Eru is often found asking open questions. Open questions typically indicate a sincere interest in learning, and as such signal empathy, much like Eru asking why Aulë created (*Silmarillion*, 32), and God asking Adam where he hid (Gen 3:9).[57] Ilúvatar shows empathy and love toward the Elves in an early version of the story of Thingol (*LT 2*, 42) and in making a "dwelling place" for the Quendi in Aman (*Morgoth*, 87). Finally, there are comments in the legendarium that sound explicitly Christian; for example, while even the Valar "were not informed by the will or design of Eru" about the master plan for Arda, Eru "appears in the Elvish tradition to demand two things from His Children (of either Kindred): belief in Him, and proceeding from that, hope or trust in Him (called by the Eldar *estel*).[58] Eru "has no further role in the action" *yet*, as time is not up and "the last chord of Eru" has not yet sounded (*Morgoth*, 99). Thus, it is not Eru's oneness that makes him "unknowable and unreachable," it is his transcendence, which implicates his holiness, which demonstrates his goodness whenever he acts within his creation.[59]

The primary motif of Tolkien's creation account is music. Within this motif we see not only Tolkien's medievalism but also his apophatic tendencies come to the fore. In Genesis' creation account, God creates the universe, and as his Spirit moves over creation, God begins to speak into creation (Gen 1:1–3). Tolkien's account modulates this, with Eru creating the Ainur, who are "angelic created beings appointed to the government of the world," (*Letters*, 286), from whom the seeds of creation were sung. As the Ainur learn to sing, Ilúvatar introduces a "mighty theme" that brings the Ainur to worship the Creator by bowing before him and remaining silent (*Silmarillion*, 3; cf. Ps 62:1, 62:5). Although music is not included in the Genesis account of creation, it is a motif that later interpreters introduce—perhaps most notably in God's answer to Job. Here God asks Job the open question, "Where wast thou when I laid the foundations of the earth? . . . When the morning stars sang together" (Job 38:4–7; cf. Sir 46:17, Luke 2:13–14). In Tolkien's creation story, the Ainur sing together as Eru Ilúvatar lays the foundation for Middle-earth. Following Job, Gregory of Nyssa believes there is a "wonderful harmony of the heavens [that] proclaims the wisdom which shines forth in the creation and sets forth the great glory of God."[60] When Moses ascends the mountain to speak to God, the Israelites hear the sound of a trumpeting horn (Exod 19:16), a musical aspect of God's proclamation.[61] Singing is often heard as a response to God for his creation (1 Chr 16:23–26) or activity (Exod 15). In Tolkien's creation story, Ilúvatar speaks, "propounding"—trumpeting?— "themes of music" to the Ainur, "and they sang before him" (*Silmarillion*, 3). Considering all of this, it is possible to argue simply that Tolkien maps later musical reflections and motifs back onto the biblical creation story, but there is something more at work here; unlike in biblical stories, Tolkien almost completely avoids cataphatic statements about Eru and hides him throughout the rest of *The Silmarillion*, *The Hobbit*, and *The Lord of the Rings*. Music, however, is part of the *"non*-verbal vocabulary of theology."[62] With music one need never *say* anything about God all the while *experiencing* God. Music (sound) is not in and of itself apophatic,[63] nor theological, but by its nature can permit one access to the transcendence of God—"music 'speaks' by speaking, apophatically, what cannot be spoken."[64] The same is true, if not more, of silence; it is "the ultimate apophatic expression."[65] Using the motifs of music and silence—in the *Ainulindalë* and the *Valaquenta*—and modes of music—throughout the remainder of his work, Tolkien followed his apophatic tendencies to 'speak' of God without ever saying anything about God. An example of this is the song *A Elbereth Gilthoniel*, a hymn to Varda Elentári, Queen of the Blessed Realm, that 'speaks' in the same way a Roman Catholic hymn to Mary 'speaks' of the faithfulness of God. The hymn appears only in Sindarin, as Tolkien insisted, its meaning unknowable and unreachable to Tolkien's audience. This is because Tolkien believed people could experience through language (phonologically) even what they could not rationally understand in words (semantically), and to that end, "he clearly believed that *untranslated* elvish would do a job that English could not."[66] Thus, we are back to the root of Tolkien's apophatic tendencies— his acute awareness of the inability of language to provide meaning about God. The medieval philosopher John Scotus Erigena (810–877) reflects this same attitude according to William Franke: "No language, with its parts and articulation, can properly convey the absolute simplicity of the divine nature, though that does not prevent us from having some experience of it as a 'beautiful and ineffable harmony.'"[67] Tolkien's readers can experience the glory of God in the beautiful and ineffable harmony of an Elvish hymn, even if they cannot rationally understand the words.

This complements a second, less frequent motif that Tolkien also relies upon that reveals his apophatic tendencies—darkness and light. Light and darkness is an extremely common motif in Christian-influenced Western culture so much of which derives from the light and darkness motifs of the Genesis creation account (Gen 1) along with the later complement in John's Gospel (esp. John 1:5) (cf. *Letters*, 131). Most of Tolkien's use of this motif follows this typical approach (which culture abbreviates as light = good, darkness = evil). For example, Tolkien mimics Genesis when he writes in the *Ainulindalë* that after the music, the Ainur see "a light, as it were a cloud with a living heart of flame; and they knew that this was no vision only, but that Ilúvatar had made a new thing: Eä, the World that Is" (*Silmarillion*, 10).[68] However, there are examples of darkness in biblical literature that later theologians read apophatically that bleed over into Tolkien's thinking.[69] For example, at one point when Moses goes to speak to God for his people, "Moses went to the dark cloud wherein God was" (Exod 20:21 DRB). Although Western cultural inclinations would expect God to be robed in light, not hidden in darkness (but see 1 Kgs 8:12, Ps 18:11, 97:2), Gregory of Nyssa understood this darkness "to indicate divine incomprehensibility."[70] Gregory also believes Moses' journey is theotic, for knowledge of God means becoming more like God.[71] Paul picks up this apophatic (and theotic) tendency when he writes, "We see now through a glass in a dark manner: but then face to face. Now I know in part: but then I shall know even as I am known" (1 Cor 13:12 DRB). These apophatic uses of darkness indicate the complete and total inability of creatures to know and understand the Creator,[72] but it is not because God is himself dark, it is because God's light is so bright that to medieval theologians this darkness represents "the superabundance of light."[73] This also builds off Paul's argument that Christ "inhabiteth light inaccessible: whom no man hath seen, nor can see" (1 Tim 6:16 DRB). An example of this occurs in the "Tale of Adanel," Tolkien's version of the fall of humanity for Middle-earth (*Morgoth*, 345–49; cf. Gen 3). Shortly after the creation of Men, they hear the Voice of Ilúvatar but are fearful and come to believe it is the Dark (and therefore, against them). During this time a beautiful lord of gold and silver light (Melkor) shows up and convinces Men to build a temple to him and worship him. Echoing the Exodus story, people fear the real God veiled in "dark cloud" with a thunderous Voice, but are willing to worship the beautiful, golden calf (Exod 32). At another point in the legendarium, Tolkien has Gelmir reply to Tuor with an apophatic aphorism: "'Through darkness one may come to the light'" (*UT*, 21).[74]

One final example from the legendarium illuminates Tolkien's apophatic theology quite plainly. In an earlier version of the Music of the Ainur, omitted from *The Silmarillion* but published in *The Book of Lost Tales, Part One*, the man Eriol sails to Tol Eressëa where he meets a number of Elves who reveal to him mysteries of Middle-earth. One of Eriol's earliest encounters is with Rúmil, the elven door-ward of the Cottage of Lost Play. As Rúmil teaches Eriol the *Ainulindalë*, Tolkien records the beginning of their conversation:

> But Rúmil said: "Ilúvatar was the first beginning, and beyond that no wisdom of the Valar or of Eldar or of Men can go."
> "Who was Ilúvatar?" said Eriol. "Was he of the Gods?"
> "Nay," said Rúmil, "that he was not, for he made them. Ilúvatar is the Lord for Always who dwells beyond the world; who made it and is not of it or in it, but loves it." (*LT 1*, 49)

In order to explain Eru Ilúvatar to Eriol, Rúmil takes a largely apophatic tack. He states that Ilúvatar is the one who precedes all else (Ainur and creation), and as a consequence, created beings from high to low, from Valar to Men, cannot understand him.[75] Apparently, Rúmil believes the starting point for discussing Ilúvatar is his darkness, his unknowableness. This confuses Eriol, who is only aware (vaguely) of the Ainur. Again, Rúmil's response to Eriol is apophatic, stating that Ilúvatar is not one of the Ainur, and cannot be, because he is their creator. In saying this, Rúmil stresses what God is not, not what God is. He continues to explain that Ilúvatar does not live within the confines of the universe, because he made it, and therefore is neither similar to creation nor within the confines of creation—all negative statements about Eru. To conclude, Rúmil pivots to tell Eriol that even though Eru is unknowable, and is not related to the world except through his creative work, Eru still loves the world. Akin to a medieval Christian theologian, Rúmil moves from an apophatic perspective on God to the possibility of a relational experience with God. As this story is among the earliest versions of the *Ainulindalë*, we can see from the first beginning that Tolkien's creation account is thoroughly rooted in an imaginative Christian faith,[76] albeit in a medieval style and in an apophatic mode. Tolkien, moving from philology to theology in his conscious development of his epics (*Letters*, 142), does well what philosopher George Steiner later put to words:

> It is decisively the fact that language does have frontiers, that it borders on three other modes of statement—light, music, and silence—that gives proof of a transcendent presence in the fabric of the world. It is just because we can go no further, because speech so marvellously fails us, that we experience the certitude of a divine meaning surpassing and enfolding ours. What lies behind man's word is eloquent of God.[77]

CONCLUSION

In his letters, Tolkien records the surprise of one reader with a "dimly dawning religious feeling" who wrote him, wondering how Tolkien was able to "create a world in which some sort of faith seems to be everywhere without a visible source, like light from an invisible lamp" (*Letters*, 413). This keen observation by an unknown reader returns us to the opening questions of this essay: Where *is* God in *The Lord of the Rings*? Why do readers so often *feel* that Tolkien is religious, spiritual, and theological when there is virtually no mention of God or religious activity (outside of his creation accounts)?

In this essay, I have argued that so much of this relates to Tolkien's apophatic tendencies. As a trained philologist, he was well aware—perhaps even humbled by—human languages when it came to speaking of a transcendent and holy God. This causes Tolkien to hide God from the reader, even as he acknowledges God's magnificence in doxology and at creation. There are other avenues where one could explore Tolkien's apophatic tendencies beyond these, such as his apophatic name for the Holy Spirit of Middle-earth, the Flame Imperishable, or his decision to create "gods" of the Ainur who would govern in Eru's stead. Apophaticism is *not* a key that unlocks a hidden meaning in Tolkien's works; it is an unfamiliar mode of thinking about God that Tolkien submerses in a fairy-story with tremendous success, allowing his readers to absorb truth about God. Much like an apophatic theologian, Tolkien is not planning to reveal God to his readers, but merely hoping to create "the receptacle of revelation" so that his readers can "arrive at the personal presence of a hidden God."[78] This is critical, because as a Christian, it is not possible to say something about God without saying something about Christ—Christ is the incarnate God who is the only way to God. Or, as John puts it, "no one comes to the Father except through" Jesus (John 14:6). Because Tolkien cannot speak of the Son in his works, he must be careful to speak of the Father in his works.[79] In summation, apophatic theology is not an unusual branch of theology, but a perfect complement to cataphatic theology that reorients one to an even greater understanding of God.[80] We cannot know to what degree Tolkien was aware of apophatic theology, but from his philological study, the influence of Newman in his early years, his engagement with medieval tradition, his awareness of *The Cloud of Unknowing*,[81] his interest in mystical thought, to his deep reverence for and faith in the God of Abraham, Isaac, and Jacob, Tolkien was immersed in apophatic thought and this shines through his work. Whether we readers realize it or not, these apophatic tendencies that saturate the Secondary World of Middle-earth influence us to adore God in the Primary World.[82] Tolkien's supreme appreciation for the limits of language causes him to write this way, so that our spirit is touched, not of a rational knowledge of God, but so that we can experience him the way his characters do, "in the brilliant darkness of a hidden silence."[83]

NOTES

1. For example, see John Cox, "Tolkien's Platonic Fantasy," *VII* 5 (1984): 53; Verlyn Flieger, "Naming the Unnameable: The Neoplatonic 'One' in Tolkien's *Silmarillion*," in *Diakonia: Studies in Honor of Robert T. Meyer*, ed. Thomas P. Halton and Joseph P. Williman (Washington, D.C.: Catholic University of America Press, 1986), 128; and Jonathan S. McIntosh, *The Flame Imperishable: Tolkien, St. Thomas, and the Metaphysics of Faërie* (Kettering, OH: Angelico, 2017); respectively.

2. Michael D. C. Drout, "Towards a Better Tolkien Criticism," in *Reading* The Lord of the Rings: *New Writings on Tolkien's Classic*, ed. Robert Eaglestone (London: Continuum, 2005), 21.

3. Cf. Carrol Fry, "'Two Musics about the Throne of Ilúvatar': Gnostic and Manichaean Dualism in *The Silmarillion*," *TS* 12 (2015): 78.

4. This argument supports Tolkien's own theological musings about reincarnation (*Letters*, 153; cf. *Morgoth*, 363–65). It is not that Tolkien rejects Roman Catholic doctrine or Christian theology; it is that he imagines how God would act in different times and places, with "different biology" scenarios, outside of, but not in rejection of, *formalized* (and orthodox) Christian theology. Protestants have similar musings, such as the question of whether or not extraterrestrials can be "saved."

5. Cox, "Tolkien's Platonic Fantasy," 63.

6. It does not seem possible for a fiction writer to create a Secondary World that would cohere completely with the Primary World unless the Secondary World *was* the Primary World, and any divergences between the two would naturally, unavoidably, and (in worthy literature) profitably create tensions for the reader to imagine.

7. Fleming Rutledge, *The Battle for Middle-earth: Tolkien's Divine Design in* The Lord of the Rings (Grand Rapids: Eerdmans, 2004), 3.

8. Douglas Estes, introduction to *Theology and Tolkien: Practical Theology*, ed. Douglas Estes (Lanham: Lexington Books / Fortress Academic, 2023), 2.

9. Gregory of Nyssa, *The Life of Moses*, II.163 (Malherbe and Ferguson, CWS).

10. Interestingly, many reference resources on theology omit a discussion on apophaticism; two that include one are Bradley Nassif, "Apophatic Theology," in *New Dictionary of Theology: Historical and Systematic*, ed. Martin Davie et al., 2nd ed. (Downers Grove: IVP Academic, 2016), 52–53; and Ian A. McFarland, "Apophatic Theology," in *The Cambridge Dictionary of Christian Theology*, ed. Ian A. McFarland et al. (Cambridge: Cambridge University Press, 2011), 25–27.

11. Bruce Milem, "Four Theories of Negative Theology," *HeyJ* 48 (2007): 187.

12. For example, apophaticism drives the atheistic theology of Martin Heidegger. Jacques Derrida believes there are three discernible paradigms in apophatic thought: Greek, Christian, and Heideggerian, developed in his "How to Avoid Speaking: Denials," in *Derrida and Negative Theology*, ed. Harold Coward and Toby Foshay (Albany: SUNY Press, 1992), 100–131, esp. 122. Modern Western philosophy's take on apophaticism is of limited value here.

13. Charles Freeman, *A New History of Early Christianity* (New Haven: Yale University Press, 2009), 68; and Tomasz Stępień and Karolina Kochańczyk-Bonińska, *Unknown God, Known in His Activities: Incomprehensibility of God during the Trinitarian Controversy of the 4th Century*, European Studies in Theology, Philosophy and History of Religions 18 (Berlin: Peter Lang, 2018), 26.

14. On Newman's influence on Tolkien, Bradley Birzer writes that when Tolkien's mother Mabel passed away, leaving Tolkien "in the care of Father Francis Morgan, a Roman Catholic priest at the Birmingham Oratory, which had originally been founded by John Henry Newman," in *J.R.R. Tolkien's Sanctifying Myth: Understanding Middle-earth* (Washington, D.C.: Regnery, 2002), 2; see also Yannick Imbert, *From Imagination to Faërie: Tolkien's Thomist Fantasy* (Eugene: Pickwick, 2022), 137; Pat Pinsent, "Religion: An Implicit Catholicism," in *A Companion to J.R.R. Tolkien*, ed. Stuart D. Lee, 2nd ed. (Hoboken: Wiley Blackwell, 2022), 425–26; and on Tolkien's "affinity" with Balthasar, see the thoughts of Lisa Coutras, *Tolkien's Theology of Beauty: Majesty, Splendor, and Transcendence in Middle-earth* (New York: Palgrave

Macmillan, 2016), esp. 14. For overview, see Holly Ordway, *Tolkien's Faith: A Spiritual Biography* (Elk Grove Village: Word on Fire, 2023).

15. Von Balthasar extensively studied the works of Gregory of Nyssa; see Martin Laird, *Gregory of Nyssa and the Grasp of Faith: Union, Knowledge, and Divine Presence*, OECS (Oxford: Oxford University Press, 2004), 15–16.

16. See for example, Oliver Davies and Denys Turner, introduction to *Silence and the Word: Negative Theology and Incarnation*, ed. Oliver Davies and Denys Turner (Cambridge: Cambridge University Press, 2004), 1–2; William Franke, preface to *On What Cannot Be Said: Apophatic Discourses in Philosophy, Religion, Literature, and the Arts*, Vol. 1: *Classic Formulations*, ed. William Franke (Notre Dame: University of Notre Dame Press, 2007), 3; and Robert Woźniak, "Apophasis and System: Dogmatic Theology in Apophatic Perspective," *Verbum Vitae* 41 (2023): 813.

17. Woźniak, "Apophasis and System," 822–23.

18. Karen Kilby, *God, Evil and the Limits of Theology* (London: T&T Clark, 2020), 145.

19. Deirdre Carabine, *The Unknown God: Negative Theology in the Platonic Tradition: Plato to Eriugena*, Louvain Theological and Pastoral Monographs 19 (Louvain: Peeters, 1995), 149.

20. Deepa Majumdar, *Plotinus on the Appearance of Time and the World of Sense: A Pantomime* (Aldershot: Ashgate, 2007), 215.

21. For a similar critique of Heidegger's atheistic negative theology, see Woźniak, "Apophasis and System," 815.

22. Vladimir Lossky, *Orthodox Theology: An Introduction*, trans. Ian and Ihita Kesarcodi-Watson (Crestwood, NY: St Vladimir's Seminary Press, 1978), 20.

23. Lossky, *Orthodox Theology*, 21.

24. Cf. Lossky, *Orthodox Theology*, 23.

25. Humphrey Carpenter, *Tolkien: A Biography* (Boston: Houghton Mifflin, 1977), 92.

26. Lossky, *Orthodox Theology*, 21.

27. Pseudo-Dionysius, *The Divine Names*, 593B (Franke).

28. Paul S. Fiddes, "The Quest for a Place Which is 'Not-a-Place': The Hiddenness of God and the Presence of God," in *Silence and the Word: Negative Theology and Incarnation*, ed. Oliver Davies and Denys Turner (Cambridge: Cambridge University Press, 2002), 43.

29. For examples, see Hamish Williams' recently edited volume, *Tolkien and the Classical World*, Cormarë 45 (Zurich: Walking Tree, 2021).

30. Derek Shank, "'The Web of Story': Structuralism in Tolkien's 'On Fairy-stories,'" *TS* 10 (2013): 148.

31. Shank, "'Web of Story,'" 148.

32. Richard Bourne and Imogen Adkins, *A New Introduction to Theology: Embodiment, Experience and Encounter* (London: T&T Clark, 2020), 124.

33. Pseudo-Dionysius, *The Mystical Theology*, 1033B (Rolt); in Dionysius the Areopagite, *The Mystical Theology*, trans. C.E. Rolt (London: SPCK, 1920), 197–98.

34. Timothy Cleveland, *Beyond Words: Philosophy, Fiction, and the Unsayable* (Lanham: Lexington, 2022), 21–22.

35. It is possible to assume that Eru represents an impersonal descriptor of God (such as the English word "God," when directed at Yʜwʜ) and Ilúvatar represents a personal description of God (such as the English phrase "Heavenly Father"). However, Petri Tikka argues that Eru is actually a highly personal *name* of God, similar to Yʜwʜ, in which case, Elvish does not seem to have an impersonal descriptor of God as English does; see "God's Name in Elvish," in *Arda Philology 3: Proceedings of the Third International Conference on J.R.R. Tolkien's Invented Languages*, ed. Anders Stenström Beregond (Stockholm: Arda Society, 2011), 32.

36. God also hides himself when his children are disobedient (Mic 3:4), but this motive seems to be a minimal part in Tolkien's work.

37. Vladimir Lossky, *The Mystical Theology of the Eastern Church* (London: James Clarke, 1957), 42.

38. Cyril of Alexandria, *Commentary on Luke*, Homily 81.

39. See the example in Estes, *Theology and Tolkien*, 1.

40. Gregory of Nyssa, *Life of Moses*, II.158.

41. This begs the question as to why Tolkien would introduce reincarnation into his stories—a theme that would undermine Christian theology (which Tolkien admits is in fact "bad *theology*" [*Letters*, 153]). Tolkien seems to suggest that it is merely a peculiar biological feature of his fairy-story, and not meant to be theological. Thus, from this perspective, just as the near-immortal lives of Elves do not damage Christian ideas about eternal life, reincarnation in Middle-earth should not damage Christian ideas about life, death, and resurrection. Both are merely peculiar biological features of the people of Middle-earth, same as "woolly-footed" Hobbits who need no shoes (*TT*, III, viii).

42. Meister Eckhart, "Sermon 83," in *Meister Eckhart: The Essential Sermons, Commentaries, Treatises and Defense*, trans. Edmund Colledge and Bernard McGinn, CWS (Mahwah: Paulist, 1981), 207.

43. Nassif, "Apophatic Theology," 52–53.

44. Of course, as a skilled author Tolkien may have omitted repetitive practices so as to not bog down the story.

45. See for example, Philip Rousseau, "Pagan, Paganism," in *The Oxford Classical Dictionary*, ed. Simon Hornblower and Antony Spawforth, 3rd ed. (Oxford: Oxford University Press, 1996), 1091; and see Tolkien's own discussion of "inherited paganism" among "'primitive' peoples" (*OFS*, 44n2).

46. Thomas Jürgasch notes it was only in the fourth century AD that the Latin term *"paganus"* began to take on the pejorative sense of "non-Christian," in "Christians and the Invention of Paganism in the Late Roman Empire," in *Pagans and Christians in Late Antique Rome: Conflict, Competition, and Coexistence in the Fourth Century*, ed. Michele Renee Salzman, Marianne Sághy, and Rita Lizzi Testa (Cambridge: Cambridge University Press, 2016), 116.

47. Jürgasch, "Christians and the Invention of Paganism," 117.

48. Heather Elkins, "Liturgies," in *The Encyclopedia of Christian Literature*, Vol 1, ed. George Thomas Kurian and James D. Smith III (Lanham: Scarecrow, 2010), 91.

49. Sameer Yadav, "Mystical Experience and the Apophatic Attitude," *Journal of Analytic Theology* 4 (2016): 22.

50. Fiddes, "Quest for a Place," 43.

51. Nicolas Ayo, *Gloria Patri: The History and Theology of the Lesser Doxology* (Notre Dame: University of Notre Dame Press, 2007), 115.

52. Horace, *Ars Poetica*, 147.

53. John William Houghton, "Augustine in the Cottage of Lost Play: The *Ainulindalë* as Asterisk Cosmogony," in *Tolkien the Medievalist*, ed. Jane Chance, RSMRC 3 (London: Routledge, 2003), 172.

54. Bradford Lee Eden, "The 'Music of the Spheres': Relationships between Tolkien's *The Silmarillion* and Medieval Cosmological and Religious Theory," in *Tolkien the Medievalist*, ed. Jane Chance, RSMRC 3 (London: Routledge, 2003), 192–93.

55. Flieger, "Naming the Unnameable," 132.

56. In this chapter I use the Douay-Rheims Bible (DRB) since this is the translation we have confidence to believe Tolkien was most familiar with. For example, in Letter 92, Tolkien refers to the Canaanite god "Moloch," a transliteration with /o/, same as the DRB, LXX, the Vulgate, and Wycliffe. In contrast, virtually all other versions render the transliteration "Molech" with /e/, including the KJV, RSV, Lutherbibel, Geneva Bible, ASV, and almost all modern translations.

57. For an extended discussion of the semantics and pragmatics of open questions, see Douglas Estes, *Questions and Rhetoric in the Greek New Testament: An Essential Reference Resource for Exegesis* (Grand Rapids: Zondervan, 2017), 149–54.

58. In the NT, the semantic range of πίστις (which we gloss as "faith") includes both "belief" and "trust" (in the sense of commitment and action).

59. It is a pervasive and persistent fallacy in popular Christian theology to render the word *holy* in the sense of *set apart*. *Holy* points to the complete and integral nature of God, his aseity, his *completeness apart from and outside of creation* (e.g., Isa 6:3, 57:15). Things which are, and people who are holy are consecrated to God, and as a result, are therefore *set apart* from things and people divorced from God (e.g., Rom 7:12).

60. Gregory of Nyssa, *Life of Moses*, II.168. If we were to trace this musical creation motif from the Bible into Western culture to Tolkien, we would include Dante Alighieri (1265–1321), John Milton (1608–1674), John Dryden (1631–1700), and C.S. Lewis; see David J. Kendall, *The Music of the Spheres in the Western Imagination* (Lanham: Lexington, 2022), 67.

61. Although readers often understand the trumpet as a metaphor for the volume and timbre of God's voice, Exodus never states that the trumpet is God's voice, nor that God is the one sounding the trumpet; see John I. Durham, *Exodus*, WBC 3 (Dallas: Word, 1987), 270–71.

62. Denys Turner, *The Darkness of God: Negativity in Christian Mysticism* (Cambridge: Cambridge University Press, 1995), 20.

63. Eduardo de la Fuente, "Music as Negative Theology," *Thesis Eleven* 56 (1999): 75.

64. Andrew W. Hass, Laurens ten Kate, and Mattias Martinson, *The Music of Theology: Language—Space—Silence*, Routledge New Critical Thinking in Religion, Theology and Biblical Studies (London: Routledge, 2024), 151.

65. Franke, *On What Cannot Be Said*, 2.

66. Tom Shippey, *The Road to Middle-earth*, rev. exp. ed. (New York: Houghton Mifflin, 2003), 114.

67. Franke, *On What Cannot Be Said*, 183, citing John Scotus Erigena, *Periphyseon*, 517c.

68. Similarly, in the *Valaquenta*, "Ilúvatar made visible the song of the Ainur, and they beheld it as a light in the darkness" (*Silmarillion*, 17).

69. See also Austin M. Freeman, *Tolkien Dogmatics: Theology through Mythology with the Maker of Middle-earth* (Bellingham: Lexham, 2022), 37.

70. Laird, *Gregory of Nyssa*, 49, also 27.

71. Laird, *Gregory of Nyssa*, 49–50.

72. Clement of Alexandria, *Strom.* 5.12.

73. Hubert Cunliffe-Jones, ed. *A History of Christian Doctrine: In Succession to the Earlier Work of G.P. Fisher* (Philadelphia: Fortress, 1978), 217. Also see Pseudo-Dionysius' explanation in *Mystical Theology*, 997B.

74. George Herring writes: "This paradox, central to Tolkien's world, is also at the heart of the Christian spiritual life. The journey to the light of God can also be made through darkness . . . This apophatic or negative way of approaching God has a long history in Christian mysticism, and is at the heart of the works of the great English spiritual writers of the fourteenth century," in "The Symbolism of Light and Darkness in *The Lord of the Rings*," in *A Hidden Presence: The Catholic Imagination of J.R.R. Tolkien*, ed. Ian Boyd and Stratford Caldecott (South Orange, NJ: Chesterton Press, 2003), 75.

75. It is possible that Tolkien uses the unusual phrase "first beginning" as a play on the Greek word ἀρχή, which we can gloss in English as either "beginning" or "first."

76. Michaël Devaux, "The Origins of the *Ainulindalë*: The Present State of Research," in *The Silmarillion—Thirty Years On*, ed. Allan Turner, Cormarë 15 (Zurich: Walking Tree, 2007), 106.

77. George Steiner, *Language and Silence* (London: Faber, 1967), 58–59.

78. Lossky, *Orthodox Theology*, 32.

79. See similar arguments in Lossky, *Orthodox Theology*, 34. An exception to this occurs in the *Athrabeth Finrod ah Andreth* (*Morgoth*, 303–366), where Tolkien hints that one day "Eru will himself enter into Arda and heal Men and all the Marring" (*Morgoth*, 351–52). However, this prophecy sounds like an explicit retelling of the Christian incarnation.

80. McFarland, "Apophatic Theology," 26.

81. Special thanks to Austin Freeman for his suggestions and critiques of this chapter.

82. Cf. Woźniak, "Apophasis and System," 823.

83. Pseudo-Dionysius, *Mystical Theology*, 997B (Luibheid); in Pseudo-Dionysius, *The Complete Works*, trans. Colm Luibheid, CWS (New York: Paulist, 1987), 135.

BIBLIOGRAPHY

Ayo, Nicolas. *Gloria Patri: The History and Theology of the Lesser Doxology*. Notre Dame: University of Notre Dame Press, 2007.

Birzer, Bradley. *J.R.R. Tolkien's Sanctifying Myth: Understanding Middle-earth*. Washington, D.C.: Regnery, 2002.

Bourne, Richard, and Imogen Adkins. *A New Introduction to Theology: Embodiment, Experience and Encounter*. London: T&T Clark, 2020.

Carabine, Deirdre. *The Unknown God: Negative Theology in the Platonic Tradition: Plato to Eriugena*. Louvain Theological and Pastoral Monographs 19. Louvain: Peeters, 1995.

Carpenter, Humphrey. *Tolkien: A Biography*. Boston: Houghton Mifflin, 1977.

Cleveland, Timothy. *Beyond Words: Philosophy, Fiction, and the Unsayable*. Lanham: Lexington, 2022.

Coutras, Lisa. *Tolkien's Theology of Beauty: Majesty, Splendor, and Transcendence in Middle-earth*. New York: Palgrave Macmillan, 2016.

Cox, John. "Tolkien's Platonic Fantasy." *VII* 5 (1984): 53–69.

Cunliffe-Jones, Hubert, ed. *A History of Christian Doctrine: In Succession to the Earlier Work of G.P. Fisher*. Philadelphia: Fortress, 1978.

Cyril of Alexandria. *A Commentary upon the Gospel According to Saint Luke*, Part 2. Translated by R. Payne Smith. Oxford: Oxford University Press, 1859.

Davies, Oliver, and Denys Turner, eds. *Silence and the Word: Negative Theology and Incarnation*. Cambridge: Cambridge University Press, 2004.

Derrida, Jacques. "How to Avoid Speaking: Denials." Pages 73–142 in *Derrida and Negative Theology*. Edited by Harold Coward and Toby Foshay. Albany: SUNY Press, 1992.

Devaux, Michaël. "The Origins of the *Ainulindalë*: The Present State of Research." Pages 81–110 in *The Silmarillion—Thirty Years On*. Edited by Allan Turner. Cormarë 15. Zurich: Walking Tree, 2007.

Dionysius the Areopagite. *The Divine Names* and *The Mystical Theology*. Translated by C.E. Rolt. London: SPCK, 1920.

Drout, Michael D. C. "Towards a Better Tolkien Criticism." Pages 15–28 in *Reading The Lord of the Rings: New Writings on Tolkien's Classic*. Edited by Robert Eaglestone. London: Continuum, 2005.

Durham, John I. *Exodus*. WBC 3. Dallas: Word, 1987.

Eden, Bradford Lee. "The 'Music of the Spheres': Relationships between Tolkien's *The Silmarillion* and Medieval Cosmological and Religious Theory." Pages 183–93 in *Tolkien the Medievalist*. Edited by Jane Chance. RSMRC 3. London: Routledge, 2003.

Elkins, Heather. "Liturgies." Pages 91–94 in *The Encyclopedia of Christian Literature, Vol 1*. Edited by George Thomas Kurian and James D. Smith III. Lanham: Scarecrow, 2010.

Estes, Douglas. "Gandalf the Grey, Apostle to Men and Elves." Pages 83–102 in *Theology and Tolkien: Practical Theology*. Edited by Douglas Estes. Lanham: Lexington Books / Fortress Academic, 2023.

————. *Questions and Rhetoric in the Greek New Testament: An Essential Reference Resource for Exegesis*. Grand Rapids: Zondervan, 2017.

Estes, Douglas, ed. *Theology and Tolkien: Practical Theology*. Lanham: Lexington Books / Fortress Academic, 2023.

Fiddes, Paul S. "The Quest for a Place Which is 'Not-a-Place': The Hiddenness of God and the Presence of God." Pages 35–60 in *Silence and the Word: Negative Theology and Incarnation*. Edited by Oliver Davies and Denys Turner. Cambridge: Cambridge University Press, 2002.

Flieger, Verlyn. "Naming the Unnameable: The Neoplatonic 'One' in Tolkien's *Silmarillion*." Pages 127–32 in *Diakonia: Studies in Honor of Robert T. Meyer*. Edited by Thomas P. Halton and Joseph P. Williman. Washington, D.C.: Catholic University of America Press, 1986.

————. *Splintered Light: Logos and Language in Tolkien's World*. Rev. ed. Kent, OH: Kent State University Press, 2002.

Franke, William, ed. *On What Cannot Be Said: Apophatic Discourses in Philosophy, Religion, Literature, and the Arts*. 2 Vols. Notre Dame: University of Notre Dame Press, 2007.

Freeman, Austin M. *Tolkien Dogmatics: Theology through Mythology in Middle-earth*. Bellingham: Lexham, 2022.

Freeman, Charles. *A New History of Early Christianity*. New Haven: Yale University Press, 2009.

Fry, Carrol. "'Two Musics about the Throne of Ilúvatar': Gnostic and Manichaean Dualism in *The Silmarillion*." *TS* 12 (2015): 77–93.

Fuente, Eduardo de la. "Music as Negative Theology." *Thesis Eleven* 56 (1999): 57–79.

Gičić Puslojić, Marija A. "Mythopoetic Imaginarium of J.R.R. Tolkien." PhD diss., University of Belgrade, 2015.

Gregory of Nyssa. *The Life of Moses*. Translated and introduced by Abraham J. Malherbe and Everett Ferguson. CWS. New York: Paulist, 1978.

Hägg, Henny Fiskå. *Clement of Alexandria and the Beginnings of Christian Apophaticism*. OECS. Oxford: Oxford University Press, 2006.

Halsall, Michael John. *Creation and Beauty in Tolkien's Catholic Vision: A Study in the Influence of Neoplatonism in J.R.R. Tolkien's Philosophy of Life as 'Being and Gift.'* Cambridge: Lutterworth, 2020.

Hass, Andrew W., Laurens ten Kate, and Mattias Martinson. *The Music of Theology: Language—Space—Silence*. Routledge New Critical Thinking in Religion, Theology and Biblical Studies. London: Routledge, 2024.

Herring, George. "The Symbolism of Light and Darkness in *The Lord of the Rings*." Pages 69–80 in *A Hidden Presence: The Catholic Imagination of J.R.R. Tolkien*. Edited by Ian Boyd and Stratford Caldecott. South Orange, NJ: Chesterton Press, 2003.

Horace. *Satires, Epistles*, and *Ars Poetica*. Translated by H. Rushton Fairclough. LCL. Cambridge: Harvard University Press, 1926.

Hornblower, Simon, and Antony Spawforth, eds. *The Oxford Classical Dictionary*. 3rd ed. Oxford: Oxford University Press, 1996.

Houghton, John William. "Augustine in the Cottage of Lost Play: The *Ainulindalë* as Asterisk Cosmogony." Pages 171–82 in *Tolkien the Medievalist*. Edited by Jane Chance. RSMRC 3. London: Routledge, 2003.

Imbert, Yannick. *From Imagination to Faërie: Tolkien's Thomist Fantasy*. Eugene: Pickwick, 2022.

Jürgasch, Thomas. "Christians and the Invention of Paganism in the Late Roman Empire." Pages 115–38 in *Pagans and Christians in Late Antique Rome: Conflict, Competition, and Coexistence in the Fourth Century*. Edited by Michele Renee Salzman, Marianne Sághy, and Rita Lizzi Testa. Cambridge: Cambridge University Press, 2016.

Kazimierczak, Karolina Agata. "Unfolding Tolkien's Linguistic Symphony: Relations Between Music and Language in the Narratives of J.R.R. Tolkien, and in Compositions Inspired by Them." Pages 56–79 in *Arda Philology 2: Proceedings of the Second International Conference on J.R.R. Tolkien's Invented Languages*. Edited by Anders Stenström Beregond. Stockholm: Arda Society, 2009.

Kendall, David J. *The Music of the Spheres in the Western Imagination*. Lanham: Lexington, 2022.

Kilby, Karen. *God, Evil and the Limits of Theology*. London: T&T Clark, 2020.

Korpua, Jyrki. *The Mythopoeic Code of Tolkien: A Christian Platonic Reading of the Legendarium*. CESFF 75. Jefferson, NC: McFarland, 2021.

Laird, Martin. *Gregory of Nyssa and the Grasp of Faith: Union, Knowledge, and Divine Presence*. OECS. Oxford: Oxford University Press, 2004.

Lossky, Vladimir. *The Mystical Theology of the Eastern Church*. London: James Clarke, 1957.

———. *Orthodox Theology: An Introduction*. Translated by Ian and Ihita Kesarcodi-Watson. Crestwood, NY: St Vladimir's Seminary Press, 1978.

Madsen, Catherine. "Light from an Invisible Lamp: Natural Religion in *The Lord of the Rings*." *Mythlore* 53 (1988): 43–47.

Majumdar, Deepa. *Plotinus on the Appearance of Time and the World of Sense: A Pantomime*. Aldershot: Ashgate, 2007.

McBride, Sam. *Tolkien's Cosmology: Divine Beings and Middle-earth*. Kent, OH: Kent State University Press, 2020.

McFarland, Ian A. "Apophatic Theology." Pages 25–27 in *The Cambridge Dictionary of Christian Theology*. Edited by Ian A. McFarland, David A. S. Fergusson, Karen Kilby, and Iain R. Torrance. Cambridge: Cambridge University Press, 2011.

McIntosh, Jonathan S. *The Flame Imperishable: Tolkien, St. Thomas, and the Metaphysics of Faërie*. Kettering, OH: Angelico, 2017.

Meister Eckhart. *Meister Eckhart: The Essential Sermons, Commentaries, Treatises and Defense*. Translated by Edmund Colledge and Bernard McGinn. CWS. Mahwah: Paulist, 1981.

Milem, Bruce. "Four Theories of Negative Theology." *HeyJ* 48 (2007): 187–204.

Nassif, Bradley. "Apophatic Theology." Pages 52–53 in *New Dictionary of Theology: Historical and Systematic*. Edited by Martin Davie, Tim Grass, Stephen R. Holmes, John McDowell, and T. A. Noble. 2nd ed. Downers Grove: IVP Academic, 2016.

Ordway, Holly. *Tolkien's Faith: A Spiritual Biography*. Elk Grove Village: Word on Fire, 2023.

Pinsent, Pat. "Religion: An Implicit Catholicism." Pages 424–36 in *A Companion to J.R.R. Tolkien*. Edited by Stuart D. Lee. 2nd ed. Hoboken: Wiley Blackwell, 2022.

Pseudo-Dionysius. *The Complete Works*. Translated by Colm Luibheid. CWS. New York: Paulist, 1987.

———. *The Divine Names* and *The Mystical Theology*. Translated and introduced by John D. Jones. Mediæval Philosophical Texts in Translation 21. Milwaukee: Marquette University Press, 1999.

Rutledge, Fleming. *The Battle for Middle-earth: Tolkien's Divine Design in* The Lord of the Rings. Grand Rapids: Eerdmans, 2004.

Shank, Derek. "'The Web of Story': Structuralism in Tolkien's 'On Fairy-stories.'" *TS* 10 (2013): 147–65.

Shippey, Tom. *The Road to Middle-earth*. Rev. exp. ed. New York: Houghton Mifflin, 2003.

Steiner, George. *Language and Silence*. London: Faber, 1967.

Stępień, Tomasz, and Karolina Kochańczyk-Bonińska. *Unknown God, Known in His Activities: Incomprehensibility of God during the Trinitarian Controversy of the 4th Century*. European Studies in Theology, Philosophy and History of Religions 18. Berlin: Peter Lang, 2018.

Tikka, Petri. "God's Name in Elvish." Pages 26–37 in *Arda Philology 3: Proceedings of the Third International Conference on J.R.R. Tolkien's Invented Languages*. Edited by Anders Stenström Beregond. Stockholm: Arda Society, 2011.

Turner, Denys. *The Darkness of God: Negativity in Christian Mysticism*. Cambridge: Cambridge University Press, 1995.

Williams, Hamish, ed. *Tolkien and the Classical World*. Cormarë 45. Zurich: Walking Tree, 2021.

Woźniak, Robert. "Apophasis and System: Dogmatic Theology in Apophatic Perspective." *Verbum Vitae* 41 (2023): 813–31.

Yadav, Sameer. "Mystical Experience and the Apophatic Attitude." *Journal of Analytic Theology* 4 (2016): 17–43.

Chapter 5

Gandalf, Sauron, Melian, and the Balrog as Angels

A Study of J.R.R. Tolkien's Maiar in the Context of Biblical Angelology

Charlie Trimm

When one thinks of what angels might look like in J.R.R. Tolkien's Middle-earth, it at first seems that angels are missing—especially if one only reads *The Hobbit* and *The Lord of Rings*. However, it becomes clear when reading some of his less well-known writings on Middle-earth and his letters that Tolkien intended his world to have a category of beings equivalent to angels. Indeed, in his mythology he created two great categories of spirits: the Valar and the Maiar. The Valar, such as Manwë, Tulkas, and Melkor, were the more powerful spirits, while the Maiar, such as Sauron, Gandalf, and Saruman, were less powerful: "With the Valar came other spirits whose being also began before the World, of the same order as the Valar but of less degree. These are the Maiar, the people of the Valar, and their servants and helpers" (*Silmarillion*, 30). In a letter, Tolkien describes Gandalf as "an angelic emissary of the angelic governors (Valar) of the Earth" (*Letters*, 268).

Given this association, this chapter will study the Maiar in the context of biblical angelology not just to understand the Maiar better, but also to imaginatively provide some possibilities for gaps in the biblical view of angels. Tolkien's work is certainly not inspired Scripture, but his rich imagination can help us envision angels in ways that we might not have thought of before. Gavin Ortlund has followed a similar path in his work defending what he calls the "angelic fall hypothesis" that entails seeing the beginning of evil in the fall of the angels.[1] Ortlund appeals to Tolkien's creation story as a possible model for what this hypothesis might look like: "his fictional meta-physics may serve to stretch the imagination toward new possibilities within the realm of orthodox metaphysics."[2] Likewise, Austin Freeman has argued that Tolkien's work helps us understand the Bible better in the area of angelology: "Tolkien's views (whether purely fictional or intended to reflect an actual belief) are in fact much more consonant with the biblical picture than our more modern, pared down picture. Our angelology is actually deficient."[3]

Even though the Valar are more powerful than the Maiar, Tolkien provided far more material about the latter through the characters of Gandalf, Saruman, Sauron, Melian, and the Balrogs.[4] At first glance, Tom Shippey's skepticism that Gandalf is similar to an angel rings true:

> During the action of *The Lord of the Rings*, though, Gandalf never looks very much like an angel, or at least not one of the normal iconographic kind. He is too short-tempered, for one thing, and also capable of doubt, anxiety, weariness, fear. Obviously too strong a flurry of angelic wings, too ready recourse to miracles or to Omnipotence, would instantly diminish the stature of the characters, devalue their decisions and their courage.[5]

Gandalf also does not appear like an angel in the Jackson's film versions of *The Lord of the Rings*. In spite of this, Gandalf and the other Maiar are more similar to angels than it might first appear. In this chapter we will begin by looking at the continuities between the Maiar and biblical angels before looking at some discontinuities.

But first, it is important to look at the background of the Maiar. The Maiar are the later versions of the elemental spirits like fays, pixies, and leprechauns in Tolkien's earliest writings in *The Book of Lost Tales*.[6] The first reference to them in the *Silmarillion* is in the context of the Valar: "And the Valar drew unto them many companions, some less, some well nigh as great as themselves, and they laboured together in the ordering of the Earth and the curbing of the tumults" (*Silmarillion*, 21). Identifying Middle-earth characters as Maiar is relatively simple in some cases, as Tolkien identifies several beings as Maiar, including Ossë, Uinen, Melian, and Gandalf, who is called Olórin (*Silmarillion*, 30–31).[7] The Balrogs, Sauron, and Arien (who was appointed to guide the sun) are directly called Maiar (*Silmarillion*, 31–32, 99, 285). Since Tolkien named Gandalf a Maia, presumably the other Wizards were also Maiar. This is supported by Tolkien describing the Wizards as "messengers sent to contest the power of Sauron" (*RK*, Appendix B). In a separate essay that was not published until 1980, Tolkien declares that all the Wizards are Maiar:

We must assume that they [the Istari] were all Maiar, that is persons of the 'angelic' order, though not necessarily of the same rank. The Maiar were 'spirits,' but capable of self-incarnation, and could take 'humane' (especially Elvish) forms. Saruman is said (e.g. by Gandalf himself) to have been the chief of the Istari—that is, higher in Valinórean stature than the others. Gandalf was evidently the next in order. Radagast is presented as a person of much less power and wisdom. Of the other two nothing is said in published work save the reference to the Five Wizards in the altercation between Gandalf and Saruman [*The Two Towers* III 10]. Now these Maiar were sent by the Valar at a crucial moment in the history of Middle-earth to enhance the resistance of the Elves of the West, waning in power, and of the uncorrupted Men of the West, greatly outnumbered by those of the East and South. It may be seen that they were free each to do what they could in this mission; that they were not commanded or supposed to act *together* as a small central body of power and wisdom; and that each had different powers and inclinations and were chosen by the Valar with this in mind. (*UT*, 394)

However, other beings in Middle-earth could also be Maiar, but are not called by this term. In a late writing Tolkien says that "Huan and Sorontar could be Maiar" (*Morgoth*, 410). In another late writing, he also calls the eagles Maiar (*Nature*, 308). Scholars have suggested a variety of other characters are Maiar, such as Tom Bombadil and Ents.[8]

Turning to the biblical material, in Hebrew the common word to refer to supernatural messengers is מַלְאָךְ (*mal'āk*), while in Greek the word is ἄγγελος (*angelos*). The Old Testament material is further complicated by the very frequent use of the term מַלְאַךְ יהוה ("angel of YHWH"), ἄγγελος κυρίου in the LXX, who occupies a special place between YHWH and the angels.[9] Since the angel speaks in the first person for YHWH, some scholars view the angel as a manifestation of YHWH.[10] A popular Christian tradition sees the angel as a Christophany: an appearance of Jesus before the incarnation.[11] However, others view the angel as a separate being from YHWH.[12] Michael Hundley suggests that the narrator is intentionally withholding the identity of the angel of YHWH from us as readers.[13] The angel of YHWH texts will be included in the discussion, but will be marked as such. Texts about demons—in traditional Western understanding those angels who have turned evil—will be included in the database of potential references.[14]

CONTINUITIES: MESSENGERS OR AGENTS

The first continuity between angels and Maiar is that both groups function as *messengers* or *agents* in some fashion. Tolkien called the Maiar "the people of the Valar, and their servants and helpers" (*Silmarillion*, 30). Elsewhere he

Charlie Trimm

Table 5.1. Continuities and Discontinuities of Angels between Tolkien and the Bible

	Tolkien	Bible
Continuities		
Role	Messengers and agents	Messengers and agents
Nature	Spirit Beings	Spirit Beings
Shift from Good to Evil	Able to shift from good to evil	Able to shift from good to evil
Level and Use of Power	Great power to help mortal beings	Great power to help mortal beings
Discontinuities		
Connection to Bodily Form	Potentially strong connection	Weak connection
Ability to Die	Able to die	Not able to die
Gender and Marriage	Female angels; angels able to marry	No female angels; no angels who marry
Negative Emotions	Negative Emotions	Very few negative emotions

By Charlie Trimm

described the Maiar as the Valar's "attendant lesser angels" (*Letters*, 153). Melian is said to be "a Maia who served both Vána and Estë" (*Silmarillion*, 30). Similarly, Tolkien describes the Wizards as "messengers sent to contest the power of Sauron" (*RK*, Appendix B) and "emissaries . . . from the Lords of the West, the Valar" (*UT*, 406). After his defeat of the Balrog, Gandalf said he was "sent back—for a brief time, until my task is done" (*TT*, III, v). While the identity of the one who sent him is left implied in *The Lord of the Rings*, elsewhere Tolkien says "it is clearly from Valinor that the emissaries came who were called the Istari (or Wizards)" (*UT*, 412). As a representative of evil Maiar, Sauron became "the greatest and most trusted of the servants of the Enemy, and the most perilous" (*Silmarillion*, 285).

The Hebrew word commonly glossed into English as *angel* (מלאך) more broadly refers to any kind of messenger. For example, Jacob sent *messengers* (מלאך) to Esau when he returned to Canaan (Gen 32:3). Most commonly in the Old Testament supernatural angels perform an action on YHWH's behalf, and this is especially true of the angel of YHWH (Num 22:22). Actions by angels other than the angel of YHWH include the rescue of Lot and his family from Sodom (Genesis 19), the guarding of the garden by cherubim (Gen 3:24), and the use of the coal by a seraph (Isa 6:6). However, they also sometimes communicate to humans on behalf of YHWH. Once again, this is particularly common for the angel of YHWH (Gen 16:7–12; Judg 2:1–5). In the New Testament, the word *angelos* refers to messengers in general, such as John the Baptist (Matt 11:10) and the messengers of John the Baptist (Luke 7:24). However, NT writers most commonly use the word to refer to supernatural messengers. Angels served Jesus in the wilderness (Mark 1:13).

The angel of the Lord spoke to Joseph (Matt 1:21–22) and Zechariah (Luke 1:19–20), and the angel Gabriel spoke to Mary (Luke 1:26–37). An angel of God spoke to Peter about interacting with Gentiles (Acts 10). The author of Hebrews describes angels as servants of those who are being saved (Heb 1:14), such as seen in the angels appearing to the women at the empty tomb (John 20:12–13).

CONTINUITIES: SPIRIT BEINGS

Second, both groups are *spirit beings*. Later we examine one of the discontinuities between the two groups in regards to the level of connection they have with a bodily form, but this section will focus on their core essence. Austin Freeman refers to them as "non-spatial spiritual beings" who have an "immaterial state."[15] Tolkien's introductory sentence in his paragraph on the Maiar says "with the Valar came other spirits" (*Silmarillion*, 30). In a late text he says, "The Valar and the Maiar were essentially 'spirits,' according to Elvish tradition given being before the making of Eä" (*Nature*, 244). In letters, Tolkien refers to Sauron as "a spirit, a minor one but still an 'angelic' spirit" (*Letters*, 200) and "an immortal (angelic) spirit" (*Letters*, 183). Likewise, he describes Gandalf as "possibly a spirit that existed before in the physical world" (*Letters*, 181). In the *Silmarillion* Sauron is called a spirit (31–32), as is Arien (100). As we will discuss below, even though Sauron lost his human form several times his spirit could still flee and later take on material form again.[16]

The evidence for angels as incorporeal is mostly based on texts that refer to angels as spirits: "The Old Testament makes it clear that the members of God's heavenly host are spirit beings—entities that, by nature, are not embodied, at least in the sense of our human experience of being physical in form."[17] In the meeting of the divine council witnessed by Micaiah, a spirit came forward and volunteered his service for the task at hand (1 Kgs 22:21). Similarly, various spirits assaulted Saul on behalf of YHWH (1 Sam 18:10; 19:9). YHWH had to open Balaam's eyes in order for him to see the angel of YHWH (Num 22:31) and Elisha prayed that YHWH would open the eyes of his servant to see the horses and chariots of fire (2 Kgs 6:17). In the New Testament, Hebrews 1:14 calls angels "ministering spirits." The Gospels often refer to the demons with the term "spirits" (Matt 8:16; 10:1; Luke 4:36), a trend that continues in the book of Acts (5:16; 19:12). Paul might refer to angels as invisible (Col 1:16).[18]

CONTINUITIES: POTENTIAL SHIFT
FROM GOOD TO EVIL

Third, both groups *started out as good, but some members became evil.*[19] The shift from good to evil is clear in Middle-earth. In a draft of a letter, Tolkien addresses this topic: "in this 'mythology' all the 'angelic' powers concerned with this world were capable of many degrees of error and failing between the absolute Satanic rebellion and evil of Morgoth and his satellite Sauron, and the faineance of some of the other higher powers" (*Letters*, 156). Elsewhere he says that the Wizards, "being clad in bodies of Middle-earth, might even as Men and Elves fall away from their purposes, and do evil, forgetting the good in the search for power to effect it" (*UT*, 407).

An early example of this in Middle-earth is Ossë, who was drawn to the power of Melkor for a time and caused great destruction. However, his wife Uinen restrained him and brought him to Ulmo, where he returned to following Ilúvatar (*Silmarillion*, 30). However, many other Maiar followed Melkor permanently: "For of the Maiar many were drawn to his splendor in the days of his greatness, and remained in that allegiance down into his darkness; and others he corrupted afterwards to his service with lies and treacherous gifts" (*Silmarillion*, 31). Tolkien refers to the Balrogs—whom he identifies as Maiar—as "demons of terror" (*Silmarillion*, 31). Not only did some of the Maiar follow him, some apparently even remained among the Valar and spied for him (*Silmarillion*, 36).

Sauron is an example of a shift from good to evil for Tolkien: "In the beginning of Arda Melkor seduced him [Sauron] to his allegiance" (*Silmarillion*, 285). In the narrative of *The Lord of the Rings* Tolkien provides another example with Saruman, the head of the council of Wizards sent to Middle-earth to combat Sauron. In spite of his role, Tolkien portrays Saruman leaving that path to glorify his own power instead. Elsewhere Tolkien says that four out of the five Wizards left the path allotted to them:

> Indeed, of all the Istari, one only remained faithful, and he was the last-comer [Gandalf]. For Radagast, the fourth, became enamoured of the many beasts and birds that dwelt in Middle-earth, and forsook Elves and Men, and spent his day among the wild creatures. . . . And Curunír 'Lân, Saruman the White, fell from his high errand, and becoming proud and impatient and enamoured of power sought to have his own will by force, and to oust Sauron; but he was ensnared by that dark spirit, mightier than he. (*UT*, 407–8)

The prime example of this shift from good to evil in traditional Western theology is Satan, which understands him as a powerful angel in Eden who was appointed to a high role as a beautiful singer but wanted to take the place of God. However, the biblical evidence for such a picture is minimal. In the Old Testament the fall of Satan in the Garden of Eden is seen by some in Isaiah 14 and Ezekiel 28, but these texts are referring to the kings of Babylon and Tyre.[20] Graham Cole sees the texts working on two levels: "at a literal level, they are about two kings (of Babylon and of Tyre, respectively), but at the archetypal level they reveal the sort of arrogant sin that is true of Satan."[21] Others deny that these texts have any connection with Satan.[22] Genesis 3 itself identifies the evil being only as a snake, but the New Testament connects Satan with the serpent (Rev 20:1–2).[23]

The word שָׂטָן (transliterated as *Satan*) is a Hebrew word that means *adversary* (Num 22:22, 32; 1 Sam 29:4; 1 Kgs 11:14). It occurs only three times in the Old Testament to refer to the being called Satan (Job 1–2; Zech 3:1–2; and 1 Chr 21:1). Old Testament authors generally use the article with the word, indicating that it is not a name; only the Chronicler does not use the article (1 Chr 21:1). Many Old Testament scholars see the *satan* not as an evil spirit being, but as an employee of YHWH. For example, perhaps his role was YHWH's prosecuting attorney, whose goal is not to draw people to act in an evil way, but to test people to see if they will follow God or not. The common use of the article with the word *satan* indicates that the word is functioning not as a name, but as a description of his action.[24] Others see Satan as YHWH's executioner who eventually became a symbol for evil.[25] However, many scholars continue to view Satan as a personal evil being, especially since the word appears in 1 Chr 21:1 without the article. In addition, YHWH's condemnation of Satan in Zech 3:2 sounds like he is opposed to Satan's plan here.[26] In the New Testament, Jesus enigmatically refers to seeing Satan fall from heaven (Luke 10:18). Revelation 12 also refers to something like a fall, as Satan is cast down to earth. However, commentators disagree about whether these are past or future events. In light of this evidence, a fall of a powerful spirit being later called Satan is possible, but should be described with less certainty.

According to traditional Western theology, demons are the angels who have turned evil.[27] Evil supernatural beings are rare in the Old Testament; the word we gloss as *demon* (שֵׁדִים) only appears twice and seems to refer both times to foreign gods (Deut 32:17; Ps 106:37), but the LXX translates the word as δαιμόνιον in both cases. The phrase "goat demon" in Lev 17:7, 2 Chr 11:15, and Isa 13:21 translates the common Hebrew word for goats (שְׂעִירִים), but once again the LXX translates Isa 13:21 as "demon."[28] Beyond these texts, the LXX uses "demon" in Ps 91:6, 96:5, Isaiah 34:14, and 65:3 to describe evil supernatural beings. The attention to demons increases significantly in the intertestamental period, seen not only in these LXX translations, but also in the literature written during these centuries.[29]

The origin of foreign gods is unclear in the Old Testament, but it is possible to identify them as angels who became demons.[30] Several texts refer to a divine council in the Old Testament, which consists of YHWH and the angels (1 Kgs 22:19; Job 1–2). According to Deuteronomy, Moses said that YHWH "set the bounds of the peoples according to the number of the children of God" (32:8), which most likely refers to the idea of appointing angels over certain countries and peoples.[31] These beings are attested in Daniel in the form of the Prince of Persia and the Prince of Greece (10:13, 20).[32] However, their judgment might be recorded in Psalm 82, when God judged them for ignoring justice for the poor and oppressed.[33] Likewise, Isaiah says that YHWH will punish the host of heaven (Isa 24:21). In sum, it appears that the foreign gods were angels appointed to be patron deities of non-Israelite nations to help them serve YHWH better. However, these beings desired to receive worship themselves and became evil, leading to their judgment.

CONTINUITIES: GREAT POWER
TO HELP MORTAL BEINGS

Fourth, they *had great power, but their power was restrained because their primary goal was to empower Men (and Elves).*[34] The Maiar clearly have great power. One example is Uinen, the spouse of Ossë, who showed great power over the sea: "to her mariners cry, for she can lay calm upon the waves, restraining the wildness of Ossë. The Númenóreans lived long in her protection, and held her in reverence equal to the Valar" (*Silmarillion*, 30). On the march of the Quendi west early in the history of Middle-earth, Tolkien notes that the presence of the Maiar on the east bank of the Anduin "drives off evil, and the place is rich in flowers and food" (*Nature*, 50). Melian set up the enchanted Girdle of Melian around Doriath that protected it from enemies for a long time (*Silmarillion*, 97).

In the Third Age, the Maiar continue to demonstrate great power, such as Gandalf does even before his return.[35] Faramir says of him that "it is hard indeed to believe that one of so great wisdom, and of power—for many wonderful things he did among us—could perish" (*TT*, IV, v). However, narratively little of this power is seen on display before his death except in his defeat of the Balrog (*FR*, II, v). Tolkien says that his power increased greatly when he returned from death: "Both his wisdom and his power are much greater. When he speaks he commands attention; the old Gandalf could not have dealt so with Théoden, nor with Saruman . . . where the physical powers of the Enemy are too great for the good will of the opposers to be effective he can act in emergency as an 'angel'—no more violently than the release of St. Peter from prison" (*Letters*, 156). Gandalf fought the Nazgûl outside

Minas Tirith to rescue Faramir: "it seemed to Pippin that he raised his hand, and from it a shaft of white light stabbed upwards" (*RK*, V, iv).

In spite of this great power, Maiar are quite restricted in its use. One example is the role of Ossë and Uinen after the Kinslaying at Alqualondë: "And Olwé called upon Ossé, but he came not, for it was not permitted by the Valar that the flight of the Noldor should be hindered by force" (*Silmarillion*, 87). The Wizards also experience restricted power. Tolkien says that they were "to unite all those who had the will to resist him; but they were forbidden to match his power with power, or to seek to dominate Elves and Men by force and fear" (*RK*, Appendix B). Elsewhere he says of the Wizards that they "were forbidden to reveal themselves in forms of majesty, or to seek to rule the wills of Men or Elves by open display of power, but coming in shapes weak and humble were bidden to advise and persuade Men and Elves to good, and to seek to unite in love and understanding all those whom Sauron, should he come again, would endeavor to dominate and corrupt" (*UT*, 406). In one intriguing text about the fall of Númenor Tolkien says that "Men (the Followers or Second Kindred) came second, but it is guessed that in the first design of God they were destined (after tutelage) to take on the governance of all the Earth, and ultimately to become Valar, to 'enrich Heaven,' *Ilúve*" (*Sauron*, 401). In light of this, perhaps the restricted power of the Maiar was part of the training of Men to take on the role of the Valar: if the Valar used their full power, they would overwhelm Men and prevent their growth. Tolkien also says that the Valar became less actively involved in Middle-earth as time went on: "The wiser they became the less power they had to *do* anything—save by counsel" (*Morgoth*, 405).

In the biblical text the angel of YHWH clearly has great power (Numbers 22; Judges 6; 2 Sam 24:16; 2 Kings 19:35). The power of angels other than the angel of YHWH is not as common (Gen 24:40). In the New Testament the angel of the Lord rescued the apostles from prison (Acts 5:19) and struck down Herod (Acts 12:23). While it is clear that angels (especially the angel of YHWH) have great power, they only have a restricted power. The limited number of stories about their power demonstrates that if they were given free reign, then they could easily defeat any enemy force that Israel or the church might face. However, stories about their powerful exploits are relatively rare and tend to happen at significant points in Israelite/early church history. As the author of Hebrews says, angels are servants of those who are being saved (Heb 1:14). If angels were allowed to use their great power on behalf of humans, then it would overwhelm any human ability and inhibit their growth.

DISCONTINUITIES: CONNECTION TO BODILY FORM

Even though the Maiar are similar to angels of the Bible in many ways, some discontinuities are also seen between them. We will now examine four of these discontinuities. The most prominent discontinuity is that the Maiar have *much stronger connections with a bodily form* than angels in the Bible. As noted above, Maiar are spirit beings without a material form.[36] However, they can take on physical forms and appear to the inhabitants of Middle-earth. The Maiar in particular often have a sustained connection with their human form, which Freeman calls an incarnation rather than merely an angelophany.[37] Tolkien notes that the Valar took on material forms based on their vision of what the Children of Ilúvatar would look like, which might be a model for the Maiar as well.

> Now the Valar took to themselves shape and hue; and because they were drawn into the World by love of the Children of Ilúvatar, for whom they hoped, they took shape after that manner which they had beheld in the Vision of Ilúvatar, save only in majesty and splendor. Moreover their shape comes of their knowledge of the visible World, rather than of the World itself; and they need it not, save only as we use raiment, and yet we may be naked and suffer no loss of our being. Therefore the Valar may walk, if they will, unclad, and then even the Eldar cannot clearly perceive them, though they be present. (*Silmarillion*, 21)

One letter refers to the physical bodies of the angels in Middle-earth as clothes, "except that they were more than are clothes the expression of their desires, moods, wills and functions" (*Letters*, 200). In a late text Tolkien says that the Valar do not make strong connections with bodies; Melkor is an exception but only because of the evil deeds he did in his body (*Nature*, 210). In the same text, he discusses more about the bodies of the Maiar (the text is written as a summary of the historian Pengolodh). In brief he says that though in origin a "self-arraying," it may tend to approach the state of "incarnation," especially with the lesser members of that order (the Maiar):

> It is said that the longer and the more the same *hröa* is used, the greater is the bond of habit, and the less do the 'self-arrayed' desire to leave it. As raiment may soon cease to be adornment, and becomes (as is said in the tongues of both Elves and Men) a 'habit,' a customary garb. Or if among Elves and Men it be worn to mitigate heat and cold, it soon makes the clad body less able to endure these things when naked. (*Nature*, 209–10)

Pengolodh also cites the opinion that if a "spirit" (that is, one of those not embodied by creation) uses a *hröa* for the furtherance of its personal purposes, or (still more) for the enjoyment of bodily faculties, it finds it increasingly difficult to operate without the *hröa*. The things that are most binding are those that in the Incarnate have to do with the life of the *hröa* itself, its sustenance and its propagation. Thus, eating and drinking are binding, but not the delight in beauty of sound or form. Most binding is begetting or conceiving (*Nature*, 210).

Looking at several specific examples of the Maiar illustrates their strong connection with a body. The case of Melian is particularly prominent: not only did she have human form, but she married the elf Thingol and had children. Tolkien says this about her:

> But Melian, having in woman-form borne a child after the manner of the Incarnate, desired to do this no more: by the birth of Lúthien she became enmeshed in 'incarnation,' unable to lay it aside while husband and child remained in Arda alive, and her powers of mind (especially foresight) became clouded by the body through which it must now always work. To have borne more children would still further have chained her and trammeled her. In the event, her daughter became mortal and eventually died, and her husband was slain; and she then cast off her 'raiment' and left Middle-earth. (*Nature*, 21)

Unlike the majority stream of the history of interpretation in both Christian and Jewish circles that forbids intercourse between humans and angels, having sexual intercourse with a Maia in Middle-earth is not evil. The evil relationship between the sons of God and the daughters of men serves as a base text for the rejection of the idea in biblical reception history (Gen 6:1–4), but Tolkien has approved of such a relationship and not only portrays the angel as the female partner rather than the male partner but even consistently shows that Melian is much wiser than her Elf husband.

Tolkien provides more details about the bodies of the Wizards.[38] A text in *Unfinished Tales* notes that the bodies of the Wizards were "real and not feigned" bodies (*UT*, 406). Indeed, the people of Middle-earth thought that they were Men until they never died, at which point they thought that they were Elves (*UT*, 405–6). McBride suggests that the bodies of the Wizards prevent Sauron from recognizing them as Maiar.[39] The Wizards are strongly connected to their bodies, and remain recognizable over time. The one exception is Gandalf when he returned after his death. He was unrecognizable to Aragorn, Gimli, and Legolas at first (*TT*, III, v). However, when others who knew him previously see him, they apparently have no problems recognizing him, such as Merry and Pippin at Isengard (*TT*, III, viii) and Sam and Frodo in Ithilien (*RK*, VI, iv). It is also possible that the connection with a bodily form makes the wizards more prone to mistakes of judgment.[40]

At the fall of Númenor, even though Sauron lost his body he did not go out of existence:

But Sauron was not of mortal flesh, and though he was robbed now of that shape in which he had wrought so great an evil, so that he could never again appear fair to the eyes of Men, yet his spirit arose out of the deep and passed as a shadow and a black wind over the sea, and came back to Middle-earth and to Mordor that was his home. There he took up again his great Ring in Barad-dûr, and dwelt there, dark and silent, until he wrought himself a new guise, an image of malice and hatred made visible; and the Eye of Sauron the Terrible few could endure. (*Silmarillion*, 280–81)

Later he suffered a similar fate when he lost the Ring in the battle against Gil-galad and Elendil: "Then Sauron was for that time vanquished, and he forsook his body, and his spirit fled far away and hid in waste places; and he took no visible shape again for many long years" (*Silmarillion*, 294). In a letter Tolkien says that the process of recovering his physical body took longer this time: "I suppose because each building-up used up some of the inherent energy of the spirit, which might be called the 'will' or the effective link between the indestructible mind and being and the realization of its imagination" (*Letters*, 200). He goes on to say that it would have been impossible for Sauron to rebuild after the Ring was destroyed (*Letters*, 200).

Several stories in the Bible record angels taking on human form (Gen 19; Num 22; Judg 6). In some cases, humans in these stories seem to view these angels as men, especially in the encounter with Abram (Gen 19). However, these bodies do not seem to be intrinsic to their identity in the same way that they are for humans. No story in biblical literature records a human recognizing an angel based on their human form. Angels can appear in other forms as well; for example, the angel of God who went before Israel in the wilderness seems to be identified with the pillar of cloud (Exod 14:19).[41]

At the same time, Tolkien's vision could be true for biblical angels given the limited amount of data available. In particular, in this area Tolkien's angels bear a strong resemblance to the angel Raphael in the deuterocanonical book of Tobit, who took on human form for a long period of time.[42] When Tobias first met Raphael, the narrator notes that he did not recognize that Raphael was an angel and indeed thought he was an Israelite male (Tob 5:4, 9). Raphael does not enlighten either Tobias or his father Tobit, going so far as to create an identity for himself as an Israelite with a genealogy (5:13). Raphael goes with Tobias on his journey, stating that he had often traveled the path to Media (5:10). He helps Tobias with many adventures on the journey, such as catching a demon (8:2–3), before finally revealing his angelic identity at the end of the story (12:15). While I am unaware of any evidence that Tolkien wrote about Tobit, as a scholarly Catholic he surely was aware of the book. While unprovable with published material from Tolkien, perhaps Raphael served as a model for the Maiar in this area.

DISCONTINUITIES: ABILITY TO DIE

Another discontinuity concerns their *ability to die*. In Middle-earth the Maiar are able to die, though the meaning of this death appears to be unlike human death. Tolkien's description of the Wizards leaves this somewhat ambiguous: "Clad in bodies as of Men, real and not feigned, but subject to the fears and pains and weariness of earth, able to hunger and thirst and be slain; though because of their noble spirits they did not die" (*UT*, 406). However, this reference to deathlessness seems to be similar to elvish deathlessness: they might not die from natural causes, but they can be killed. The most famous example is Saruman, who was killed by Gríma Wormtongue. The cloud that rises after his death tries to go west, but is denied entry to Valinor.

> To the dismay of those that stood by, about the body of Saruman a grey mist gathered, and rising slowly to a great height like smoke from a fire, as a pale shrouded figure it loomed over the Hill. For a moment it wavered, looking to the West; but out of the West came a cold wind, and it bent away, and with a sigh dissolved into nothing. (*RK*, VI, viii)

It is unclear what exactly happened to the Balrog that Gandalf defeated, but it appears that he died as Gandalf said "I threw down my enemy, and he fell from the high place and broke the mountain-side where he smote it in his ruin" (*TT*, III, v). Several Balrogs die in the *Silmarillion*, especially connected with the fall of Gondolin (*Silmarillion*, 242–43). Given the lack of further clarity from Tolkien on the ultimate origin of these Maia, we can only speculate that Saruman and the Balrogs were annihilated. Perhaps, given his Christian background, Tolkien would have included some kind of future judgment of demonic beings.

Gandalf is the most famous example of a Maia dying. In his account, Gandalf does not specify that he died: "Then darkness took me, and I strayed out of thought and time, and I wandered far on roads that I will not tell" (*TT*, III, v). However, Tolkien provides more specifics elsewhere. In the *Unfinished Tales* Tolkien said Gandalf "was slain, and being sent back from death for a brief while was clothed then in white, and became a radiant flame (yet veiled still save in great need). And when all was over and the Shadow of Sauron was removed, he departed for ever over the Sea" (*UT*, 408). Tolkien provided more details in a private conversation with Edmund Fuller:

> In response to my question he said, unhesitatingly, 'Gandalf is an angel.' He went on to explain that Gandalf had voluntarily accepted incarnation to wage the battle against Sauron. Gandalf the Gray does indeed die in the mortal flesh

in the encounter with the Balrog in the Mines of Moria. Gandalf the White, who returns, is the angel in the incorruptible body of resurrection.[43]

More directly, in a letter to Robert Murray, S.J., Tolkien wrote, "Gandalf really 'died'" (*Letters*, 156).

As noted above, angels are able to fall by means of turning against God and becoming demons. However, the biblical angels are not said to die in the same way as humans: The Bible never records an angel even suffering injury, let alone dying. One possible exception is in Psalm 82, which begins with YHWH in his divine council surrounded by other divine beings, who appear to be angels. However, he judges these angels because of their lack of attention to helping the oppressed. Their judgment is as follows: "I said, 'You are gods, sons of the Most High, all of you; nevertheless, like men you shall die, and fall like any prince'" (Ps 82:6–7). However, it is unclear what this death means, and the referent of Psalm 82 has been highly debated. Another possible exception is the final destiny of demons: "For if God did not spare angels when they sinned, but cast them into hell and committed them to chains of gloomy darkness to be kept until the judgment" (2 Pet 2:4). Revelation refers to the lake of fire in which the devil is thrown; this would presumably also include the demons (Rev 20). While it is unclear if angels can die, Psalm 82 might reflect the death of angels in a fashion similar to Middle-earth.

DISCONTINUITIES: GENDER AND MARRIAGE

While most of the Maiar who are named are male, at least some of the Maiar are female.[44] Tolkien says of the Valar that they "take upon them forms some as of male and some as of female; for that difference of temper they had even from the beginning, and it is but bodied forth in the choice of each, not made by the choice, even as with us male and female may be shown by the raiment but is not made thereby" (*Silmarillion*, 21). Presumably the same is true of the Maiar. Tolkien refers in passing to the Maia "Ilmarë, the handmaid of Varda" (*Silmarillion*, 30), but she never appears again. Uinen is another named female Maia, who mainly appears in connection with her husband Ossë (*Silmarillion*, 30, 40, 58). Her sole action recorded in the narrative that is without her husband is weeping for the Teleri after the Kinslaying at Alqualondë (87). A female Maia named Arien was chosen to guide the vessel of the sun (*Silmarillion*, 99–101). The most prominent among these female Maiar is Melian, who married Thingol and bore Lúthien.[45]

In the Bible, all of the angels are portrayed as male and lacking familial relationships. For those who discuss the topic, scholars sometimes lean toward the view that angels are sexless.[46] Jesus says directly that angels do not marry (Matt 22:30). One possible exception is the story of the sons of God and the daughters of men (Gen 6), but the interpretation of that text is unclear as the sons of God are understood as human rulers by some interpreters. Another possible exception is the female characters in Zechariah 5:9, who might be angels. Michael Heiser denies that these characters are angels because the following verse records Zechariah talking to an angel, implying that he is a different kind of being that the two women.[47] However, the reference to a male angel in the following verse is not conclusive evidence that the two women are not female angels. The lack of data permits the speculation that the angels are gendered and an entire world of female angels exist that are not described in the Bible.

DISCONTINUITIES: NEGATIVE EMOTIONS

Finally, the emotional state of angels is different.[48] As noted earlier, Shippey is skeptical that Gandalf is like an angel. His main reason is this discontinuity: "He is too short-tempered, for one thing, and also capable of doubt, anxiety, weariness, fear."[49] For example, one of the earliest encounters with Gandalf in *The Fellowship of the Ring* from Frodo's perspective is that "the old wizard looked unusually bent, almost as if he was carrying a great weight" (*FR*, I, i). Shortly later, Frodo notes that Gandalf looked "worried" (*FR*, I, iii). Gandalf himself admits he made a mistake when he allowed Gollum to go free (*FR*, I, ii). The incarnation of the Wizards in bodies played a role in this: "being incarnate [they] were more likely to stray, or err" (*Letters*, 156). Tolkien does not make us privy to the emotions of the enemy, such as the Balrogs. Aragorn said that Sauron experienced fear and doubt, which he learned after he looked into the Palantír (*RK*, V, ii). Gandalf likewise says that Sauron was afraid after Aragorn's use of the Palantír (*RK*, V, iv).

Angels do not seem to have many emotions, at least as described in the biblical texts. This could be seen as evidence of not having emotions. However, it could also be the side effect of the attention of the biblical author being elsewhere. In at least some places, they appear to have positive emotions, such as joy. For example, in the parable of the lost coin Jesus said "there is joy before the angels of God over one sinner who repents" (Luke 15:10). However, this statement is in a parable, which means that it might be part of the imaginative aspect of the parable and not a definitive statement about the nature of angels. The singing of the angels praising God might imply emotion (Rev 5:11–12), as does the praise of the angels when speaking to the shepherds (Luke 2:10–14).[50] In a few texts angels contradict or even rebuke someone, such as Gabriel's pronounced judgment of Zechariah for not trusting his words (Luke 1:19–20). A stronger rebuke is Michael's rebuke of the devil when arguing about the body of Moses: "The Lord rebuke you!" (Jude 9). Likewise, an angel rebuked John twice for falling to his feet to worship him (Rev 19:10; 22:8–9). Angels are said to "long to investigate" things about the good news (1 Peter 1:12). However, how much emotion can be seen in these texts is difficult to determine, and even if these texts depict angelic emotion they remain positive emotions of those obedient and in tune with YHWH. One case of apparent angelic distress is the angel who lamented to YHWH about the lengthy amount of time YHWH was angry with Jerusalem and not showing compassion (Zech 1:12). In response, YHWH provided the angel with "comforting words" (Zech 1:13). Most likely, the lack of references to the emotions of angels in the Bible is due to the small sample size rather than an actual lack of emotion; the emotions of the Maiar are most likely a helpful guide for us to creatively imagine the emotional life of the angels (such as we see in Zech 1:12–13).

CONCLUSION

Tolkien's portrayal of the Maiar provides readers of the biblical text with rich comparative data. A study of the Maiar as a group offers many interesting perspectives on events in Middle-earth and how Ilúvatar and the Valar direct events, especially through the Wizards. However, comparing and contrasting the Maiar with angels in the Bible helps us to see more clearly the characteristics of biblical angels. For example, the strong connection of the Maiar with a body offers an imaginative possibility for biblical angels: Could this happen in our world as well? Likewise, while the Bible does not include any explicitly female angels, perhaps Jesus' reference to angels not marrying implies the existence of female angels, not totally unlike Tolkien's vision of female Maiar.

NOTES

1. Gavin Ortlund, "On the Fall of Angels and the Fallenness of Nature: An Evangelical Hypothesis Regarding Natural Evil," *EvQ* 87 (2015): 114–36.

2. Ortlund, "On the Fall," 128.

3. Austin M. Freeman, *Tolkien Dogmatics: Theology through Mythology with the Maker of Middle-earth* (Bellingham, WA: Lexham, 2022), 126.

4. Ironically, Tolkien says in *The Silmarillion* that "the Maiar have seldom appeared in form visible to Elves and Men" (30).

5. Tom Shippey, *The Road to Middle-earth: How J.R.R. Tolkien Created a New Mythology*, 2nd ed. (Boston: Houghton Mifflin, 2003), 151.

6. Dimitra Fimi, *Tolkien, Race, and Cultural History: From Fairies to Hobbits* (New York: Palgrave, 2010), 48. For more on the textual history of the Maiar and the Valar, see Elizabeth A. Whittingham, *The Evolution of Tolkien's Mythology: A Study of the History of Middle-earth*, CESFF 7 (Jefferson, NC: McFarland, 2007), 70–73, 83–91.

7. For background on the Wizards, see Sam McBride, *Tolkien's Cosmology: Divine Beings and Middle-earth* (Kent, OH: Kent State University Press, 2020), 52–71.

8. See Suzanne Jacobs, "Tolkien's Tom Bombadil: An Enigma '(Intentionally),'" *Mythlore* 38.2 (2020): 82–83; and Freeman, *Tolkien Dogmatics*, 134, respectively.

9. The translation of YHWH as "lord" (*kurios*) in the LXX is the standard way of rendering the divine name in the LXX.

10. Stephen L. White, "Angel of the Lord: Messenger or Euphemism?" *TynBul* 50 (1999): 299–305; Andrew S. Malone, "Distinguishing the Angel of the Lord," *BBR* 21 (2011): 297–314.

11. Robert P. Lightner, "Angels, Satan, and Demons: Invisible Beings that Inhabit the Spiritual World," in *Understanding Christian Theology*, ed. Charles R. Swindoll and Roy B. Zuck (Nashville: Thomas Nelson, 2003), 567–71.

12. René A. López, "Identifying the 'Angel of the Lord' in the Book of Judges: A Model for Reconsidering the Referent in Other Old Testament Texts," *BBR* 20 (2010): 1–18. For a study of the topic in early Jewish sources—which shows that no interpretation was dominant in the early period—see Camilla Hélena von Hei-jne, *The Messenger of the Lord in Early Jewish Interpretations of Genesis*, BZAW 412 (Berlin: De Gruyter, 2010). For example, Tobit refers to the angel Raphael as the angel of the Lord, which leans toward the separate being view: Phillip Muñoa, "Raphael the Savior: Tobit's Adaptation of the Angel of the Lord Tradition," *JSP* 25 (2016): 232.

13. Michael Hundley, "Of God and Angels: Divine Messengers in Genesis and Exodus in Their Ancient Near Eastern Contexts," *JTS* 67 (2016): 21.

14. Other beings, such as cherubim and seraphim, are sometimes included in the overarching category of angels as well and will be included below.

15. Freeman, *Tolkien Dogmatics*, 140. Elsewhere Freeman describes angels as having bodies, but bodies that occupy higher dimensions and so are completely different kinds of bodies from human bodies; see Austin M. Freeman, "Celestial Spheres: Angelic Bodies and Hyperspace," *TheoLogica* 2.2 (2018): 168–86.

16. A detailed study of the textual history of Tolkien's work shows that he placed greater emphasis on the physical forms of the Valar earlier in his writings, but removed some of that material in later versions; see Whittingham, *Evolution*, 73–83. Whittingham argues that Tolkien intentionally shifted them to conform more closely to biblical angels, but it is more likely that the earlier material was not repudi-ated but rather assumed in the background as part of the summarizing genre of the newer tellings of the legends; see Charlie Trimm, "Tolkien's War Gods: Studying Tolkien's View of War through the Characterization of Makar and Tulkas," in *Tolkien 2019 Proceedings*, ed. Will Sherwood (Edinburgh: Luna, 2024).

17. Michael S. Heiser, *Angels: What the Bible Really Says about God's Heavenly Host* (Bellingham, WA: Lexham, 2018), 2.

18. For more on the incorporeality of angels, see Graham A. Cole, *Against the Darkness: The Doctrine of Angels, Satan, and Demons*, Foundations of Evangelical Theology (Wheaton: Crossway, 2019), 35–38.

19. Freeman, *Tolkien Dogmatics*, 144–47.

20. Lightner, "Angels, Satan, and Demons," 573–76.

21. Cole, *Against the Darkness*, 93.

22. John H. Walton and J. Harvey Walton, *Demons and Spirits in Biblical Theology: Reading the Biblical Text in Its Cultural and Literary Context* (Eugene: Cascade, 2019), 217–22.

23. Romans 16:20 is most likely also connected Satan with the serpent.

24. Walton and Walton, *Demons and Spirits in Biblical Theology*, 212–17.

25. Ryan E. Stokes, *Satan: How God's Executioner Became the Enemy* (Grand Rapids: Eerdmans, 2019).

26. Lightner, "Angels, Satan, and Demons," 572–82; Cole, *Against the Darkness*, 97–100.

27. Lightner, "Angels, Satan, and Demons," 583–88; Cole, *Against the Darkness*, 111–27.

28. Leviticus 17:7 uses the word we gloss as "worthless things" and 2 Chronicles 11:15 uses two phrases for the one word: "worthless things and idols."

29. Stokes, *Satan*, 48–119; Loren T. Stuckenbruck, *The Myth of Rebellious Angels: Studies in Second Temple Judaism and New Testament Texts* (Grand Rapids: Eerdmans, 2017); and Heiser, *Angels*, 85–115.

30. For the argument for this view, see Michael S. Heiser, *The Unseen Realm: Recovering the Supernatural Worldview of the Bible* (Bellingham, WA: Lexham, 2015), 110–15.

31. This verse has a textual problem, as many translations follow the standard Hebrew text with the translation "sons of Israel." However, both the Greek translation and a Dead Sea scroll of Deuteronomy read "sons of God." For a discussion of the textual problem and its relation to the divine council motif, see Michael S. Heiser, "Deuteronomy 32:8 and the Sons of God," *BSac* 158 (2001): 52–74.

32. For the argument that these beings are not evil, see Walton and Walton, *Demons and Spirits*, 186–97.

33. Ellen White, *YHWH's Council: Its Structure and Membership*, FAT 2.65 (Tübingen: Mohr Siebeck, 2014), 30–34. However, many commentators see these beings as humans rather than angels. For a contrary view, see Walton and Walton, *Demons and Spirits*, 197–208.

34. For a study of the relative power between different angelic beings in Middle-earth and the extent of the power of these angelic powers, see Freeman, *Tolkien Dogmatics*, 129–31, 139–43.

35. For a detailed study of Gandalf's power, see McBride, *Tolkien's Cosmology*, 57–71.

36. Tolkien also talks about the powerful Maiar being able to act upon physical objects without the use of their bodies (*Nature*, 236).

37. Freeman, *Tolkien Dogmatics*, 149.

38. Some texts suggest that Tolkien considered not only making Melian one of the wizards, but their chief (*Nature*, 95).

39. McBride, *Tolkien's Cosmology*, 53.

40. McBride, *Tolkien's Cosmology*, 53.

41. Some texts could portray angels in non-human forms if beings such as the *seraphim* or *cherubim* are included (Isaiah 6).

42. Muñoa, "Raphael the Savior."

43. Edmund Fuller, "The Lord of the Hobbits: J.R.R. Tolkien," in *Tolkien and the Critics: Essays on J.R.R. Tolkien's* The Lord of the Rings, ed. Neil D. Isaacs and Rose A. Zimbardo (Notre Dame: University of Notre Dame Press, 1968), 35.

44. The role of women in Tolkien's writing has been the topic of much recent scholarship; for example, see Janet Brennan Croft and Leslie A. Donovan, eds., *Perilous and Fair: Women in the Works and Life of J.R.R. Tolkien* (Altadena, CA: Mythopoeic, 2015).

45. For more on the textual history of the female Valar and Maiar, see Whittingham, *Evolution*, 91–98.

46. Lightner, "Angels, Satan, and Demons," 629–30.

47. Heiser, *Angels*, 164–67.

48. Earlier texts also portray the Valar as making the occasional mistake, but Tolkien changes his mind on this in later writing and emphasizes how it only appeared that they made mistakes; for a summary of these texts see Freeman, *Tolkien Dogmatics*, 144–47. Since these texts do not directly involve the Maiar, this essay will not engage this area.

49. Shippey, *Road*, 151.

50. Cole, *Against the Darkness*, 37–38.

BIBLIOGRAPHY

Cole, Graham A. *Against the Darkness: The Doctrine of Angels, Satan, and Demons.* Foundations of Evangelical Theology. Wheaton: Crossway, 2019.

Croft, Janet Brennan, and Leslie A. Donovan, eds. *Perilous and Fair: Women in the Works and Life of J.R.R. Tolkien.* Altadena, CA: Mythopoeic, 2015.

Fimi, Dimitra. *Tolkien, Race, and Cultural History: From Fairies to Hobbits.* New York: Palgrave, 2010.

Freeman, Austin M. "Celestial Spheres: Angelic Bodies and Hyperspace." *TheoLogica* 2.2 (2018): 168–86.

———. *Tolkien Dogmatics: Theology through Mythology with the Maker of Middle-earth.* Bellingham, WA: Lexham, 2022.

Fuller, Edmund. "The Lord of the Hobbits: J.R.R. Tolkien." Pages 17–39 in *Tolkien and the Critics: Essays on J.R.R. Tolkien's* The Lord of the Rings. Edited by Neil D. Isaacs and Rose A. Zimbardo. Notre Dame: University of Notre Dame Press, 1968.

Heijne, Camilla Hélena von. *The Messenger of the Lord in Early Jewish Interpretations of Genesis.* BZAW 412. Berlin: De Gruyter, 2010.

Heiser, Michael S. *Angels: What the Bible Really Says about God's Heavenly Host.* Bellingham, WA: Lexham, 2018.

———. "Deuteronomy 32:8 and the Sons of God." *BSac* 158 (2001): 52–74.

———. *The Unseen Realm: Recovering the Supernatural Worldview of the Bible.* Bellingham, WA: Lexham, 2015.

Hundley, Michael. "Of God and Angels: Divine Messengers in Genesis and Exodus in Their Ancient Near Eastern Contexts." *JTS* 67 (2016): 1–22.

Jacobs, Suzanne. "Tolkien's Tom Bombadil: An Enigma '(Intentionally).'" *Mythlore* 38.2 (2020): 79–108.

Lightner, Robert P. "Angels, Satan, and Demons: Invisible Beings that Inhabit the Spiritual World." Pages 539–640 in *Understanding Christian Theology.* Edited by Charles R. Swindoll and Roy B. Zuck. Nashville: Thomas Nelson, 2003.

López, René A. "Identifying the 'Angel of the Lord' in the Book of Judges: A Model for Reconsidering the Referent in Other Old Testament Texts." *BBR* 20 (2010): 1–18.

Malone, Andrew S. "Distinguishing the Angel of the Lord." *BBR* 21 (2011): 297–314.

McBride, Sam. *Tolkien's Cosmology: Divine Beings and Middle-earth.* Kent, OH: Kent State University Press, 2020.

Muñoa, Phillip. "Raphael the Savior: Tobit's Adaptation of the Angel of the Lord Tradition." *JSP* 25 (2016): 228–43.

Ortlund, Gavin. "On the Fall of Angels and the Fallenness of Nature: An Evangelical Hypothesis Regarding Natural Evil." *EvQ* 87 (2015): 114–36.

Shippey, Tom. *The Road to Middle-earth: How J.R.R. Tolkien Created a New Mythology.* 2nd ed. Boston: Houghton Mifflin, 2003.

Stokes, Ryan E. *Satan: How God's Executioner Became the Enemy.* Grand Rapids: Eerdmans, 2019.

Stuckenbruck, Loren T. *The Myth of Rebellious Angels: Studies in Second Temple Judaism and New Testament Texts.* Grand Rapids: Eerdmans, 2017.

Trimm, Charlie. "Tolkien's War Gods: Studying Tolkien's View of War through the Characterization of Makar and Tulkas." Forthcoming in *Tolkien 2019 Proceedings.* Edited by Will Sherwood. Edinburgh: Luna, 2024.

Walton, John H., and J. Harvey Walton. *Demons and Spirits in Biblical Theology: Reading the Biblical Text in Its Cultural and Literary Context.* Eugene: Cascade, 2019.

White, Ellen. *YHWH's Council: Its Structure and Membership.* FAT 2.65. Tübingen: Mohr Siebeck, 2014.

White, Stephen L. "Angel of the Lord: Messenger or Euphemism?" *TynBul* 50 (1999): 299–305.

Whittingham, Elizabeth A. *The Evolution of Tolkien's Mythology: A Study of the History of Middle-earth.* CESFF 7. Jefferson, NC: McFarland, 2007.

PART II
Erebor

Chapter 6

The Marian Valkyrie

Tolkien's Theology of the Heroic Feminine

Lisa Coutras

Within the realm of Tolkien scholarship, an area of fervent debate revolves around the portrayal and significance of women in J.R.R. Tolkien's mythic world. While audiences of Peter Jackson's cinematic masterpiece may readily recognize Galadriel, Éowyn, and Arwen as prominent female characters, a deeper exploration of Tolkien's literary works unveils a tapestry rich with compelling female figures. Consider, for instance, Lúthien, an Elven princess of the ancient world, whose tale unfolds against the backdrop of a land ensnared by the malevolent Morgoth. Lúthien's narrative is a captivating study of the power of transcendent love, as she willingly relinquishes her immortality for the sake of Beren, a mortal Man. Similarly, the figure of Haleth emerges as a noteworthy character—a female warrior and tribal leader loved and honored by Elves and Men. Beyond the cinematic glamour, the nuanced portrayal of women in Tolkien's writings present a complex interplay of femininity, strength, and agency in Tolkien's mythology, inviting us to delve deeper into their roles and significance within the literary landscape.

Tolkien's multifaceted portrayal of women resonates with a dual influence, one rooted in Germanic mythological imagery and the other in his Catholic devotion. As Leslie Donovan notes, many of Tolkien's female characters reflect aspects of the Germanic Valkyrie figure, with images of cup-bearing, weaving, personal cost, and martial skill.[1] Simultaneously, these characters are infused with the essence of Tolkien's deeply cherished devotion to the Virgin Mary, with attributes of humility, wise counsel, motherhood, healing, and the renunciation of power.[2] In my full-length work, *Tolkien's Theology of*

Beauty, I suggest that Tolkien blends the Valkyrie motif with Marian theology, effectively creating the Marian Valkyrie.[3] That is to say, Tolkien utilized Germanic mythological imagery to create heroic women of remarkable fortitude and resolve, who make free choices at great personal cost, at times renouncing their own power so as to overthrow evil and bring healing. Some of these women are martial warriors while others are not; yet all show active bravery and personal abnegation. Éowyn's character demonstrates overt attributes of the Valkyrie figure, simply by virtue of her role as a Germanic shield-maiden in battle.[4] Others, such as Galadriel and Arwen, emanate Valkyrie-like qualities in their unwavering fortitude and strength of will, alongside their self-sacrifice, sorrow, and great personal loss.[5]

Tolkien's deep Marian devotion finds its most luminous manifestation in the character of Galadriel, the high Elven Lady of Lothlórien. In a letter from 1953, Tolkien responds to Father Robert Murray's observation of Galadriel's resemblance to Mary. He writes,

> I think I know exactly what you mean by the order of Grace; and of course by your references to Our Lady, upon which all my own small perception of beauty both in majesty and simplicity is founded. *The Lord of the Rings* is of course a fundamentally religious and Catholic work; unconsciously so at first, but consciously in the revision. (*Letters*, 142)

Tolkien wholly acknowledged and embraced the influence of his Marian devotion upon the character. Indeed, Galadriel's affinity with Mary has inspired a number of scholars to explore the parallels and influence.[6] In conjunction with her spiritual dimension, Tolkien endows Galadriel with a multifaceted history—one that weaves athleticism, military prowess, ambition, and—in earlier renditions—a rebellious and stubborn pride. He describes the young Galadriel as "proud, strong, and self-willed," desiring "far lands and dominions that might be her own" (*UT*, 230; *Peoples*, 337). When the Noldor rebelled against the Valar, Galadriel was "the only woman of the Noldor to stand that day tall and valiant among the contending princes, [and] was eager to be gone" (*Silmarillion*, 83–84; *Morgoth*, 112). Such was her pride that "once she set foot upon the road of exile she would not relent" (*UT*, 230). Even in later versions of her history when he removed her rebellion, she remained both valiant and proud.[7]

In the convergence of these two facets—transcendent spirituality and martial prowess—Galadriel emerges as a quintessential exemplar of the Marian Valkyrie, a theologically complex mythological warrior woman that challenges both ancient and modern concepts of power and womanhood. This essay explores the nuanced landscapes of Tolkien's literary universe, wherein the Marian Valkyrie takes center stage, serving as a lens through which we explore the theological underpinnings of Galadriel within the rich tapestry of Middle-earth.

GALADRIEL AND THE MARIAN ARCHETYPE

In *Tolkien's Theology of Beauty*, I suggest that Tolkien's use of the Valkyrie motif is an extension of the Marian archetype. The Marian archetype is largely characterized by humility, courage, self-giving, and sorrow. As the "handmaid of the Lord," Mary exemplifies humble obedience and proactive fortitude (Luke 1:38). In courage, she offers herself to the will of God and endures immeasurable suffering.[8] Her humble self-sacrifice ultimately enables the defeat of evil and brings healing to humankind through the Son she bears.

Hans Urs von Balthasar notes that "the Marian experience is one of dispossession."[9] As the Mother of Sorrows, Mary is honored as one who suffered intensely, participating with Christ in the work of salvation.[10] As the Mother of Jesus, she stood at the foot of the cross, witnessing the suffering and death of her Son (John 19:25–27). Nevertheless, she endured suffering with courageous resolve, retaining her integrity in steadfastness of spirit. The Medieval understanding of Mary's humility gave way to the title, "Woman of Valor" (Prov 31:10), a rendering of the Latin *mulier fortis*.[11] Jaroslav Pelikan states that Mary's identity as the meek and humble Handmaid of the Lord is inseparable from her identity as the courageous Woman of Valor, for she is the Second Eve who would "crush the head of the serpent" (Gen 3:15).[12] He observes that in the Middle Ages her identity as the Woman of Valor grew into that of a "warrior and champion, [a] conqueror and leader."[13] Some scholars have since compared Mary to the Biblical warrior women of the Old Testament, namely Deborah, Jael, and Judith.[14] Stefano Manelli suggests that Deborah, with the help of Jael, delivers the Israelites and thus prefigures Mary's role as Co-redemptrix in God's work of salvation. Additionally, Judith's act of cutting off the head of Holofernes prefigures Mary's crushing of the serpent's head.[15] Judith displays "Purity and beauty, together with courage and audacity," which then prefigures Mary as "the 'invincible warrior woman' who crushes the head of the enemy."[16] Some even suggest that Mary's *Magnificat* is modeled as an Israelite war song celebrating God's victory.[17]

Pelikan ties Mary's role as warrior to her identity as "Lodestar," or the guiding North Star to seafarers. As Lodestar, she would not only guide, but triumphantly overcome enemies and storms.[18] One will recall the phial that Galadriel gave to Frodo; this housed the light of Eärendil's star and served to guide Frodo in the darkness of Shelob's lair, while utilizing light as a protection. Interestingly, Cynewulf's *Christ*, the pivotal work that inspired Tolkien's creation of Eärendil, describes Mary as "full of triumph."[19] With these descriptions of Mary in the background of Tolkien's religious devotion, it is no surprise that he wrote Galadriel as a motherly protector with martial undertones.[20]

GALADRIEL AND THE VALKYRIE MOTIF

While Galadriel is deeply Marian, she also exemplifies a martial maiden of Germanic literature. In particular, Galadriel bears a striking resemblance to the character of Wealhtheow in *Beowulf*. In *Beowulf's Wealhtheow and the Valkyrie Tradition*, Helen Damico explores the deeper connotations behind the character of Wealhtheow, the king's wife who charges Beowulf to seek out and defeat Grendel. Damico argues that the Valkyrie parallels are unmistakable, from ceremonial cup-bearing, to publicly testing Beowulf and inciting him to battle, to demanding a solemn vow.[21] Building on Damico's premise, Donovan notes Galadriel's similarities to Wealhtheow, expanding further on traditional Valkyrie imagery in Galadriel's narrative, such as radiance, a ring of power, gift-giving, ceremonial cup-bearing, weaving, testing the heroes, and inciting a quest.[22]

Damico suggests that Wealhtheow has a small role at first glance, acting as a simple catalyst to move the story forward. Upon closer inspection, however, there is far more to her character. In the foreground, she is a courtly and hospitable queen; in the background, there are clear references to her martial role. Not only is she "renowned," but is accompanied by a "troop of maidens" while the warriors "unambiguously . . . pay her homage."[23] Damico carefully expounds upon Wealhtheow's martial presence within the court, showing striking parallels between the queen and the warriors.

As a scholar well-versed in the Germanic, and most notably his extensive expertise in *Beowulf*, Tolkien would likely have noticed these references. The subtlety of a courteous martial queen in the court of warriors mirrors Galadriel's first appearance. While Galadriel is indeed stately, queenly, and a woman of the court, she, like Wealhtheow, has a military background. In the published *Silmarillion*, Tolkien writes of her part in Fëanor's rebellion:

> Galadriel, the only woman of the Noldor to stand that day tall and valiant among the contending princes, was eager to be gone. . . . She yearned to see the wide unguarded lands and to rule there a realm at her own will. (*Silmarillion*, 83–84)

In the *Unfinished Tales*, he describes her thus:

Galadriel was the greatest of the Noldor, except Fëanor maybe, though she was wiser than he . . .

She was strong of body, mind, and will, a match for both the loremasters and the athletes of the Eldar in the days of their youth.

She was proud, strong, and selfwilled . . . She had dreams of far lands and dominions that might be her own to order as she would without tutelage. (*UT*, 229–30)

Similarly, in a letter to Catharine Findlay (1973), Tolkien remarks that Galadriel was "of Amazon disposition" in her youth (*Letters*, 348). Galadriel's various names are likewise descriptive of her nature. Her name, Galadriel, meant "maiden crowned with gleaming hair," referring to the manner in which she would braid her hair like a crown when competing in athletic games (*Letters*, 348). The name her mother gave her was Nerwen, meaning, "man-maiden," a reference to her ability to thrive in masculine activities (*UT*, 337).[24] Indeed, Tolkien describes her as a formidable force in athleticism, military might, political power, and force of will.

Like a Valkyrie, the young Galadriel was headstrong and proud, daring to defy the command of the Valar, even embracing banishment and threat of death to seek out a dominion of her own. While she did not act in malice, she was a prominent leader in Fëanor's revolt, the violent flight of the Noldoran Elves from Valinor. Later in life, when she had established her dominion in Middle-earth, Tolkien notes that Galadriel looked upon the Dwarves "with the eye of a commander, seeing in them the finest warriors to pit against the Orcs" (*UT*, 235). She strategized with the thought of a military leader, making valuable alliances that would aid her in the fight against Sauron.

GALADRIEL AS ONE DIVIDED

We thus see two sides of Galadriel that Tolkien created from the character's first conception. In *The Lord of the Rings*, she is an ethereal, queenly, and maternal figure whose purity and sanctity is likened to Mary. In Tolkien's various writings outside of *Lord of the Rings*, including the published *Silmarillion*, Galadriel is a powerful political figure with a stubborn will and rebellious spirit, capable of martial feats and ambitiously seeking her own kingdom. She is cursed with the Noldor and banished from Valinor; when offered forgiveness, she defiantly refuses pardon (*UT*, 230–31; *Letters*, 407).

In the essay, "The Fall and Repentance of Galadriel," Romuald Lakowski carefully and thoughtfully traces the details of Galadriel's evolution in

Tolkien's writing. He notes that the various drafts and letters that elaborate on the detail of Galadriel's story were written between the years of 1967–1971 and are largely in agreement. Galadriel was involved in the rebellion of Fëanor, fell under the curse, and refused forgiveness. She ultimately repented and was granted permission to return to Valinor because of her resistance to Sauron and her rejection of the Ring. However, as Lakowski notes, in 1973, the last year of his life, Tolkien made "bewildering" changes to the nature of Galadriel: "Gone is Galadriel's rebellious pride: she is exonerated from all blame and only falls under the Ban of the Valar on a technicality."[25] While these were only projected changes, Tolkien had now reimagined Galadriel's history, erasing any vestiges of rebellion or desire for power. In a letter written in 1973, Tolkien underscores Galadriel's purity, stating that she was "'unstained': she had committed no evil deeds" (*Letters*, 431). His use of the word "unstained" is telling, as it connects her to the Catholic doctrine of Mary's sinlessness.[26] His son, Christopher, suggests that this version of Galadriel was purely "philosophical" and inconsistent with all other materials.[27] Tom Shippey argues that Tolkien's change to Galadriel's character was based on a "soft-heartedness," an aversion to darkening a character's narrative.[28] Alternatively, Stratford Caldecott suggests that Tolkien felt the "pressure of the Marian archetype" as he developed Galadriel's history.[29]

Tolkien clearly struggled to craft a consistent narrative for Galadriel's character development that took into account both her purity and her power. If Caldecott is correct in that Tolkien felt the pressure of the Marian archetype, it is unsurprising that Tolkien felt deep discomfort over Galadriel's rebellious pride and selfish ambition. However, the apparent inconsistency of virtue and pride point to a realistic character trait: Galadriel's inner struggle between light and dark. Over the course of her long life, she lives as one divided. In particular, her ambition and pride come into direct conflict with her continued devotion to the Valar and her innate goodness. For although she was "proud, strong, and selfwilled" with "dreams of far lands and dominions that might be her own," she nevertheless had a "noble and generous spirit . . . and a reverence for the Valar that she could not forget" (*UT*, 230). Her ambition drives her forward and her pride resists repentance, yet both these elements are held in check by an overarching piety and virtue. It is only when offered the ultimate temptation to fulfill her life's ambition that she is forced to choose. On the one hand, her ambitious pride can be fulfilled by absolute power. On the other hand, her devotion and goodness can only be fulfilled by the renunciation of that power.

Galadriel's virtue and pride are held in constant tension throughout her recorded history. Her devotion to the Valar is first seen in the narrative of *The Lord of the Rings*. When the Fellowship departs from Lothlórien, her song speaks of Varda, the high queen of the Valar, with great reverence and longing (*FR*, II, viii). In keeping with this, Tolkien carefully notes that she did not take the Oath of Fëanor (*Silmarillion*, 84). Her rebellion was not one of malice, but of foolish ambition. She was young, headstrong, and filled with dreams of power. Although she revered the Valar in her heart, this was overshadowed by youthful dreams and willful anger. Compare Galadriel's actions to those of Fëanor's wife, Nerdanel. Nerdanel's faithfulness to the Valar overrules even family ties. As Sandra Miesel notes, this choice exacts a tremendous sacrifice, for Nerdanel's husband and seven sons will die in Middle-earth.[30] Galadriel, on the other hand, throws herself headlong into the disarray. When Fëanor and his sons launch an attack on the sea-Elves to seize their ships, Galadriel "fought fiercely against Fëanor" to defend the sea-Elves, for they were her mother's family (*UT*, 230). Yet, even in the atrocity of the Kinslaying, Galadriel would not relent. Her pride and ambition of her youth were greater than her devotion. When later offered pardon, she "proudly refused forgiveness" (*Letters*, 320), for the thought of returning as one defeated and humiliated was more than her pride could bear (*UT*, 230). Compare this to her father, Finarfin, the half-brother of Fëanor. He never condones the rebellion, yet sets out for love of family (*Silmarillion*, 84). Even following the Kinslaying, he continues on, just as Galadriel does. When the curse is declared by the Valar, however, Finarfin repents and turns back to Valinor, where he is pardoned (*Silmarillion*, 88). His devotion to the Valar ultimately outweighs his other allegiances.

As discussed above, Tolkien eventually removes Galadriel's outright rebellion, rendering a version where she sets out separately from Fëanor, having no tie to Fëanor's revolt (*UT*, 231–33). Nevertheless, even in separating Galadriel's intentions from the rebellion itself, I would argue that her pride remains. She willfully chooses ambition over faithfulness, for even in this version she departs Valinor with full knowledge that this would not be permitted (*Silmarillion*, 232). In contrast, Nerdanel and Finarfin each chose devotion and wisdom amidst the trying circumstances—whereas the "purified" Galadriel did not. In view of this, one notes that Tolkien's efforts to purify Galadriel did not remove her willful nature or proud ambition. For in Tolkien's imagination, Galadriel was in her essence a political leader and military commander whose martial valor and spiritual might were instrumental in the fight against Sauron.

However, Tolkien's inability to truly erase Galadriel's guilt does not indicate that he failed to create a compelling character with a complexity of virtue and pride, who then grows in wisdom over the course of her long life. Parallel to the ambition and willful nature of her earlier narratives, Galadriel retained a strong element of virtue. She did not align herself with evil nor did she commit murder in the name of any cause. She did not curse the Valar nor ultimately reject them. Indeed, we see that in the published *Silmarillion*, she speaks with Queen Melian, an incarnate angelic Maia; their conversations suggest an ongoing reverence toward the Valar.[31] She is careful to clarify that she had no part in any evil nor does she condone the actions of Fëanor (*Silmarillion*, 127). As the long years pass, she fosters wisdom and virtue. When she at last establishes her own longed-for dominion of Lothlórien, she does not take up the title of Queen, considering herself only a guardian (*UT*, 245).

Galadriel thus maintains wisdom and virtue, coupled with an ongoing political ambition. For the long ages of her life, she walks upon a tightrope, looking long into the lures of power. When given the choice to take the One Ring, she knows she can use that power to destroy Sauron and all current forms of evil in Middle-earth (*FR*, II, vii; and cf. *Letters*, 246). It is this inner conflict that makes her temptation for the Ring compelling and definitive. Her long-standing desire for political power naturally aligns with the One Ring, yet she also wants what is good.

Galadriel's inner conflict extends beyond the complexities of her political ambition. She is divided between her desire to control outcomes and her commitment to the Good. She used her own ring of power for the good of the Elves and of Middle-earth. With it, she beautified and fortified Lothlórien, halting the natural decay of time. While her virtue framed her actions, her desire for power drove her motives. Despite the transcendent beauty of Lothlórien, one finds that it is merely "propped up" by the power of Galadriel's ring. Without that power, it becomes subject to decay like any other forest in Middle-earth.[32] In a letter, Tolkien remarks that such beauty is an "embalming," a selfish desire to stop growth and change (*Letters*, 154). Verlyn Flieger writes, "There is a concealed sting in Lórien's beauty. . . . It is a cautionary picture, closer in kind to the Ring than we'd like to think, shown to us in all its beauty to test if we can let it go. . . . Lórien's beauty is crystalized. It is frozen. And in its perfection is its flaw."[33] On the one hand, Galadriel's power is used for good, in that it offers protection and infuses immortal beauty into mortal lands. On the other hand, the immortal beauty is deceptive, serving instead as a temptation to remain in Middle-earth and resist the call to Valinor. This plays directly into Galadriel's pride and ambition, for she desires to retain her kingdom, her power, and the beauty she has created.

While Galadriel is enticed by power and political reputation, this is not her greatest desire. Consider her words to Frodo. When he asks her what she "wishes," she responds, "That what should be shall be." This appears to be a resignation to fate, but she qualifies it: "The love of the Elves for their land and their works is deeper than the deeps of the Sea . . . Yet they will cast all away rather than submit to Sauron" (*FR*, II, vii). Beyond resignation, there is another element at play: the love of beauty and its relation to the Good. Von Balthasar writes, "In a world without beauty . . . the good also loses its attractiveness, the self-evidence of why it must be carried out." Without an awareness of the Beautiful, "the proofs of the truth have lost their cogency."[34] Galadriel's statement is significant, for she connects her reaction to good and evil with an understanding of beauty. The works of the Elves are beautiful and love-worthy, and the Elves possess an intense love for that beauty. Nevertheless, they would prefer to sacrifice that beauty than to succumb to evil. Beauty is thus set in direct contrast to evil. By contrasting beauty and evil, she is insinuating that beauty is related to goodness. However, in sacrificing created beauty in an effort to resist evil, she is suggesting that there is a Beauty higher and deeper than created beauty, a beauty that correlates to the Good. For Galadriel, the correlation of the Beautiful to the Good outweighs her desire for power. While pride and ambition are an undercurrent throughout her history, her virtue is ultimately greater.

THE RENUNCIATION OF POWER AND THE INTEGRATION OF BEING

Throughout her story, Galadriel lived as one divided. She grew in wisdom and goodness, and in her love for true Beauty. Nevertheless, her dreams of power remained. In Galadriel's character we see two types of power exercised. The first is her life-long desire to rule, along with the temptation to dominate other wills—the will to power. The second is the sheer power of her will to confront, wrestle with, and ultimately overcome the temptation to misuse power. When she is confronted by her long-held desire, she is forced to choose, wholly and completely. In this moment, she declares all that could be and what she has dreamed to become: a queen "beautiful and terrible" that is loved and feared (*FR*, II, vii).

Ultimately, Galadriel's inner conflict is not between virtue and martial strength. Rather, her conflict is between wisdom and pride. In wisdom, she retained her virtue; in pride she rebelled. In wisdom, she resisted Sauron; in pride, she coveted his power. In wisdom, she ruled Lothlórien as a guardian and brought forth beauty; in pride, she embalmed that beauty in an effort to imitate Valinor, and so avoid returning in disgrace. When presented with the One Ring, the two sides of her character are brought to the forefront and a choice demanded.

One notes, however, that her choice has already been made. Only moments earlier, she held up her hands in a "gesture of rejection" toward Mordor (*FR*, II, vii). She then told Frodo that she desired that "what should be shall be." In this declaration, she does not make an active choice, but a resigned one. She knows what is good, and in her wisdom has chosen the Good. However, in Frodo offering her the One Ring, the fulfillment of all her desires, that choice is tested and her true being laid bare.

As Galadriel rightly notes, to embrace the power of the One Ring would eventually turn to great ruin. The only path to salvation for herself, and Middle-earth at large, is to renounce that power. As Enright remarks, the "inversion of power exhibit[s] a virtue that . . . is crucial to salvation—the choice of love over pride."[35] She had already resolved that she will not forcibly take the Ring from Frodo; she will not actively pursue that power. In reality, she had made a greater choice, a choice to relinquish her dreams of power—now ruthlessly tested. So great is the test that the two sides of her nature are forced into alignment, for good or for evil. Her resolve requires absolute integrity, a holistic and unreserved integration of being. Wisdom and power, once at odds within her, now join. Her ambition that began in self-service now finds its fulfillment in the love and preservation of the Good. She is indeed the guardian of Lothlórien, and as the guardian she knows that she and her people would sacrifice created beauty for an Everlasting Beauty. In this moment of testing, her wisdom brings her ambition into its rightful place: she is a guardian and not a queen; she is a warrior in service to the Good and not in service to herself. She is offered a choice that demands a holistic integrity of being, one that exacts an extreme personal loss—and she passes the test. At the crux, she releases her desire for the sake of the Good and for love of the Beautiful. If Beauty is the deepest and greatest motivation to Goodness, as von Balthasar suggests, then Galadriel has chosen the greater Beauty, an everlasting Beauty. Tolkien notes that Galadriel's rejection of the One Ring was due to the growth of her wisdom, suggesting a maturity had come to fruition within her (*UT*, 231). She is no longer divided, but whole.

In passing the test, she declares, "I will remain Galadriel, and diminish." This has a direct tie to her previous statement, wherein she laments that if Frodo destroys the Ring, the "power [of the Elves] is diminished." In rejecting the Ring, she willingly chooses this fate—for the Elves, and for herself. She relinquishes her dream to become a powerful queen, and instead embraces her own identity as, simply, Galadriel. She submits her pride to receive the pardon of the Valar. She is choosing to release her effort to control outcomes. Galadriel's use of power in this moment manifests as a relinquishing of power, a diminishing.[36] This free action brings all her associations of power into an appropriate ordering. True power, situated in the beauty of the good, plays out in an inversion of power. Galadriel enacts the power of her will to overcome the temptation to dominate other wills. In tremendous fortitude of mind and resolve of spirit, she resists the temptation of the One Ring. In great power, she renounces power.

CONCLUSION

In *The Lord of the Rings*, the reader encounters Galadriel at the conclusion of her known narrative. She is grave and ethereal; a queenly figure, wise in her vast foresight, and compassionate even to Dwarves. The Fellowship approach her with an awe and reverence that is deeply Marian. However, in comparing Galadriel to Wealhtheow, it becomes evident that Tolkien had always imagined Galadriel as a warrior woman with political ambition. Recognizing the Marian archetype in her narrative, he later endeavored to purify her, spanning back to the beginning of her days. Nevertheless, he could not reconcile the pieces of her narrative, for even in making her "stainless," he did not remove her boldface choice to defy the Valar's command. He could not truly make her sinless.[37] For indeed, Galadriel was modeled after a Valkyrie, thereby retaining the typical characteristics of headstrong pride, courageous resolve, and political ambition. Yet even in this, in all versions of her story she retained goodness and virtue. While she sought to preserve earthly beauty, even to the point of "embalming" it, she ultimately recognized that there was a greater Beauty.

Undoubtedly, Tolkien addresses power and its uses and misuses in various ways throughout his *legendarium*. His female characters, in particular, give a telling commentary on his approach to power. In contrast to traditional power revealed in force and domination, these characters show that true power is found in abnegation, in self-giving. Such an approach is modeled after the Virgin Mary in her humble self-giving, a choice enacted with courage and driven by love. This is the heart of Tolkien's female characters, as modeled in Galadriel's characterization in *The Lord of the Rings*. However, Tolkien was a man steeped in the Germanic mythologies of the ancient past. As such, it is no surprise that his female characters often take the form of the Germanic Valkyrie, whether it be in ritual, temperament, or martial prowess. Galadriel is no exception. However, Tolkien takes the Valkyrie motif and reshapes it within the Marian archetype.

The Marian archetype challenges common perceptions of power, showing the renunciation of power to be the greater might. In Germanic mythology, power and renunciation are often caricatures; female warriors are shown to be "masculine" and capable of martial activities only prior to marriage, after which they become "meek" and domestic.[38] Galadriel's narrative challenges this portrayal of Valkyries. In her youth, she does indeed embody the typical Valkyrie behavior of martial prowess, rebellion, and pride, contending with male warriors on an equal plain. Yet she retains her athleticism and military might even in marriage, unlike traditional Valkyries. As she matures in wisdom over the long ages, she grows in power. She counsels her husband while governing as his equal, yet demonstrates greater spiritual power and political reputation. Upon the downfall of Sauron, she marches out with her husband's army and, in her own power, destroys Sauron's fortress of Dol Guldur (*RK*, Appendix B).

Tolkien models Galadriel after the mythological Valkyrie yet changes the traditional approach to power. As one with a natural talent and desire for power, Galadriel craves and ambitiously pursues it in her youth. Yet, within the Marian archetype, she tempers that appetite by increasing her wisdom and virtue over time. When tested by the offer of absolute power, she renounces it wholly and resolutely, choosing the Good with humility and self-sacrifice. Her martial abilities and leadership remain intact, but her power finds an appropriate place: in humility and resilience in service to the Good.

Tolkien's conflicting drafts reflect the dividedness of Galadriel's character, showing a realism of the character's inner struggle. This mirrors the long and painful process of renouncing selfish ambition. Like a Valkyrie, a choice was exacted that would bring tremendous personal loss. Like Mary, she sacrificed her own desires in the name of the Good and in the fight against Evil. While she loved the earthly beauty that she had created, she chose instead a higher Beauty. In so doing, she "sacrificed all" to bring the mere *hope* of salvation to Middle-earth—much like Mary in bringing the hope of salvation to human-kind through the birth of her Son.

Galadriel's use of power is distinctly Marian. Compare her state-ment: "What should be shall be" with Mary's "May it be to me as you have said" (Luke 1:38 NIV). Both indicate a seemingly passive submission, but each are enacted with great power of the will, an active submission to the Good as a free but deliberate choice of the will. It is not ultimately a choice of resignation, as it first appears, but a choice actively and resolutely chosen with courage and resolve. Rather than passively accepting her fate, each of these women actively enacts her fate, putting into motion an overarching sal-vation. Both situations demand a great personal sacrifice. Galadriel chooses the greater Beauty, yet acknowledges the loss that comes with such a choice. For Mary, the loss was the death of her Son, an unspeakable bereavement. For Galadriel, the loss was the forfeiture of her very world, the beauties she had created, the kingdom she had built through ages of struggle and suffering. Just as Mary's humility and self-giving enables Satan's defeat, so also does Galadriel relinquishing of power enable Sauron's downfall. Her loss and her choice to "diminish" opens the way—not only to victory for Middle-earth, but also for forgiveness and pardon for herself. In obtaining a full integration of being, she can now honor the Valar without the shadow of rebellion or pride.

Tolkien's love and reverence for Mary resonate throughout his literary works, but nowhere more evident than in the character of Galadriel. In his *legendarium*, Ilúvatar is the God-figure with whom Sauron contends. Tolkien explained that *The Lord of the Rings* is fundamentally "about God, and His sole right to divine honour," for "Sauron desired to be a God-King" (*Letters*, 183). When Frodo offers Galadriel the One Ring, she is tempted to take Sauron's place as the God-king vying against Ilúvatar. In her wisdom, she saw that to seek such power was not only foolish, but was not her ultimate desire. Her greatest desire was for the higher Beauty of Goodness despite the anguish of loss. In this, we see echoes of Tolkien's much beloved "theory of courage," the hail of the hero to sacrifice all despite certain defeat. So also with Galadriel, who believed that she was fighting "the long defeat" (*FR*, II, vii). For Galadriel, the Marian Valkyrie enacts her power at great cost for the sake of the Good because of the Beautiful.

NOTES

1. Leslie A. Donovan, "The Valkyrie Reflex in J.R.R. Tolkien's *The Lord of the Rings*: Galadriel, Shelob, Éowyn, and Arwen," in *Perilous and Fair: Women in the Works and Life of J.R.R. Tolkien*, ed. Janet Brennan Croft and Leslie A. Donovan (Altadena, CA: Mythopoeic Press, 2015), 221–57.

2. Nancy Enright, "Tolkien's Females and the Defining of Power," in Croft and Donovan, *Perilous and Fair*, 118–35; Michael Maher, "'A Land Without Stain': Medieval Images of Mary and Their Use in the Characterization of Galadriel," in *Tolkien the Medievalist*, ed. Jane Chance, RSMRC (London: Routledge, 2003), 225–36; Stratford Caldecott, *The Power of the Ring: The Spiritual Vision Behind* The Lord of the Rings *and* The Hobbit (New York: Crossroad, 2005), 52; Romuald Ian Lakowski, "The Fall and Repentance of Galadriel," in Croft and Donovan, *Perilous and Fair*, 161–72; see also Marjorie Burns, *Perilous Realms: Celtic and Norse in Tolkien's Middle-earth* (Toronto: University of Toronto Press, 2005), 152.

3. Lisa Coutras, *Tolkien's Theology of Beauty: Majesty, Splendor, and Transcendence in Middle-earth* (New York: Palgrave Macmillan, 2016).

4. Donovan, "Valkyrie Reflex," 243; and Burns, *Perilous Realms*, 143. Interestingly, in describing maiden warriors of Germanic literature, Jenny Jochens highlights the maiden warrior Hervor, who not only preferred military activities to feminine ones, but, like Éowyn, joined the male warriors, taking on the garb and name of a man, and accomplished unprecedented feats in battle; see Jenny Jochens, *Old Norse Images of Women*, Middle Ages (Philadelphia: University of Pennsylvania Press, 1996), 99.

5. Donovan, "Valkyrie Reflex," 221–57.

6. Some examples are as follows: Sandra Miesel, "Life-Giving Ladies: Women in the Writings of J.R.R. Tolkien," in *Light Beyond All Shadow: Religious Experience in Tolkien's Work*, ed. Paul E. Kerry and Sandra Miesel (Madison: Fairleigh Dickinson University Press, 2013), 139–52; Stratford Caldecott, *Power of the Ring*; Nancy Enright, "Tolkien's Females," 118–35.

7. Consider, for example, the final version of Galadriel's narrative, in which she set forth from Valinor separately from the rebelling Noldor, on her own and with "legitimate" reasons. I argue later in this chapter that she demonstrated pride when she departs secretly and against the wishes (or expected wishes) of the Valar (*UT*, 231–32; *Letters*, 431).

8. For a brief summary and commentary on Mary's suffering, see Arthur Burton Calkins, "Mary Co-Redemptrix: The Beloved Associate of Christ," in *Mariology: A Guide for Priests, Deacons, Seminarians, and Consecrated Persons*, ed. Mark Miravalle (Goleta, CA: Seat of Wisdom, 2008), 393–95.

9. Hans Urs von Balthasar, *The Glory of the Lord: A Theological Aesthetics*, vol 1: *Seeing the Form* (Edinburgh: T&T Clark, 1983), 332–33.

10. This tradition first originated in the writings of St. Irenaeus of Lyons, who introduced the concept of Mary as a participant in redemption with Christ. He stated that she reversed Eve's disobedience with obedience, becoming the "New Eve" in the saving work of Christ, the "New Adam." St. Bernard further developed the tradition of Mary as co-redeemer and co-sufferer, for she offered her Son to the Father "for the reconciliation of the world." According to Calkins, Mary had an "active but subordinate role" in Christ's saving work, including his suffering; see Calkins, "Mary Co-Redemptrix," 350, 365, 353; see also Irenaeus, *Epid.* 33.

11. Modern translations render this as "capable wife" (NRSV), "excellent wife" (ESV, NASB), or "a wife of noble character" (NIV). Pelikan notes that "the Hebrew vocable did allow for the meaning 'valor'; and both the Greek translation in the Septuagint, *andreia* (this being the word for the classical virtue 'fortitude'), and the Latin translation in the Vulgate, *fortis*, understood it that way"; see Jaroslav Pelikan, *Mary Through the Centuries* (New York: History Book Club, 2005).

12. Pelikan, *Mary*, 44–45, 85.

13. Pelikan, *Mary*, 91.

14. Stefano Manelli, "The Mystery of the Blessed Virgin Mary in the Old Testament," in *Mariology: A Guide for Priests, Deacons, Seminarians, and Consecrated Persons*, ed. Mark Miravalle (Goleta, CA: Seat of Wisdom, 2008), 29–32; Julie Walsh, "Jael's Story as Initial Fulfillment of Genesis 3:15," *Priscilla Papers* 33.4 (2019): 22–27; J. Clinton McCann, *Judges*, Interpretation (Louisville: Westminster John Knox, 2011); see also Dorota Filipczak, "Éowyn and the Biblical Tradition of a Warrior Woman," *Text Matters* 7 (2017): 405–15.

15. Manelli, "Mystery," 29–32.

16. Manelli, "Mystery," 32.

17. McCann, *Judges*, 21, 58; J. Massyngbaerde Ford, *My Enemy Is My Guest: Jesus and Violence in Luke* (Eugene: Wipf and Stock, 2010), 5; Walsh, "Jael's Story," 24.

18. Pelikan, *Mary*, 94.

19. Cynewulf, *Cynewulf's Christ: An Eighth Century English Epic*, ed. Israel Gollancz (London: David Nutt, 1892), 9; see also Marjorie Burns, "Saintly and Distant Mothers," in *The Ring and the Cross: Christianity and* The Lord of the Rings, ed. Paul E. Kerry (Madison: Fairleigh Dickinson University, 2010), 250–52.

20. Another interesting connection is Éowyn's similarity to Jael and Judith as Biblical warrior women, who in turn prefigure Mary as a Jael-Judith figure. See Filipczak, "Éowyn."

21. Helen Damico, *Beowulf's Wealhtheow and the Valkyrie Tradition* (Madison: University of Wisconsin Press, 1984), 6.

22. Donovan, "Valkyrie Reflex," 230–38.

23. Damico, *Wealhtheow*, 5–6.

24. The Septuagint translates Prov 31:10 with γυναῖκα ἀνδρείαν ("woman of courage"). While the word ἀνδρεῖος means "heroic" or "awesome," especially when referring to women, at its root is ἀνδρ-, which indicates "man" or "masculine"—or, seemingly very similar to what Tolkien means by Nerwen, "man-maiden."

25. Lakowski, "Fall and Repentance," 166.

26. Manfred Hauke explains that Mary was preserved from original sin in light of the Incarnation, so as to consecrate her for divine motherhood, in "The Mother of God," in *Mariology: A Guide for Priests, Deacons, Seminarians, and Consecrated Persons*, ed. Mark Miravalle (Goleta, CA: Seat of Wisdom, 2008), 199.

27. Christopher Tolkien describes a "projected revision" wherein his father completely reimagined Galadriel's departure from Valinor as a separate and innocent event, thereby removing any guilt or tainted motive. Christopher surmises that his father's intention was to re-draft Galadriel's entire history based on this purely "philosophical" conception (*UT*, 231–32).

28. Tom Shippey, *The Road to Middle-earth: How J.R.R. Tolkien Created a New Mythology* (New York: Houghton Mifflin, 2003), 375n13.

29. Caldecott, *Power of the Ring*, 54; see also Enright, "Tolkien's Females and the Defining of Power," 127–28.

30. Miesel, "Life-Giving Ladies," 149.

31. In other texts, Tolkien states that Galadriel "received the love of Melian" and "there was great love between them" (*Jewels*, 178, 35).

32. After Aragorn's death, Arwen goes to the "fading" Lothlórien (*RK*, Appendix A).

33. Verlyn Flieger, *A Question of Time: J.R.R. Tolkien's Road to Faërie* (Kent, OH: Kent State University Press, 1997), 112, 114.

34. Von Balthasar, *Glory of the Lord*, 1:19.

35. Enright, "Tolkien's Females," 121.

36. Romuald Lakowski makes the insightful connection between Galadriel's words, "I will diminish," and John the Baptist's statement, "I must diminish," in "Fall and Repentance," 163.

37. See Christopher Tolkien's comments in *UT*, 232. See also *Letters*, 431.

38. Jochens, *Old Norse Images*, 101, 112.

BIBLIOGRAPHY

Balthasar, Hans Urs von. *The Glory of the Lord: A Theological Aesthetics.* Vol 1: *Seeing the Form.* Edinburgh: T&T Clark, 1983.

Burns, Marjorie. *Perilous Realms: Celtic and Norse in Tolkien's Middle-earth.* Toronto: University of Toronto Press, 2005.

———. "Saintly and Distant Mothers." Pages 246–58 in *The Ring and the Cross: Christianity and* The Lord of the Rings. Edited by Paul E. Kerry. Madison: Fairleigh Dickinson University, 2010.

Caldecott, Stratford. *The Power of the Ring: The Spiritual Vision Behind* The Lord of the Rings *and* The Hobbit. New York: Crossroad, 2005.

Calkins, Arthur Burton. "Mary Co-Redemptrix: The Beloved Associate of Christ." Pages 349–409 in *Mariology: A Guide for Priests, Deacons, Seminarians, and Consecrated Persons.* Edited by Mark Miravalle. Goleta, CA: Seat of Wisdom, 2008.

Coutras, Lisa. *Tolkien's Theology of Beauty: Majesty, Splendor, and Transcendence in Middle-earth.* New York: Palgrave Macmillan, 2016.

Croft, Janet Brennan, and Leslie A. Donovan, eds. *Perilous and Fair: Women in the Works and Life of J.R.R. Tolkien.* Altadena, CA: Mythopoeic Press, 2015.

Cynewulf. *Cynewulf's Christ: An Eighth Century English Epic.* Edited by Israel Gollancz. London: David Nutt, 1892.

Damico, Helen. *Beowulf's Wealhtheow and the Valkyrie Tradition.* Madison: University of Wisconsin Press, 1984.

Donovan, Leslie A. "The Valkyrie Reflex in J.R.R. Tolkien's *The Lord of the Rings*: Galadriel, Shelob, Éowyn, and Arwen." Pages 221–57 in *Perilous and Fair: Women in the Works and Life of J.R.R. Tolkien.* Edited by Janet Brennan Croft and Leslie A. Donovan. Altadena, CA: Mythopoeic Press, 2015.

Enright, Nancy. "Tolkien's Females and the Defining of Power." Pages 118–35 in *Perilous and Fair: Women in the Works and Life of J.R.R. Tolkien.* Edited by Janet Brennan Croft and Leslie A. Donovan. Altadena, CA: Mythopoeic Press, 2015.

Filipczak, Dorota. "Éowyn and the Biblical Tradition of a Warrior Woman." *Text Matters* 7 (2017): 405–15.

Flieger, Verlyn. *A Question of Time: J.R.R. Tolkien's Road to Faërie.* Kent, OH: Kent State University Press, 1997.

Ford, J. Massyngbaerde. *My Enemy Is My Guest: Jesus and Violence in Luke.* Eugene: Wipf and Stock, 2010.

Hauke, Manfred. "The Mother of God." Pages 167–212 in *Mariology: A Guide for Priests, Deacons, Seminarians, and Consecrated Persons.* Edited by Mark Miravalle. Goleta, CA: Seat of Wisdom, 2008.

Irenaeus. *On the Apostolic Preaching.* Translated by John Behr. Crestwood, NY: St Vladimir's Seminary Press, 1997.

Jochens, Jenny. *Old Norse Images of Women.* Middle Ages. Philadelphia: University of Pennsylvania Press, 1996.

Lakowski, Romuald Ian. "The Fall and Repentance of Galadriel." Pages 153–67 in *Perilous and Fair: Women in the Works and Life of J. R. R. Tolkien.* Edited by Janet Brennan Croft and Leslie Donovan. Altadena, CA: Mythopoeic, 2015.

Maher, Michael. "'A Land Without Stain': Medieval Images of Mary and Their Use in the Characterization of Galadriel." Pages 225–36 in *Tolkien the Medievalist.* Edited by Jane Chance. RSMRC 3. London: Routledge, 2003.

Manelli, Stefano. "The Mystery of the Blessed Virgin Mary in the Old Testament." Pages 1–43 in *Mariology: A Guide for Priests, Deacons, Seminarians, and Consecrated Persons*. Edited by Mark Miravalle. Goleta, CA: Seat of Wisdom, 2008.

McCann, J. Clinton. *Judges*. Interpretation. Louisville: Westminster John Knox, 2011.

Miesel, Sandra. "Life-Giving Ladies: Women in the Writings of J.R.R. Tolkien." Pages 139–52 in *Light Beyond All Shadow: Religious Experience in Tolkien's Work*. Edited by Paul E. Kerry and Sandra Miesel. Madison: Fairleigh Dickinson University Press, 2013.

Pelikan, Jaroslav. *Mary Through the Centuries*. New York: History Book Club, 2005.

Shippey, Tom. *The Road to Middle-earth: How J.R.R. Tolkien Created a New Mythology*. New York: Houghton Mifflin, 2003.

Walsh, Julie. "Jael's Story as Initial Fulfillment of Genesis 3:15." *Priscilla Papers* 33.4 (2019): 22–27.

Chapter 7

Songs of Light and Darkness

*Theological Imagination and
Metaphor in J.R.R. Tolkien*

Beth M. Stovell

While many scholars have explored the themes and metaphors of
J.R.R. Tolkien, few have compared the theology implicit in Tolkien's specific metaphors of light and darkness using modern theories of conceptual
metaphor.[1] Yet key aspects of Tolkien's theological imagination arise through
his uses of metaphors of light and darkness and related metaphors of geo-
spatial and meteorological manifestations that create light (stars, fire, etc.),
obscure light (mist, shadow, hiding, etc.), or create darkness (rain, storm, ash,
etc.) for theological ends. A crucial example of this is the light of Eärendil's
star within Galadriel's phial in the battle against Shelob (a creature of darkness) in *The Two Towers,* which will be the focus of this chapter. Probing the
background of Eärendil as a literary figure in Tolkien's imagination and the
essential role of Eärendil in Tolkien's Middle-earth mythology allows for the
contextualization of Eärendil's star. These depictions of light and darkness
show striking similarities to biblical language in the Hebrew Bible and New
Testament, intertwined with other mythological stories. Tolkien's unique
theological imagination becomes evident in the way he builds on this imagery
in the genre of fantasy.

METHODOLOGY

This essay uses conceptual blending theory to approach the ways that
Tolkien conceptualizes light and darkness in *TT* and as a way of exploring

the conceptions of light and darkness in specific biblical texts influencing Tolkien's work. Using conceptual blending theory is useful in studying Tolkien's work because it allows for study of the specific ranges of language that Tolkien uses to describe the concepts of light and darkness and other related concepts. This allows for analysis of Tolkien's imagery as part of a wider system alongside a close observance of the way such language is used in a specific part of Tolkien's writing.

While conceptual blending theory developed within cognitive linguistics, many scholars in biblical studies and in literary studies have used this approach in recent years.[2] Conceptual blending theory has several central features.[3] Fauconnier and Turner describe their theory in terms of network. They are concerned with "the on-line, dynamical cognitive work people do to construct meaning for local purpose of thought and action."[4] According to Fauconnier and Turner, conceptual blending is the central process by which this cognitive work of meaning construction occurs. A key element of conceptual blending is "mental spaces." Mental spaces are "small conceptual packets constructed as we think and talk, for purposes of local understanding and action."[5] These mental spaces contain partial elements from conceptual domains and from the given context.[6] In conceptual blending theory, mental spaces make up the input structures, generic structures, and blending structures in the network. Generic space is the mental space that describes the connection drawn between the two input spaces allowing them to blend with one another. The blended space is the result of the connections created between the two input spaces. To put it another way, this new mental space called "blended space" contains the results of "blending" the two inputs, while the mental space called "generic space" contains the means for this blending.

An example in Scripture would be the terms "Son of God," "Father," and "King of Israel" in John 1:14, 18, and 49. Because "Son of God" was associated with Davidic kingship and with the "Father-Son" familial metaphor in the Hebrew Scriptures, it allows for conceptual blending between "Father" and "King of Israel" through the generic space of kingship.[7] In *Two Towers*, one can do a similar conceptual blending study of how Tolkien speaks of darkness. At times, Tolkien uses semantic terms directly associated with darkness such as "dark, black," and other times he uses elements that create darkness or are associated with darkness such as "shadow," "mist," and "ash" or uses physical sensations to convey the *weight* of this darkness such as "heavy" (*TT*, IV, i–ii).[8] All of these different aspects of Tolkien's language provide us with a picture of how he conceptualizes darkness more broadly.

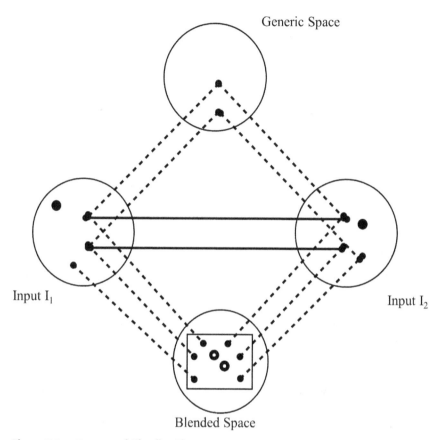

Figure 7.1. Conceptual Blending Theory.
By Beth M. Stovell

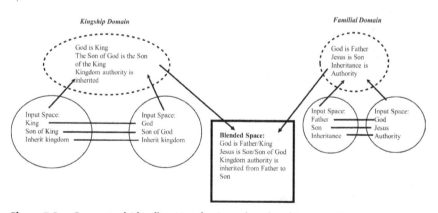

Figure 7.2. Conceptual Blending Map for Son of God and Jesus as King.
By Beth M. Stovell

CONCEPTUALIZING LIGHT AND
DARKNESS IN *THE TWO TOWERS*

We will first examine light and darkness in Tolkien's theological imagination found in *TT,* IV, ix. In this scene, the spider-like monstrous figure of darkness Shelob attacks Frodo and Sam. The light of Eärendil's star within Galadriel's phial saves them. But as is typical of Tolkien's work, the story of Galadriel's phial and the light of Eärendil's star within it does not start with *TT,* but flows from an extensive literary background in other parts of Tolkien's work. We begin this exploration by pointing to the contents of Galadriel's phial, the light of Eärendil's star. This use of light associated with Eärendil is noteworthy for literary historical reasons, narrative reasons, and theological reasons.

The Literary Background of Eärendil

Thus, to understand how the light from Eärendil's star pushes away the darkness of Shelob in the *TT,* we must explore aspects of the background of Eärendil himself. However, a single story of Eärendil is complicated by Tolkien's multiple retellings and the incomplete notes on Eärendil. As Christopher Tolkien notes in *The Book of Lost Tales, Part Two,* when he gathered his father's notes on Eärendil, there seemed to be at least 5 different strands of Eärendil's story, which C. Tolkien designated A, B, C, D, and E (*LT 2,* 252–77). While much could be said of Eärendil as "lover of the sea" and his seaward journeys, particularly as they are chronicled in "The Lay of Eärendil" and elsewhere in Tolkien's writings, our discussion focuses on the key parts of Eärendil's story related to the light of Eärendil's star.

Eärendil is a figure who appears in many of Tolkien's works (including *Silmarillion, FR, TT, RK, LT 2,* and *Lays*). *The Silmarillion* describes Eärendil's birth and life thus:

> In the spring of the year after was born in Gondolin Eärendil Halfelven, the son of Tuor and Idril Celebrindal; and that was five hundred years and three since the coming of the Noldor to Middle-earth. Of surpassing beauty was Eärendil, for a light was in his face as the light of heaven, and he had the beauty and the wisdom of the Eldar and the strength and hardihood of the Men of Old; and the Sea spoke ever in his ear and heart, even as with Tuor his father. (*Silmarillion,* 249)

While the narrator explicitly describes Eärendil as "Halfelven" and half-human, his beauty comes from his connection to light. Prior to being associated with a star, as will later occur, Eärendil's face has a light compared to "the light of heaven." This is one of four characteristics describing Eärendil by way of association: 1. His association with light ("as the light of heaven"), 2. His association with the Eldar (via "beauty and wisdom"), 3. His association with Men (via "strength and hardihood") and 4. His association with the Sea.[9] Each of these associations will influence Eärendil's adventures as they play out from Tolkien's earliest poem about Eärendil dating to September 1914[10] to his re-telling and explanation of Eärendil's story in a 1967 letter from Tolkien, only a few years prior to his death.[11] To give context for these dates, this places Tolkien's earliest poem about Eärendil roughly sixteen years before Tolkien began writing *The Hobbit* in around 1930 (published in 1937) and forty years before the publication of *Fellowship of the Ring*. It also places this earliest poem in the same year that Britain entered the Great War, which Tolkien joined in 1915. Tolkien mentions 1914 as a momentous date in his foreword to *FR:* "One has indeed personally to come under the shadow of war to feel fully its oppression; but as the years go by it seems now often forgotten that to be caught in youth by 1914 was no less hideous an experience than to be involved in 1939 and following years. By 1918 all but one of my close friends were dead."[12] The spark of Eärendil's story came before Tolkien's personal experiences of war, but the development of Eärendil's story interwoven into Tolkien's other works became shaped by Tolkien's wartime experiences.

Some have argued that Eärendil sparked for Tolkien what would "become the seed of his mythology of Middle-earth."[13] As Zaleski and Zaleski explain,

> it was here [at Gelding, Nottinghamshire], in a register yet dimly understood, that his imaginary cosmos first found voice. Tolkien had been reading—without much interest—the Anglo-Saxon poem *Crist* (formerly attributed to the poet Cynewulf) from the tenth-century Exeter Book, when his attention was caught by the following line, which evoked in him "a curious thrill, as if something had stirred in me, half wakened from sleep":

> *éala éarendel, engla beorhtast / ofer middangeard monnum sended*
> "Hail Éarendel, brightest of angels, / Sent unto men upon Middle-earth."[14]

The poem itself is based upon the fifth of the Latin "O" Antiphons sung at Vespers during the season of Advent . . . but who is *Éarendel*? This mysterious Old English word looks like a proper name; Albert Cook, in his 1900 edition of *Crist*, which Tolkien would have known, translates it as "rising sun," which would seem to point to Christ. Yet in the tenth-century Blickling Homilies, as Tolkien would note later, *eorendel* (as it is spelled there) refers to John the Baptist in his role as herald of Christ, the rising sun. The image has biblical roots (Luke 1:68–79): John the Baptist is "brightest of angels" by virtue of being the messenger (in Greek, ἄγγελός) of Christ, and he is the morning star—namely Venus—by virtue of being forerunner of the dawn. Tolkien thought he could see, in these associations, the baptized version of an astral myth.[15]

Here Zaleski and Zaleski provide a few key factors pertinent to this essay. First, Tolkien experienced this "thrill" while reading an Anglo-Saxon poem and connecting it with the biblical story. This combination of Anglo-Saxon and biblical themes forms a substantial part of Tolkien's continuing theological imagination throughout his works. Second, in both the Blickling Homilies and in Tolkien's work this figure "Éarendel" refers to John the Baptist due to "his role as herald of Christ" (language found in *FR* to describe Eärendil as we will discuss below).[16] Third, Eärendil becomes a forerunner for the dawn, language that builds both on the astral myth of Venus and on the language in Luke 1 about John the Baptist. Thus, there are intertwined biblical roots for Tolkien's imagery of light built into this first creative moment in the emergence of Eärendil. Fourth, as Zaleski and Zaleski will point out later:

> the keen-eyed reader will also note, in the original lines from *Crist* that gave rise to Tolkien's poem, the word *middangeard*, cognate with the Old Norse *Miðgarðr* (Midgard), the middle 'yard' where humans dwell, linked by its similar sound to the Old English *eorðe*, 'earth': hence Middle-earth, which Tolkien would adopt for his mythology.[17]

Thus, Eärendil's arrival in Tolkien's imagination coincides with Tolkien's development of Middle-earth itself. This explains the prevalence of Eärendil as a figure throughout Tolkien's writings and as an essential part of Tolkien's theologically-informed imaginative vision.

Eärendil's Star in *The Lord of the Rings*

Eärendil's star plays a key role in each of the books in *The Lord of the Rings*. After Frodo wakes to find his companions and Bilbo in the house of Elrond in Rivendell, Bilbo sings a song about Eärendil (*FR*, II, i). The song describes Eärendil's seafaring ways, his adventures, and how he became a star. Bilbo shares how Aragorn told him "that if I had the cheek to make verses about Eärendil in the house of Elrond, it was my affair." This points to Elrond's relationship with Eärendil, who was his father.

This earlier scene with Bilbo provides the narrative background to interpret the later reference to Eärendil in Lothlórien when Frodo and Sam meet with Galadriel at her Mirror. After Frodo sees the Eye of Sauron in the Mirror, he is tempted to be afraid, but Galadriel explains that while the Dark Lord "gropes ever to see" her and her thoughts, "but still the door is closed!" Her gestures that follow point to this rejection of the Dark Lord, as she "spread her hands out towards the East in a gesture of rejection and denial" (*FR*, II, vii).[18] Her denial of this Dark Lord and the darkness he portends is met with a hopeful light from the West: Eärendil's star.

> Eärendil, the Evening Star, most beloved of the Elves, shone clear above. So bright was it that the figure of the Elven-lady cast a dim shadow on the ground. Its rays glanced upon a ring about her finger; it glittered like polished gold overlaid with silver light, and a white stone in it twinkled as if the Even-star had come down to rest upon her hand. (*FR*, II, vii)

The light of Eärendil, the Evening Star, shows Frodo a sign of hope after the terrifying "black abyss" and "fire" of Sauron's Eye in the Mirror moments earlier. The narrator suggests that it is as if Eärendil as "Even-star had come down to rest upon [Galadriel's] hand" and in doing so moves Frodo from "horror" to "awe; for suddenly it seemed to him that he understood." Understanding and awe come as responses to the light that Eärendil's star brings. Frodo finds some measure of clarity that helps him to make a decision to journey with the Ring.

This encounter with Eärendil's star at Galadriel's Mirror serves as the backdrop for Galadriel's gift to Frodo as he leaves Lothlórien (*FR*, II, viii). The "small crystal phial" that Galadriel gives Frodo "glittered as she moved it, and rays of white light sprang from her hand." She explains that "in this phial . . . is caught the light of Eärendil's star, set amid the waters of [her] fountain" (*FR*, II, viii). This suggests that Galadriel may have caught this light on the night when Frodo came to the Mirror and Eärendil's star shone upon her. This hypothesis is further evidenced by Galadriel's call to "Remember Galadriel and her Mirror!" by way of this phial. She explains that "it will shine still brighter when night is about you" and she prays, "may it be a light to you in dark places, when all other lights go out." Indeed, it is this prayer and the experience of viewing the phial's bright light that reminds Sam of the phial when he and Frodo encounter Shelob (*TT*, IV, ix). This moves us to our close examination of this scene with Shelob in *TT*.

Literary and Conceptual Analysis of Darkness and Light in Shelob's Lair

Tolkien begins this chapter with a description of the depths of darkness as Gollum, Frodo, and Sam move closer to Shelob's cave (*TT*, IV, ix). The darkness is so intense that "it may indeed have been daytime now, as Gollum said, but the hobbits could see little difference . . . " The narrator clarifies that there may be some mild variance in the level of darkness "less utterly black" and more like a "grey blurring shadow shroud[ing] a stony world around them" and less like "the darkness of deep night." Yet the narrator undercuts even this decrease in darkness by pointing to the way the "darkness of the deep night" "lingered still in cracks and holes."

Several conceptions of darkness are at play in Tolkien's description of approaching Shelob's lair. Darkness is described with color adjectives such as "black" "grey," with adjectives of extent such as the repeated use of "deep," with adjectives and verbs that picture darkness as a tangible weight, "heavy" "loomed" "shrouded," and darkness is compared to "a great roof of smoke." The path leading to this stage of Frodo, Sam, and Gollum's journey also included similar comparisons between smoke and darkness (*TT*, IV, ii). The Hobbits describe the awful smell associated with Shelob's cave. The heaviness of the darkness and the intensity of the smell increase as they draw closer.

In a similar way to Eärendil's backstory, Shelob also has an extensive backstory that we will only cover in brief here.[19] Shelob is "an evil thing in spider-form . . . [the] last child of Ungoliant to trouble the unhappy world" (*TT*, IV, ix). Where Eärendil is characterized by light, Shelob and her mother Ungoliant are explicitly creatures of darkness. The *Silmarillion* speaks of Ungoliant's creation: "in ages long ago before she descended from darkness that lies in Arda . . . in the beginning she was one of those who [Melkor/ Morgoth] corrupted to his service" (*Silmarillion,* 65).[20] Ungoliant desired to "feed her emptiness" and hated the light so she "took shape as a spider of monstrous form . . . there she sucked up all light that she could find, and spun it forth again in dark nets of strangling gloom, until no light more could come to her abode" (*Silmarillion,* 65–66). In doing so, Ungoliant becomes the reason for the darkening of Valinor, lamented with such pathos in the *Silmarillion* (*Silmarillion,* 65–68). Shelob, her child, is similarly a monstrous spider creature, who creates an "utter and impenetrable dark" in her lair (*TT*, IV, ix). The narrator speaks of this darkness as "deeper and denser" than "the lightless passages of Moria," the underground mines of the Dwarves. The narrator provides a series of words describing the experience of this darkness: "the air was still, stagnant, heavy," "sound fell dead," "a black vapour wrought of veritable darkness itself" when breathed "brought blindness not only to the eyes but to the mind." Such darkness leaves the breather believing "night always had been, and always would be, and night was all" (*TT*, IV, ix).

In this imagery, we can identify two conceptions of darkness: DARKNESS IS AN ADVERSARY and DARKNESS IS A SUBSTANCE. Regarding the first of these conceptions, Shelob is figuratively depicted as a monster of darkness as her mother Ungoliant before her. She uses darkness as a trap to draw in her prey. But Shelob is also empowered by this darkness as the narrator explains speaking of Shelob: "But other potencies there are in Middle-earth, powers of night, and they are old and strong" (*TT*, IV, ix). In this way, Shelob embodies the darkness that she inhabits, making darkness itself an enemy to Sam and Frodo. As the chapter later explains "all living things were her food, and her vomit darkness" (*TT*, IV, ix). This contributes to the conception that DARKNESS IS AN ADVERSARY, as it is not only *in* the darkness that Shelob attacks, but *by way of the power* of this darkness.

Regarding the second conception, DARKNESS IS A SUBSTANCE, Tolkien's conception of darkness pictures immaterial darkness in terms of a physical substance with weight, depth, and density. While in English we often speak of darkness "shrouding" or "looming," such phrases are by their nature figurative. Darkness can cover a surface by obscuring light, but darkness does not physically create weight or density on the surface it covers. Darkness itself is not *actually* tangible even if we commonly speak as though darkness is. Manifestations of darkness and the causes of darkness such as smoke, ash, etc., can be tangible, but darkness itself cannot.[21] This is evident in Frodo and Sam's experience of Shelob's darkness as "deeper," "denser," and "heavy" (*TT*, IV, ix).

Yet this darkness does not ultimately succeed in *TT*. When Sam realizes that Gollum has led Frodo and him into a trap, he sees a light: "a light in his mind, almost unbearably bright at first, as a sun-ray to the eye of one long hidden in a windowless pit."[22] In this moment, Sam remembers Galadriel's phial, which he calls "the star-glass." He remembers Galadriel's description of the help this would give. Frodo, reminded of the phial, remembers Galadriel's words, "*A light when all other lights go out!*" and realizes that "light alone can help us." Light is the means to life in this dark place with this dark monster that intends their death. Thus, LIGHT IS LIFE becomes a repeated conception in the passages about the light of Eärendil's star in Galadriel's phial. When Frodo holds the phial aloft in Shelob's lair, the light begins to glimmer faintly and is compared to "a rising star struggling in heavy earthward mists." When the light begins to burn, it becomes like "a silver flame" "a minute heart of dazzling light." As the burgeoning light is compared to "a rising star," now the glowing light is compared to Eärendil coming to earth: "as though Eärendil had himself come down from the high sunset paths with the last Silmaril on his brow" (*TT*, IV, ix). The description of Eärendil as walking on "high sunset paths" teamed with Frodo and Sam's literal journey points to the metaphorical conception of LIFE AS A JOURNEY. This metaphorical conception is frequently found throughout Tolkien's work and often collocated with imagery of light.[23] The light of Eärendil's star in Galadriel's phial is then compared to sparkling "white fire." The figure of Eärendil becomes so near that it seems that his starry presence is actually in the lair with Frodo and Sam.

This notion of the phial bringing Eärendil close appears again in the next chapter as Sam fights and kills Shelob using Galadriel's phial and the

Elven-blade. The phial first blazes "like a white torch in his hand" and then "it flamed like a star that leaving from the firmament sears the dark air with intolerable light" (*TT*, IV, x). This light enters Shelob's wounds and spreads like a "dreadful infection of light spread from eye to eye" (*TT*, IV, x), leading to her death and Frodo and Sam's escape.

In the initial encounter in Shelob's lair, Frodo calls out in Quenya, "*Aiya Eärendil Elenion Ancalima!*" translated as "Hail Eärendil, brightest of angels." Frodo speaks these words that in their Anglo-Saxon counterpart lit Tolkien's imagination to create a character named Eärendil and a place called Middle-earth. As he speaks, "another voice spoke through his, clear, untroubled by the foul air of the pit" and it may be Galadriel's voice that speaks through his, using her native language. This exclamation from Frodo also occurs in *RK* when Frodo and Sam feel "the malice of the Watchers beating on them" in the Tower of Cirith Ungol, on either side of the gate. By Sam using Galadriel's phial and Frodo crying out "*Aiya elenion ancalima!*" ("Hail, brightest of angels!"), they are able to break the will of the Watchers (*RK*, VI, i). Eönwë, herald of Manwë, exclaims similar words in the narratively earlier story "Of the Voyage of Eärendil and the War of Wrath" in *The Silmarillion*.[24] Eönwë cries out: "Hail Eärendil, of mariners most renowned, the looked for that cometh at unawares, the longed for that cometh beyond hope! Hail Eärendil, bearer of light before the Sun and Moon! Splendour of the Children of Earth, star in the darkness, jewel in the sunset, radiant in the morning!" (*Silmarillion*, 256). The calls by Frodo of these similar words appear to build on the earlier calls to Eärendil and draw the power of his star and his light near. In each context with Frodo and Sam, this light becomes a means toward life and protection for them.

Thus, our conceptual analysis of Frodo and Sam's encounter with Shelob shows a few recurring conceptions of darkness and light in Tolkien's work. As a creature of darkness, Shelob represents in her very body the metaphorical concept DARKNESS IS AN ADVERSARY. The darkness that surrounds her and is used by her is conceptualized with the language of depth, density, and weight leading to the metaphorical concept DARKNESS IS A SUBSTANCE. The light that Frodo and Sam use from Eärendil's star in Galadriel's phial becomes a means toward life, leading to a LIGHT IS LIFE metaphorical conception. The phial and Frodo's call beckon Eärendil's presence and their rescue depends on his strength.

BIBLICAL ASSOCIATIONS

The light of Eärendil's star in Galadriel's phial and the darkness of Shelob show considerable similarities to the conceptions of light and darkness present in two biblical creation stories in Genesis 1 and John 1 and the further developments on these themes of light and darkness in Genesis, Exodus, John's Gospel, and Luke's Gospel. Such conceptions include LIGHT IS LIFE, DARKNESS IS A POTENTIAL ADVERSARY, which MUST BE ORDERED BY GOD and DARKNESS IS A SUBSTANCE. In John's Gospel and in Luke's Gospel, metaphors of LIGHT AS LIFE are found alongside an associated metaphor, LIFE IS A JOURNEY. As we demonstrate below, Tolkien's work shows engagement with each of these metaphorical conceptions as fuel for his theological imagination in *The Two Towers.*

Genesis and Exodus: LIGHT IS LIFE and DARKNESS IS A POTENTIAL ADVERSARY and DARKNESS IS A SUBSTANCE

Genesis 1 establishes the picture of light and darkness that frames the remainder of the Hebrew Bible and New Testament. Genesis 1 begins as God creates the heavens and the earth in v. 1 and by v. 3 God creates the light through his spoken word. God declares this light as "good" (Gen 1:4).[25] The goodness of this light, which is also called "Day," (Gen 1:5) and God's creation of other lights, which are also declared as "good" (Gen 1:14–18), initiates the picture of light as associated with goodness. God gives light before creating plant and animal life, suggesting that light leads to or is necessary for life.[26] This will play into a key conception in Scripture that LIGHT IS LIFE.

In Genesis 1, darkness is not depicted explicitly as an enemy, but is separated from the light. The darkness itself is not described as "good," rather the light is (Gen 1:4). Further, God creates a greater and lesser light to rule the day and night respectively and to "separate the light from the darkness" (Gen 1:16–18). Thus, in Genesis 1, darkness when sequestered to its proper place is part of the order of the good creation. Yet darkness itself in Genesis 1 is not necessarily always depicted as purely "good." Genesis 1:2 hints at the potential of darkness as an adversary, particularly when read in light of the ancient Near Eastern traditions surrounding the people at the time of Genesis' writing. Genesis 1:2 describes the earth's emptiness and how "darkness covered the face of the deep," pointing to the common notion in ANE traditions of the waters of chaos that threaten creation.[27] In Genesis 1:2, a wind from God (also translated "the Spirit of God")[28] was sweeping or hovering over the waters. The cultural context of this description—and God's subsequent ordering of the darkness and the waters in vv. 4 and 6—suggests that God's wind or Spirit's actions of sweeping/hovering are directing these potentially dangerous chaotic waters. Thus, in Genesis 1, while darkness has the potential of becoming an adversary, it is ordered by God's ultimate power. We can summarize these conceptions of darkness in Genesis 1 as twofold: DARKNESS IS A POTENTIAL ADVERSARY and DARKNESS MUST BE ORDERED BY GOD.

While Genesis 1 does not make the dangerous nature of darkness explicit, Genesis eventually does give us a more explicit picture of darkness as a prelude to danger. Genesis 15:12 highlights the fear associated with darkness when Abram falls into a "deep sleep" and "a deep and terrifying darkness descended upon him." Following the descension of this darkness, the Lord warns Abram of the enslavement and oppression of the people God has promised to give him through his descendants, only a few verses prior. This connection between Egyptian enslavement of the Hebrew people and darkness continues in the book of Exodus as darkness is the ninth plague against Egypt (Exod 10). This plague of darkness describes darkness that can be "felt" and is "dense" (Exod 10:21–22). This conception of darkness as tangible with density connects to the common metaphor that DARKNESS IS A SUBSTANCE. This depicts immaterial darkness with physical properties like a substance often including depth, density, and tangibility, as we have seen in Tolkien.

John 1 and 8: LIGHT IS LIFE, LIFE IS A JOURNEY, and DEATH IS AN ADVERSARY

John 1's depiction of light builds on Genesis 1 and conceptualizes light in several key ways that impact Tolkien's theological imagination. First, light is associated with the act of creation and the giving of life through the actions of the Word in John 1:1–3. We can describe this metaphorical conception as LIGHT IS LIFE.[29] In John 1:1, the language "in the beginning" links John 1:1 to Genesis 1:1 and then shifts the focus of the story of creation from God's creation of the world to creation by the Word, who "was God." The Word's act of creation produces life, which is immediately associated with "the light of all people" (John 1:4). John's idea that LIFE IS LIGHT has the conceptual equivalency that LIGHT IS LIFE. Two associations arising from this depiction are found in other parts of John's Gospel. First, LIGHT IS LIFE arises again in John's repeated language of Jesus as "the light of the/ this world"/"light into the world" found four times in John's Gospel (John 8:12, 9:5, 11:9, 12:46).

The connection between Jesus as "light of the world" and LIGHT AS LIFE is made explicit in the first appearance of the phrase: "Again Jesus spoke to them, saying, 'I am the *light of the world*. Whoever follows me will never walk in darkness but will have *the light of life*'" (John 8:12). Here John joins two metaphorical conceptions: LIFE IS A JOURNEY and LIGHT IS LIFE. The first of these metaphorical conceptions LIFE IS A JOURNEY is also sometimes called "the Way metaphor" and is present throughout the Hebrew

Bible, especially in the biblical prophets and in Wisdom Literature. The metaphor LIFE IS A JOURNEY in the Hebrew Bible frequently uses nouns such as "path," "track," "way" and verbs such as "follow," "walk" to describe how one lives their life, whether in righteous ways associated with wise thinking and behavior leading to life, or in wicked ways associated with foolish thinking and behavior leading to death.[30] In this way, life is compared to a road or a path that one takes.[31] John 8:12 joins this typical "way" metaphor of life as journey to LIGHT IS LIFE in two ways. First, John describes Jesus as the light of the world, drawing back on John 1:4 where the Word's creative act brings light to all people and then speaks of "following" Jesus, using a typical verb associated with journeying. Second, John speaks of the alternative to following Jesus as "walk[ing] in darkness." This plays on the frequent image of two paths/ways for someone's life to follow: the way of wisdom/light, which is life or the way of folly/darkness, which is death.[32] The links between LIFE IS A JOURNEY and LIGHT IS LIFE can also be found in Tolkien's work as we will discuss below.

After the depiction of the Word creating the world and giving life and light to all in John 1:1–5, John 1:6 shifts the reader's attention to another figure: John the Baptist. His relationship to "the light" becomes the focus in John 1:6–9. John is first introduced as "a man sent from God" even before we are given John's name. This places John the Baptist's role as God's messenger as the priority even over his own name. John 1:7 further describes John the Baptist's role as "a witness to testify to the light, so that all might believe through him." This begins a repeated metaphorical framework of witness and testimony that will permeate the rest of John's Gospel.[33] John the Baptist's ability to "testify to the light" as a "witness" engages not only lawsuit language, but also points to the visual nature of light, which can be seen and then testified about. John 1:8 clarifies John the Baptist's position in relation to the light: "He himself was not the light, but he came to testify to the light." In other words, John the Baptist functions as an emissary of the light or as a witness to the light. John the Baptist's two roles as messenger and witness play into the larger frameworks of royal metaphors (John as messenger for Jesus who is King) and judicial metaphors (John as witness in a trial asserting Jesus' identity).[34] While there may be historical reasons why John the Baptist's role needed to be clarified,[35] the description of John the Baptist as witness to the light pushes the reader toward the subsequent verse, which itself witnesses to the Word's identity: "The true light, which enlightens everyone, was coming into the world" (John 1:9). Jesus' identity as the "true light" and "the light of the world" is frequently associated not only with life, but with knowledge and with sight. Describing light as what "enlightens" in 1:9 fits with the language of light as what allows the way (and deeds) to be "exposed" (John 3:20), "clearly seen" (John 3:21), which keeps the people from "stumbling" in darkness (John 11:9, 10). According to John, then, the way light gives life is by illuminating the "way" toward safety.

Zaleski and Zaleski have argued that Tolkien's depiction of Eärendil as John the Baptist takes precedence from Luke 1's depiction of him.[36] John the Evangelist's picture of John the Baptist adheres well to Luke's vision of John the Baptist, particularly in the song of Zechariah about John the Baptist's role in Luke 1:76–79:

> And you, child, will be called the prophet of the Most High;
>> for you will go before the Lord to prepare his ways . . .
> By the tender mercy of our God,
>> the dawn from on high will break upon us,
> to give light to those who sit in darkness and in the shadow of death,
>> to guide our feet into the way of peace.

In Luke's description of John the Baptist, we see John's role as messenger placed centrally as it was in John's Gospel in the words, "you will go before the Lord to prepare his ways." As in John's Gospel, the conception of LIGHT IS LIFE is present in Luke 1:79 where light is given to those who sit in darkness and this light gives life rather than "the shadow of death" that darkness is associated with. As in John's Gospel, LIGHT IS LIFE is joined with the conception of LIFE IS A JOURNEY, as Luke describes how John will "prepare his *ways*" (Luke 1:76) and "the dawn from on high" will "*guide our feet* into the *way* of peace*" (Luke 1:79). As noted above, Tolkien saw Eärendil as a John the Baptist figure. We will explore in more detail below how the conceptions of light and darkness associated with John the Baptist in John and Luke give additional insight into Tolkien's depiction of light and darkness.

In John 1, as soon as light is compared to life, it faces an adversary: darkness. DARKNESS IS AN ADVERSARY is a conception that arises from the language in John 1:5. Here John describes how the light, which is life, "shines in the darkness and the darkness did not overcome it." Unlike Genesis, where darkness is only a *potential* adversary, the language of darkness potentially overcoming the light attests to some kind of battle between light and darkness assumed in John's Gospel. This conception of DARKNESS IS AN ADVERSARY is found in other parts of John's Gospel as well. For example, John 12:35 pictures darkness "overtak[ing]" a person who walks in the darkness and "does not know where [they] are going." Here darkness is pictured both as what obscures the person's view and also as an assailant who takes advantage of this obscurement to overtake the person on the path. As with light, the conception LIFE IS A JOURNEY plays a role in conceptualizing darkness using the language of "walk" in darkness in John 8:12 and 12:35 and the picture of a pathway that can be darkened and therefore create situations of stumbling. This notion is present in John 11:10, which uses the language of "at night" compared to the "day" to compare walking in light to walking in darkness, which can produce stumbling. Tolkien also joins DARKNESS IS AN ADVERSARY to LIFE IS A JOURNEY in his depiction of Shelob and the Hobbits' journey into her lair.

TOLKIEN'S THEOLOGICAL IMAGINATION

Tolkien explicitly connects Eärendil to John the Baptist as he explains this figure in his 1967 letter, but evidence of this allusion is present with a close reading of Eärendil's depictions in the *LOTR* and elsewhere among Tolkien's work. One striking example is the song about Eärendil that Bilbo sings. The song describes how Elwing comes to Eärendil using the language of "flame" in "the darkness lit." This light is "more bright than light of diamond" and is described as a "the fire upon her carcanet." This connects to the Silmaril, which she binds to him and, in doing so, she "crowned him with the living light." His head is then described as a "burning brow" (*FR,* II, i).

In Tolkien's imagery, we see the brightness of the Silmaril's true light shine in the darkness and the darkness cannot overcome it. This light is described as "living light" similar to John 1's description of light as life. The specific similarities to John the Baptist increase with another set of lines in the song where he is described as "a herald" who is "on an errand that should never rest." This errand is "to bear his shining lamp afar/the Flammifer of Westernesse" (*FR,* II, i).

Essential to the connection between Eärendil and John the Baptist in John 1 is the association with the light that both John the Baptist and Eärendil have: John 1 describes John the Baptist in terms of his role as "a witness to testify to the light so that all might believe" (John 1:7) and Bilbo's song describes Eärendil in terms of his role as bearer of the light afar so that all might see ("to bear his shining lamp afar"). Both John the Baptist and Eärendil function in John 1 and Bilbo's song as messengers. John the Baptist is "a man sent from God" (John 1:6) for the express purpose of testifying to the light (language many scholars have linked to the messenger language used of prophets in the Hebrew Bible);[37] in Bilbo's song, Eärendil is "ever still a herald on/an errand that should never rest" and that errand is "to bear his shining lamp afar" (*FR,* II, i). Eärendil as "herald" to Christ, the rising sun, fits with how Tolkien describes the impetus for Eärendil's name and his story in his 1967 letter.[38] In Luke 1, John the Baptist is the forerunner to the dawn, who is Christ, imagery that sparked Tolkien's imagination by way of its use in *Crist.* Thus, both John the Baptist and Eärendil are described in terms of their roles as "heralds" who witness to the great, true light. Such depictions of John the Baptist are present in both John's Gospel and in Luke's and resonate with Tolkien's portrayal of Eärendil.

Shifting to the conception of darkness in Tolkien's work, the encounter with Shelob and the darkness leading up to her lair demonstrates Tolkien's frequent use of DARKNESS IS AN ADVERSARY and DARKNESS IS A SUBSTANCE as we have noted in the conceptual analysis above. These conceptions show striking similarities to John's picture of the darkness that attempts to overcome the light just as Shelob attempts to overcome Frodo and Sam. The tangible nature of Tolkien's darkness and its recessing at the light of Eärendil's star points to the theme of DARKNESS IS A SUBSTANCE present in Genesis and Exodus.

CONCLUSION

Tolkien's conceptions of light and darkness are built on biblical themes and biblical figures such as creation imagery in Genesis 1 and John 1, the figure of John the Baptist in John 1 and Luke 1, and the plague of darkness in Exodus 10. The figure of Eärendil holds a particularly important place in Tolkien's theological imagination as part of the seed for Tolkien's Middle-earth mythology and as a recurring figure from Tolkien's earliest literary writings before Tolkien endured the Great War to near the end of Tolkien's life. The role of Eärendil's star in *FR, TT*, and *RK* builds on several biblical conceptual ideas of LIGHT IS LIFE and LIFE IS A JOURNEY. Meanwhile the darkness of Shelob that Eärendil's star combats in *TT* builds on the biblical conceptual ideas of DARKNESS IS A SUBSTANCE and DARKNESS IS AN ADVERSARY. Through this metaphorical schema, Tolkien presents a theological picture of hope amidst the darkness, where light, beauty, and awe can transform one's perception to realize the temporary nature of the darkness one may currently face. In emphasizing the transitory nature of this "Shadow," and showing the power of the light, Tolkien both acknowledges the potential horror of the darkness, but does not let that horror be the final word. Instead, repeatedly Eärendil's star pierces the darkness, bringing light and hope and thereby life to all who see it. As Eärendil's star points to a greater light beyond, the rising Sun, so John the Baptist points to the greater light of Christ. In this way, Tolkien's theological imagination becomes deeply Christological, pointing to the ultimate light in the darkness seen in John 1:14: the Word who "became flesh and lived among us," Christ the Son of God.

NOTES

1. Sources on Tolkien's themes and metaphors of light and darkness include Amanda Laís Jacobsen de Oliveira and Adriana Yokoyama, "O mundo no círculo de fogo: Questões da visão em Tolkien," *Revista Abusões* (2017): 151–71; and Leslie A. Donovan, "The Valkyrie Reflex in J.R.R. Tolkien's *The Lord of the Rings*: Galadriel, Shelob, Éowyn, and Arwen" in *Perilous and Fair: Women and the Works of J.R.R. Tolkien*, ed. Janet Brennan Croft and Leslie A. Donovan (Altadena, CA: Mythopoeic Press, 2015), 221–57. For scholarship specifically on Shelob and the imagery of darkness, see Lavinia Scolari, "Representations of the Mythical Figure of the Spider in the Literary Corpus of J.R.R. Tolkien," *Amaltea* 3 (2011): 241–52.

2. In biblical studies, see Bonnie Howe and Joel B. Green, eds., *Cognitive Linguistic Explorations in Biblical Studies* (Berlin: De Gruyter, 2014). In literary studies, see Paul B. Armstrong, *How Literature Plays with the Brain: The Neuroscience of Reading and Art* (Baltimore: Johns Hopkins University Press, 2013). For an example of using a form of conceptual blending theory specifically on Tolkien, see Liliia Kh. Shaiakhmetova and Leysan Kh. Shayakhmetova, "The Representation of the Concept 'Journey' in the Author's Picture of the World of J. Tolkien (By Example of His Novel *Hobbit or There and Back Again*)," *Journal of Language and Literature* 7.3 (2016): 91–95.

3. I have a similar description of conceptual blending theory in several of my works including Beth M. Stovell, "Son of God as Anointed One? Johannine Davidic Christology and Second Temple Messianism," in *Reading the Gospel of John's Christology as Jewish Messianism: Royal, Prophetic, and Divine Messiahs*, ed. Benjamin E. Reynolds and Gabriele Boccaccini, AJEC 106 (Leiden: Brill, 2018), 149–77. At times, Fauconnier and Turner simply call this theory "conceptual blending" and at other times the "network model of conceptual integration." See Gilles Fauconnier and Mark Turner, "Mental Spaces: Conceptual Integration Networks," in *Cognitive Linguistics: Basic Readings*, ed. Dirk Geeraerts, Cognitive Linguistics Research 34 (Berlin: Mouton de Gruyter, 2006), 312; Gilles Fauconnier and Mark Turner, *The Way We Think: Conceptual Blending and the Mind's Hidden Complexities* (New York: Basic Books, 2002).

4. Fauconnier and Turner, "Mental Spaces," 312.

5. Fauconnier and Turner, "Mental Spaces," 307–8.

6. Fauconnier and Turner, "Mental Spaces," 331. For a more detailed discussion of the definition, use, and influence of "mental spaces," see Fauconnier and Eve Sweetser, *Spaces, Worlds, and Grammar: Cognitive Theory of Language and Culture* (Chicago: University of Chicago Press, 1996); Fauconnier, *Mental Spaces: Aspects of Meaning Construction in Natural Language* (Cambridge: MIT Press, 1985); Fauconnier, *Mappings in Thought and Language* (Cambridge: Cambridge University Press, 1997).

7. See my extended discussion of this topic in Beth M. Stovell, *Mapping Metaphorical Discourse in the Fourth Gospel: John's Eternal King*, LBS 5 (Leiden: Brill, 2012), 135–80.

8. Tolkien uses this range of words in his descriptions of Mordor (*TT*, IV, i–ii).

9. As Zaleski and Zaleski point out, Eärendil functions as a mediator between Men and Elves (Halfelven as his surname), between the Valar and Men and Elves (begging on behalf of Men and Elves). See Philip Zaleski and Carol Zaleski, *The Fellowship: The Literary Lives of the Inklings: J.R.R. Tolkien, C. S. Lewis, Owen Barfield, Charles Williams* (New York: Farrar, Straus and Giroux, 2015), 64.

10. This poem was originally entitled "The Voyage of Éarendel the Evening Star," but was eventually renamed "*Éalá Éarendel Engla Beorhtast*" "The Last Voyage of Eärendel." See *LT 2*, 267.

11. See *Letters*, 297. Here Tolkien explains "*Eärendil*, being in part descended from Men, was not allowed to set foot on Earth again, and became a star shining with the light of the Silmaril."

12. See Tolkien's explanation in the foreword to revised edition of *FR*.

13. Zaleski and Zaleski, *Fellowship*, 63. Humphrey Carpenter points to this connection, which is foundational to Zaleski and Zaleski's claims: Humphrey Carpenter, *Tolkien: A Biography* (Boston: Houghton Mifflin, 1977), 64. For an extension of Carpenter's philological suggestions of the naming of Eärendil, see Carl F. Hostetter, "Over Middle-earth Sent Unto Men: On the Philological Origins of Tolkien's Eärendel Myth," *Mythlore* 65 (1991): 5–10.

14. Zaleski and Zaleski, *Fellowship*, 63.

15. Zaleski and Zaleski, *Fellowship*, 63–64.

16. The name for this figure is spelled in several ways in Tolkien including Éarendel and Eärendil. This is in part due to Tolkien's translation of this name from Anglo-Saxon to his invented language of Quenya with different spellings. Such changes are quite common in Tolkien's work with characters with multiple names in different languages and various spellings. For this essay, I will use Eärendil as the spelling generally unless I am directly quoting the name from a source that uses a different spelling. I have chosen this spelling because it is the spelling used in the final manuscripts of the *LOTR* and the *Silmarillion.*

17. Zaleski and Zaleski, *Fellowship*, 65.

18. Scholars have pointed out that Tolkien's praise of the West and his denigration of the East has potential racial and ethnic issues. See Robert Gehl, "Something Is Stirring in the East: Racial Identity, Confronting the 'Other,' and Miscegenation in *Othello* and *The Lord of the Rings*," in *Tolkien and Shakespeare: Essays on Shared Themes and Language*, ed. Janet Brennan Croft, CESFF 2 (Jefferson, NC: McFarland & Company 2007), 251–67.

19. For more on the mythical figure of spider in Tolkien using a conceptual approach, see Scolari, "Representations," 241–52.

20. Further exploration of the darkness of Shelob in relation to the darkness of Morgoth and Sauron can be found in other explorations of Tolkien's imagery of light and darkness such as Jacobsen and Yokoyama, "O mundo," 151–71, and Scolari, "Representations," 241–52.

21. Fabian Horn makes a similar point when Horn uses a conceptual metaphor approach to examine the use of darkness imagery in depictions of death in Early Greek poetry. As Horn explains, "In all these instantiations, the immaterial concept of darkness/night is envisioned as a kind of substance by means of an ontological

metaphor: darkness/night is reified and conceptualised as a physical entity"; see Fabian Horn, "'Entering the House of Hades': The Formulaic Language of Metaphors of Death and the Question of Deliberateness in Early Greek Poetry," in *Drawing Attention to Metaphor: Case Studies across Time Periods, Cultures and Modalities,* ed. Camilla Di Biase-Dyson and Markus Egg, FTL 5 (Amsterdam: John Benjamins, 2020), 159–187, citation on 169.

22. Notably Sam also thinks of Tom Bombadil in this moment. Jane Beal argues that Tom is a figure of healing who resembles both the Old Adam and the New Adam, Jesus, and that the light we see within Frodo at different stages in Tolkien's work is the Christ-light. See Jane Beal, "Who Is Tom Bombadil? Interpreting the Light in Frodo Baggins and Tom Bombadil's Role in the Healing of Traumatic Memory in J.R.R. Tolkien's *Lord of the Rings*," *JTR* 6 (2018): 1–34.

23. LIFE AS A JOURNEY is a common metaphor in Tolkien's work more broadly from Bilbo's language (and experience) of journey in *The Hobbit* with his book title, *There and Back Again*, to the journeys taken by major characters in *The Lord of the Rings* to the many themes and experiences of journey in the *Silmarillion,* including the sea journeys of Eärendil mentioned above. For more on Tolkien and this concept of journey, see Shaiakhmetova and Shayakhmetova, "Representation," 91–95.

24. While *The Silmarillion* was largely written and was published after the *LOTR,* it tells stories that are narratively prior to the stories in the *LOTR.*

25. This chapter uses NRSV as its English biblical translation. Any use of other translations will be noted in the endnotes.

26. John Goldingay provides an extensive explanation of the implications of God's creation of light. See John Goldingay, *Old Testament Theology*, Vol 1: *Israel's Gospel* (Downers Grove: InterVarsity Press, 2003), 49–92.

27. Robin Routledge points to the unresolved tension when comparing Gen 1:1 and 1:2 around the origin of this chaos. Routledge agrees with scholars who argue that Gen 1:2 depicts a picture of God's subduing of chaos that both engages the ANE myths of the author's time, while also shows God's unique power over these chaotic forces. See Robin Routledge, "Did God Create Chaos? Unresolved Tension in Genesis 1:1–2," *TynBul* 61 (2010): 69–88.

28. NRSV and CEB use "wind from God" and "swept over the waters" while KJV, NKJV, ASV, NIV, ESV, NASB, and many others use "Spirit of God" with "moving" or "hovering" over the face/surface of the waters. Jewish translations tend to either leave the phrase untranslated as a name *Ruach Elohim* (in Hebrew רוּחַ אֱלֹהִים) most commonly understood as "the Spirit of God" or translate the phrase as "the Spirit of God" directly. However, there is substantial debate over whether this phrase should be translated as "Spirit of God" or not based on both lexical and contextual criteria. For more on this debate, see Richard S. Hess, "Bezalel and Oholiab: Spirit and Creativity," in *Presence, Power and Promise: The Role of the Spirit of God in the Old Testament,* ed. David G. Firth and Paul D. Wegner (Downers Grove: IVP Academic, 2011), 161–72.

29. Alternatively, this could be described as LIGHT AS CREATION LIFE as in John 1 this picture of LIGHT AS LIFE is rooted on the creation account, but in the

rest of John's Gospel, the idea of LIGHT AS LIFE in its basic form is a recurring symbol.

30. Many scholars have argued for this metaphor in the Psalms, Proverbs, and prophets such as Isaiah. See for example Phil Botha, "Following the 'Tracks of Righteousness' in Psalm 23," *OTE* 28 (2015): 283–300; Kent Aaron Reynolds, *Torah as Teacher: The Exemplary Torah Student in Psalm 119*, VTSup 137 (Leiden: Brill, 2010), 53–140; Øystein Lund, *Way Metaphors and Way Topics in Isaiah 40–55*, FAT 2.28 (Tübingen: Mohr Siebeck, 2007); Bo H. Lim, *The 'Way of the Lord' in the Book of Isaiah*, LHBOTS 522 (New York: T&T Clark, 2010).

31. George Lakoff and Mark Johnson describe LIFE IS A JOURNEY as one of the most common metaphors in the English language. Lakoff and Johnson explore this conceptual metaphor in their book *Metaphors We Live By* (Chicago: University of Chicago Press, 1980). Katz and Taylor demonstrate how this conceptual metaphor is shown as data output related to semantic and episodic memory, studying the metaphor from a psychological perspective. See Albert N. Katz and Tamsen E. Taylor, "The Journeys of Life: Examining a Conceptual Metaphor with Semantic and Episodic Memory Recall," *Metaphor and Symbol* 23 (2008): 148–73.

32. For example, these themes are present in the depictions of Lady Wisdom and Dame Folly in Proverbs. These themes were further developed in the Second Temple period at Qumran in the Dead Sea Scrolls. See Sidnie White Crawford, "Lady Wisdom and Dame Folly at Qumran," *DSD* 5 (1998): 355–66.

33. For more on testimony and witness in John's Gospel and its relationship to the imagery of a trial, see Andrew T. Lincoln, *Truth on Trial: The Lawsuit Motif in the Fourth Gospel* (Peabody: Hendrickson, 2000).

34. Tom Thatcher discusses the role of John the Baptist in John's prologue (John 1:1–18) and how this relates to John the Baptist's confession immediately following the prologue. See Tom Thatcher, "The Riddle of the Baptist and the Genesis of the Prologue: John 1:1–18 in Oral/Aural Media Culture," in *The Fourth Gospel in First Century Media Culture,* ed. Anthony Le Donne and Tom Thatcher, LNTS 426 (New York: T&T Clark, 2011), 29–48.

35. The Gospel of John attests to people wondering whether John the Baptist was the Messiah rather than Jesus (John 1:20). For more on explorations of John the Baptist and Messianic conceptions, see Joel Marcus, *John the Baptist in History and Theology* (Columbia: University of South Carolina Press, 2018).

36. Zaleski and Zaleski, *Fellowship*, 64.

37. For more on this, see Marcus, *John the Baptist.*

38. Hostetter describes Eärendil as herald as one of his characteristics and points to the etymological elements of this; see Hostetter, "Over Middle-earth," 7–8.

BIBLIOGRAPHY

Armstrong, Paul B. *How Literature Plays with the Brain: The Neuroscience of Reading and Art*. Baltimore: Johns Hopkins University Press, 2013.

Beal, Jane. "Who Is Tom Bombadil? Interpreting the Light in Frodo Baggins and Tom Bombadil's Role in the Healing of Traumatic Memory in J.R.R. Tolkien's *Lord of the Rings.*" *JTR* 6 (2018): 1–34.

Botha, Phil. "Following the 'Tracks of Righteousness' in Psalm 23." *OTE* 28 (2015): 283–300.

Carpenter, Humphrey. *Tolkien: A Biography*. Boston: Houghton Mifflin, 1977.

Crawford, Sidnie White. "Lady Wisdom and Dame Folly at Qumran." *DSD* 5 (1998): 355–66.

Donovan, Leslie A. "The Valkyrie Reflex in J.R.R. Tolkien's *The Lord of the Rings*: Galadriel, Shelob, Éowyn, and Arwen." Pages 221–57 in *Perilous and Fair: Women and the Works of J.R.R. Tolkien*. Edited by Janet Brennan Croft and Leslie A. Donovan. Altadena, CA: Mythopoeic Press, 2015.

Fauconnier, Gilles. *Mental Spaces: Aspects of Meaning Construction in Natural Language*. Cambridge: MIT Press, 1985.

———. *Mappings in Thought and Language*. Cambridge: Cambridge University Press, 1997.

Fauconnier, Gilles, and Eve Sweetser. *Spaces, Worlds, and Grammar: Cognitive Theory of Language and Culture*. Chicago: University of Chicago Press, 1996.

Fauconnier, Gilles, and Mark Turner. "Mental Spaces: Conceptual Integration Networks." Pages 303–71 in *Cognitive Linguistics: Basic Readings*. Edited by Dirk Geeraerts. Cognitive Linguistics Research 34. Berlin: Mouton de Gruyter, 2006.

———. *The Way We Think: Conceptual Blending and the Mind's Hidden Complexities*. New York: Basic Books, 2002.

Gehl, Robert. "Something Is Stirring in the East: Racial Identity, Confronting the 'Other,' and Miscegenation in *Othello* and *The Lord of the Rings.*" Pages 251–67 in *Tolkien and Shakespeare: Essays on Shared Themes and Language*. Edited by Janet Brennan Croft. CESFF 2. Jefferson, NC: McFarland & Company 2007.

Goldingay, John. *Old Testament Theology*, Vol 1: *Israel's Gospel*. Downers Grove: InterVarsity Press, 2003.

Hess, Richard S. "Bezalel and Oholiab: Spirit and Creativity." Pages 161–72 in *Presence, Power and Promise: The Role of the Spirit of God in the Old Testament*. Edited by David G. Firth and Paul D. Wegner. Downers Grove: IVP Academic, 2011.

Horn, Fabian. "'Entering the House of Hades': The Formulaic Language of Metaphors of Death and the Question of Deliberateness in Early Greek Poetry." Pages 159–87 in *Drawing Attention to Metaphor: Case Studies across Time Periods, Cultures and Modalities*. Edited by Camilla Di Biase-Dyson and Markus Egg. FTL 5. Amsterdam: John Benjamins, 2020.

Hostetter, Carl F. "Over Middle-earth Sent Unto Men: On the Philological Origins of Tolkien's Eärendel Myth." *Mythlore* 65 (1991): 5–10.

Howe, Bonnie, and Joel B. Green, eds. *Cognitive Linguistic Explorations in Biblical Studies*. Berlin: De Gruyter, 2014.

Jacobsen de Oliveira, Amanda Laís, and Adriana Yokoyama. "O mundo no círculo de fogo: Questões da visão em Tolkien." *Revista Abusões* (2017): 151–71. doi:10.12957/abusoes.2017.30298.

Katz, Albert N., and Tamsen E. Taylor. "The Journeys of Life: Examining a Conceptual Metaphor with Semantic and Episodic Memory Recall." *Metaphor and Symbol* 23 (2008): 148–73.

Lakoff, George, and Mark Johnson. *Metaphors We Live By*. Chicago: University of Chicago Press, 1980.

Lim, Bo H. *The 'Way of the Lord' in the Book of Isaiah*. LHBOTS 522. New York: T&T Clark, 2010.

Lincoln, Andrew T. *Truth on Trial: The Lawsuit Motif in the Fourth Gospel*. Peabody: Hendrickson, 2000.

Lund, Øystein. *Way Metaphors and Way Topics in Isaiah 40–55*. FAT 2.28. Tübingen: Mohr Siebeck, 2007.

Marcus, Joel. *John the Baptist in History and Theology*. Columbia: University of South Carolina Press, 2018.

Reynolds, Kent Aaron. *Torah as Teacher: The Exemplary Torah Student in Psalm 119*. VTSup 137. Leiden: Brill, 2010.

Routledge, Robin. "Did God Create Chaos? Unresolved Tension in Genesis 1:1–2." *TynBul* 61 (2010): 69–88.

Scolari, Lavinia. "Representations of the Mythical Figure of the Spider in the Literary Corpus of J.R.R. Tolkien." *Amaltea* 3 (2011): 241–52.

Shaiakhmetova, Liliia Kh., and Leysan Kh. Shayakhmetova. "The Representation of the Concept 'Journey' in the Author's Picture of the World of J. Tolkien (By Example of His Novel *Hobbit or There and Back Again*)." *Journal of Language and Literature* 7.3 (2016): 91–95.

Stovell, Beth M. *Mapping Metaphorical Discourse in the Fourth Gospel: John's Eternal King*. LBS 5. Leiden: Brill, 2012.

———. "Son of God as Anointed One? Johannine Davidic Christology and Second Temple Messianism." Pages 149–77 in *Reading the Gospel of John's Christology as Jewish Messianism: Royal, Prophetic, and Divine Messiahs*. Edited by Benjamin E. Reynolds and Gabriele Boccaccini. AJEC 106. Leiden: Brill, 2018.

Thatcher, Tom. "The Riddle of the Baptist and the Genesis of the Prologue: John 1.1–18 in Oral/Aural Media Culture." Pages 29–48 in *The Fourth Gospel in First Century Media Culture*. Edited by Anthony Le Donne and Tom Thatcher. LNTS 426. New York: T&T Clark, 2011.

Zaleski, Philip, and Carol Zaleski. *The Fellowship: The Literary Lives of the Inklings: J.R.R. Tolkien, C. S. Lewis, Owen Barfield, Charles Williams*. New York: Farrar, Straus and Giroux, 2015.

Chapter 8

Christianity and Paganism in *The Silmarillion* and *The Lord of the Rings*

A Typology Based on Niebuhr's Christ and Culture

Allan M. de Novaes, Milton L. Torres,
and João Fernando O. Barboza

Literature and religion have had a close relationship for a long time. Those who write fiction and fantasy often take advantage of Christian symbols—imbued as they are with distinct meanings—and either use them in ways similar to their use in the original texts or transform them into something new by importing a different meaning into their new textual location. J.R.R. Tolkien does the latter in the legendarium, his mythopoeic writing that forms the background to his primary creations, *The Hobbit* and *The Lord of the Rings*. Tolkien uses Christian symbols as well as Norse and Faërie mythology to create one of the greatest high fantasy works of the twentieth century.[1]

Starting with his origin story *The Silmarillion*, Tolkien uses references to biblical, Norse, and Anglo-Saxon traditions to imagine a single creator God. Many of these features are absent, however, from *The Lord of the Rings*, and this fact fascinates the scholars who study his work. During his lifetime, Tolkien was frequently confronted by readers with the presence of non-Christian symbols in his work and was often criticized for using Northern European pagan symbolism as a believing Roman Catholic.

To better understand these issues, this chapter presents a review of the criticism that readers made to Tolkien about his usage of both Christian and pagan elements in his stories. To do this, we adopt a typology derived from the work of H. Richard Niebuhr (1894–1962), an American theologian who wrote *Christ and Culture*, one of the most impressive Christian books of the last century.[2] Published in 1951, the book tries to make sense of the different types of attitudes and stances that Christians resort to in order to relate to culture in general.[3] Niebuhr's seminal work addresses an "enduring problem," since it describes "a many-sided debate about the relations of Christianity and civilization" that "moves between the poles of Christ and culture."[4] Niebuhr posits that the challenge of considering the relationship between Christ and culture necessitates a fivefold solution that includes responses such as opposition (the *Christ against culture*), acceptance (the *Christ of culture*), tension (the *Christ in paradox with culture*), synthesis (the *Christ above culture*), and transformation (the *Christ who transforms culture*). Of course, typologies become imprecise as they confront differing nuances within reality. Niebuhr was aware of this epistemological limitation, but still defended—as we also do—the relevance of his method. He argues that there remains "the advantage of calling to attention the continuity and significance of the great *motifs* that appear and reappear in the long wrestling of Christians with their enduring problem."[5]

Therefore, this chapter takes up Niebuhr's assessment of what he calls an "enduring problem" to an analysis of Tolkien's work. What is the relationship between Christianity and Northern European paganism in Tolkien's literature according to those who critique it? This question can be roughly equated as follows: As far as *The Silmarillion* and *The Lord of the Rings* are concerned, who is the author (Tolkien)? A Christian? A traditional Anglo-Saxon? Or a syncretic mixture of both?[6] By bringing together the criticism of Tolkien and Niebuhr, we expect to design a useful, hermeneutical starting point for the study of the relationship between Christianity and paganism in Tolkien's legendarium. The arguments of *Christ and Culture* suggest that there is no simple answer to this question. In fact—as often is the case—interpretations vary according to the assumptions that underlie them. Several scholars, including Ronald Hutton, allow for the presence of pagan symbols that precede Christianity, while others, including Joseph Pearce, argue conversely that all symbols in Tolkien's work come from a Christian background.[7]

Responses to the presence of pagan symbolism in Tolkien's literary corpus, just like Niebuhr's typology, can be placed in categories or groups. Two indispensable studies that successfully attempt to create a typology of the relationship between Christianity and paganism in Tolkien's works are those by Claudio Testi, which strongly influenced this chapter.[8] According to Testi, scholars argue for one of four different ways to understand that relationship, each of which can be subsumed in one of the following categories: (1) "Tolkien's work is Christian," (2) "Tolkien's work is pagan," (3) "Tolkien's work is pagan and Christian," and—finally—(4) "Tolkien's work is pagan although in harmony with Christianity" (the view that Testi himself defends). We propose three different categories instead: (1) "Tolkien's work is more pagan than Christian," (2) "Tolkien's work is Christian but also pagan," and (3) "Tolkien's work is inherently Christian."[9]

The claim that Tolkien had a linguistic focus which utilized both pagan and Christian symbols in a "more-pagan-than-Christian" approach derives from scholars such as Hutton, as well as Catherine Madsen, Tom Shippey, Jane Chance, and Brian Rosebury.[10] The claim that Tolkien's literature can have a Christian application—but not necessarily a Christian interpretation—belongs to a second category, which includes Testi, plus Stephen Morillo, Elizabeth Whittingham, and Ralph Wood.[11] That is the "Christian-but-also-pagan" category. Finally, the claim that Tolkien's work was essentially Christian belongs to a third category, which includes Pearce, along with Peter Kreeft, Bradley Birzer and Nils Ivar Agøy, who think that Tolkien wanted his books to convey his religious sentiments, even if he sometimes used pagan symbols.[12]

The present study is divided into three parts: (1) an overview of criticism to Niebuhr's typology in *Christ and Culture*; (2) a typology of how recent scholarship address Tolkien's use of pagan and Christian elements in *The Silmarillion* and *The Lord of the Rings*; and (3) a comparison of the two typologies.

AN INTERPRETIVE TYPOLOGY OF NIEBUHR'S *CHRIST AND CULTURE*

Niebuhr sees the Christ/culture problem, above all, as a question of authority and loyalty. His view of the history of Western civilization clearly expresses that there has always been a fierce antagonism between allegiance to one of two masters: *Christ* and *culture*. Choosing to obey one or the other is the essence of the "enduring problem." Christians and non-Christians, according to Niebuhr, take one of these stances. In fact, there is some dispute even among Christians as to which beliefs and practices can be construed as loyalty to Christ or to culture. Thus, Niebuhr systematically outlines the stances from which Christians have faced the Christ/culture problem throughout history. Niebuhr then offers a descriptive analysis of the five types of response to the Christ/culture problem by Christians: rejection of culture, affirmation of it through assimilation, and three intermediary positions.[13] For each type of response, he offers historical examples, naming theologians and Christian movements that arguably embraced each.

Niebuhr calls the first type of response the *Christ against culture* approach, because it highlights an opposition between Christ and culture no matter what human customs and achievements are under analysis. This response is one that argues for Christ's sovereign and exclusive authority over the believer, implying complete rejection of culture. The second type of response is the *Christ of culture* approach, because it takes the opposite view, and proposes that there is a fundamental agreement between Christ and culture. Christ would be part of culture, in the sense that he himself is part of the social heritage that Christians should transmit and preserve. Christ is therefore seen as a great educator and thinker. The other three types of responses lie between the two extremes of the first and second types. They show some agreement between Christ and culture, but they seek to maintain that they are somehow different from the two previous positions.

The third type is the *Christ above culture* approach, which understands the relationship between Christ and culture in a similar way to the second type but also holds that, in addition to Christ being the great hero of human history, there is also something in him that neither comes directly from culture nor contributes directly to it. An understanding of culture from this perspective follows the following logic: culture is both divine and human, holy and sinful, and its domain pertains to both reason and revelation. Therefore, the Christ above culture response does not have to choose between Christ and culture, because it believes that a divine element is present in both.

The fourth type or the *Christ and culture in paradox* approach acknowledges that both Christ and culture have authority over Christians, but also allows for the tension that stems from this requirement of double obedience. Adherents to this stance refuse to compromise the biddings of Christ to those of secular society as do, they think, advocates of the second and third groups. Thus, human beings are subject to two sources of authority, and it is in a tension between Christ and culture that life must be lived.

The fifth and last type Niebuhr labels the *Christ the transformer of culture* approach. It resolves the Christ-culture tension by assuming, as the first and fourth type do, that human nature is corrupt and fallen, and that this perversion does not just lie in culture, but is transmitted by it. It sees Christ as the Redeemer of human beings in—and not apart from—culture and society since there is no human nature apart from culture and no point of conversion for people outside society. Christians of the Christ the transformer of culture stance also believe that culture lies under the sovereign government of God and that Christians must reach society in obedience to Christ's commission.

Although this general overview of the fivefold typology of Christ and culture is widely known among English-speaking theologians, there is an indispensable aspect of the Niebuhrian typology that said theologians often underestimate in its complexity and depth; and this aspect has become nearly invisible to critics and commentators: the identification of the theological elements that constitute each of the types.

Among the leading commentators and critics of *Christ and Culture*, Douglas Ottati and D. M. Yeager are the only ones who have identified the theological elements as important components of Niebuhr's typology.[14] In fact, Ottati goes so far as to say that *Christ and Culture* readers often pay *too much* attention to the five types and *too little* attention to the detailed theological analysis that Niebuhr offers about them.[15] Ottati and Yeager help explain how the typology of Niebuhr structures *Christ and Culture* and, as a result, how readers should read and understand the book. Specifically, Niebuhr organizes the theological elements of his typology as *binomials*. In previous publications, I (Allan Novaes) proposed a synthesis of Niebuhr's binomials based on Otatti's and Yeager's analysis that we represent here in the following structure:

1. Yet vs. not yet, a binomial from an eschatological (i.e., end-time) perspective;
2. Reason vs. revelation, a binomial from an epistemological (i.e., knowledge-based) perspective;
3. Nature vs. grace, a binomial from a perspective based on the doctrines of creation and the Godhead;
4. Sin vs. good, a binomial from an anthropological perspective combined with a hamartiological (i.e., sin-based), and soteriological (i.e., salvation-based) perspective;
5. Law vs. gospel, a binomial from an ethical and moral perspective;
6. Church vs. world, a binomial from an ecclesiological (i.e., church-based) and missiological (i.e., mission- and *kerygma*-based) perspective.[16]

We can also depict these binominals in table 8.1.

It is these six theological binomials that Niebuhr uses as criteria to qualify Martin Luther (1483–1546) and Tertullian (ca. 155–220), for example, as belonging to the *Christ and culture in paradox* and *Christ against culture* types, respectively. The six theological criteria of *Christ and Culture* are

Table 8.1. Niebuhr's Binomials in *Christ and Culture*

Binomial	Perspective	Foundation
Yet vs. Not Yet	eschatological	end-time-based
Reason vs. Revelation	epistemological	knowledge-based
Nature vs. Grace	relational	history-based
Good vs. Evil	anthropological, hamartiological, and soteriological	salvation-based
Law vs. Gospel	ethical	moral-based
Church vs. World	ecclesiological and missiological	*kerygma*-based

By Allan M. de Novaes, Milton L. Torres, and João Fernando O. Barboza and based on preliminary work by Douglas Otatti and D. M. Yeager instantiations of the "enduring problem," the persistent dilemma that prompts Christians to choose between following the authority of Christ or the mandates that foster human civilization—without which we cannot adequately understand the logic and *modus operandi* of the typology of *Christ and Culture*.

Although there are a large number of publications that explicitly or implicitly reflect Niebuhrian typology, it is three American researchers who polarized the most recent debate on *Christ and Culture*: John Howard Yoder, George Marsden, and James Gustafson.[17] In fact, Gustafson responded to Yoder and Marsden in the preface to the commemorative edition of the work's fiftieth anniversary.[18] The fertile period of 1996–2001, marked by tributes to Niebuhr's legacy, brought with it the possibility of establishing a typology of recent academic reactions to *Christ and Culture*. Such categories were first elaborated by Glanzer, later adapted by Novaes,[19] and now updated here as a typology of a typology:

a. Rejection: Yoder rejects Niebuhr's typology and its assumptions, generally denying its applicability.[20] According to this view, Niebuhr's typology is useless.

b. Acceptance: Gustafson accepts Niebuhr's typology as useful and defends the applicability of Niebuhr's categories, generally proposing small and modest modifications.[21] According to this view, Niebuhr's typology is useful as it is.

c. Transformation: Marsden thinks that Niebuhr's typology is useful within certain limitations and proposes his own categories.[22] According to this view, Niebuhr's typology is useful to a certain extent.

Whatever the reactions to Niebuhr's typology in *Christ and Culture* may be, criticism of it always revolves around three main aspects:

1. *Niebuhr's definitions and terminology.* One can argue, for instance, against the imprecision of Niebuhr's use of the terms *Christ* and *culture*. What Christ does Niebuhr present? The Christ from the New Testament? The historical Jesus? The Christ of liberals or conservatives? The Christ of Protestants or Catholics?

2. *Niebuhr's purpose and argument.* Niebuhr can be criticized for avoiding the debate on the term *culture*, and for simultaneously adopting an overly broad and inclusive definition. From this perspective, the major problem with Niebuhr's use of the terms *Christ* and *culture* would be the assumption that there is a dichotomy between them. To defend Niebuhr's terminological choice, one can argue that his critics fail to adequately appreciate how Niebuhr's terminology relates to the

typology that he proposes. Niebuhr does not seek to create a polarity of concepts; rather, his aim is to describe and analyze complex manifestations of a single *pole*: the Christ/culture problem. On the question of Niebuhr's implicit argument, one can argue that Niebuhr prefers the fifth and last type, the Christ who transforms culture. Thus, his typology is so biased that its categories can only be used to recommend the transformation stance.

3. *The legitimacy and accuracy of his typology.* One can argue against possible historical inaccuracies among his examples that illustrate each of the types, which thus invalidate the whole typology.

It is necessary, however, to understand the ideal types as *heuristic concepts*, thus avoiding a confusion between taxonomy and typology.

Adapting the theological criteria from Niebuhr's typology to another context and another enduring problem may require that we resort to new binomials. In fact, the "enduring problem" that we address here is the tension between Christianity and paganism in Tolkien's work. For that reason, understanding Niebuhr's Christ/culture typology and the criticism it has received can shed light on the relationship between Christianity and paganism in Tolkien's work by pointing to elements that help form a typology that works as a hermeneutic key for the study of epistemological polarizations and interpretive cruces.

AN INTERPRETIVE TYPOLOGY OF TOLKIEN'S *THE SILMARILLION* AND *THE LORD OF THE RINGS*

The first part of the chapter introduced the "enduring problem"—whether Tolkien's inspiration for his work is Christian, pagan, or both, and pointed to two important aspects of the method we chose to attempt to solve this dilemma. First, we established that we would begin with Niebuhr's fivefold typology of the interplay between religion and culture. Then, we discussed that such typology was illuminating, but not sufficient to address the problem under study. Because of such insufficiency, we moved to a set of six Niebuhrian "polar tensions"—or binomials, as we call them—proposed by Novaes.[23] We must bear in mind, however, that the typology that our analysis proposes is neither to be applied directly to Tolkien nor to be directly derived from Niebuhr. We use Niebuhr's fivefold classification of the relationship between religion and culture as a starting point to foster our own analysis, which we believe is a more simple and productive way to describe how recent scholars see that aspect in Tolkien's works.

Now, as we turn to our analysis proper, we must define a corpus to circumscribe our typology from Christianity as a whole to two of Tolkien's works—*The Silmarillion* and *The Lord of the Rings*. We chose not to work with all his works mainly because they are not all included in the criticism that other authors direct against him in this regard. In addition, consideration was given to the instruction given by Tolkien in the preface to the second edition of the first book in *The Lord of the Rings*. According to him, his work was not an allegory. Therefore, outside of this parameter, no attempts should be made to narrow the scope of the way readers could take his narrative (*FR*, I, xxviii). This position entails a discussion on the sources that Tolkien resorted to so he would find inspiration for the symbols he uses.[24]

Another reason to limit our inquiry to *The Silmarillion* and *The Lord of the Rings* is that these works show closer connections to a Christian framework. Kreeft sees Frodo, for instance, as someone who bears the weight of evil in order to destroy it, a possible analog to Christ.[25] Another example is the *Ainulindalë*, the creation song that appears in the beginning of *The Silmarillion*, which can be considered a nod to the biblical genesis. When we say that we are restricting our analysis of the "enduring problem" to these two books, we do not mean to say that we will not resort to other works that form the legendarium. In fact, other works will be mentioned when they can be helpful in the analysis of our corpus.

Our next section undertakes a brief survey of Tolkien scholarship, focusing on scholars who address the relationship between Christianity and paganism in Tolkien's writings. We hope our classification will help us group such scholars according to their themes and arguments.

More Pagan than Christian

Those who argue that Tolkien is more pagan than Christian support their assumption by saying that *The Silmarillion* and *The Lord of the Rings* show a religiosity that is only tangential. Therefore, it is not possible to consider Tolkien a Christian writer since he makes little use of systematic doctrines or rituals. Some of these critics point to the fact that *The Lord of the Rings* is a work that was intended for the public-at-large, a fact that would have possibly led the author to remove any overt Christian symbols from the book.

For example, Rosebury claims that making the Ring that Frodo wears a reference to salvation in Christ is inconsistent because Frodo somehow succumbs to the power of the Ring.[26] For him, that fact weakens the analogy beyond repair and is not in tandem with Catholicism. He acknowledges, however, that there are a few religious elements in *The Lord of the Rings*, such as Tom Bombadil's relationship with the earth, which bears much resemblance to that of Adam with the garden of Eden. In his opinion, Tolkien uses religious symbols, but they do not refer to a specific religion. In fact, *The Silmarillion* has pervasive mystical elements, but Tolkien does not seem to be using them as systematized features that could point coherently to Catholicism.

Rosebury is emphatic to say that the Middle-earth has its own ethical system that came into being after Melkor fell and decided to turn away from Eru, thus rebelling against creation.[27] Therefore, religion is an integral part of the historical construction of Middle-earth. On the other hand, both Hutton and Rosebury state that the period when Tolkien wrote *The Lord of the Rings* was decisive for his creation of a universe where religion played only a small part.[28] According to Hutton, Tolkien admitted in one of his letters that his created mythology could be less dissonant from what someone, included himself, believed to be "the truth."[29] To add to this, Rosebury sees the twentieth century as extremely distant from any institutionalized religion.[30] Tolkien knew that his books would not sell if he created too much room for religion in them.

Madsen sees *The Lord of the Rings'* religion as a natural religion, which grew and developed from the history of Middle-earth.[31] For that reason, she emphasizes that if Tolkien had restricted his religious symbols to Christianity, he would have imposed limitations to his own work and would have curtailed its relevance to non-Christian readers. In fact, Madsen argues that *Beowulf*, a landmark in medieval literature, does not contain any Christian symbols because the presence of such symbols would have amounted to an anachronism.[32] The same thing supposedly happened to Tolkien's creation of *The Lord of the Rings*. Since Tolkien wanted his story to belong to a pre-Christian era, he removed all Christian symbols to make that aspect more believable. It would be extremely damaging to the narrative if Tolkien had spelled out any overt Christian symbols. However, she argues that there is "a natural religion" in *The Lord of the Rings* that comes into existence in Middle-earth to play a part in its development.

Shippey, like Madsen, is skeptical of the presence of any Christian symbolism—in an apologetical way—in Tolkien's narrative.[33] He assumes that there are few similarities between Tolkien's myth and biblical literature and focuses on the differences instead. Shippey understands that the Valar would clearly represent the angels, especially in *Silmarillion*, as they have the responsibility to take care of the earth and the beings that inhabit it.[34] Yet, differently from the biblical angels, the Valar show creative skills and chant Arda—the planet Earth—into existence, even though there is a divine order by Eru that they should not create life, only protect it. Even so, Aulë—the blacksmith Valar—creates the Dwarves before the awakening of the Elves. Ilúvatar finds out and mercifully makes the Dwarves fall asleep until the time is right. He also forgives Aulë for his act of disobedience. Because of these differences,

Shippey sees *The Lord of the Rings* as neither Christian nor religious.[35] On the other hand, Shippey says that it would be too difficult for Tolkien to move away from all the symbols he was acquainted with and—probably even unconsciously—included a few of them in one form or another in the narrative.[36] Such similarities do not mean, however, that Tolkien wanted to use them as a means of spreading his religious beliefs.

Thus, scholars such as Hutton, Rosebury, Madsen, and Shippey admit that there are religious symbols—broadly speaking—that point to the sacred in the universe of the Middle-earth.[37] For Hutton and Rosebury, a part of Tolkien's literature can be called Christian since it clearly contains Christian elements, but not the entire work.[38] Hutton summarizes this view, stating that there are essentially "three elements found in Tolkien's personal mythology: the Christian, the pagan, and the faerie."[39] Madsen and Shippey consider Tolkien's universe to lie far away from human or Christian reality.[40] For them, the creation of Middle-earth was an imaginative and complex process, in which Tolkien prescinded from all meaning external to *The Lord of the Rings* scenario.

Chance takes a slightly different stance from that of the previous scholars.[41] Basing her considerations upon an article written by Tolkien (*Monsters*, I), titled "The Monsters and the Critics," she analyzes Tolkien's work in the same way that Tolkien analyzed the Beowulf legend. By doing so, she concludes that the *LOTR* creates and supports its own universe. Nevertheless, she allows for the presence of as many Christian symbols as pagan elements in *The Lord of the Rings*. Chance maintains that Tolkien thought of Beowulf when he wrote his own epic.[42] As a result, he resorted to both pagan and Christian symbols. An evaluation of the symbolism of good and evil is evidence for this, since Frodo—from the start—takes on the simultaneous role of monster and hero. In the second book, Saruman adopts the monster position and thus incorporates Christian and Germanic expectations of evil. Chance is relatively successful in her analysis of the *LOTR*, but she is not able to apply her assumption to *The Silmarillion*, since it lacks a royal character, or a Lord, or even a central hero who could represent the medieval tradition.[43]

Scholars who adhere to the "more pagan than Christian" approach to Tolkien's symbolism do not deny that there was some Christian influence behind *The Silmarillion* and *The Lord of the Rings*. But they categorically affirm that these works are not to be compared to Lewis' *The Chronicles of Narnia* or Chesterton's short stories, which clearly allegorized Christian themes.

Christian but also Pagan

Scholars who embrace the "Christian but also pagan" approach to Tolkien's writings acknowledge that the word *interpretation* is key to any plausible understanding of his symbolism. In fact, Tolkien himself makes the following statement in the introduction to his first book:

> Other arrangements could be devised according to the tastes or views of those who like allegory or topical reference. But I cordially dislike allegory in all its manifestations, and always have done so since I grew old and wary enough to detect its presence. I much prefer history, true or feigned, with its varied applicability to the thought and experience of readers. I think that many confuse "applicability" with "allegory"; but the one resides in the freedom of the reader, and the other in the purposed domination of the author. (*FR*, I, xxviii)

Thus, Tolkien points out the complexities surrounding authorial inspiration and says that any attempt to pinpoint what exactly inspired him to create a certain setting or character would be speculation. Scholars who subscribe to the "Christian but also pagan" approach often argue for a more reality-oriented application, since they do not limit their understanding to personal interpretations, and therefore make no exhaustive attempt to try to prove what inspired Tolkien to write *The Silmarillion* and to create Middle-earth. These authors argue that literary influence is a personal experience and reject any interpretation that becomes mandatory for a general public. For them, individual theoretical contexts should always predominate in any approach to interpret Tolkien's works. Thus, Testi, Whittingham, and Wood focus on the Christian aspect of Tolkien's works, but as stated above, they do not try to establish a single interpretation as a rule to define which symbols are Christian and which ones are pagan, since they understand the contingent nature of any interpretation that can be offered in this regard.[44]

Testi, on one hand, tries to reconcile arguments against a Christian interpretation of Tolkien's works with biblical evidence that favor it.[45] In order to do that, he reviews what scholars say to dismiss a Christian interpretation for those works and concludes by echoing Honegger's argument that Tolkien's work "is meant neither for a single nation (England) nor a specific religion (be it Christian or Pagan), but for all of Mankind."[46]

Whittingham, on the other hand, seeks to map the possible sources of inspiration for different characters and situations whether mythological, historical, or religious.[47] She refers to symbols such as those that can be seen in the eschatology of Middle-earth, in its creation mythology, in the general mythology in which divine beings play an important role, in the concept of immortality, and beyond. She seeks to better understand the story itself by assessing its symbolism in less well-known works such as *The Return of the*

Shadow, The Treason of Isengard, The War of the Ring, Sauron Defeated and other works within the twelve volumes of *The History of Middle-earth.* In fact, she includes the entire legendarium in her analysis, to a greater extent than the other representative authors, since she attempts a deeper analysis of details found in Tolkien's twelve history books. However, she does not seem to include Tolkien's personal writings—such as his letters—in her corpus of study. She considers the creation of Middle-earth as a whole, and therefore mainly as a myth that interprets itself, but which came under the influence of other myths that were part of Tolkien's background. She seeks to decode Tolkien's narrative from a personal perspective because her objective is not to impose one single interpretation on the reader, but simply to state her own. To do so, she links individual aspects of his works to possible sources of influence.

Wood presents a possible Christian interpretation for Tolkien's works, without meddling with much of the academic debate.[48] He focuses on the similarities between aspects of the Christian gospel and Tolkien's myth. According to him, "this great work enables us to escape into reality," that is, myth enables readers to look at reality from a different perspective from their own.[49]

Morillo, unlike Testi, Whittingham, and Wood, argues for a more general interpretation for Tolkien's writings.[50] By pointing out that Tolkien was a linguist and not a theologian, Morillo asserts that Tolkien's concern was to avoid writing an allegorical book like those by fellow Inkling C.S. Lewis, and to avoid trying to use his literature with the overt purpose of converting people to the Christian faith. Morillo does not deny that Tolkien's personal devotion played a part in his books, but it did not have a great impact on the narrative. According to Morillo,

> the spirituality of *Lord of the Rings* cannot convincingly be taken as specifically Christian. Nor, I think, did Tolkien wish it to be taken that way. The spirituality of Middle-earth may have been, for him, compatible with Christian spirituality—indeed, what else was he going to say, or feel, about the issue, as a devout as well as spiritual man? But he did not wish to write allegory, as his friend C.S. Lewis did, and nothing but allegory could capture a specifically Christian spirituality in a story such as that in *Lord of the Rings*, so he believed in compatibility at a level abstract enough that it is also compatible with most other major forms of spirituality.[51]

For Morillo, Tolkien's work should be interpreted internally.[52] Tolkien clearly points to the ineffectiveness of trying to understand the plot of *The Lord of the Rings* and the entire legendarium from any point of view other than the literary one, and Morillo is correct when he says that Tolkien's work was mainly informed by his academic research, and not by his religious devotion.[53] The New Criticism of Tolkien's time started in the 1920s, and one of its main goals was to allow a text to express itself. Tolkien was well aware that an author was not able to determine a reader's interpretation of his work. That is why he wrote in the preface to *The Lord of the Rings* that he did not like allegories that would impose limitations to his imagination, thus encouraging readers to enjoy their freedom to read the narrative through their own lenses. In support of this argument, Morillo notes that Tolkien was often willing to oblige to the interpretation that his friends offered to his work.[54]

The "Christian but also Pagan" approach is considerably more impartial regarding the interpretation that can be proposed for Tolkien's books, since it does not assume one only correct way to interpret them and tries to avoid radical conclusions about Tolkien's intentions for the symbols he used or created to tell his story of Middle-earth.

Inherently Christian

The *inherently Christian* approach is the view of those scholars who assume that Tolkien's intention was to create a Christian epic under the guise of a world with complex symbolism. For them, not only is Tolkien's inspiration Christian, but his characters are clear allusions to Christian personae. These scholars back their argument on a quotation from Tolkien in one of his letters to his friend and Jesuit priest, Robert Murray:

> *The Lord of the Rings* is of course a fundamentally religious and Catholic work; unconsciously so at first, but consciously in the revision. That is why I have not put in, or have cut out, practically all references to anything like "religion," to cults or practices, in the imaginary world. For the religious element is absorbed into the story and the symbolism. (*Letters*, 172)

We chose the four scholars in our study based on the Christian, and often biblical, emphasis that they place on Tolkien's work. Pearce, Kreeft, Birzer, and Agøy maintain that it would be unlikely for Tolkien to ignore in his work the Christian and Roman Catholic traditions that he so valued in his personal life.[55] For these scholars, Tolkien was a committed Christian, and as a result, it would be impossible for him to distance himself from his religious beliefs even when he was writing fiction.

Based on this idea, Kreeft states that the supernatural emphasis that exists in Tolkien's narrative comes from Christianity.[56] Thus, if Tolkien belonged to any other religion or followed any other philosophy, his narrative would have come out completely different. For this reason, these scholars relate some aspects of Tolkien's narrative to classical ideas, such as the ideas of Plato and

Aristotle, who greatly influenced the church fathers and Catholic thought. For example, Kreeft argues that *The Lord of the Rings* characters are so platonic, that they are like archetypes in the mind of God.[57]

There is another common aspect in the way these scholars see the issue: they understand Tolkien's works as trying to mirror the real world. Birzer says that Tolkien's mythologization of the world helps us see the beauty and sacramentality of biblical creation.[58] That is, starting from the book one can have a new vision, or a more refined vision of reality, even biblical reality. For Birzer, Tolkien's inspiration came from God, and he implicitly acknowledges that he was an instrument for God to write the story (e.g., *Letters*, 79, 231, 252, and 258).[59]

Pearce seems to agree with Birzer and emphasizes the obviousness of Tolkien's Christian symbols.[60] To prove it, he compares a biblical scene and a scene from *The Lord of the Rings*. In *The Return of the King*, Frodo falls from exhaustion (*RK*, VI, iii). He is on his way to the Mount Doom, and the One Ring weighs on his neck. The One Ring is small, but very powerful and tempting. Upon seeing this, Sam offers to help carry it. This scene for Pearce shows a clear parallel with Christ carrying the cross.[61] In both cases, a heavy object is carried for humanity to be saved.

Agøy has something in common with Pearce, Kreeft, and Birzer: a strong attitude toward those who deny a inherently Christian interpretation or application for Tolkien's work.[62] In fact, Agøy tries to rebut Hutton by stating that in this debate all of Tolkien's statements should be considered, not only his primary fictional works.[63] These scholars do not prioritize received form and content, but rather the influences that led Tolkien to write his works. They often refer to "On Fairy-Stories," an essay that Tolkien published in 1947 to present his definition of mythology as the transposition of reality. There, Tolkien assumes that mythology is just another way of looking at common things. Nevertheless, it is only when a story is taken out of its context and reworked as fantasy or myth, that the reader—or listener—can understand it comprehensively. For that reason, Kreeft uses the example of Arda, which is where Middle-earth is located in the universe.[64] According to him, the world Arda was flat before its fall, which was intended to be a symbol of supernaturalistic metaphysics. As a divine punishment, Arda is changed from flat to round, representing that our worldview was changed from supernaturalism to naturalism.

The *inherently Christian* approach is sponsored primarily by theologians and philosophers who ultimately judge Tolkien's fiction to be a Christian work. Therefore, they emphasize that any other interpretation given to the Middle-earth narrative impoverishes the myth Tolkien created.

Considering the different aspects we analyzed, it is fair to conclude that the three views on Tolkien's religious symbolism in *The Silmarillion* and

The Lord of the Rings are sustained by different assumptions and research methods. Two of them value interpretive freedom while a third one stresses authorial intention. Scholars in the first and second groups tend to have literary credentials, while those in the third group bear more theological ones. The literary criticism of the first two groups of scholars depends on a reader's response emphasis or puts its stress on text forms and content. Scholars in the third group emphasize religious traditions. Our solution to this conundrum is to consider all alternatives. Attempts to understand the symbols that are present in *The Silmarillion* and *The Lord of the Rings* must proceed from an acknowledgment of their complexity, and consider how they affect form and content, in addition to the response those texts incite as well as their fit into religious traditions, whether Christian or pagan. Because so many affinities exist between the three critiques of *Christ and Culture* and the three critiques of *The Silmarillion* and *The Lord of the Rings*, the interpretive typology of *Christ and Culture* can shed light on the hermeneutic challenges for the interpretative typology of *The Silmarillion* and *The Lord of the Rings*.

INTERPRETIVE TYPOLOGIES FOR NIEBUHR AND TOLKIEN: A COMPARISON

Our discussion of the different critiques to *Christ and Culture* as well as to *The Silmarillion* and *The Lord of the Rings* begins with the acknowledgment that both typologies are threefold and commensurable. One type of critique disavows the theological significance of the works under study while another category allows for their significance; a final type admits some significance to them.

Therefore, the comparison between the categories reveals that there is a natural distribution of stances in which one can defend, reject, or partially accept the theological significance of the works under study. This also ensues

Table 8.2. Scholarly Criticism to the Theological Significance of Niebuhr's and Tolkien's Works

Niebuhr		Tolkien	
Typology	*Critique*	*Typology*	*Critique*
Rejection	Useless	More pagan than Christian	Useless
Acceptance	Useful	Christian but also pagan	Useful to a certain extent
Transformation	Useful to a certain extent	Inherently Christian	Useful

By Allan M. de Novaes, Milton L. Torres, and João Fernando O. Barboza the appearance of binomials that can become useful hermeneutic indicators for the investigation of interpretive typologies and for the systematization of an author's thought.

Another aspect to be observed in the critiques directed to the works of the two authors under study concerns the origin of these critiques, as table 8.3 describes. The sensitive point of the discussion regarding the question of symbolism and the influence of Christianity and paganism in Tolkien's work is the nature and interpretation of symbols. This again raises the question: Does the symbolism in Tolkien's works refer to the Catholic Christian tradition or to a pagan mythology? Is the symbolism present explicitly and unequivocally, or implicitly and subtly, Christian? Because responses may differ, Tolkien's works are described as ranging from Christian epics to Norse and Faërie mythology-based novels. The terminological issue concerning *Christ* and *culture* in Niebuhr's work was directly linked to literary paradigms, even if they led to theoretical and philosophical discussions. In a similar fashion, the discussion of how allegorical or explicit the Christian symbolism is in Tolkien is ultimately a literary one.

The underlying discussion here is the dichotomous assumption that underlies this debate, namely, the logic of exclusion and opposition: Christ *vs.* culture, in Niebuhr's case, and Christian *vs.* pagan symbolism, in Tolkien's case. In both cases, a more consistent hermeneutic solution should lead us to replace exclusion and opposition with pertinence and collaboration when we want to define terms and/or interpret symbols.

When dealing with the question of indoctrination or proselytism, the Christian vs. pagan debate about Tolkien's work focuses on his intentionality. Did he move away from Christian symbols to reach a larger audience and avoid resistance from readers? Did he embrace Catholicism to the point of making his works catechetical literary pieces? Do Tolkien's works resemble or distance themselves from the biblical allegorism of C.S. Lewis? Similarly, Niebuhr's critics have speculated how much he constructed his narrative to favor one of his categories—Christ the transformer of culture—and how intentional he was in trying to disqualify the other types. Whether the debate is about how liberal or conservative Niebuhr was or how Catholic or pagan Tolkien was, the nature of the debate is religious and—to a greater or lesser degree—belongs to the realm of apologetics.

Table 8.3. The Origin of the Critique to Niebuhr's and Tolkien's Works

Origin	Niebuhr	Tolkien
Literature	Terminology	Symbolism
Theology	Argument	Indoctrination
Epistemology	Typology	Logic

Finally, when dealing with the narrative, regardless of the categories in which they are framed, the critiques stream from a third point of origin: their rationale for interpretation. Should Tolkien's works be read by themselves, as literary pieces, or must they be interpreted from a religious point of view? What version of Tolkien is more manifest in *The Silmarillion* and *The Lord of the Rings*—the linguist or the Catholic? His work's narrative structure and literary genre bring us here to a discussion of his method. His penchant for neologisms, his development of characters, the mythology he created for his Powers, the languages he brought into existence from scratch, the history and the geography he designed—all these aspects demonstrate that Tolkien engaged in a well-articulated method for creating his literary narrative. Knowing for what purpose Tolkien developed this method—whether purposedly Catholic propaganda or an exercise in literary mastery—is the answer that must be sought.

Similarly, the critique of Niebuhr's *Christ and Culture* pushes us for a discussion of his method and of the applicability of typologies as tools to help us make sense of the relationship between Christianity and culture. Any answer must contemplate both literary theory and theology when we address the typologies that are useful to compare Niebuhr and Tolkien from a religious and cultural perspective.

CONCLUDING REMARKS

We began this chapter with an elucidation of Niebuhr's typology of how different Christians perceive their relationship to culture. Based on his typology, we created a similar typology to address the problem of how different scholars make sense of religious symbols in Tolkien's *Silmarillion* and *Lord of the Rings*. Although Tolkien's personal writings that give anecdotes about his motivation for writing seem to be at times self-contradictory, we established three views: a view that emphasizes the multiple sources of inspiration from which Tolkien may have gathered his ideas, and sees Tolkien as "more pagan than Christian"; a view that prioritizes text and history and tries to interpret it for itself, considering Tolkien as "Christian, but also pagan"; and, finally, a view that sees his work as "inherently Christian" and believes that Christianity is the only background against which a reader can reach the full meaning of *The Silmarillion* and *The Lord of the Rings*.

After our analysis, it seems clear that the scholars in the first group value plurality and consider many possible interpretations for Tolkien's work, assuming he received influences from various sources. Their argument stems from their study of Tolkien's works against the backdrop of his academic tradition. By doing so, they refrain from using a reader's response approach and focus on Tolkien's writing process.

Scholars in the second group resort to the ideas that came with the New Criticism movement and argue for much freedom to contextually interpret Tolkien's works. They value textual form and content, and often start from individual assumptions, thus emphasizing that literary works are not limited by what they say, but to what the reader can read out of the text.

Scholars in the third group defend a Christian interpretation for Tolkien's works, and see them as philosophically- and theologically-oriented toward Christian concepts with Catholic symbolism. These scholars insist that there can essentially be no other interpretation for Tolkien's work besides the Christian one. Any other interpretations would deprive the reader of any real understanding of the symbols which Tolkien employed.

Considering the different aspects we analyzed, it is fair to conclude that the three views on Tolkien's religious symbolism in *The Silmarillion* and *The Lord of the Rings* are sustained by different assumptions and research methodologies. Two of them value interpretive freedom while a third one stresses authorial intention. Scholars in the first and second groups tend to have literary credentials, while those in the third group usually bear the mark of theological training. The literary criticism of the first two groups of scholars depends on a reader's response emphasis or puts its stress on textual form and content. Scholars in the third group emphasize religious traditions. Our solution to this conundrum is to consider all alternatives. Any serious attempt to understand the symbols that are present in *The Silmarillion* and *The Lord of the Rings* must proceed from an acknowledgment of their complexity, and consider how they affect form and content, the response those texts incite as well as how they fit religious traditions, whether Christian or pagan.

NOTES

1. Ronald Hutton, "The Pagan Tolkien," in *The Ring and the Cross: Christianity and* The Lord of the Rings, ed. Paul E. Kerry (Madison: Fairleigh Dickinson University Press, 2011), 63.

2. H. Richard Niebuhr, *Christ and Culture* (New York: Harper & Row, 1951).

3. The insight to look to Niebuhr's *Christ and Culture* for a typology of Christian attitudes to culture comes from the work of Allan Novaes; see for example, Allan Novaes, "O Problema Adventismo-Televisão: Uma Análise do Pensamento Adventista Sobre a TV a Partir da Tipologia de H. Richard Niebuhr em *Cristo e Cultura*," (Tese de doutorado, Pontifícia Universidade Católica de São Paulo, 2016); and Allan Novaes, *Cristo e Cultura: Uma Introdução Crítica* (Campinas: Fonte Editorial, 2019).

4. Niebuhr, *Christ and Culture*, 1.

5. Niebuhr, *Christ and Culture*, 44.

6. As Tolkien seems to intend little distinction between himself as author and the implied author.

7. For example, Hutton, "Pagan Tolkien," 69; and Joseph Pearce, *Tolkien: Man and Myth* (San Francisco: Ignatius Press, 1998), 81, respectively.

8. Claudio A. Testi, "Tolkien's Work: Is It Christian or Pagan? A Proposal for a Synthetic Approach," *TS* 10 (2013): 1–47; and also, Claudio A. Testi, *Pagan Saints in Middle-earth*, Cormarë 38 (Zurich: Walking Tree, 2018).

9. In this new categorization, we find that Testi's approach now belongs to the second category.

10. Hutton, "Pagan Tolkien," 57–70; Catherine Madsen, "Light from an Invisible Lamp: Natural Religion in *The Lord of the Rings*," *Mythlore* 14.3 (1988): 43–47; Tom Shippey, *J.R.R. Tolkien: Author of the Century* (New York: Harper Collins, 2000); Jane Chance, *Tolkien's Art: A Mythology for England* (Louisville: University Press of Kentucky, 2001); and Brian Rosebury, *Tolkien: A Cultural Phenomenon* (London: Palgrave Macmillan, 2003).

11. Testi, "Tolkien's Work," 1–47; Stephen Morillo, "The Entwives: Investigating the Spiritual Core of *The Lord of the Rings*," in Kerry, *The Ring and the Cross*, 106–118; Elizabeth A. Whittingham, *The Evolution of Tolkien's Mythology: A Study of the History of Middle-earth*, CESFF 7 (Jefferson, NC: McFarland, 2008); and Ralph C. Wood, introduction to *Tolkien Among the Moderns* (Notre Dame: University of Notre Dame Press, 2015), 1.

12. Pearce, *Tolkien*, 82; Peter J. Kreeft, *The Philosophy of Tolkien: The Worldview Behind* The Lord of the Rings (San Francisco: Ignatius Press, 2005); Bradley J. Birzer, *J.R.R. Tolkien's Sanctifying Myth: Understanding Middle-earth* (Wilmington: ISI Books, 2002), 25–26; and Nils Ivar Agøy, "The Christian Tolkien: A Response to Ronald Hutton," in Kerry, *The Ring and the Cross*, 71–89.

13. Niebuhr, *Christ and Culture*, 40–44.

14. Douglas F. Ottati, "Christ and Culture," *American Presbyterians* 66 (1988); Douglas F. Ottati, "*Christ and Culture*: Still Worth Reading after All These Years," *JSCE* 23.1 (2003): 121–32; and Douglas F. Ottati, *Meaning and Method in H. Richard Niebuhr's Theology* (Washington, D.C.: University Press of America, 1982); and D. M. Yeager, "H. Richard Niebuhr's *Christ and Culture*," in *The Oxford Handbook of Theological Ethics*, ed. Gilbert Meilaender and William Werpehowski (Oxford: Oxford University Press, 2005), 466–86.

15. Ottati, "Christ and Culture," 1988, 325.

16. Novaes, *Cristo e Cultura*; and Novaes, "Problema Adventismo-Televisão."

17. John Howard Yoder, "How H. Richard Niebuhr Reasoned: A Critique of *Christ and Culture*," in *Authentic Transformation: A New Vision of* Christ and Culture, ed. Glen Stassen, D. M. Yeager and John Howard Yoder (Nashville: Abingdon, 1996), 31–90; George Marsden, "Christianity and Cultures: Transforming Niebuhr's Categories," *Insights* 115.1 (1999): 4–15; and James M. Gustafson, preface to *Christ and Culture*, by H. Richard Niebuhr (New York: HarperSanFrancisco, 2001), xxi–xxxvi.

18. Gustafson, preface, xxi–xxxv.

19. Perry L. Glanzer, "Christ and the Heavy Metal Subculture: Applying Qualitative Analysis to the Contemporary Debate about H. Richard Niebuhr's *Christ and Culture*," *JRS* 5 (2003); Novaes, *Cristo e Cultura*; and Novaes, "Problema Adventismo-Televisão."

20. Yoder, "Niebuhr Reasoned," 31–90.

21. Gustafson, preface, xxxiv–xxxv.

22. Marsden, "Christianity and Cultures," 4–15.

23. Novaes, *Cristo e Cultura*; and Novaes, "Problema Adventismo-Televisão."

24. Some interesting studies about symbols in Tolkien's works are David Harvey, *The Song of Middle-earth: J.R.R. Tolkien's Themes, Symbols and Myths* (London: HarperCollins, 1985); Craig Bernthal, *Tolkien's Sacramental Vision: Discerning the Holy in Middle-earth* (Kettering: Second Spring, 2014); and Lisa Coutras, *Tolkien's Theology of Beauty: Majesty, Splendor, and Transcendence in Middle-earth* (London: Palgrave Macmillan, 2016).

25. Kreeft, *Philosophy*, 43.

26. Rosebury, *Tolkien*, 171.

27. Rosebury, *Tolkien*, 43.

28. Hutton, "Pagan Tolkien," 65; and Rosebury, *Tolkien*, 153.

29. Hutton, "Pagan Tolkien," 68–69.

30. Rosebury, *Tolkien*, 153.

31. Madsen, "Invisible Lamp," 44.

32. Madsen, "Invisible Lamp," 45.

33. Shippey, *Tolkien*, 171–72; and Madsen, "Invisible Lamp," 44, respectively.

34. Shippey, *Tolkien*, 173–74.

35. Shippey, *Tolkien*, 169.

36. Shippey, *Tolkien*, 174.

37. Hutton, "Pagan Tolkien," 59; Rosebury, *Tolkien*, 182; Madsen, "Invisible Lamp," 45; and Shippey, *Tolkien*, 174.

38. Hutton, "Pagan Tolkien," 69; and Rosebury, *Tolkien*, 182.

39. Hutton, "Pagan Tolkien," 90.

40. Madsen, "Invisible Lamp," 43; and Shippey, *Tolkien*, 173.

41. Chance, *Tolkien's Art*, 92.

42. Chance, *Tolkien's Art*, 92–93.

43. Chance, *Tolkien's Art*, 3–4.

44. Testi, "Tolkien's Work," 29; Whittingham, *Evolution*, 200; and Ralph C. Wood, *The Gospel According to Tolkien: Visions of the Kingdom in Middle-earth* (Louisville: Westminster John Knox, 2003), 1.

45. Testi, "Tolkien's Work," 30.

46. Thomas Honegger, "A Mythology for England—the Question of National Identity in Tolkien's Legendarium," *Hither Shore* 3 (2006): 25.

47. Whittingham, *Evolution*, 8–9.

48. Wood, *Tolkien Among the Moderns*, 1.

49. Wood, *Gospel According to Tolkien*, 1.

50. Morillo, "Entwives," 120; contra Testi, "Tolkien's Work," 29–30; Whittingham, *Evolution*, 5–6; and Wood, *Gospel According to Tolkien*, 2–4.

51. Morillo, "Entwives," 114.
52. Morillo, "Entwives," 117–18.
53. Morillo, "Entwives," 116.
54. Morillo, "Entwives," 114.
55. Pearce, *Tolkien*, 43; Kreeft, *Philosophy*, 19–20; Birzer, *Sanctifying Myth*, 26; and Agøy, "Christian Tolkien," 79.
56. Kreeft, *Philosophy*, 19.
57. Kreeft, *Philosophy*, 20.
58. Birzer, *Sanctifying Myth*, 23.
59. Birzer, *Sanctifying Myth*, 26.
60. Pearce, *Tolkien*, 45.
61. Pearce, *Tolkien*, 45.
62. For example, Agøy, "Christian Tolkien," 71; Pearce, *Tolkien*, 43–45; Kreeft, *Philosophy*, 9–11; and Birzer, *Sanctifying Myth*, 1–4.
63. Agøy, "Christian Tolkien," 73; and Hutton, "Pagan Tolkien," 60, respectively.
64. Kreeft, *Philosophy*, 19 and 36.

BIBLIOGRAPHY

Agøy, Nils Ivar. "The Christian Tolkien: A Response to Ronald Hutton." Pages 71–89 in *The Ring and the Cross: Christianity and* The Lord of the Rings. Edited by Paul E. Kerry. Madison: Fairleigh Dickinson University Press, 2011.

Bernthal, Craig. *Tolkien's Sacramental Vision: Discerning the Holy in Middle-earth.* Kettering: Second Spring, 2014.

Birzer, Bradley J. *J.R.R. Tolkien's Sanctifying Myth: Understanding Middle-earth.* Wilmington: ISI Books, 2002.

Carpenter, Humphrey. *The Letters of J.R.R. Tolkien.* Boston: Houghton Mifflin Harcourt, 2013.

Chance, Jane. *Tolkien's Art: A Mythology for England.* Louisville: University Press of Kentucky, 2001.

Coutras, Lisa. *Tolkien's Theology of Beauty: Majesty, Splendor, and Transcendence in Middle-earth.* London: Palgrave Macmillan, 2016.

Glanzer, Perry L. "Christ and the Heavy Metal Subculture: Applying Qualitative Analysis to the Contemporary Debate about H. Richard Niebuhr's *Christ and Culture.*" *JRS* 5 (2003).

Gustafson, James M. Preface to *Christ and Culture*, by H. Richard Niebuhr. New York: HarperSanFrancisco, 2001.

Harvey, David. *The Song of Middle-earth: J.R.R. Tolkien's Themes, Symbols and Myths.* London: HarperCollins, 1985.

Honegger, Thomas. "A Mythology for England—the Question of National Identity in Tolkien's Legendarium." *Hither Shore* 3 (2006): 13–26.

Hutton, Ronald. "The Pagan Tolkien." Pages 57–70 in *The Ring and the Cross: Christianity and* The Lord of the Rings. Edited by Paul E. Kerry. Madison: Fairleigh Dickinson University Press, 2011.

Hutton, Ronald. "Can We Still Have a Pagan Tolkien? A Reply to Nils Ivar Agøy." Pages 90–105 in *The Ring and the Cross: Christianity and* The Lord of the Rings. Edited by Paul E. Kerry. Madison: Fairleigh Dickinson University Press, 2011.

Kreeft, Peter J. *The Philosophy of Tolkien: The Worldview Behind* The Lord of the Rings. San Francisco: Ignatius Press, 2005.

Lewis, C.S. *Mere Christianity*. Rev. and enl. ed. San Francisco, CA: HarperOne, 2009.

Madsen, Catherine. "Light from an Invisible Lamp: Natural Religion in *The Lord of the Rings*." *Mythlore* 14.3 (1988): 43–47.

Marsden, George. "Christianity and Cultures: Transforming Niebuhr's Categories." *Insights* 115.1 (1999): 4–15.

Morillo, Stephen. "The Entwives: Investigating the Spiritual Core of *The Lord of the Rings*." Pages 106–118 in *The Ring and the Cross: Christianity and* The Lord of the Rings. Edited by Paul E. Kerry. Madison: Fairleigh Dickinson University Press, 2011.

Niebuhr, H. Richard. *Christ and Culture*. New York: Harper & Row, 1951.

Novaes, Allan. *Cristo e Cultura: Uma Introdução Crítica*. Campinas: Fonte Editorial, 2019.

———. "O Problema Adventismo-Televisão: Uma Análise do Pensamento Adventista Sobre a TV a Partir da Tipologia de H. Richard Niebuhr em *Cristo e Cultura*." Tese de doutorado, Pontifícia Universidade Católica de São Paulo, 2016.

Ottati, Douglas F. "*Christ and Culture*." *American Presbyterians* 66 (1988): 320–25.

———. "*Christ and Culture*: Still Worth Reading after All These Years." *JSCE* 23.1 (2003): 121–32.

———. *Meaning and Method in H. Richard Niebuhr's Theology*. Washington, D.C.: University Press of America, 1982.

Pearce, Joseph. *Tolkien: Man and Myth*. San Francisco: Ignatius Press, 1998.

Rosebury, Brian. *Tolkien: A Cultural Phenomenon*. London: Palgrave Macmillan, 2003.

Shippey, Tom. *J.R.R. Tolkien: Author of the Century*. New York: HarperCollins, 2000.

Testi, Claudio A. *Pagan Saints in Middle-earth*. Cormarë 38. Zurich: Walking Tree, 2018.

———. "Tolkien's Work: Is It Christian or Pagan? A Proposal for a Synthetic Approach." *TS* 10 (2013): 1–47.

Whittingham, Elizabeth A. *The Evolution of Tolkien's Mythology: A Study of the History of Middle-earth*. CESFF 7. Jefferson, NC: McFarland, 2008.

Wood, Ralph C. *The Gospel According to Tolkien: Visions of the Kingdom in Middle-earth*. Louisville: Westminster John Knox, 2003.

Wood, Ralph C., ed. *Tolkien Among the Moderns*. Notre Dame: University of Notre Dame Press, 2015.

Yeager, D. M. "H. Richard Niebuhr's *Christ and Culture*." Pages 466–86 in *The Oxford Handbook of Theological Ethics*. Edited by Gilbert Meilaender and William Werpehowski. Oxford: Oxford University Press, 2005.

Yoder, John Howard. "How H. Richard Niebuhr Reasoned: A Critique of *Christ and Culture*." Pages 31–90 in *Authentic Transformation: A New Vision of* Christ and Culture. Edited by Glen Stassen, D. M. Yeager and John Howard Yoder. Nashville: Abingdon, 1996.

Chapter 9

Perceiving the Material and Immaterial in Middle-earth

Adam B. Shaeffer

Christian theology has a long tradition that situates our ability to perceive immaterial realities within spiritual corollaries to our physical senses.[1] Whether he was intentionally engaging with this tradition or not, J.R.R. Tolkien's legendarium contributes to this project and deserves a place at the table.[2] In *The Lord of the Rings*, Tolkien narrates possibilities for spiritual sight that both parallel and expand upon the existing tradition. These possibilities in Tolkien's secondary world invite us to reconsider what's possible in the primary world.[3]

One strand of the tradition, especially as seen in Hans Urs von Balthasar's reading of Origen (ca. 184–253 CE), emphasizes the nature of all perception as a joint spiritual-corporeal endeavor because humans, by their very nature, are spiritual-corporeal unities.[4] Tolkien's imagination assumes such a unity and presents a range of possibilities for its expression: from physical far-sightedness to a spiritual perception that sees Arda's providential nature. In addition to exploring Tolkien's presentation of perception as both spiritual and corporeal, this chapter also attends to the need for community if the spiritual senses are to be developed, the possibility of becoming proficient in their use by growing in virtue, and their availability at all stages of the spiritual journey.

PERCEPTION AS SPIRITUAL-CORPOREAL ENDEAVOR

Bodies matter for Tolkien. We need only look at the difference in grandeur between Melkor of the *Ainulindalë* and Morgoth who is finally led away in

185

chains. The two are so unlike as to be in some sense different people. So too, Sauron loses the ability to appear in a pleasing form before finally losing his ability to take a form at all except for that of the lidless eye. These examples point toward the inherent weakness of physical bodies because of the Melkor-ingredient resident within all matter—and this holds true for even "incarnate spirits" such as the Istari (*UT*, 390 and *Letters*, 202)—but physical bodies are not just a liability for Tolkien. They are part of Ilúvatar's design, and they are good. For the Ainur, they present opportunities to engage in fellowship with the created order in a different mode than when they are in their natural disembodied forms.

In Tolkien's work, outer appearance mirrors inner reality and in that light, body and soul are deeply connected. The body bears witness to the soul's state. The physical difference between Elves and Orcs demonstrates this, as do the "bodies" of the Nazgûl.[5] Perhaps this is clearest as Frodo looks upon Saruman's dead body, "for as he looked it seemed that long years of death were suddenly revealed in it, and it shrank, and the shriveled face became rags of skin upon a hideous skull" (*RK*, VI, viii). This is because, in Tolkien's work as in von Balthasar's,[6] the human person is a "sensory-spiritual totality."[7] In other words, the human person is both an embodied soul and an ensouled body, and neither the body nor the soul takes precedence over the other.[8] To be a Child of Ilúvatar is to exist as this unity-in-duality, and this is by design. The Children are made to interact with all things as embodied creatures, whether Elves or Dwarves, Ainur or beasts.

This is just as true in the primary world, where the body is not an unfortunate side-effect of creaturehood, but is essential and valuable, and it does more than inform and enrich the spiritual life. We experience the spiritual through the physical. The world around us is comprised of both the physical and the spiritual, and so it is only fitting that we would be equipped to perceive more than just physical realities. As von Balthasar writes, "It is with both body and soul that the living human being experiences the world and, consequently, also God."[9]

So, too, in Tolkien's legendarium there is a spiritual reality undergirding everything, and beyond the obvious manifestation of spiritual evil in Sauron, the more subtle spiritual realities can also be perceived by those who have eyes to see. When Faramir peers into the depths of Gollum's soul, finding "locked doors and closed windows" with "dark rooms behind them" (*TT*, IV, vi), his perception reveals a parallel between Tolkien and von Balthasar. For both, it is through the physical senses that the spiritual senses work. Tolkien makes no attempt to describe or explain how this seeing happens, but it appears to be in and through Faramir's physical sight. He sees more clearly and more deeply than many. He sees Gollum's soul through the physical body before him.

SPIRITUAL PERCEPTION AND COMMUNITY

For von Balthasar, the spiritual senses are primarily experienced in interpersonal encounters with "the Thou" rather than in solitary mystical encounters, and Tolkien shares this perspective, narrating community's power to influence the kind of people we become.[10]

Look, for example, at Gandalf's power to shape those around him into certain kinds of people, into ennobled souls, and conversely at Saruman's power to twist and break relational bonds, isolating and marring those he brings under his sway. The communities Gandalf fosters offer a kind of narrated metaphor for the role of community in developing the spiritual senses. As Frodo and Sam spend time with Gandalf, and later with only each other, they experience the growth and ennoblement of their ability to perceive. Sam's ennoblement offers a particularly striking example of this point. When Sam first appears in *The Fellowship of the Ring*, he is a humble hobbit who is so fascinated by the Elves that he eavesdrops on Gandalf and Frodo's conversation to hear more about the Elves and the wider world (*FR*, I, ii). This same Sam grows into someone who perceives spiritual truths as the Elves do as he is shaped by the fellowship of Gandalf, Aragorn, and Frodo.[11] As I discuss in more detail later, he exhibits spiritual sight after he and Frodo encounter Gollum, but the transformative work preparing him to see in such a way had already been happening since the journey began. The ability to perceive in this way is latent within him at the beginning, but his community draws it out and breathes life into it.

GROWING IN VIRTUE

Tolkien imagines ennobled perception as something that can be learned, even if that training is accomplished without explicit instruction. Gandalf never sits his friends down to teach them how to see and experience the world as he does, yet they learn it nonetheless. As they are ennobled in their community, they are equipped to perceive more than just physical realities. In Tolkien's epic, virtue and spiritual perception are closely connected, which means that growth in virtue brings about a corresponding growth in spiritual perception.

In discussing Gregory of Nyssa's engagement with the spiritual senses, Sarah Coakley suggests, "our very acts of visual perceiving and sensual response might be affected by our moral fiber."[12] The same can be said of those living in Middle-earth. While it is true that in Tolkien's work the Children of Ilúvatar are, by nature, capable of spiritual perception, those who have been most ennobled are most likely to see with spiritual sight.[13] In a letter from 1956, Tolkien writes that *The Lord of the Rings* is "primarily a study of the ennoblement (or *sanctification*) of the humble" (*Letters*, 237, emphasis added). So, when Tolkien writes of ennoblement, he has sanctification (or growth in holiness) in mind.[14] And this ennoblement has direct implications on his characters' ability to perceive spiritual things.

Coakley reads Gregory as suggesting "a capacity for the sense organs to develop from 'small-souled' to 'large-souled' apprehensions; yet what is also given is the simultaneous temptation 'completely to close' down the spiritual senses."[15] The inhabitants of Arda Marred have an analogous potential. As embodied creatures, their sense organs can be developed and grown from "small-souled" perception, where sight is limited to the material world around them, to "large-souled" perception, where sight's physical limitations are gradually removed. Origen suggests this potential in comparing the value of physical exercise to having "the senses of my soul trained to perceive."[16] Karl Rahner helpfully summarizes Origen: "The physical faculties are strengthened by constant practice; it is just the same with the spiritual senses. The efforts of the bodily senses must be followed by the mastery of spiritual faculties, where indeed a great deal of training is required."[17] The need for training is significant. Gregory observes that it is possible for people to close their "eyes completely to the perceptions of the soul" and erect walls "which prevent small-souled folk through their own fault from the contemplation of the intelligible."[18] Coakley sees in Gregory an insight that holds true for Tolkien too: "the view being proposed is that our perceptual capacities have labile and transformative possibilities, but ones that not all activate—whether through sin, laziness, blindness or philosophical obtuseness."[19] While all can live out these "large-souled" capacities, not all do. And while it is not necessarily sin that prevents hobbits from seeing with spiritual sight, it might be called laziness, or at least excessive comfort. Their life in the Shire is good and pleasant and has not pressed them to see beyond its borders. Neither has it inspired them to look for things deeper or higher than what they already know.[20]

But even those who exhibit "large-souled" perception are not immune from the temptations Coakley mentions. This is most evident in Denethor and Saruman. Denethor is of true Númenórean descent with all that entails (*RK*, V, i) and Saruman is one of the Maia, so both are capable of seeing both farther (physically) and deeper (spiritually) than most. But both have their perceptual capacities diminished and clouded. Both think they are seeing more clearly than others, while, in reality, they are seeing falsehoods and partial truths. Though they should see more clearly and more deeply, their sight has been diminished. It is ironic that the downfall of both characters and the clouding of their perception and judgment comes about because of their inappropriate use of the *palantíri*, or seeing stones of Númenor. These ancient artifacts were made to enable communication and sight across great distances, and what they reveal is true. As Gandalf states, "The Stones of Seeing do not lie, and not even the Lord of Barad-dûr can make them do so" (*RK*, V, ix). They were used to further extend the Númenóreans' already super-human capacities (*TT*, III, xi), but for Denethor and Saruman, they result in the opposite.

Both use a *palantír* to look afield, and both turn their empowered gaze on Sauron who deceived them (*RK*, V, vii; *RK*, V, ix). Sauron's deception takes what was native within them and turns it to their destruction, so that Denethor sees only defeat (*RK*, Appendix A, I, iv) and Saruman sees only tools *(UT*, 413).[21] For Saruman, in particular, his vision is a domineering and imperialist form of sight that lacks the ability to see and respect things as other than himself and with their own right to exist (*FR*, II, ii; *Morgoth*, 413, 418–19; *UT*, 413).[22] Further, neither Saruman nor Denethor sees with hope, and neither sees the providential ordering of the world.

The contrast between these two and Aragorn is stark. Their diminished virtue and weakened spiritual perception prevent them from seeing clearly, both physically and spiritually, through the *palantír*. While the Stone cannot lie to them, Gandalf speculates that Sauron could "maybe, by his will choose what things shall be seen by weaker minds, or cause them to mistake the meaning of what they see" (*RK*, V, ix). Saruman's corruption and Denethor's despair can be tied to this (*TT*, III, xi; *RK*, V, vii). Aragorn, on the other hand, is the virtuous true king and he can wrest control of the *palantír* from Sauron and use it as it was intended. His sight is extended so far that he can face off with Sauron in Mordor and demonstrate his moral fiber. His "large-souled" perception in everyday life has prepared him to properly extend his perception through the *palantír*.[23]

Considering the connection between outer appearance and inner reality in Tolkien's work, it is not surprising that there is also a connection between virtue and perception. Since characters perceive—physically and spiritually—through their physical senses, it is fitting that their ability to perceive would be affected by the state of their souls. As spiritual-corporeal unities, outer appearance and perceptual capacities are reflections of interior realities, and so as characters become more ennobled their capacity to exercise the spiritual senses increases.[24] Similarly, when their physical and spiritual senses are trained in the wrong direction, their ability to perceive with those senses diminishes. But as their spiritual senses are strengthened, they are equipped to perceive Ilúvatar's providential ordering of reality.

PERCEIVING PROVIDENCE

Perceiving the ways Ilúvatar is at work in Arda Marred (*Morgoth*, 396) takes two different forms: one sees the plot of Arda Marred with hope because it perceives the potential for redemption in any situation (for the Ring to be destroyed, for instance), and the other sees people with hope because it perceives the potential for Ilúvatar to redeem them. One of the most instructive ways Tolkien presents this second kind of perception of Providence is in Gandalf's refusal to close off the potential for others to grow and change. Empowered by humility and a genuine love for people, Gandalf is equipped to perceive Ilúvatar's providential work in the world and fulfill his mission as a transformative force in Middle-earth.

Where Saruman's downward spiral might lead some to write him off, Gandalf holds out hope, recognizing that Saruman's degradation was not inevitable. Gandalf, and later Frodo, still have hope that Saruman can be restored to his intended purpose and place in the world. A section in *Unfinished Tales* explores the scenes surrounding Gandalf's escape from Orthanc. In one of the drafts, Tolkien describes the internal battle in which Saruman considers repenting and returning to the light. In Christopher Tolkien's summary of this scene, he writes: "In this account, Saruman, in fear and despair, and perceiving the full horror of service to Mordor, resolved suddenly to yield to Gandalf, and to beg for his pardon and help," though Gandalf's escape foils this and causes Saruman's "pride [to reassert] itself in anger" (*UT*, 346). This would have marked a drastic change within Saruman's heart and mind and would have fundamentally altered the narrative as we know it. But the possibility existed in Tolkien's mind for this kind of change to occur. It is the kind of thing that can happen in Arda Marred, even to one so far along Sauron's path of domination and destruction.

Gandalf's hope for Saruman's restoration is not unfounded. In Tolkien's imagining, Saruman could have been restored and redeemed, offering his help to Ilúvatar's children rather than continuing to oppose them for his own benefit. Gandalf knows that Ilúvatar's providential activity in the world means that hearts *can* change, repentance and restoration *are* possible, and so he can never close off the possibility for others to change. This deep belief and understanding of the way Arda works motivates Gandalf's generous open-handedness with Saruman (*TT*, III, x), and it also motivates his hope for Gollum's healing.

From the beginning of *The Lord of the Rings*, Gandalf encourages pity for Gollum and an openness to what Providence may have in store for him. When Frodo learns of the Ring's history and how it came into Gollum's hands, his immediate response is one of horror and loathing. But Gandalf replies, "I think it is a sad story . . . and it might have happened to others, even to some hobbits that I have known" (*FR*, I, ii). Gandalf sees in Bilbo's interaction with Gollum hints that Gollum "was not wholly ruined" and that "there was a little corner of his mind that was still his own" (*FR*, I, ii). This gives him hope for Gollum's restoration. If any piece of his mind and will remain his own, then the possibility for redemption necessarily exists. As a Maia, Gandalf is a child of Ilúvatar's thought and so he knows Ilúvatar intimately. Sauron and Saruman did once, but their corruption has obscured even the faintest remaining traces of that knowledge. Gandalf knows of Ilúvatar's ongoing providential interaction with the world, and so Gandalf expects to see Ilúvatar continuing to work in that manner (*FR*, I, ii). He knows something of the mind of the Maker, even if his knowledge and experience are limited. Even Melkor can be redeemed and forgiven. In fact, many of the Valar believe that Melkor's feigned repentance and restoration are genuine.[25] They, like Gandalf, have been sub-creatively involved in the shaping of Arda from the beginning and know that redemption and restoration are woven into the fabric of the world. They know the mind of Ilúvatar and so they know that restoration and redemption are characteristic of the way he works.[26] Knowing all this, they believe that Melkor had truly been reformed since his apparent restoration matches the pattern they recognize from the Great Music.

Since Gandalf knows that redemption is part of the way Ilúvatar works within the marred world, he also knows that Ilúvatar's redemptive activity is not limited to individuals and extends to the events and story of Arda itself. And so, when he tells Frodo that there was more than one power at work when Bilbo found the Ring (*FR*, I, ii) he recognizes the providential hand of Ilúvatar. He commends Bilbo for his pity and mercy, seeing in them the reason Bilbo suffered so little harm from his long possession of the Ring (*FR*, I, ii) and sees in them again the working of Providence. From this foundation, Gandalf makes a kind of providential prophecy of Gollum's future role in the grand scheme of things. It is because he has not closed off the potential for Gollum's redemption and because he perceives Providence at work in the world that he can say:

> I have not much hope that Gollum can be cured before he dies, but there is a chance of it. And he is bound up with the fate of the Ring. My heart tells me that he has some part to play yet, for good or ill, before the end; and when that comes, the pity of Bilbo may rule the fate of many—yours not least. (*FR*, I, ii)

Gandalf recognizes that Ilúvatar's providential restoration of individuals can play a part in his restoration of Arda Marred. But Ilúvatar does not force redemption on individuals, and so Gollum and Saruman resist his redemptive activity. Even so, the Ring is destroyed. Despite Saruman's attempts at domination and destruction, the Ring eludes him. Despite Gollum's loss of self and resistance to the power of transformative community, he is ultimately responsible for the Ring's destruction. The world is saved precisely because Gollum so desired the Ring that he would stop at nothing to have that all-consuming desire sated. In Ilúvatar's Providence, Gollum finishes the task that was beyond Frodo's limited strength.

Perceiving the World

In *The Lord of the Rings*, spiritual perception is tied to growth in virtue, and transformative community fosters this kind of growth. Because of this, the Children of Ilúvatar can learn to see and experience the world on both a physical and a spiritual level. Here, Tolkien fits within the Christian tradition surrounding spiritual perception, but he builds upon it, too. Where the tradition typically posits that the object of spiritual sight is the person of God,[27] Tolkien shows that we can also see the world and its inhabitants with this spiritual sight.

This is clear in Sam Gamgee, who is ennobled through his fellowship with Frodo, but does not attain the kind of Elvishness that Frodo does, and this is good. Sam's narrative demonstrates that everyone can learn to perceive spiritual things, while demonstrating that the hobbitish way of perceiving the world also carries spiritual weight—not despite its humility, but precisely because of it. The insight of Hobbits, rather than being a kind of perception that they must grow out of, offers a way of viewing the world that attends to its fabric and aims to live in harmony with it. Rather than seeing through the things around them to the deeper spiritual realities they contain, hobbits see the ordinary in things.[28] They can see through the lofty and great to the humble within. It is no accident that it is Merry and Pippin who find food, drink, and tobacco in the flotsam of Isengard, and not Aragorn or Legolas (*TT*, III, ix).

Despite their appearances, hobbits are tough and willing to endure hardship and loss when they must. This readiness to go without further spurs their love for and enjoyment of the good things in life, which is born out of the peace they inhabit and their contentment with the ordinary things in life. This close familiarity with the ordinary empowers them to see the ordinary in all things.

Hobbits are not disposed to seeing the grand picture, the heights or the depths, in part because they recognize that is not truly their place, that is not where they belong—not because of any fault in hobbit nature or inability to shape world events, but because on the heights their simple, ordinary life can be lost from view and it is in the ordinary and peaceful that they truly thrive.[29] They value the prosaic and see in it a good that the tradition of the spiritual senses might be prone to miss. Tolkien sanctifies the everyday, where the tradition around spiritual perception might want to see through it to what's beyond. The hobbits' narrative in *The Lord of the Rings* demonstrates the dual reality of spiritual sight: that a vision of the heights and depths is available to everyone, and that the vision of the ordinary between those heights and depths is also good. Both are ways of seeing the world in the light of God, even though they differ. Where one can see the grand narrative of redemption, the other sees the constant goodness of creation. This touches on Tolkien's assertions in *On Fairy Stories* that fantasy should aid in our recovery:

> We should look at green again, and be startled anew (but not blinded) by blue and yellow and red. We should meet the centaur and the dragon, and then perhaps suddenly behold, like the ancient shepherds, sheep, and dogs, and horses— and wolves. (*OFS*, 83)

Tolkien believed that fantasy could help us to see the world around us with new eyes, and that is just what the perspective of Hobbits can do. It can remind us of the good around us, the pleasure in simple things, the joy in good food and good company. The perspective of Hobbits offers the remedy to greed and possessiveness in that hobbits see the world "as we are (or were) meant to see [it]—as [something] apart from ourselves" (*OFS*, 83).[30] This kind of vision ennobles and re-enchants the world.

As with the perception of Providence, this perception of the world has at least two facets. One, which I have been discussing, has to do with perceiving the ordinary as good in itself, valuing it and appreciating it. It is seeing things as ingredients in our ordinary good life. The other re-enchants the world. By appreciating and loving the world as something other than themselves, the hobbits can also perceive the mystery of the world around them. Because it is something other than them that has a life of its own beyond them, they can live in peace with it as being more than they can know or grasp. These two visions of the ordinary must go together. To live well in a hobbit-like way means living in harmony with things that we do not control and respecting their otherness. The hobbits' vision balances a sacramental appreciation for the mystery of the world with a recognition of its ordinariness. They are at home with the mystery of the world as other than them and with the world as familiar.

Hobbits are specially equipped through their intimacy with the earth, their natural peace-loving nature, and their contentment with the ordinary to really see the mundane around them. They are able, as Sam is with the Southron (*TT*, IV, iv), to become in some sense one with the object of their perception. They can perceive along with rather than in isolation from what they attend to, precisely because they can appreciate and respect the other as other.

Perceiving the Other

Another facet of spiritually perceiving the world—perceiving it as both mysterious and mundane—is perceiving the others who inhabit that world with spiritual sight. While this is related to perceiving Providence—particularly in seeing others with hope and recognizing the potential for redemption within the world and within others—this is less about perceiving possibilities than it is about perceiving realities. While spiritual sight can see the possibility for redemption, it can also see the actuality of their souls.

Frodo's ennoblement is evident to those who look on him with this kind of sight. Gandalf sees it (*FR*, II, i), Galadriel sees it (*FR*, II, vii), and Faramir sees it (*TT*, IV, v). They see it in his ability to perceive that which is hidden, in an Elvish air about him, and in the light growing stronger and brighter within him. When Gandalf sees this light in Frodo, he recognizes that it is in direct contrast to the Ring's influence and recognizes that if Frodo's body had continued to thin out, it would have done nothing to dim the brightness of his soul. In fact, Gandalf perceives that his thinning might only make his ennoblement more obvious since his body would become translucent and thereby unable to obscure the brightness of the soul housed within (*FR*, II, i). But this kind of perception is narrated most often through Sam, who also sees the actual ennoblement of Frodo's soul, especially in contrast to Gollum's corruption.

Sam sees Frodo's suffering, sees how heavy the burden of bearing the Ring becomes, and sees that these cannot diminish the brightness, but only cause it to grow stronger. Before the hobbits encounter Faramir and his men in Ithilien, Sam watches Frodo sleep, and "he was reminded suddenly of Frodo as he had lain, asleep in the house of Elrond, after his deadly wound. Then as he had kept watch Sam had noticed that at times a light seemed to be shining faintly within; but now the light was even clearer and stronger" (*TT*, IV, iv). Frodo's resistance to the Ring's temptations seems to have increased the brightness Sam already saw within him so many months before. But this increasing brightness is even more clear when Sam sees Frodo and Gollum together. Then it is as though a veil is lifted and rather than seeing just the physical bodies in front of him, he sees the souls within. In the end, this even allows him to see Gollum with pity (*RK*, VI, iii).

Sam sees Frodo and Gollum in this way on two occasions. In both, the contrast between Frodo's ennoblement and Gollum's corruption is clear. Sam sees the echo of this reality in their bodies, of course, but he also sees more deeply into the reality of the two souls before him than he typically does. He sees the lowliness of Gollum's withered soul in contrast to the ennobled gleam of Frodo's, which is being constantly tested and pressed by the temptations of bearing the Ring. Sam first demonstrates this sight during the taming of Sméagol, when,

> For a moment it appeared to Sam that his master had grown and Gollum had shrunk: a tall stern shadow, a mighty lord who hid his brightness in grey cloud, and at his feet a little whining dog. Yet the two were in some way akin and not alien: they could reach one another's minds. (*TT*, IV, i)

Here, Sam's spiritual sight is revealed in two parts: first in recognizing the state of their souls, but also in recognizing their kinship. He sees that Frodo and Gollum can understand each other in a way that he cannot. They both know what it is to bear the Ring and to suffer under its oppressive weight. The first recognition is of the ennoblement of Frodo's soul and the corruption of Gollum's. These are truths Sam would surely have known and acknowledged, but to see them so clearly is not typical. He sees deeply and does not just mentally acknowledge what he already knows to be true. This is an actual sight into what is normally only demonstrated in words and deeds.

The second recognition is perhaps the deeper of the two since it sees the commonality between two such disparate souls. It is a recognition of the potential for transformative community between them. It is telling that Sam does not share in this kinship, and so he never fully trusts Gollum because he cannot understand him as Frodo does. While it demonstrates the potential for Gollum to be ennobled and to become like Frodo, it also emphasizes Frodo's potential to become like Gollum.

The second instance intentionally echoes the first, and Sam himself acknowledges the resonance. After Gollum's attack on Frodo and Sam on the path up Mount Doom Tolkien writes,

> Then suddenly, as before under the eaves of the Emyn Muil, Sam saw these two rivals with other vision. A crouching shape, scarcely more than the shadow of a living thing, a creature now wholly ruined and defeated, yet filled with a hideous lust and rage; and before it stood stern, untouchable now by pity, a figure robed in white, but at its breast it held a wheel of fire. Out of the fire there spoke a commanding voice. (*RK*, VI, iii)[31]

Frodo draws on the power of the Ring at this point just as he warned Gollum he would (*TT*, IV, i), which explains the voice and its origin, but not the white robes.[32] The wheel of fire stands in contrast to the pure white robes that Saruman once wore and Gandalf now wears. This should not be read as the Ring making Frodo into an anti-Gandalf, but rather as demonstrating Frodo's ennoblement into the "image" of Gandalf, or at least into a more Elvish hobbitness in line with the ennoblement of the humble that is Tolkien's key interest. Wood is right to see a kind of transfiguration in this scene; he is right to assert that Sam is "given a sudden mystical vision of his friend"; but the glimpse is not of "a new Saruman who has returned to replace Gandalf."[33] Rather, it is a glimpse of Frodo's ennobled spirit. The inner brightness Sam has seen growing in him now suffuses Frodo's whole being. His outer appearance, at least to Sam's eyes, matches the inner reality of his soul.

CONCLUSION

By highlighting the goodness of a lowly, hobbitish engagement with spiritual sight, Tolkien offers a unique perspective on spiritual perception that reinforces facets of the tradition while helpfully expanding it. The lives of hobbits demonstrate the unity of body and spirit that define humanity, and emphasize the reality that earthy, common things are just as rich with spiritual meaning as the high and lofty. By narrating the value of directing spiritual perception toward the world and the other, Tolkien makes a powerful endorsement for allowing spiritual perception to be directed toward objects other than the divine.

Since we are spiritual-corporeal entities and our fiction will be populated with people like us in many respects, it is fitting that these fictional others would be able to disclose spiritual truths through their lives and actions. As they perceive their secondary world, their spiritual eyes may see truths that can enlighten and enliven us in the primary world. Perhaps in reading *The Lord of the Rings* we will be empowered to see the world as hobbits do, humbly perceiving the mundane in all things and through that humility gaining a new knowledge of ourselves. Or perhaps we will find hope in seeing Providence at work. But, if nothing else, our close association with these uniquely embodied individuals allows us to perceive those around us with clearer sight, and in seeing them more clearly come to feel the pity and compassion for them that Gandalf and Frodo exemplified.

NOTES

1. See Trevor B. Williams, "Nazgûl and the Perversion of Spiritual Senses," in *Theology and Tolkien: Practical Theology*, ed. Douglas Estes (Lanham: Lexington/Fortress, 2023), 191–207.

2. Adapted from my PhD thesis, "Spiritual Formation in Tolkien's Legendarium."

3. "It was in fairy-stories that I first divined the potency of the words, and the wonder of the things, such as stone, and wood, and iron; tree and grass; house and fire; bread and wine" (*OFS*, 86).

4. "What is at stake is always man as a spiritual-corporeal reality in the concrete process of living." Hans Urs von Balthasar, *The Glory of the Lord: A Theological Aesthetics I: Seeing the Form*, ed. Joseph Fessio, S.J., and John Riches, trans. Erasmo Leiva-Merikakis (Edinburgh: T&T Clark, 1982), 384.

5. Germaine Paulo Walsh sees physical dissolution as paradigmatic for all the evil creatures within Tolkien's mythology. She writes, "All of the evil characters in the *legendarium* undergo a process of physical alteration, losing their original beauty and wholesomeness, and this loss is a sign of more fundamental loss of the capacity for wisdom and sympathetic understanding, for creativity, for love and friendship." Germaine Paulo Walsh, "Philosophic Poet: J.R.R. Tolkien's Modern Response to an Ancient Quarrel," in *Tolkien among the Moderns*, ed. Ralph C. Wood (Notre Dame: University of Notre Dame Press, 2015), 24.

6. Many scholars have noted connections between Tolkien and von Balthasar. For just a few, see: Lisa Coutras, *Tolkien's Theology of Beauty: Majesty, Splendor, and Transcendence in Middle-earth* (New York: Palgrave Macmillan, 2016); Jeffrey L. Morrow, "J.R.R. Tolkien and C.S. Lewis in Light of Hans Urs Von Balthasar," *Renascence* 56.3 (2004): 180–96; Mark Sebanc, "J.R.R. Tolkien: Lover of the Logos," *Communio* 20 (1993): 84–106; and Williams, "Nazgûl."

7. Von Balthasar, *Seeing the Form*, 405. In *Morgoth's Ring* Tolkien makes the connection between body and soul explicit when he observes that "their bodies had an effect upon their spirits" (*Morgoth*, 400).

8. For a similar perspective, see Maximus Confessor, *Maximus Confessor: Selected Writings*, ed. John Farina, trans. George C. Berthold, CWS (Mahwah: Paulist, 1985), 196. In "The Church's Mystagogy," Maximus likens the relationship between the visible and invisible to that of body and soul, saying that in both cases, "neither of these elements joined to the other in unity denies or displaces the other according to the law of the one who has bound them together." Frederick D. Aquino summarizes Maximus' perspective nicely, noting that for Maximus, "the natural state of the self, as intended by God, entails continuity, not division, between body and soul." Frederick D. Aquino, "Maximus the Confessor," in *The Spiritual Senses: Perceiving God in Western Christianity*, ed. Paul L. Gavrilyuk and Sarah Coakley (Cambridge: Cambridge University Press, 2012), 108.

9. Von Balthasar, *Seeing the Form*, 406. Yves De Maeseneer helpfully explores the relevance of this line of thinking, writing: "Today, von Balthasar would have to stress more than he did in a context of 'anti-incarnational' tendencies that the spiritual senses are not only bodily, but also spiritual." Yves De Maeseneer, "Retrieving the Spiritual Senses in the Wake of Hans Urs von Balthasar," *Communio Viatorum* 55.3 (2013): 287.

10. In *Seeing the Form*, von Balthasar refers to perception "as a fully human act of encounter" (365) and to humanity's essential state as "being-with-others" (381) in which "Man always finds himself within the real, and the most real reality is the Thou—his fellow-man and the God who created him and who is calling him" (405).

11. Robert Stuart brings up some valid points about Sam's ennoblement in his *Tolkien, Race, and Racism in Middle-earth* (New York: Palgrave Macmillan, 2022), 316. However, Stuart's critique, narrowly focused as it is, does not account for the

spiritual dimension of ennoblement (*Letters*, 237). For Tolkien, ennoblement is not just an elevation of standing among the peoples of Middle-earth. It is also the sanctification—setting apart and making holy—of those who experience it. In this context, ennoblement is available to everyone regardless of hierarchy, and has nothing to do with superiority or subordination. Unsurprisingly, it is in keeping with the Beatitudes (Matt 5:3–11) and the *Magnificat* (Luke 1:46–55).

12. Sarah Coakley, "Gregory of Nyssa," in Gavrilyuk and Coakley, *Spiritual Senses*, 55. Coakley has Gregory's "On the Soul and the Resurrection" squarely in focus, particularly Macrina's emphasis on the inability of "small-souled folk" to see with spiritual sight; see Gregory of Nyssa, "On the Soul and the Resurrection," in *Saint Gregory of Nyssa: Ascetical Works*, trans. Virginia Woods Callahan, FC 58 (Washington, DC: Catholic University of America Press, 1967), 202.

13. See, for example, Faramir's interaction with Gollum (*TT*, IV, vi) and Sam's description of meeting with Galadriel (*FR*, II, vii).

14. In equating ennoblement and sanctification, Tolkien may be drawing on the language of the *Catechism of the Catholic Church* and Vatican II documents such as *Lumen gentium*. These documents state that the Church "purifies, strengthens, elevates and ennobles" people (*Lumen gentium* 13), that "Like any other human activity, art is not an absolute end in itself, but is ordered to and ennobled by the ultimate end of man" (*CCC* 2501), and perhaps most tellingly, "It is in Christ, Redeemer and Savior, that the divine image, disfigured in man by the first sin, has been restored to its original beauty and ennobled by the grace of God" (*CCC* 1701).

15. Coakley, "Gregory of Nyssa," 48. See Gregory, "On the Soul and the Resurrection," 202.

16. Origen, "The Two Eagles, the Cedar, the Flourishing Vine (Ezekiel 17:1–7)," in *Origen: Homilies 1–14 on Ezekiel*, ed. Dennis D. McManus, trans. Thomas P. Scheck, ACW 62 (New York: Newman Press, 2010), 137.

17. Karl Rahner, "The 'Spiritual Senses' According to Origen," in *Theological Investigations XVI: Experience of the Spirit: Source of Theology*, trans. David Morland O.S.B. (London: Darton, Longman and Todd, 1979), 87.

18. Gregory, "On the Soul and the Resurrection," 202.

19. Coakley, "Gregory of Nyssa," 48.

20. I am *not* saying that there is anything inherently wrong with this hobbitish sense of the world. In fact, there is something good and right about the ordinariness of Hobbit vision as I discuss later.

21. Saruman and Denethor had already taken steps down this path before their encounters with Sauron through the *palantíri*. See, for example, "Saruman's integrity 'had been undermined by purely personal pride and lust for the domination of his own will. His study of the Rings had caused this, for his pride believed that he could use them, or It, in defiance of any other will. He, having lost any devotion to other persons or causes, was open to the domination of a superior will, to its threats, and to its display of power'" (*UT*, 413). See also, "In the days of his wisdom, Denethor would not presume to use it to challenge Sauron, knowing the limits of his own strength. But his wisdom failed; and I fear that as the peril of his realm grew he looked in the Stone and was deceived" (*RK*, V, vii).

22. In *Cry of the Earth, Cry of the Poor*, Leonardo Boff could have easily been describing Saruman in his discussion of power and its relationship to the natural world: "The issue is the will to power as domination. This will to domination is sometimes manifested as annihilating the power of the other (oppression), sometimes as subjecting it (subordination), and sometimes as co-opting and harnessing it (hegemony). Power is established as the point around which everything is organized. This domination strategy stirs the impulses to command everything, control everything, force everything, make everything fit, and subject everything." Leonardo Boff, *Cry of the Earth, Cry of the Poor* (Maryknoll, NY: Orbis, 1997), 74.

23. Frodo's moral fiber also prepares him for his encounter with the mirror of Galadriel. That Sam is also invited to look in the Mirror demonstrates that, for Tolkien, the spiritual senses are available to all, even the lowliest.

24. This does not mean that *only* the large-souled and ennobled can perceive in these kinds of ways. I discuss this below, in the final two sections of this chapter.

25. Tolkien writes, "it seemed to Manwë that the evil of Melkor was cured. For Manwë was free from evil and could not comprehend it, and he knew that in the beginning, in the thought of Ilúvatar, Melkor had been even as he; and he saw not to the depths of Melkor's heart, and did not perceive that all love had departed from him forever" (*Silmarillion*, 65–66).

26. The *Ainulindalë* narrates this reality (*Silmarillion*, 15–22). Melkor's marring of Arda neither breaks it nor destroys it, despite his intentions. When Ilúvatar shows the Ainur a vision of Arda before speaking it into existence, he tells them "that no theme may be played that hath not its uttermost source in me, nor can any alter the music in my despite. For he that attempteth this shall prove but mine instrument in the devising of things more wonderful, which he himself hath not imagined" (*Silmarillion*, 17). What Melkor intends for evil, Ilúvatar redeems. This redemptive potential is inherent in the very fabric of Arda Marred.

27. Or the person of God as communicated through the Eucharist, the Church, or the beatific vision. The tradition takes biblical passages like Matt 5:8, 1 Cor 13:12, and 2 Cor 2:18 seriously, and recognizes that since God is spirit, this kind of seeing requires more than mere physical sight. The beatific vision is often discussed in terms like those Aquinas used when he wrote, "The supreme and perfect happiness of the intellectual nature consists in seeing God." Thomas Aquinas, *Summa Contra Gentiles, Books I–IV*, trans. Laurence Shapcote, vol. 12 of *Latin/English Edition of the Works of St. Thomas Aquinas* (Steubenville, OH: Emmaus Academic, 2018), 109. In summarizing the moves early scholastic theologians made, Gavrilyuk and Coakley observe "a sharper focus, for example, [on] the relation of the spiritual senses to the Eucharist, the ecclesial 'mystical body of Christ' and the beatific vision"; from the introduction to Gavrilyuk and Coakley, *Spiritual Senses*, 14.

28. Much is made, particularly in the Prologue to *The Lord of the Rings*, of the peaceful existence hobbits enjoyed. Tolkien writes that hobbits "love peace and quiet and good tilled earth: a well-ordered and well-farmed countryside was their favorite haunt" (*FR*, Prologue); have "*a close friendship with the earth*" (*FR*, Prologue, emphasis mine); "were, as a rule, generous and not greedy, but contented and moderate" (*FR*, Prologue); and "usually kept the laws of free will, because they were The

Rules (as they said), both ancient and just" (*FR*, Prologue). Similarly, "at no time had Hobbits of any kind been warlike, and they had never fought among themselves" (*FR*, Prologue), yet "ease and peace had left this people still curiously tough. They were, if it came to it, difficult to daunt or to kill . . . Though slow to quarrel, and for sport killing nothing that lived, they were doughty at bay" (*FR*, Prologue). It is precisely in this peaceful, bucolic existence that the hobbits' strength resides, which is why Bilbo gives the story of *The Hobbit* the alternate title of *There and Back Again* (*RK*, VI, ix), why "The Scouring of the Shire" is such an important ending for *The Lord of the Rings* (*RK*, VI, viii), and why Frodo's inability to remain in the Shire is so tragic for him and his friends.

29. Merry and Pippin recognize this to be true in the Houses of Healing (*RK*, V, viii).

30. Even Pippin's desire to look into the *palantír* is not out of a desire to possess or acquire, but out of curiosity, a desire to *know*.

31. Ralph Wood sees this as the voice of the Ring speaking through Frodo's mouth, a kind of demonic ventriloquism at work. Ralph C. Wood, "Tolkien and Postmodernism," in *Tolkien among the Moderns*, ed. Ralph C. Wood (Notre Dame: University of Notre Dame Press, 2015), 265. I think, in line with Hammond and Scull, this is taking things too far. While the Ring is an embodiment of Sauron himself—it is in fact the greater part of his power and self, distilled into one small object—it is not presented as having the power of speech: a power reserved for living things. Giving the Ring the power of speech is "to argue for a sentience within the Ring beyond its ability, established early in the story, to 'look after itself' with the aim of eventual return to Sauron." Wayne G. Hammond and Christina Scull, *The Lord of the Rings: A Reader's Companion* (London: HarperCollins, 2014), 616. The Ring is clearly presented as having a will, but its power to affect that will is limited. Some may cite the Witch-King's pause upon leaving Minas Morgul as evidence of the Ring's ability to speak: "Maybe it was the Ring that called to the Wraith-lord, and for a moment he was troubled, sensing some other power within his valley" (*TT*, IV, viii). Rather than giving voice to the Ring, this passage seems to convey the Nazgûl's sensitivity to the *power* of the Ring. It can work on the one who bears it and on the evil thoughts and bents of those around it, but there is no indication that it can act in the way Wood suggests.

32. This scene points toward the very real potential for ennoblement and corruption to be at work concurrently within one soul, pulling it in opposing directions.

33. Wood, "Tolkien and Postmodernism," 265.

BIBLIOGRAPHY

Aquinas, Thomas. *Summa Contra Gentiles, Books I–IV*. Translated by Laurence Shapcote, Volume 12 of *Latin/English Edition of the Works of St. Thomas Aquinas*. Steubenville, OH: Emmaus Academic, 2018.

Aquino, Frederick D. "Maximus the Confessor." Pages 104–20 in *The Spiritual Senses: Perceiving God in Western Christianity*. Edited by Paul L. Gavrilyuk and Sarah Coakley. Cambridge: Cambridge University Press, 2012.

Balthasar, Hans Urs von. *The Glory of the Lord: A Theological Aesthetics Vol. 1: Seeing the Form*. Edited by Joseph Fessio, S.J., and John Riches. Translated by Erasmo Leiva-Merikakis. Edinburgh: T&T Clark, 1982.

Boff, Leonardo. *Cry of the Earth, Cry of the Poor*. Ecology and Justice. Maryknoll, NY: Orbis, 1997.

Catholic Church. *Catechism of the Catholic Church*. 2nd ed. Vatican City: Libreria Editrice Vaticana, 1997.

Catholic Church. "Dogmatic Constitution on the Church: Lumen Gentium," in *Vatican II Documents*. Vatican City: Libreria Editrice Vaticana, 2011.

Coakley, Sarah. "Gregory of Nyssa." Pages 36–55 in *The Spiritual Senses: Perceiving God in Western Christianity*. Edited by Paul L. Gavrilyuk and Sarah Coakley. Cambridge: Cambridge University Press, 2012.

Coutras, Lisa. *Tolkien's Theology of Beauty: Majesty, Splendor, and Transcendence in Middle-earth*. New York: Palgrave Macmillan, 2016.

De Maeseneer, Yves. "Retrieving the Spiritual Senses in the Wake of Hans Urs von Balthasar." *Communio Viatorum* 55.3 (2013): 276–90.

Gregory of Nyssa. "On the Soul and the Resurrection." Pages 195–272 in *Saint Gregory of Nyssa: Ascetical Works*. Translated by Virginia Woods Callahan. FC 58. Washington, DC: Catholic University of America Press, 1967.

Hammond, Wayne G., and Christina Scull. *The Lord of the Rings: A Reader's Companion*. London: HarperCollins, 2014.

Kisor, Yvette. "Incorporeality and Transformation in *The Lord of the Rings*." Pages 36–66 in *The Body in Tolkien's Legendarium: Essays on Middle-earth Corporeality*. Edited by Christopher Vaccaro. Jefferson, NC: McFarland, 2013.

Komornicka, Jolanta N. "The Ugly Elf: Orc Bodies, Perversion, and Redemption in *The Silmarillion* and *The Lord of the Rings*." Pages 132–52 in *The Body in Tolkien's Legendarium: Essays on Middle-earth Corporeality*. Edited by Christopher Vaccaro. Jefferson, NC: McFarland, 2013.

Maximus Confessor. *Maximus Confessor: Selected Writings*. Edited by John Farina. Translated by George C. Berthold. CWS. Mahwah: Paulist, 1985.

Morrow, Jeffrey L. "J.R.R. Tolkien and C.S. Lewis in Light of Hans Urs von Balthasar." *Renascence* 56.3 (2004): 181–96.

Origen. "Homily 11: The Two Eagles, the Cedar, the Flourishing Vine (Ezekiel 17:1–7)." Pages 137–146 in *Origen: Homilies 1–14 on Ezekiel*. Edited by Dennis D. McManus. Translated by Thomas P. Scheck. ACW 62. New York: Newman Press, 2010.

Rahner, Karl. "The 'Spiritual Senses' According to Origen." Pages 81–103 in *Theological Investigations, Vol. 16 Experience of the Spirit: Source of Theology*. Translated by David Morland O.S.B. London: Darton, Longman and Todd, 1979.

Sebanc, Mark. "J.R.R. Tolkien: Lover of the Logos." *Communio* 20 (1993): 84–106.

Stuart, Robert. *Tolkien, Race, and Racism in Middle-earth*. New York: Palgrave Macmillan, 2022.

Walsh, Germaine Paulo. "Philosophic Poet: J.R.R. Tolkien's Modern Response to an Ancient Quarrel." Pages 7–49 in *Tolkien among the Moderns*. Edited by Ralph C. Wood. Notre Dame: University of Notre Dame Press, 2015.

Williams, Trevor B. "Nazgûl and the Perversion of Spiritual Senses." Pages 191–207 in *Theology and Tolkien: Practical Theology*. Edited by Douglas Estes. Lanham: Lexington/Fortress, 2023.

Wood, Ralph C. "Tolkien and Postmodernism." Pages 247–77 in *Tolkien among the Moderns*. Edited by Ralph C. Wood. Notre Dame: University of Notre Dame Press, 2015.

Chapter 10

A Chance for Metanarrative to Prove Its Quality

Jeremy M. Rios

Popular culture is characterized by hunger—especially, in the West, of hunger for identity. Disenchantment, the rise of individualism, and the demise of Christendom have left people without key reference points from which to draw their sense of self. The result is a gnawing hunger that drives, in the consumption of media, a high demand for vast quantities of metanarrative—exhibited especially in Star Wars, Harry Potter, the Marvel Cinematic Universe, and, of course, *The Lord of the Rings*. Metanarrative, in this sense, identifies an "archetypal story, which provides a schematic world view upon which an individual's experiences and perceptions may be ordered."[1] Each of the above story-worlds functions in this way, offering the consumer a sense of scale, a place of pilgrimage, and, ultimately, a framework in which uncertain identity may discover temporary comfort. With respect to this, Peter Jackson's *The Lord of the Rings* films are exemplar, exhibiting a wide and ongoing influence in watch parties, imaginative subconscious, and memes.

In a striking turn, each of these metanarrative replacements now occupy a space formerly filled by Scripture—they are viewed repeatedly, memorized, and utilized in the interpretation of experience. But whereas the Scriptural metanarrative was (and remains) critical of culture, these media metanarratives are often merely reflective of the culture that produced them. Of course, pop culture is not a neutral producer of consumable metanarrative. Instead, it subtly influences the creation of such media to fit metrics of sale-ability and popularity, metrics that, upon examination, are ulterior to the (traditionally) critical function of metanarrative.

This essay argues that key differences between Tolkien's original works and Jackson's films illustrate the difference between critical and reflective metanarratives. Tolkien's original books are a consciously sub-created meta-narrative that innately criticizes modern culture. We witness elements of this criticism, for example, in Tolkien's prioritization of certain goods (e.g., plain food, deindustrialization, gardening), and against the flash and allure of modern excitements (e.g., in the character of Saruman). We also witness it in his thematic convictions regarding death and self-resignation (for example, in Frodo and Théoden). In contrast to this, Jackson's films present a metanarrative that appears to be more reflective of culture, a transition that is accounted for when we attend to key adaptations in the films—especially those treating of Treebeard, Théoden, and Faramir. These alterations seem to betray the intruding influence of a market-driven pop culture—evidenced especially both in its inability to represent the good and in its projective psychologizing. In the process, Jackson's films end up offering merely a reflective metanarrative that ultimately denudes Tolkien's works of their implicitly critical edge.

In the following sections, I will explore the nature and hunger for metanarrative and point to how Tolkien's books have attained a surprising ascendancy. Following this, I will articulate key differences between critical and reflective metanarratives. Finally, we will turn to Tolkien and Jackson in order to document how their respective works illuminate these metanarrative types.

THE HUNGER FOR METANARRATIVE AND THE (SURPRISING) ASCENDANCY OF TOLKIEN

Over the past fifty years, the concept of 'metanarrative' has come to encapsulate something intrinsic to human identity: it points to the meaning super-structures within which we interpret our human experience. It is perhaps ironic that the emergence of the discourse surrounding metanarratives coincided with the conviction that no such meaning structures were real. This is the sense with which Lyotard picks up the concept of metanarrative in *The Postmodern Condition*, where it makes "an explicit appeal to some grand narrative, such as the dialectics of Spirit, the hermeneutics of meaning, the emancipation of the rational or working subject, or the creation of wealth."[2] In other words, in view of the perceived inadequacy of the metanarratives of Hegel, Gadamer, Marx, and Adam Smith, Lyotard describes what is essential to the postmodern perspective: "I define postmodern as incredulity toward metanarratives."[3] His convictions do not emerge from nothing—in the background, Lyotard is responding specifically to the events of the *Shoah*.[4] It is this framework of horrendous suffering that renders all metanarrative frameworks suspicious, or even invalid. Confronted by such horrors, how could we any longer believe in such superstructures of meaning?

For more than 1,000 years the regnant metanarrative of Western society had been that of Christendom, typified especially in the Christian Scriptures. But seismic changes in the landscape of the self—especially under the influence of the Enlightenment and Freud—have effected an alteration in our approach to meaning. It will be worthwhile to trace these changes, even if in brief.

Charles Taylor's *Sources of the Self* describes a seismic shift in the consciousness of the self throughout history. He documents the transition from an ancient self—which was an integrated, holistic self, bound together in a network of polis, nature, household, and religion—to the disintegrated, individualistic self that is today characterized by autonomy, atomism, and a concept of 'freedom.' The transition between these characterizations—from integrated and communal to atomized and individualist—was the process Weber called *disenchantment*, i.e., "the dissipation of our sense of the cosmos as a meaningful order."[5] To be disenchanted is to have lost one's connection to that former, unifying sense of order.

With this new sense of self arose new anthropologies; regnant among them in the modern world is a Freudian concept of "psychological man," what sociologist Philip Rieff describes as "the latest, and perhaps the supreme—individualist."[6] Where formerly a person might seek wholeness by appeal to a larger frame of meaning, psychological man is isolated and alone; the quest for identity is now inscribed purely within the boundaries of the self. Rieff goes on to describe a new kind of what he calls "theory" that emerges in this situation. Since there is no longer any metanarrative, theory (a way of interpreting the world) "becomes actively concerned with mitigating the daily miseries of living rather than with a therapy of commitment to some healing doctrine of the universe." Therapy in such a context does not deal with faith, "but, rather, power. A good theory becomes the creator of power."[7] Under this new rubric, metanarratives are not forces of intrinsic order but of personal empowerment—used and discarded based on our perception of their benefit. In other words, individualism framed in a milieu that rejects ultimate meaning strives for therapies of power rather than of health or restoration. Disenchanted and individualist man is therefore a solitary psychological entity; cut off from a grand metanarrative, he picks and chooses narratives based on their perceived usefulness to his present circumstances.

These Enlightenment shifts, combined with the rise of individualist man, and responses to horrors like the *Shoah*, have left modern man right where Lyotard described him: incredulous toward metanarratives. Inasmuch as Christian Scripture is understood as such a metanarrative, it is de facto out of court. Rieff writes that "Western culture has had a literary canon, through which its character ideals were conveyed. What canons will replace the scriptural? None, I suppose. We are probably witnessing the end of a cultural history dominated by book religions and word-makers."[8] And yet, the loss of trust *in* metanarrative has not eliminated the hunger *for* metanarratives. The human creature, as Pascal mused, is like a vacuum—seeking to be filled. It is an absence that "he tries in vain to fill with everything around him,"[9] inaugurating what Evelyn Underhill called the "pilgrim longing."[10] The hunger for meaning points to our deep need for meaning—a need, theologically, on par with that for water, food, and shelter. With traditional sources of meaning removed, humans will attempt to fill the gap with other and inferior things. Removed from traditional metanarratives, we will inevitably generate new ones.

"That a new myth of man is developing," observes Rieff, "seems evident to me."[11] If metanarratives are those story superstructures that give meaning and direction to a society—the interpretive framework through which we examine events, find identity, and make decisions—then deprived of such metanarrative, humans will create and adopt new metanarratives. The throne of meaning will not suffer itself to be left vacant. This we have seen conspicuously in the consumption of modern media. The Star Wars *universe*, the Harry Potter *universe*, the Marvel Cinematic *universe*; it is worth stressing that in all three cases the word 'universe' is acting as a kind of cypher for metanarrative. People gather for watch parties, plan weekends to marathon these films, debate the proper order in which they should be watched, develop and distribute fan-fiction and fan-theories, debate which elements are canonical, dispute about minutiae, visit conventions in which they dress (liturgically?) as their favorite characters, quote the books and films endlessly, and generate memes as a means of (prophetic?) critical cultural commentary.[12] In the case of each cinematic (and literary) metanarrative, a fan base is treating its sources with an attention formerly given to Scripture. Metanarrative has not gone away; it has merely been supplanted by lesser lights.[13]

All of these metanarrative functions are fulfilled, today, by *The Lord of the Rings*. Indeed, Tolkien's works have come to occupy a cultural space that would have astonished Tolkien. Middle-earth offers a story-world in which humans locate meaning and significance, whose primary texts are read and re-read as a kind of Scripture, within which its adherents develop theologies and intellectual superstructures that are advanced, debated, and, in a way, even believed. The continuing growth of his readership, combined with the now twenty-year cultural impact of Jackson's films, have boosted his story to heights previously unimaginable. Tolkien's world now possesses a unique, even trenchant space, in our cultural subconscious.

It is a shift that would no doubt alarm Tolkien immensely: *The Lord of the Rings* now occupies a metanarrative space formerly occupied almost solely by Christendom. It has, like these other metanarratives, filled the gap left by the retreat of Scripture. In one respect, this is an unsurprising outcome of Tolkien's genius. Writing about his concept of sub-creation, Tolkien is explicit that the power of creation comes from the Creator; that no author creates his own work, but creates instead by repurposing the work of God:

> Probably every writer making a secondary world, a fantasy, every sub-creator, wishes in some measure to be a real maker, hopes that he is drawing on reality: hopes that the peculiar quality of this secondary world (of not all the details) are derived from Reality, or are flowing into it. If he indeed achieves a quality that can fairly be described by the dictionary definition: 'the inner consistency of reality,' it is difficult to conceive how this can be, if the world does not in some way partake of reality.[14]

No created work comes from nothing, save that creative work originating in the Creator. All human creation is a repurposing of those original materials. And yet humans are given unprecedented freedom in our creative efforts—freedom expressed most clearly in our ability to invent imaginary worlds, languages, histories, and stories. Tolkien puts these convictions into narrative form when he documents the creation of the Dwarves in *The Silmarillion*. There, Aulë is cast in the role of sub-creator, mimicking the creative work of Ilúvatar, who rebukes him: "Why dost thou attempt a thing which thou knowest is beyond thy power and thy authority? For thou hast from me as a gift thy own being only, and no more" (*Silmarillion*, 43). Aulë's creatures have no life of their own; they depend solely on the limited life of Aulë, who nevertheless answers Ilúvatar's challenge sufficiently: "Yet the making of things is in my heart from my own making by thee; and the child of little understanding that makes a play of the deeds of his father may do so without thought of mockery, but because he is a son of his father" (*Silmarillion*, 43). It is difficult not to hear echoes of autobiography in Aulë's words—that Tolkien, in giving life to his creation (Middle-earth), was enacting a loving imitation of the Father's creative power.

On Tolkien's own accounting, his work has life inasmuch as it draws that life from a deeper source. It is on account of this explicitly derivative connection to the Primary World that the metanarratival function of Tolkien's works bears greater similarity to that of Scripture than the function of more recent cultural metanarratives. To be explicit: Tolkien's *The Lord of the Rings* has been so successful at its "inner consistency of reality" that for many of its consumers it is now an easy replacement for Scripture in the primary creation. This is the situation that would doubtless fill Tolkien with alarm. And yet there are critical differences between the two sets of metanarratives—differences that lie in the distinction between critical and reflective metanarratives.

CRITICAL AND REFLECTIVE METANARRATIVES

What are critical and reflective metanarratives, and how are they developed? On the discarded, premodern model, metanarrative provided a theory of being—a way to interpret life and events, a story into which the human person, rightly aligned, would fit him or herself. In this framework, Reiff writes, "Things being what we know them to be, the intellectual and emotional task of life is to make our actions conform to the right order, so that we too can be right."[15] This is the sense in which metanarratives can be understood as critical; they condemn distortion in our world by pointing to what is right. Scripture is a prime example (and remnant) of such a critical metanarrative; its overarching story presents a piercing criticism of our present world order. The Scriptural metanarrative offered a vision for how God viewed reality and how we were to align ourselves with that divine vision, often *against* the comfortable ways of the *status quo*.

That Christian Scripture represents a metanarrative critical of culture is in this respect obvious, and yet it may also be an underexamined premise. We can amass any number of texts which show how God criticizes the world order—condemnations of idolatry (Ps 115), sin (Gen 4:10), compromise with culture (Rev 3:16), of confusion about the nature of God (Ps 50:21). But these discrete texts do not constitute the metanarrative force of Scripture's criticism. In fact, as readers today we are such entrenched individualists that we struggle at times to envision the nature of that criticism. What I mean is that we read the Scriptures, the Word of God, *as disenchanted individualists*. We read for our own personal devotion, as atomized people who approach the text in an atomized way—my verse of the day, my word from the Lord, my inspiration for the moment. We must recall that the whole basis of frustration with misinterpretation of certain Bible texts (such as frequent hullabaloo over Jeremiah 29:11) lies in the reading of the atomized verse apart from its broader context. If Scripture is a true metanarrative (it is!), then its metanarratival characteristics will be embodied in its whole counsel, which offers an unwavering testimony to the otherness of God's ways and the criticism of the world's.

The Lord's Prayer is a superb example of this kind of criticism. Often, it is recited as a kind of mantra—a set of words repeated in obedience, but without much thought given to the individual requests. Attentive readers might focus on the clauses of the prayer as a series of personal petitions, in which the pray-er seeks God's favor in a variety of somewhat disconnected ways. But a closer look reveals two important features. First, that each of the clauses of the prayer is voiced in the imperative; that is, each clause is a clear petition for God to *do* something. Second, that Jesus's prayer falls nicely into two halves. The first four petitions—that God's name be made holy, that God's will be done, that God's Kingdom come, that things on earth be as they are in heaven—*align the human heart with the Kingdom of God*. The second four petitions—for bread, forgiveness, for protection from temptation, and for protection from the evil one—*supply us with what we need to fulfil that Kingdom mission*. Perceived this way, the Lord's Prayer can be apprehended for the critical text that it is: we do not pray it to get what we want, we pray it to align ourselves with God's story *against* the world's. The Lord's Prayer, then, ceases to be a list of individual requests and becomes instead an aperture through which the light of God's Kingdom shines down with critical power upon our world. In this respect, the Lord's Prayer is an archetypal text for critical metanarrative.[16]

Critical metanarrative draws its critical power from what Kierkegaard called the "infinite qualitative difference."[17] There exists, in other words, an infinite, transcendent gap between God and the world. To acknowledge that gap is to admit that the Kingdom of God—by its very otherness, transcendence, and superiority—criticizes us. Transcendently-sourced metanarratives cannot but be critical of imminent reality. By contrast, reflective metanarratives are birthed from imminence, and, in our modern context, from a situation that stands in bold *rejection* of holistic and traditional models. Instead of metanarrative drawing from and then pointing to a higher order (one that is sublime) in which humans find an ultimate right-relatedness, or even cure, now imminent metanarratives are useful or useless depending almost solely on their empowerment. Theory, remember, is only good when it empowers. The result, however, is that instead of modern metanarratives drawing their strength from an otherworldliness, they become simple projections of a limited this-worldly perspective. Malleable and impressionable, they are especially susceptible to the influence of three features: hunger, ego, and marketing.

Hunger we have treated already—the absence of a metanarrative does not eliminate the need for metanarrative; the throne of meaning will not suffer vacancy. But hunger is not a discriminating producer of value. In this respect, Proverbs is instructive: "A sated man loathes honey, but to a famished man any bitter thing is sweet" (Prov 27:7 NASB). To those who are starving for meaning, any meaning—even thin, poorly constructed, immature, vulgar, uncharitable, bad meaning—will suffice. Hunger's drive to fill the vacancy of meaning will not, on its own, necessarily gravitate to either nutritious or satisfying meanings.

In addition to hunger driving the creation of metanarratives, there is the impact of an invasive ego. C.S. Lewis describes two different kinds of reading in *An Experiment in Criticism*. In the first, "Egoistic Castle Building," a given reader reads from a starting point of selfishness in order to experience all the benefits of the author's world, while laying aside all the liabilities; he travels to the Alps, wins the girl, or is the hero of the adventure. He reads to insert himself—his preferences and tastes—*into* the work. Lewis calls the second kind of reading "Disinterested Castle Building." Here, the reader experiences the book as a spectator—the ego has been sidelined, and the author's purposes are given foreground.[18] It is not difficult to imagine how Rieff's psychological man, in his trenchantly individualist outlook, prefers egoistic narratives that favor power rather than holism. Heroes and villains alike in modern metanarratives must have satisfying backstories and motivations that are explicitly psychological. Tony Stark, Anakin Skywalker, and Harry Potter are each explicitly shaped by their common psychological profiling: loss of parents. With respect to this, their narratives are not crafted to 'fit' with respect to an overarching aesthetic whole, but present a magnified (and simplistic) representation of our own neuroses. Perhaps nowhere does this ego projection appear more clearly than in Jung's psychological mythology (which sits explicitly behind *Star Wars*)—that within anima, shadow, mother, and father, the troubled human can discover a tailor-made sense of well-being.[19]

Lastly, reflective metanarrative is crafted under the influence of a market—of sale-ability. Manufacture of these stories are subject to indexes of popularity, universality, and marketability. (As if identity were subject to the dictates of supply and demand!) Naturally, metanarratives birthed from a dominating market context will curtail any critical aspect. Prophets, after all, are regularly stoned for the messages they are tasked to bring. And so, the feel-good supplants the discomfiting, wide appeal dismisses the particularity of a vision of the good, and an ugly democratization of 'what sells to the masses' replaces a commitment to the true.

Reflective metanarratives are thus intrinsically imminent: they are the products of hunger, ego, and the market; bound to a naturalistic ethos, they are of necessity more mirror than window; like the well into which we look deeply and see our own faces reflected back at us. They are culturally comfortable, and not culturally challenging. In their imminence, they cannot be properly critical.

Under the influence of reflective metanarratives, we experience a dual confusion: about what is life-giving, and about goodness. Baron Friedrich von Hügel articulates a vision for what is life-giving when he distinguishes between 'zest' and 'excitement.' *Zest*, in his thinking, refers to those life-giving elements that provide "balance and centrality," a "natural warmth." By contrast, *excitement* "is the pleasure which comes from breaking loose, from fragmentariness, from losing our balance and centrality." Ironically, the pursuit of excitement only enervates our spirit, leaving us merely to "long for more excitement."[20] Zest characterizes the life-giving, the nourishing, the wholesome; it is the reward for attending to the critical metanarrative. Excitement appeals to us, but is ultimately life-draining; it is the fragmented pursuit of a psyche hungry for distraction. The difference between these two is illustrated even more clearly in reflective metanarrative's approach to goodness. With a keen perception into this dynamic, Simone Weil writes that "imaginary evil is romantic and varied; real evil is gloomy, monotonous, barren, boring. Imaginary good is boring; real good is always new, marvelous, intoxicating."[21] Weil's insight has been proved again and again, as a catena of films, books, and television shows cater to the simplicity of attractive evil and repeat ad nauseum the banality of good. Evil is, in fiction, mysteriously exciting; while in reality it is goodness that gives us a true zest. Reflective metanarrative, under the influence of hunger, the ego, and the market, characteristically steers away from the zestful good, trending instead toward an exciting evil.

THE LORD OF THE RINGS AS CRITICAL (BOOKS) AND REFLECTIVE (FILMS) METANARRATIVES

In light of the above discussion, we may now turn to exploring key differences between the book and film versions of *The Lord of the Rings*. This will not be an exhaustive summary of differences, nor will I engage in any substantive comparison between the media. Instead, I will highlight two exemplary aspects of critical metanarrative from the books, and then note two exemplary reflective aspects from the films, each rooted in a deviation from the book.

Tolkien's Books as Critical Metanarratives

Tolkien's original books embody many aspects of a critical metanarrative—that is, of an over-story that offers tacit criticism of our world. But we must be clear that such criticisms are never really Tolkien's conscious intent. Tolkien writes with no preconceived message, no agenda for the characters, no allegory for his ring. He is in fact explicit in his disavowal of allegory in the introduction to the books: "As for any inner meaning or 'message,' it has in the intention of the author none" (*FR*, foreword). But the books were self-consciously a sub-creation, and Tolkien is explicit that "*The Lord of the Rings* is of course a fundamentally religious and Catholic work; unconsciously so at first, but consciously in the revision" (*Letters*, 142). In other words, Tolkien's consonance with a critical metanarrative is rooted in this vital connection between Middle-earth and the Primary World. Tolkien clarifies this connective relationship further in a letter to Stanley Unwin, "do not let Rayner suspect 'Allegory.'" Instead, while his characters "contain universals . . . they never represent them as such" (*Letters*, 109). In the same way that Tolkien's characters have 'life' because they participate in certain universals, so his sub-creation offers a critical metanarrative because it participates in the deeper criticism rooted in the great Christian metanarrative.

The nature and scope of this connectivity defies simple categorization, but we might, perhaps, highlight two ways that Tolkien's literary world effects this tacit metanarratival criticism of ours: with respect to goodness and death. Doubtless there are more, but these two emerge most explicitly in contrast with the vision presented by Jackson's films.

To suggest that there is a criticism offered by goodness may at first seem strange—how can goodness criticize? But the nature of this criticism emerges most clearly when we recall Simone Weil's assessment of imaginary good and evil. In the modern Western imaginary world, evil is attractive, appealing, and fun, while good is dull, repulsive, and boring. It is therefore all the more astonishing to reflect on Tolkien's almost unparalleled ability to render goodness appealing—Lothlórien, Rivendell, Ithilien, and Hobbiton are intoxicating; Mordor, Mirkwood, and Moria are geographies of undeniable gloom. Tom Shippey, reflecting on this characteristic wholesomeness, observes that it is "remarkable that Frodo has to be dug out of no less than five 'Homely Houses' before his quest is properly launched." Entrenched in the homeliness of Bag End, Crickhollow, Tom Bombadil's House, *The Prancing Pony*, and Rivendell, Frodo requires various external pressures to move. Shippey continues, "there is a sense that the zest of the story goes not into the dangers but the recoveries."[22] In each case, Tolkien presents compelling visions of the good—embodied especially in things simple, pure, and homely.

By extension, it is worth noting that Tolkien's more explicit critiques of modernity are in fact a subset of his commitment to the goodness of simplicity. Of these, no character represents the allure of the modern more than Saruman, who engineers new orcs, perceives Fangorn as a supply depot, has a machine mind, and "innovates" with the gunpowder at Helm's Deep. But it is Saruman's despoiling of the Shire which creates the most grievous offense against the good. Here there are improvements done that improve nothing—trees cut down, rations limited, no pipe-weed, Sandyman's "new mill" (he is Saruman's most explicit acolyte). Worst of all, there's no beer (*RK*, VI, viii)! If we feel any horror or frustration at these events, it is because in them Tolkien has invested some of the innate and simple goodness of the ordinary world. In bristling at its violation, we are feeling the sting of a critical metanarrative, subtly reminding us that it is the good which is desirable and wholesome, while evil is always wasteful and banal.

The second criticism embedded in Tolkien's books might best be perceived in his attitude toward death. Kevin Aldrich argues convincingly that the primary theme underlying Tolkien's books is one of death and the acceptance of death: "Perhaps the most powerful temptation for both men and Elves in

Tolkien's world—and one which touches us because it reaches to the depths of our being—is to deal with death and time on their own terms rather than the Creator's."[23] There is a season and a time for everything, and the proper attitude of sub-created beings is to live rightly within those seasons, those times. In view of this, the Ring is not a cypher for atomic power, nor it is a metaphor for addiction.[24] Instead, the Ring represents the allure of undue preservation. On this, Tolkien is explicit:

> To attempt by device or 'magic' to recover longevity is thus a supreme folly and wickedness of 'mortals.' Longevity or counterfeit 'immortality' (true immortality is beyond Eä) is the chief bait of Sauron—it leads the small to a Gollum, and the great to a Ringwraith. (*Letters*, 212)

The power of the three Elven rings was a power of preservation—Rivendell and Lothlórien retain their ancient homeliness by virtue of their ringbearing luminaries, who recognize that the loss of the One Ring necessitates the death of what they have for so long labored to preserve. Galadriel's acceptance of that death (of a kind) is therefore a far greater sacrifice than it might appear on the surface.

Aldrich, summarizing his perspective, writes that "*The Lord of the Rings* is about immortality and escape from death. But there is no escape *from* death except *through* death, if at all."[25] The idea that we must accept death—our limitations, our desire for preservation, even our power to effect what preservations we might—is an inherently critical word. It criticizes the human desire to work all the angles, to take every advantage; it prizes a resignation where, as a culture, we refuse any appeal to go gently into that good night. Against this, almost all of Tolkien's heroes resign themselves to a kind of death—Elrond and Galadriel to the demise of their earthly habitations, Gandalf relinquishes control of the resistance to Sauron so that he can save his friends on the bridge of Khazad-dûm (*Letters*, 156). Even Frodo's ultimate failure at Mount Doom is one that Tolkien cast as a kind of meditation on "Lead us not into temptation" (*Letters*, 181). Frodo is led beyond his abilities, he is tempted—and even "apostatizes"!—but even in his failure the greater purposes are achieved, significantly because of Frodo's commitment to mercy. Had he not spared Gollum, Gollum could not have completed the mission. Beneath this there is the suggestion that even in our failures—and perhaps *because* of them—the greater purposes of God may be known. Again, in these resignations lie an ongoing criticism of human power.

I have barely scratched the surface of these two features, but I trust that these comments will sufficiently illustrate how Tolkien's books exhibit an embedded and subversive criticism of the modern world—a subversive goodness and a subversive critique of power.

Jackson's Films as Reflective Metanarratives

By contrast, Peter Jackson's film iterations of *The Lord of the Rings* exhibit the characteristics of a reflective metanarrative—that is, of a metanarrative that reflects the prevailing culture, rather than criticizing it. Such a metanarrative is birthed from hunger, circumscribed by a materialist self, and ultimately engaged in egoistic castle building under the influence of a market mentality. However, we should be explicit at the outset that Jackson's films are no more intentionally reflective metanarratives than Tolkien's books were intentionally critical metanarratives. I do not believe that Jackson has set himself consciously to reflect the preferences of a disenchanted world in his interpretation of this story. All the same, many of these characteristics are present, and they appear most clearly in the film treatments of three characters: Faramir, Treebeard, and Théoden. I will briefly discuss their treatments, then return to how these alterations appear to be the product of reflective metanarrative.

In Tolkien's *The Two Towers*, there are a series of critical junctures where the main characters—Aragorn, Legolas and Gimli, Merry and Pippin, and Frodo and Sam—from within their separate story arcs find what I call "unexpected help." When Aragorn, Legolas and Gimli meet King Théoden of Rohan, he provides unexpected help without delay after he is freed from Wormtongue's spell (*TT*, III, vi). He puts his full trust in Gandalf's counsel, and when a Gondorian messenger arrives to plead for Rohan's help, the good king acts immediately. When Merry and Pippin are swept up by Treebeard in Fangorn Forest, he provides unexpected help to the young hobbits, requiring no special rhetoric or complaint to make him fight Saruman, but making his 'hasty' decision and working steadily to convince the remaining Ents to fight as well (*TT*, III, iv). Most striking of all, Faramir, unlike his brother, when confronted with the One Ring refuses it outright, providing instead a noble and much needed ally to Sam and Frodo on their journey (*TT*, IV, v). But the film interpretation of these events could scarcely be more different. Théoden refuses to help, turning inward under the pretext of "defending his people." It is only much later, after nearly three hours of argument, that he is finally convinced to come to Gondor's aid. Treebeard resists the hobbits' pleas, simply turning back and refusing outright to assist the free peoples. It is only when he sees some burnt trees that he becomes 'angry' and (completely out of Entish character!) does something truly hasty in rushing off to war. Worst of all, Faramir is not a heroic helper—instead, he threatens the hobbits, kidnapping them, intending to bring the ring as a prize to his father, assisting them only somewhat reluctantly at the end.

There are two ways (at least) that these alterations point to the influence of a reflective metanarrative. In the first place—and drawing again from the language of von Hügel—they exhibit a preference for excitement rather than zest. Simple motivations are cinematically boring; complex motivations ratchet up tension. Lurking beneath this is a belief, expressed concisely by Rick Moranis as Dark Helmet in *Spaceballs*: "So, Lonestar, now you see that evil will always triumph, because good is dumb."[26] If good characters are dumb, and if imaginary goodness is boring, then in choosing the path of excitement Jackson's films have—however subtly—participated in the creation of an alluring but false imaginary evil. Tolkien himself detected this trend when reading an early film treatment of his work. There he perceived that there was a "preference for fights" (*Letters*, 210). The exciting (almost always, in blockbuster films) wins out over more mundane goodnesses.

But there is yet a deeper criticism to offer. Since Jackson's interpretations are birthed from a disenchanted world, they cannot tolerate unalloyed goodness. There can be no heroes in a disenchanted world; the heroes belong to the old narrative. Therefore, the simple goodness of Treebeard, redeemed Théoden, and Faramir must be spiced up, made complex with additional motives and interest. Like Saruman they have become many-colored; white was no longer good enough (*FR*, II, ii).

A second aspect of reflective metanarrative appears in the perspective of Rieff's psychological man. The human, no longer searching for his fit within a cosmic frame, strives instead for a sense of psychological inner peace. But instead of looking to that which is outside herself for identity, she engages in endless journeys of psychological self-discovery. The result is nothing more than a projection of our own cultural anxieties and weaknesses outward, rather than a reflection of eternal realities back upon us. Shippey muses that the alterations to Théoden's character might be explained by "different politico-military expectations of a 21st century audience," but surely it is just as likely that we have projected our own insecurities into Théoden's character—unable otherwise to account for his sense of duty and self-sacrifice.[27] Nowhere is this armchair psychologizing more evident than in the exposition and display of Faramir's thinly projected Freudian daddy-issues. In Tolkien's work, Faramir is self-assured, confident in his identity; it is, perhaps, his very confidence that allows him to resist the Ring. In the films, he must become a mirror of our own fears and anxieties, a weak and insecure projection of a pervasive cultural fear—the desire for paternal approval. He is no longer of the great; he is just as small as we are. In each case, these psychological interpretations betray clear examples of Lewis's egoistic castle building, where the overriding ego of the modern reader muddles the narrative with its own psychological interpretations. But the result is a metanarrative that looks too much like our world, one that in its implicit narcissism robs us of the escape that might provide a true refreshment of spirit. The Faramir of Tolkien's critical metanarrative condemns our pervasive selfishness; the Faramir of Jackson's reflective metanarrative merely imitates it.[28]

A CONCLUDING WORD

In a conversation between Walter Hooper and C.S. Lewis on the identity of Elizabeth Taylor (Lewis didn't know who she was), Hooper recalls Lewis's solid reading advice: "He recommended that if I absolutely 'must' read newspapers I have a frequent 'mouthwash' with *The Lord of the Rings* or some other great book."[29] The advice seems to me salutary on more than one front. If we *must* be saturated in modern media, in that glut of news, streams, films, and television that bloat our minds and hearts, then it is all the more critical to read books like Tolkien's, whose lingering attachment to the Real metanarrative effects a healing of the imagination. Quentin Schultze, reflecting on media use in the Christian world, observes that "in North America we tend to assume that more information and more powerful media technologies are signs of progress. Instead, they increase the likelihood that we will find our identities in fashionable media rather than in Jesus Christ."[30] It seems to me that we should keep *The Lord of the Rings* unfashionable; we should keep it safe.

"Religious man was born to be saved;" writes Philip Rieff, "psychological man is born to be pleased."[31] Reflective metanarratives might please and distract us, but only critical metanarratives—rooted as they are in a holism, an integration, and in the Primary World—can grant us a wholeness, a zest, even a kind of salvation. Tolkien's books, in their tethering to Primary Creation offer a lingering taste of that now lost critical metanarrative. Jackson's films, as reflective metanarratives shaped by hunger, ego, and the market, have curtailed the power of Middle-earth to critique us—obscuring what we might have learned or seen from what Charles Williams called, "a light that shone from behind the sun."[32]

NOTES

1. "Metanarrative, n.," in *OED Online* (Oxford University Press, December 2020), https://www.oed.com/view/Entry/245263.
2. Jean-François Lyotard, *The Postmodern Condition: A Report on Knowledge*, trans. Geoff Bennington and Brian Massumi (Manchester: Manchester University Press, 1984), xxiii.
3. Lyotard, *Postmodern Condition*, xxiv.

4. Peter Gratton, "Jean François Lyotard," in *The Stanford Encyclopedia of Philosophy* (Stanford: Metaphysics Research Lab, 2018), https://plato.stanford.edu/archives/win2018/entries/lyotard/.

5. Charles Taylor, *Sources of the Self: The Making of the Modern Identity* (Cambridge: Harvard University Press, 2012), 17.

6. Philip Rieff, *The Triumph of the Therapeutic* (Middlesex: Penguin Books, 1966), 9.

7. Rieff, *Triumph*, 74.

8. Rieff, *Triumph*, 17.

9. Blaise Pascal, *Pensées*, trans. A. J. Krailsheimer (London: Penguin Books, 1995), 45; no. 148 (428).

10. Evelyn Underhill, *Mysticism: A Study in the Nature and Development of Man's Spiritual Consciousness*, 3rd rev. ed. (New York: E. P. Dutton and Company, 1912), 151.

11. Rieff, *Triumph*, 34.

12. In a bizarre cultural moment, at an event at Bethel Church in Redding, CA, on 12 June 2020, leadership declared an end to racism in the church, utilizing a Gandalf-type staff, which was thumped onto the ground while the room chanted, "Thou shall not pass." You can watch the episode here: https://twitter.com/thebereanmillen/status/1282477294037209089.

13. For more on this displacement of meaning structures, especially with respect to cultural worship, see James K. A. Smith, *Desiring the Kingdom: Worship, Worldview, and Cultural Formation* (Grand Rapids: Baker Academic, 2009), 86 ff.

14. J.R.R. Tolkien, "On Fairy-Stories," in *Essays Presented to Charles Williams*, ed. C.S. Lewis (Oxford: Oxford University Press, 1947), 82–83. Tolkien's terminology and concepts from this essay are carefully wrought. One aspect, critically important to stress again, is Tolkien's conviction that the human creature *creates* nothing, only rearranges things already created. This is why we are "sub-creators," and why our creations invite what he calls "secondary belief." This is a critical reason why Tolkien would be alarmed to discover that his works have, for some people, replaced scripture (or, to be more accurate, a Roman Catholic metanarrative). For a discussion on how Tolkien's concept of sub-creation relates to Art, see Miguel Benitez Jr., "Art and Sub-Creation: Tolkien's Theology of Art," in *Theology and Tolkien: Practical Theology*, ed. Douglas Estes (Lanham: Lexington/Fortress, 2023), 121–34.

15. Rieff, *Triumph*, 73.

16. Most critical commentaries acknowledge the imperative tense of the clauses in the Lord's Prayer, but few (to my knowledge) divide the prayer into discrete halves. For a slightly more sustained exposition of this text, see Jeremy Michael Rios, *Ordinary Prayer: Encountering God through Our Everyday Needs* (British Columbia: CreateSpace Independent, 2012), 66ff.

17. Søren Kierkegaard, *The Sickness unto Death*, trans. Howard Hong and Edna Hong (Princeton: Princeton University Press, 1980), 126. In this passage he is writing as Anti-Climacus, Kierkegaard's pseudonym for the ideal Christian.

18. C.S. Lewis, *An Experiment in Criticism* (Cambridge: Cambridge University Press, 1961), 50–56.

19. For an extended description of these features, see Carl Gustav Jung, *Man and His Symbols* (London: Picador, 1978); Joseph Campbell, *The Hero with a Thousand Faces*, 3rd ed., Bollingen Series (Novato: New World Library, 2008).

20. Gwendolen Green, ed., *Letters from Baron Friedrich von Hügel to a Niece* (Chicago: Regnery, 1955), 159.

21. Simone Weil, *Gravity and Grace*, trans. Arthur Wills (Lincoln: University of Nebraska Press, 1997), 120.

22. Tom Shippey, *The Road to Middle-earth*, rev. and exp. ed. (London: HarperCollins, 2005), 118–19.

23. Kevin Aldrich, "The Sense of Time in J.R.R. Tolkien's *The Lord of the Rings*," *Mythlore* 15.1 (1988): 5. See also *Letters*, 181, et al.

24. Shippey, *Road*, 157.

25. Aldrich, "Sense of Time," 9.

26. *Spaceballs* (Metro-Goldwyn-Mayer, 1987).

27. Shippey, *Road*, 418–19.

28. I have highlighted Treebeard, Théoden, and Faramir as exemplary cases, but I might also have mentioned Denethor, Frodo, Gollum, Elrond, Galadriel, Arwen, and Éowyn as additional film aberrations from the critique offered by the books.

29. C.S. Lewis, *Present Concerns* (San Diego: Harcourt, Brace, Jovanovich, 2002), vii.

30. Quentin Schultze, "He-Man and the Masters of the Universe: Media, Postmodernity, and Christianity," in *Imagination and Interpretation: Christian Perspectives*, ed. Hans Boersma (Vancouver: Regent College Publishing, 2005), 161.

31. Rieff, *Triumph*, 22.

32. From "The Calling of Taliessin," in Charles Williams, *Region of the Summer Stars* (London: Editions Poetry London, 1944), 18.

BIBLIOGRAPHY

Aldrich, Kevin. "The Sense of Time in J.R.R. Tolkien's *The Lord of the Rings*." *Mythlore* 15.1 (1988): 5–9.

Benitez, Miguel, Jr. "Art and Sub-Creation: Tolkien's Theology of Art." Pages 121–34 in *Theology and Tolkien: Practical Theology*. Edited by Douglas Estes. Lanham: Lexington/Fortress, 2023.

Campbell, Joseph. *The Hero with a Thousand Faces*. 3rd ed. Bollingen Series. Novato: New World Library, 2008.

Carpenter, Humphrey, ed. *The Letters of J.R.R. Tolkien*. Boston: Houghton Mifflin Company, 1981.

Gratton, Peter. "Jean François Lyotard." In *The Stanford Encyclopedia of Philosophy*. Stanford: Metaphysics Research Lab, 2018.

Green, Gwendolen, ed. *Letters from Baron Friedrich von Hügel to a Niece*. Chicago: Regnery, 1955.

Jung, Carl Gustav. *Man and His Symbols*. London: Picador, 1978.

Kierkegaard, Søren. *The Sickness unto Death*. Translated by Howard Hong and Edna Hong. Princeton: Princeton University Press, 1980.

Lewis, C.S. *An Experiment in Criticism*. Cambridge: Cambridge University Press, 1961.

———. *Present Concerns*. San Diego: Harcourt, Brace, Jovanovich, 2002.

Lyotard, Jean-François. *The Postmodern Condition: A Report on Knowledge*. Translated by Geoff Bennington and Brian Massumi. Manchester: Manchester University Press, 1984.

"Metanarrative, n." In *OED Online*. Oxford University Press, December 2020.

Pascal, Blaise. *Pensées*. Translated by A. J. Krailsheimer. London: Penguin Books, 1995.

Rieff, Philip. *The Triumph of the Therapeutic*. Middlesex: Penguin Books, 1966.

Rios, Jeremy Michael. *Ordinary Prayer: Encountering God through Our Everyday Needs*. Vancouver: CreateSpace Independent, 2012.

Schultze, Quentin. "He-Man and the Masters of the Universe: Media, Postmodernity, and Christianity." Pages 155–77 in *Imagination and Interpretation: Christian Perspectives*, edited by Hans Boersma. Vancouver: Regent College Publishing, 2005.

Shippey, Tom. *The Road to Middle-earth*. Rev. and exp. ed. London: HarperCollins, 2005.

Smith, James K. A. *Desiring the Kingdom: Worship, Worldview, and Cultural Formation*. Grand Rapids: Baker Academic, 2009.

Spaceballs. Metro-Goldwyn-Mayer, 1987.

Taylor, Charles. *Sources of the Self: The Making of the Modern Identity*. Cambridge: Harvard University Press, 2012.

Tolkien, J.R.R. "On Fairy-Stories." Pages 38–89 in *Essays Presented to Charles Williams*. Edited by C.S. Lewis. Oxford: Oxford University Press, 1947.

Underhill, Evelyn. *Mysticism: A Study in the Nature and Development of Man's Spiritual Consciousness*. 3rd rev. ed. New York: E. P. Dutton and Company, 1912.

Weil, Simone. *Gravity and Grace*. Translated by Arthur Wills. Lincoln: University of Nebraska Press, 1997.

Williams, Charles. *Region of the Summer Stars*. London: Editions Poetry London, 1944.

PART III

Ithilien

Chapter 11

"An Encouraging Thought"

The Interplay of Providence and Free Will in Middle-earth

Devin Brown

In 1975 Cambridge University Press released a groundbreaking new work by literary critic Colin Manlove titled *Modern Fantasy*. One of Manlove's five studies was devoted to *The Lord of the Rings*. Back in 1975 most critics took the position that—despite such famous fantasy works as *The Odyssey*, *Beowulf*, and *The Tempest*—fantasy literature was not real literature and was unsuitable for serious study. As a counter to academia's entrenched bias, Manlove sought to demonstrate modern fantasy's literary value. Given his position, we might expect Manlove to take a positive view of *The Lord of the Rings*, a work many readers consider to be among the best fantasy works of all time. While Manlove praised several elements in Tolkien's fiction, he found one "glaring feature" which he claimed previous critics had either downplayed or simply ignored.[1]

What, according to Manlove, was this glaring feature—by which he meant glaring flaw—in *The Lord of the Rings*? It was "the continued presence of a biased fortune."[2]

According to Manlove, this biased fortune is not an isolated element occurring just now and then in limited spots in Tolkien's epic, but a continued presence that is found nearly everywhere—as he explains:

The story is packed with hairsbreadth escapes, many of them lacking explanation. The power opposed to the success of the quest is formidable. Sauron has his lieutenants and spies everywhere in Middle-earth; he also knows that the one Ring is in the hands of a hobbit called Baggins. At the beginning of the story, where Frodo agrees to take the Ring to Mordor, Sauron's Black Riders

223

or Nazgûl are closing in on him in the Shire. For the first part of the story he is closely pursued; for the remainder he has to evade the omnipresent vigilance of his enemies. Yet he constantly wins through; and by means which are assignable neither to his own skill nor to the bad judgment of his opponents.[3]

Manlove goes on to argue that escaping from the Black Riders, and later from the Nazgûl, is "only one strand in a whole skein of apparent coincidences and luck."[4] Merry and Pippin are rescued from Old Man Willow because they happen to become trapped on the one day in the year when Tom Bombadil happens to be in that part of the Old Forest. The fire that the Fellowship makes on the ridge in Hollin just happens to die down so that the crow spies do not see them. At the gates of Moria, Gandalf is able to remember the open-ing spell in the final moment before the Watcher in the Water would have dragged the Company to a watery death. After Merry and Pippin are taken captive by the orcs, they are able to escape because of, as Manlove puts it, a "chance-in-a-million" slaying of Grishnákh as he draws his sword and is about to kill them.[5] Likewise, Manlove claims that it is only by "constant miracles" that Frodo and Sam are able to elude the watchful gaze of the sen-tinels of Mordor.[6] And during the Battle of Cormallen, the Ring is destroyed just as the tide is turning against the West.

Midway through *The Two Towers* after Wormtongue picks up the Palantír—an object which will play a key role in defeating Sauron—and hurls it down at Gandalf narrowly missing him, the wizard observes: "Strange are the turns of fortune" (*TT*, III, x). For Manlove, the many turns of fortune in *The Lord of the Rings* are too strange—they are far too positive. He points out that even Bill the pony, the beloved animal they must to abandon in the wilderness at the entrance to Moria, is later found safe and well at Bree on their eventual return. Manlove maintains that throughout *The Lord of the Rings* "it is not mortal will but luck which is the architect of success," and concludes that Tolkien's repeated use of fortunate coincidences like these so degrades the fight against evil that it becomes "mere posturing in a rigged boat."[7]

BIASED FORTUNE OR SOMETHING ELSE?—A HINT FROM *THE HOBBIT*

In chapter three of *The Hobbit*, Gandalf, Bilbo, and the dwarves arrive at Rivendell, the end of the first leg of their journey to the Lonely Mountain. Within a few days their clothes are mended, their bags are filled with food, and they are ready to continue. The night before they are to leave, Elrond meets with them and asks to see their map. As he gazes at it in the light of a broad crescent moon, additional markings come into view. These, Elrond explains, are moon-letters, which can only be seen only when "a moon of the same shape and season as the day when they were written" shines behind them (*Hobbit*, III).

Elrond just happens to be looking at the map at the exact moment—on a midsummer's eve under a crescent moon—when the otherwise invisible letters can be seen. To make sure that readers do not miss the unlikely nature of this event, Tolkien has his narrator point out that there would not be another such astronomical alignment until "goodness knows when" (*Hobbit*, III). What is more, the letters just happen to provide critical directions for the only way to get inside the otherwise impenetrable mountain.

This is not the first highly fortunate coincidence in *The Hobbit*. Just before coming to Rivendell, Bilbo and the dwarves encountered a group of trolls and had to be rescued by Gandalf who had left the Company to investigate the road ahead. In explaining how he happened to arrive back in time to save them, Gandalf reports that he had met friends from Rivendell who told him trolls were in the area and that he "had a feeling" he was needed back and so returned just in time (*Hobbit*, II).

Does Tolkien want readers to believe—as Manlove proposes—that unlikely coincidences like these come about simply by mere chance? Or by including these incidents and others like them, first in *The Hobbit* and then to a greater extent in *The Lord of the Rings*, is the author suggesting that there is an unseen power at work in Middle-earth? This question is critical to how we read Tolkien's fiction.

The moon-letters Elrond discovers state that the keyhole to the mountain door will become visible only on the last light of Durin's Day. Thorin explains that Durin's Day takes place when the last moon of autumn and the sun are in the sky together but then adds: "This will not help us much, I fear, for it passes our skill in these days to guess when such a time will come again" (*Hobbit*, III). Eight chapters later, it seems that it is just by great (or biased) fortune that Bilbo happens to be sitting by the doorstep at just the right moment to witness the brief appearance of the keyhole, which allows them to get inside the mountain, where they will soon need to be in order to escape the enraged Smaug.

Of all the unlikely events in *The Hobbit*, the most unlikely—and thus most open to Manlove's claim of biased fortune—is the apparent chance occurrence of Bilbo's finding and picking up the ring that Gollum has lost. After he becomes separated from the others during their escape from the goblins, Bilbo ends up crawling blindly in the miles of tunnels beneath the Misty Mountains. Given the vast spaces of the goblin kingdom with its miles of passageways, the tiny fraction of the tunnels that Bilbo traverses, the fact that he can see nothing, and the extremely small space where his hand touches down—some readers may find Bilbo's coincidental finding of the Ring to be too much of a coincidence, a case of too much good fortune. As if anticipating this reaction, Tolkien has his narrator exclaim, "A magic ring . . . ! He had heard of such things, of course, in old old tales; but it was hard to believe that he really had found one, by accident" (*Hobbit*, V).

It was hard to believe that he had found one by accident. This is precisely Manlove's point and exactly the type of incident he uses to support his argument that we find an over-reliance on unbelievable occurrences in Tolkien and this is a crucial weakness on the author's part. In one sense, Manlove has a point: an over-reliance on chance would make *The Hobbit*, *The Lord of the Rings,* or any work of fiction fatally flawed, the kind of story that unskilled writers create when they are unable to get their heroes out of trouble without such contrivances. However, a careful reading of the text suggests there is another way, besides biased fortune, to understand these seemingly fortunate coincidences that take place in Middle-earth—just as there is another way to understand the highly unlikely favorable events that take place in our own world.

In Gandalf's final words on the last page of *The Hobbit*, a place of particular significance, Tolkien provides a hint of what has been behind all of these so-called lucky events. It is some years after Bilbo's return to Bag End, and one evening as the hobbit is in his study working on his memoirs, Gandalf and Balin arrive for an unexpected visit. They soon fall to talking of their times together and sharing news. On learning that the new Master of Lake-town has ushered in such prosperity that the people are making songs that say the rivers run with gold, Bilbo remarks how the old prophecies are turning out to be true.

"Surely you don't disbelieve the prophecies, because you had a hand in bringing them about yourself?" asks Gandalf. Then he adds, "You don't really suppose, do you, that all your adventures and escapes were managed by mere luck, just for your sole benefit?" (*Hobbit*, XIX). In Gandalf's second question—*You don't really suppose, do you, that all your adventures and escapes were managed by mere luck, just for your sole benefit?*—we find the first of several direct suggestions provided by Tolkien that there is more than just biased fortune at work behind the scenes.

And what is this something that is more than mere luck? As we look at Tolkien's comments about his fiction, an appropriate word for this benevolent agency that acts behinds the scenes is Providence. It will be Tolkien's practice to typically keep any hints of Providence somewhat veiled—both in the stories themselves and in comments he made about them.

In a letter written to Rayner Unwin in 1965, Tolkien broke his characteristic silence to make plainer the underlying foundations of both *The Hobbit* and *The Lord of the Rings*, as he explained:

The story and its sequel are . . . about the achievements of specially graced and gifted individuals. I would say, if saying such things did not spoil what it tries to make explicit, 'by ordained individuals, inspired and guided by an Emissary to ends beyond their individual education and enlargement.' (*Letters*, 365)

This is clear in *The Lord of the Rings*; but it is present, if veiled, in *The Hobbit* from the beginning, and is alluded to in Gandalf's last words.

Here in Tolkien's comments we find a number of relevant points. First, with his use here of the unspecified passive—a topic that will be discussed later—Tolkien leaves it unsaid exactly *by whom* Bilbo and Frodo were graced, gifted, and ordained, clearly by some greater power that chooses to work indirectly. Second, Tolkien states that the two hobbits were inspired and guided to ends that went beyond their personal growth, and here we find Gandalf's claim that Bilbo's adventures and escapes were managed by this unnamed agency *for more than his sole benefit*, arguably for the good of Middle-earth. Finally, Tolkien makes it clear that Gandalf's final words in *The Hobbit* allude to the role of Providence and that this underlying role is "clear" in *The Lord of the Rings*.

Before moving on, it is worth pointing out that Gandalf's statement to Bilbo is like something readers might say themselves as they reflect back on their own undertakings: *Surely you don't suppose, do you, that all your adventures and escapes were managed by mere luck, just for your sole benefit?*

WAYS OF SPEAKING ABOUT PROVIDENCE: THE UNSPECIFIED PASSIVE AND SO-CALLED CHANCE

John Piper opens the first chapter of his recent book, *Providence*, with the following statement:

> The reason this book is about the Providence of God rather than the sovereignty of God is that the term *sovereignty* does not contain the idea of *purposeful* action, but the term *Providence* does. Sovereignty focuses on God's right and power to do all that he wills, but in itself it does not express any design or goal. Of course, God's sovereignty *is* purposeful. It *does* have design. It *does* pursue a goal.[8]

Piper goes on to note that *Providence* has its roots in the word *provide*, and that in reference to God, *Providence* has come to mean "the act of purposefully providing for, or sustaining and governing, the world."[9] As another way to express what we mean by God's Providence, Piper offers that God "sees to it that things happen in a certain way,"[10] either directly or through use of his representatives. Sometimes a helpful distinction is made between general Providence, which refers to God's upholding of the existence and natural order of the universe, and special Providence, which refers to God's intervention in the lives of individual people.[11] As we will see, these ways of speaking about how Providence works in our world are also a good fit for the Providence found in Middle-earth.

In "The Shadow of the Past," the second chapter of *The Fellowship of the Ring*, Tolkien returns to the topic of who or what has been behind Bilbo's adventures, specifically his finding the Ring. Gandalf recounts its long history, and then using words that highlight the highly improbable nature of the event, he comes to Bilbo's "arrival just at that time, and putting his hand on it, blindly, in the dark," an event that the wizard claims to be "the strangest event in the whole history of the Ring so far" (*FR*, I, ii). Then Tolkien makes explicit what has previously been implied as Gandalf tells Frodo that the Ring was picked up by Bilbo, the "most unlikely person imaginable," not by sheer luck or blind chance but because "there was more than one power at work," something "beyond any design of the Ring-maker" (*FR*, I, ii).

In Middle-earth, as in our world, the workings of Providence are typically veiled and sometimes may be discernible only in hindsight. In words that briefly pull back this veil Gandalf tells Frodo: "Bilbo was *meant* to find the Ring, and not by its maker. In which case you also were *meant* to have it" (*FR*, I, ii). Here Tolkien uses the passive voice without specifying who it was that meant for these things to take place. The implication is it was the Creator of Middle-earth or his agents, the Valar, who intended these things to happen. To help ensure that they did, Gandalf was sent as an emissary. We are told in Appendix B that after the Wizards appeared in Middle-earth, it was said they "were messengers sent to contest the power of Sauron" and "were forbidden to match his power with power" (*RK*, Appendix B, The Third Age). Here again Tolkien leaves the agency unspecified or implied: *sent* and *forbidden* by whom?

Readers may find Tolkien's use of the unspecified passive to refer to Providence recognizable because in our world people often use it to talk about unlikely events in their own lives which seem to have been brought about by something larger than themselves. For example, in referring to a seemingly chance meeting that then led to a lifelong relationship, someone might say, "We were *meant* to meet that day."

Gandalf concludes his claim that Bilbo was meant to find the Ring and Frodo was meant to have it with the statement: "And that may be an encouraging thought" (*FR*, I, ii). With these six words Tolkien says much about the power at work behind the scenes in Middle-earth. Why might this thought be encouraging? First, Bilbo was meant to find the Ring, as Gandalf states, but "*not* by its maker" (*FR*, I, ii). Clearly this something else at work is greater in power than Sauron who "was awake once more and sending out his dark thought from Mirkwood" (*FR*, I, ii). Here Providence is able to thwart Sauron's plans for the Ring and instead put it into the hands of the Dark Lord's enemies, and this action is crucial, for if the Ring had stayed with Gollum or had simply remained lost, Sauron's armies were powerful enough to win without it. The only hope the free peoples of Middle-earth have to defeat Sauron is by destroying the Ring. Bilbo's picking it up in the darkness of the deep caverns under the Misty Mountains is one step in a great plan that will gradually be revealed. This power that meant for Bilbo to pick up the Ring both cares for the free people of Middle-earth and has the power to thwart Sauron's plans—a very encouraging thought indeed.

At the Council at Rivendell, Elrond makes a similar use of the unspecific passive to allude to the hand of Providence. He begins by asking those in attendance, "What shall we do with the Ring, the least of rings, the trifle that Sauron fancies?" (*FR*, II, ii). Then in a reference to the benevolent power at work in Middle-earth, he explains: "That is the purpose for which you are called hither. Called, I say, though I have not called you to me, strangers from distant lands. You have come and are here met, in this very nick of time, by chance as it may seem. Yet it is not so. Believe that it is so ordered that we, who sit here, and none others, must now find counsel for the peril of the world" (*FR*, II, ii).

The assorted collection of Elves, Men, Dwarves, Hobbits, and a Wizard have not arrived at Rivendell by chance. They may think that they came there individually and for other reasons, but in fact they were *called* there as a group and for a *purpose*, but not by Elrond—he makes these points explicit. But if not by Elrond, then by whom? What is more, it was *so ordered* that this specific group gathered together at this particular time and place should take council together and decide the fate of the Ring. And again we must ask—if not by Elrond, then so ordered by whom?

We are not told who has done this calling or who has ordered it so, but presumably it is the same agency which meant for Bilbo to pick up the Ring, the same agency that years ago sent the Wizards to Middle-earth to contest the power of Sauron, and the same agency that later will send Gandalf back after his battle with the Balrog—either the "One" that Arwen refers to (*RK*, Appendix A, "The Tale of Aragorn and Arwen"), or the Valar who act on his behalf.

Here again, Tolkien, the philologist, has been careful to have Elrond use words that readers themselves might use when speaking about Providence in their own lives. Sometimes we, too, may believe that we were meant to do something, to meet someone, or be somewhere. We, too, may say that we felt *called* to a certain task. Why use the unspecified passive when the most natural and more common way to state something is in active voice? Tolkien, the linguistics professor, would have been aware that while the use of active voice typically makes statements stronger and more direct, one time where the unspecified passive is correct and preferred is to describe actions where the agency behind the action is not directly known. For example, typically when we say we *were meant* to meet someone, we are expressing the fact that we do not directly know who meant this.

Why make the Providence in Middle-earth look and feel like the Providence that readers might experience in their own lives? In a 1955 letter to his publisher, Tolkien makes it clear that Middle-earth is intended to be our Earth many years ago. There he states that Middle-earth is "not a name of a never-never land without relation to the world we live in" and that the fictional events from *The Lord of the Rings* "take place in a period of the actual Old World of this planet" (*Letters,* 220). And readers need not look outside the text to see that Tolkien has set his epic in our prehistoric past. In the Prologue we are told that Hobbits "are relatives of ours" though now estranged since days "now long past" (*FR*, Prologue, I).

In a letter to Rhona Beare in 1958, Tolkien takes a step further and explains that his allusions to the divine in *The Lord of the Rings* were not intended to be "any kind of new religion" but rather, as he states, "an imaginative invention, to express, in the only way I can, some of my (dim) apprehensions of the world" (*Letters,* 283). Tolkien goes on to say that he hopes the long, undefined gap in time between the Fall of Barad-dûr and our time, a gap of about 6,000 years, is sufficient to provide literary creditability. Then he writes: "Theologically (if the term is not too grandiose) I imagine the picture to be less dissonate from what some (including myself) believe to be the truth."

While the lands and events in *The Lord of the Rings* are somewhat more "dissonate" than they might have been if Tolkien had "fitted things in with greater verisimilitude" (*Letters,* 283), the theology of Middle-earth is a much better match with what Tolkien believes to be true in our world. If so, it should come as no surprise that the language Tolkien has his characters use to describe their experience of Providence is so similar to our own. Joseph Pearce summarizes the theological connection between the two worlds, stating:

Although the characters in Middle-earth have a knowledge of God that is less complete than that which has been revealed to the Christian world, the God who is dimly discerned in Middle-earth is nonetheless the same God as the One worshipped by Tolkien himself. The God of Earth and the God of Middle-earth are One. This follows both logically and theologically from Tolkien's beliefs that his sub-created secondary world was a reflection, or a glimpse, of the truth inherent in the Created Primary World.[12]

At the conclusion of the Council meeting, Tolkien has Elrond turn again to the unspecified passive to refer to the invisible hand of Providence. After Frodo tells the Council that he will take the Ring, Elrond replies, "If I understand aright all that I have heard, I think that this task is appointed for you, Frodo; and that if you do not find a way, no one will" (*FR*, II, ii). Frodo was *appointed* to take the Ring, but not by the Council and not by Elrond. Here we see the next step in the plan Providence has to defeat Sauron. That said, we still must note that Providence works in a way that even wise guides such as Elrond cannot fully see.[13] Here we sense this incomplete understanding as Elrond says to Frodo *if I understand aright* and that he *thinks* this task has been appointed to him. Earlier Gandalf expressed the thought this way: "Even the very wise cannot see all ends" (*FR*, I, ii).

Although Boromir is present at the Council meeting, either he is not paying attention to the statements Elrond makes, or he disagrees with Elrond's assessment. Eight chapters later, Boromir will confront Frodo about the Ring and will argue that it came to Frodo not because it was meant to but only by "unhappy chance" (*FR*, II, x), and might just as easily have been his. While Boromir sees the history of the ring as nothing more than random chance— like flipping a coin that is as likely to come up tails as it is heads—Tolkien does not intend for readers to see it this way.

Besides the use of the unspecified passive, a second element from what Elrond says is worth noting. Since the Providence in Middle-earth typically chooses to work behind the scenes rather than in ways that are directly visible, some characters—such as Boromir—may see its actions as mere chance. Elrond tells the members of the Council, "You have come and are here met, in this very nick of time, by chance as it may seem. Yet it is not so" (*FR*, II, ii). Tolkien's point is that while the actions of Providence have intention and purpose, to some they may appear as just coincidences—it *may seem* that they take place by chance.

Tolkien includes several other times when far-seeing characters give voice to this same thought after critical Providential events. "Just chance brought me then, if chance you call it," Tom replies after rescuing Merry and Pippin from Old Man Willow (*FR*, I, vii). He then adds, "It was no plan of mine." And here in Tom's peculiar wording, Tolkien hints that Tom's arrival may have been the plan of someone else.

At the Council of Elrond, Gandalf uses words similar to Tom's to describe the coincidental driving of Sauron from Mirkwood in the very year that Bilbo came across the Ring, calling it "a strange chance, if chance it was" (*FR*, II, ii). After Pippin's near disaster of looking into the Palantír, Tolkien has Gandalf again make plain that Providence may appear as mere chance. "You have been saved, and all your friends too," the wizard tells Pippin, "by good fortune, as it is called" (*TT*, III, xi). Clearly Gandalf, Elrond, and Tom do not call the agency working on their behalf good fortune. They have a very different name for it.

If we turn to the Prologue at the start of *The Lord of the Rings*, we can find similar suggestions of the presence of an unseen hand behind the apparent luck in Middle-earth. There Tolkien's narrator reports that the story told in *The Hobbit* "would scarcely have earned more than a note in the long annals of the Third Age, but for an 'accident' by the way" (*FR*, Prologue, IV). What was this so-called accident, set off here by quotation marks? It is Bilbo's finding the Ring lying on the floor of the tunnel "as he groped in vain in the dark" (*FR*, Prologue, IV). In words that echo Gandalf, Tom, and Elrond, the narrator states: "It seemed then like mere luck" (*FR*, Prologue, IV). A second occurrence of what seemed like chance takes place in Bilbo's guessing game with Gollum. "In the end Bilbo won the game," the narrator explains, "more by luck (as it seemed) than by wits" (*FR*, Prologue, IV).

Tolkien provides a further example of this pattern in Appendix A. There Gandalf tells Frodo and Gimli that ruin and defeat in Middle-earth were averted all because he happened to meet Thorin one spring evening in Bree, "a chance-meeting, as we say in Middle-earth" (*RK*, Appendix A, III). In *J.R.R. Tolkien: Author of the Century*, Tom Shippey points out that here and in the examples earlier Tolkien suggests that *chance* is "just a word people use to explain things they do not understand" and that this is "a sign only of the limits of their understanding."[14] Shippey then poses the question: "What would a less limited understanding make of events?"

THE INTERPLAY OF PROVIDENCE AND FREE WILL

If, as we have seen, Tolkien weaves the actions of Providence into the underlying fabric of *The Hobbit* and *The Lord of the Rings*, he also includes an equally inextricable role for free will—the ability to choose between different possible courses of action in a voluntary way, unimpeded by the will or wishes of others. And if we look for it, we can see this emphasis again and again. Bilbo chooses to join the dwarves on their quest and later chooses to spare Gollum. Frodo chooses of his own free will to take the Ring—both at Bag End and later at Rivendell. As both Gandalf and Elrond make clear, no one (except the Black Riders) is seeking to coerce Frodo to do anything. Gandalf states, "The decision lies with you" (*FR*, I, ii), and Elrond tells him, "I do not lay it on you. But if you take it freely, I will say that your choice is right" (*FR*, II, ii).

Earlier when Frodo first learned that Sauron had risen again, he exclaimed: "I wish it need not have happened in my time!" (*FR*, I, ii). And in Gandalf's response, we find one of Tolkien's most famous statements about the importance of individual choice. "So do I," Gandalf answers, "and so do all who live to see such times. But that is not for them to decide. All we have to decide is what to do with the time that is given us" (*FR*, I, ii).

Tolkien gives us several different types of situations where characters must decide what to do with the time that is given them. In repeated occasions Tolkien shows characters choosing what is right over simply obeying orders. Merry and Pippin choose to go against the expressed wishes of Théoden and Denethor to whom they have pledged service. We see Éowyn make a similar decision. Rather than following the laws of the land, Éomer chooses to aid Aragorn, Faramir chooses to assist Frodo and Sam, and Beregond chooses to leave his post to save Faramir. In the chapter appropriately titled "The Choices of Master Samwise," Sam laments that he, all alone, must make a decision whether to take the Ring or stay with Frodo's body. But, in the words Aragorn says to Éomer, "the doom of choice" applies to Sam as it does to all individuals in Middle-earth (*TT*, III, ii).

At Parth Galen Aragorn gives voice to this point that though we might wish otherwise, there is no evading the choices that come our way. He tells Frodo: "Your own way you alone can choose. In this matter I cannot advise you. I am not Gandalf, and though I have tried to bear his part, I do not know what design or hope he had for this hour, if indeed he had any. Most likely it seems that if he were here now the choice would still wait on you" (*FR*, II, x). To put it another way, in Middle-earth the freedom and the necessity to make moral decisions is unavoidable.

Further highlighting Tolkien's position on the importance of free will, we find that seeking to dominate the will of others is seen as the greatest of evils, as evidenced in Sauron's limitless desire to *rule them all*. Saruman follows in Sauron's path as he rejects the charge the Wizards were given not "to dominate Elves or Men by force or fear" (*RK*, Appendix B, I).

Tolkien puts free will center stage in another way by providing several sets of paired characters who make opposite decisions. We are shown Gandalf and Saruman, wizards who make different choices about serving and commanding. In Aragorn and Isildur we see relatives and future kings who make opposite choices about the Ring. We also see two brothers, Boromir and Faramir, who when given an opportunity to seize the Ring by force make different choices. And in Théoden and Denethor, Tolkien shows two aging leaders who make different decisions about whether to despair or to fight.

So how do we reconcile the powerful hand of Providence that Tolkien shows us working its will behind the scenes with the free will he gives his characters? We can find Tolkien's solution in Sam's reflection on the adventures that "the wonderful folk of the stories" find themselves caught up in (*TT*, IV, viii). Looking back on these adventures, Sam describes the interplay between Providence and free will this way: "Folk seem to have been just landed in them, usually—their paths were laid that way, as you put it. I expect they had lots of chances, like us, of turning back, only they didn't" (*TT*, IV, viii).

Their paths were laid that way and *they had many chances to turn back.* Rather than making either Providence or free will responsible for what happens in Middle-earth, Tolkien has both. If, as we have seen, Frodo was chosen to bear the Ring, he also chooses to accept the role of Ringbearer and might have chosen otherwise. The same could be said for Bilbo's decision to spare Gollum. The will of Providence is never forced on anyone and never overrides a character's free will.

But what happens when individual choice goes *against* Providence? Where does Tolkien show us characters who, in Sam's words, take advantage of their chance to turn back? And, if so, what happens to the will of Providence? As Tom Shippey points out, Tolkien's characters can "say 'No' to divine Providence, though of course if they do they have to stand by the consequences of their decision."[15] Saruman may be the clearest example of a character saying no to the path that was laid out to him. Another example which Shippey offers is found in Boromir's dream. He explains: "Providence or the Valar sent the dream that took Boromir to Rivendell. But they sent it first and most often to Faramir, who would no doubt have been a better choice. It was human decisions, or human perversity, which led to Boromir claiming the journey, with what chain of ill-effects and casualties no one can tell."[16] Boromir tells the Council that the dream "came oft" to his brother and then later came once to him (*FR*, II, ii)—presumably only after it became clear that Boromir would not allow his brother to go. Faramir will later explain how Boromir went against what should have been, as he tells Frodo: "I should have been chosen by my father and the elders, but he put himself forward, as being the older and the hardier (both true), and he would not be stayed" (*TT*, IV, v).

He would not be stayed. In Boromir's decision to claim the journey for himself, we see an individual who chooses to go against the will of Providence, but then Tolkien shows how Providence still accomplishes its original purpose, albeit in a different way. It is impossible to know what would have happened if Faramir had been permitted to go, but Boromir's presence on the quest leads to several actions with positive outcomes: Frodo and Sam going to Mordor alone, Merry and Pippin reaching Fangorn, and the others coming to Meduseld and rousing Théoden and the Rohirrim. Similarly in *The Hobbit* we could say that because of the goblins' decision to capture Bilbo and the dwarves, they contrive to bring Bilbo to the exact right place deep below the mountain to find the Ring where otherwise he would never have come.

While it is beyond the scope of this chapter to also provide similar illustrations from *The Silmarillion*, in the repercussions that stem from Boromir's decision, readers familiar with that work may hear echoes of a passage which comes after Melkor rebels and chooses to interweave "matters of his own imagining that were not in accord with the theme of Ilúvatar" (*Ainulindalë*). Ilúvatar confronts him saying: "And thou, Melkor, shalt see that no theme may be played that hath not its uttermost source in me, nor can any alter the music in my despite. For he that attempteth this shall prove but mine instrument in the devising of things more wonderful, which he himself hath not imagined" (*Ainulindalë*).

When Saruman chooses to relinquish his appointed role as Saruman the White, Gandalf becomes Saruman "as he should have been" (*TT*, III, v). When Isildur chooses not to destroy the Ring, Providence devises another plan for its destruction. Galadriel alludes to this interplay that occurs between Providence and free will as she tells the Company, "Maybe the paths that you each shall tread are already laid before your feet" (*FR*, II, viii), and at the same time warns them, "Your Quest stands upon the edge of a knife. Stray but a little and it will fail" (*FR*, II, viii). As Paul Kocher states, "Their future course is indeed laid out for them, provided they themselves choose to tread it."[17]

Of course, the interplay between Providence and free will is not the only interplay of wills in Tolkien's fictional world, or in our own. The free will of others also comes into play. While many examples of this might be cited, a look at two final instances from Middle-earth must suffice.

In one choice of his rebellion, Sauron sends the Black Riders to hunt down "Baggins" and the Ring, a decision which leads Frodo to choose to go through the Old Forest rather than taking the road. In the Old Forest, Merry and Pippin are caught by Old Man Willow and subsequently freed by Tom Bombadil who later must rescue the hobbits from a Barrow-wight. Afterwards, Tom gives the hobbits long daggers from the barrow that had been forged many years ago by Men of Westernesse. Later it will be Merry's blade that helps kill the Lord of the Nazgûl, as Tolkien's narrator reports: "No other blade, not though mightier hands had wielded it, would have dealt that foe a wound so bitter" (*RK*, V, vi). And so ends a chain of events that began with Sauron choosing to send his Black Riders after Frodo. As Paul Kocher points out, Providence "not only permits evil to exist but weaves it inextricably into its purpose for Middle-earth."[18]

A second example of the interplay of Providence and the opposing wills of more than one individual can be found in the breaking of the Fellowship at the end of Book Two. Frodo has decided to leave the others and to go to Mordor alone. Sam disobeys Aragorn's command to stay nearby and runs to the riverbank just in time to fling himself at Frodo's departing boat. "So all my plan is spoilt!" Frodo tells Sam after pulling him from the water. "It is no good trying to escape you. But I'm glad, Sam, I cannot tell you how glad. Come along! It is plain that we were meant to go together" (*FR*, II, x).

It is plain that we were meant to go together. Tolkien, always careful with words, has Frodo use the same pattern used earlier by Gandalf and Elrond to speak about Providence. In Frodo's use of the unspecified passive we can hear that while he and Sam each had a plan, someone else who goes unnamed also had a plan and *meant* for them to go together. And this plan is *plain*—at least to Frodo who is willing to discern it.

In 1954 Tolkien received a letter from the manager of a Catholic bookstore in Oxford suggesting that in writing *The Lord of the Rings* Tolkien may have been guilty of "over-stepping the bounds of a writer's job," particularly when it came to "metaphysical matters" (*Letters*, 187–88). In response, Tolkien wrote that his one object as a writer was "the elucidation of truth and the encouragement of good morals in this real world" (*Letters*, 194). And if we, like Frodo, have been paying attention, we, too, may learn a truth about Providence, free will, and the interplay between them—an interplay that provides not only complexity to the worlds of Middle-earth and our own but encouragement as well.

NOTES

1. Colin Manlove, *Modern Fantasy: Five Studies* (Cambridge: Cambridge University Press, 1978), 180.

2. Manlove, *Modern Fantasy*, 181.

3. Manlove, *Modern Fantasy*, 181.

4. Manlove, *Modern Fantasy*, 182.

5. Manlove, *Modern Fantasy*, 182.

6. Manlove, *Modern Fantasy*, 183.

7. Manlove, *Modern Fantasy*, 183.

8. John Piper, *Providence* (Wheaton: Crossway, 2020), 29.

9. Piper, *Providence*, 30.

10. Piper, *Providence*, 30.

11. For an example of how Divine Providence looks in the Bible, we might turn to the account in Exodus 11 of how Pharaoh's daughter not only happens to find the baby Moses but then also (because his sister just happens to be nearby) arranges for his own mother to nurse him. We can find similar illustrations of Providence in many of the events in the life of Joseph.

12. Joseph Pearce, *Tolkien: Man and Myth* (New York: HarperCollins, 1999), 110.

13. *Deo pro nobis* or "God for us" is one of the oldest sayings of the ancient church, and it summarizes the intentions of Providence. But how exactly God is for us in the events of our lives and the people that we meet will not always be clear. We may be able to see God's Providence only looking back in hindsight.

14. Tom Shippey, *J.R.R. Tolkien: Author of the Century* (Boston: Houghton Mifflin, 2002), 144.

15. Tom Shippey, *The Road to Middle-earth: How J.R.R. Tolkien Created a New Mythology* (Boston: Houghton Mifflin, 2003), 152.

16. Shippey, *Road*, 152.

17. Paul Kocher, *Master of Middle-earth: The Fiction of J.R.R. Tolkien* (New York: Ballantine, 1977), 44.

18. Kocher, *Master*, 48.

BIBLIOGRAPHY

Elliott, Mark W. *Providence: A Biblical, Historical, and Theological Account.* Grand Rapids: Baker, 2020.

Jensen, Keith W. "Dissonance in the Divine Theme: The Issue of Free Will in Tolkien's *Silmarillion*." Pages 102–13 in *Middle-earth Minstrel: Essays on Music in Tolkien*, ed. Bradford Lee Eden. Jefferson, NC: McFarland, 2010.

Kocher, Paul. *Master of Middle-earth: The Fiction of J.R.R. Tolkien.* New York: Ballantine, 1977.

Manlove, Colin. *Modern Fantasy: Five Studies.* Cambridge: Cambridge University Press, 1978.

Pearce, Joseph. *Tolkien: Man and Myth.* New York: HarperCollins, 1999.

Piper, John. *Providence.* Wheaton: Crossway, 2020.

Shippey, Tom. *J.R.R. Tolkien: Author of the Century.* Boston: Houghton Mifflin, 2002.

———. *The Road to Middle-earth: How J.R.R. Tolkien Created a New Mythology.* Boston: Houghton Mifflin, 2003.

Chapter 12

The Redemptive Power of Love

Arwen as the Anti-Eve in Peter Jackson's The Lord of the Rings

Julie Loveland Swanstrom

The elevated role of Arwen and Aragorn's love story in Peter Jackson's film adaptations of *The Lord of the Rings* bring to the fore an important, and understated, part of Tolkien's story. Tolkien noted the importance of love stories in his monumental work and described Arwen and Aragorn's romance as the highest love (*Letters*, 131).[1] The debate over the changes Jackson made to these characters notwithstanding, the role that Arwen and Aragorn's love story plays emphasizes the redemptive power of love (*Letters*, 131).[2] Much ink has been spilled over platonic love and the redemptive power it has in *The Lord of the Rings*,[3] so in this chapter, I focus on the redemptive power infused in Arwen and Aragorn's love as expressed in Jackson's films. Despite Janet Brennan Croft's claim that Aragorn "must renounce love in order to do his job" in Jackson's films because Aragorn follows "the classic pattern established in countless westerns," I argue that neither Aragorn nor Arwen fully renounce love; instead, it is love that redeems both.[4] Arwen's love dramatically redeems Aragorn in a way that inverts Augustine's conceptualization of the fall, showing how love moves Jackson's characters to eucatastrophic victory rather than love being simply a reward for victory.[5]

ARWEN AND ARAGORN'S LOVE IN JACKSON'S FILMS VERSUS TOLKIEN'S TEXT

Jackson sought to bring Arwen's character into the main story in his film adaptation of *The Lord of the Rings* by using information from the Appendices and making changes to Arwen's and Aragorn's characterization to fit them within his larger framework for the adaptation.[6] Whereas Tolkien himself deemed the love story significant—significant enough to include Arwen and Aragorn's larger story with numerous details in the Appendices—the narrative structure of *The Lord of the Rings* did not center on this story but merely benefitted from it (*RK*, Appendix A, I, v; *Letters*, 131).[7] In Jackson's films, this story is brought to the fore, with the character development of Aragorn depending significantly on a potential love triangle between him, Arwen, and Éowyn for much of his adaptation of *The Two Towers*.[8]

These tensions, along with other revisions to Aragorn's character, lead Croft to argue that Jackson adjusted Aragorn's character to fit better with the myth of the American superhero. A part of these adjustments includes sexual renunciation on Aragorn's part; Aragorn renounces his love for Arwen "in order to do his job," and upon such a renunciation, Aragorn wins several victories.[9] The woman, therefore, becomes a temptress who tries to draw the man away from his heroic quest, and Croft provides numerous examples of the 'woman as temptress' trope, such as in the first *Superman* film when Clark Kent must remain celibate to retain his powers, in *Star Trek: The Original Series* when James T. Kirk forsakes other loves for the sake of being married (as it were) to his ship, and in *Bonanza* when the fiancées of the main characters are regularly killed off.[10] In each of these instances, a female love interest would derail the hard work the hero undertakes. Croft argues that Jackson treats Arwen as a 'Hollywood' temptress to an extent: Aragorn rejects Arwen's pendant (which she asserts he must keep); Aragorn tells Arwen to go to the Undying Lands after an angry confrontation with Elrond, her father; and it is Elrond who supports Aragorn on his path to kingship rather than Arwen, who, in the book, sends a Gondorian banner with her brothers to fight alongside Aragorn.[11]

All of this Croft contrasts with Tolkien's text, in which "Aragorn's goal is union with the goddess Arwen."[12] Throughout the books, Arwen is Aragorn's ardent supporter, sometimes to the chagrin of her father. Finding out about Arwen's betrothal to Aragorn, Elrond tells Aragorn that "she shall not be the bride of any Man less than the King of both Gondor and Arnor," which provides motivation for Aragorn to be restored to the Gondorian throne (*RK*, Appendix A, I, v).[13] Arwen sends her grandmother Galadriel a green brooch to give to Aragorn as a sign of her hope and trust in him (*FR* II, viii). Arwen makes a banner for Aragorn, sent to him by way of her broth-ers (*RK* V, ii). Arwen's faith in Aragorn does not waver. Croft rightly asserts that in Tolkien's works, "Arwen is never a temptress or a weakness keeping [Aragorn] from concentrating on his quest—she is an inspiration and source of his strength."[14] Even when Éowyn expresses interest in Aragorn, Arwen's love helps him reject her persistent demands to accompany him out of love for him (*RK* V, ii). Arwen empties herself, giving up her long life out of love for Aragorn, a sacrifice which Nancy Enright connects to Tolkien's notion of a *eucatastrophe*—a joyful denial of final defeat that still recognizes the cost and likelihood of sorrow and failure.[15]

Croft and others rightly note the difference in presentation between Arwen and Aragorn's relationship in Tolkien's text and Jackson's films, but I argue that Jackson's injection of uncertainty into Arwen and Aragorn's relationship functions to highlight the redemptive power of love. One way love redeems is by drawing someone toward what is good, and love for Arwen repeatedly draws Jackson's Aragorn toward doing the good thing—the right thing, or at least the thing that helps fulfill Aragorn's kingly potential—at crucial points in the narrative. Aragorn is initially reluctant about the throne and his role as descendant of Isildur, but Arwen confidently asserts that Aragorn will not fail as Isildur did (Jackson's *FR*, chapter 25). Arwen repeatedly expresses confidence in Aragorn and his path even as Aragorn doubts, such as when she reassures him of her confidence in his path despite his own lack of clarity, insisting that he trust their relationship if he will not trust himself (Jackson's *TT*, chapter 33). She consistently offers help to Aragorn from afar, such as when she kisses him after his clifftop fall, requesting the grace of the Valar to protect him (Jackson's *TT*, chapter 37). She also resists Elrond's attempts to get her to leave for the Undying Lands, and it is not until Elrond's particularly shocking description of all of the death—including her own—which she will face if she stays with Aragorn that she momentarily relents (Jackson's *TT*, chapter 38). Even then, Arwen is torn and reluctant; when experiencing a vision of her (possible) future child, she returns to Elrond to scold him about the slanted version he told her of her life with Aragorn (Jackson's *RK*, chapter 9). It is then, just as Arwen determines that she will stay in Middle-earth, that Arwen's immortality vanishes; in Tolkien's text, Arwen's life force does not dim until Arwen gives up her immortality after Aragorn's death, but in Jackson's version, Arwen's commitment to Aragorn triggers her mortality (*RK* Appendix A, I, v; Jackson's *RK*, chapter 10). In the films, Arwen demands that the shards of Narsil be reforged, and she sends Elrond to Aragorn with the new sword, Andúril, Flame of the West. Further, Arwen's gift of the sword makes Aragorn confident enough to take the Paths of the Dead, where he gathers an army to win the Battle of Pelennor Fields, making Arwen indirectly responsible for one of Aragorn's greatest victories

(Jackson's *RK*, chapter 10, 30). Once Elrond tells Aragorn that Arwen's life is tied to the fate of the quest to defeat Sauron and destroy the One Ring because the evil of Mordor is not something she can survive, Aragorn puts aside his doubts and moves forward with kingly intent (Jackson's *RK*, chapter 30–31). His love for Arwen—love he has not given up, for it is love that drives him to tell her to go to the Undying Lands in the first place—motivates and inspires his kingly activity. Aragorn wishes to save Arwen, if possible, even if that means that he dies in the process; or, as he tells Elrond, he keeps no hope for himself, echoing the words of his mother, Gilraen (Jackson's *RK*, chapter 30; *RK* Appendix A, I, v).

In these differences, Jackson weaves a web of redemptive love. Jackson's Aragorn is about to shirk his duties or fail to live up to his full abilities. Arwen consistently sets Aragorn back on the path toward greatness, and in this way, she helps him recover and reorient himself. Her redemption goes beyond these ordinary romantic supports: she supports him by loving him, but Arwen also gives something of herself for his success, namely her Elven immortality.[16] She is confident that he will succeed, and she quite literally puts her life on the line in order to further motivate him. The redemptive power of Arwen's love shows up in her persistent confidence in Aragorn, her constant help given to him from afar, and her recommitment to remain with him despite the death and pain that undoubtedly await her in the future.

AUGUSTINE'S REDEMPTIVE LOVE
AND ADAM'S DAMNING LOVE

Arwen's redemptive love functions in an Augustinian manner. To demonstrate this warrants a closer look at Augustine's theology of love. Following that, we will contrast a comparison of Arwen's salvific love of Aragorn with Adam's damning love of Eve. In Jackson's films, Arwen inverts the Augustinian Edenic fall, saving her partner by love—her love for him and his love for her—instead of leading him to his damnation.

Love is central to Augustine's theology.[17] In his *On Christian Doctrine*, Augustine focuses on love and asserts that love of God and neighbor is central for interpreting all of Scripture.[18] Revealed truth is tied to love, for Augustine asserts that love asks, seeks, knocks, reveals, and assures the permanence of revelation; it takes love to influence one's will and believe God's revelation.[19] The love of God—that is, God's love for God's creatures—is a referent for all other love, including familial, spousal, and platonic love.[20] Human love of God is a component of loving one's neighbor for the neighbor's own sake; without love for God, loved ones become a tool for one's self-interest.[21] Love consummates the virtues, for it is through rightly ordered love that one becomes as good as God's grace enables one to be.[22] As Étienne Gilson puts it, virtue simply is loving "what we should love" for Augustine, and it is love that sets the tone for other mental and physical acts.[23]

Augustine's Trinitarian ontology influentially centers on the notion of love. What the Father and the Son have in common is the Holy Spirit, which Augustine says can be called love. The relations within the Trinity are described as follows: love is the Holy Spirit; loving the Son is the Father; loving the Father is the Son.[24] Augustine makes ample use of 1 John 4:8, which says that "whoever does not love does not know God, for God is love" (1 John 4:8 NRSV). If we see love, then, we see God.[25] The commonplace instances of love in families and friendships allow us to get an initial glimpse of love. Such instances of loving express their own trinity between the lover, the object, and the love.[26] This trinity of love parallels the divine Trinity as described above.

As Gilson explains, love plays this central role in Augustine's theology because love is the force that constantly draws human beings to God.[27] Augustine discusses in his *Confessions* how love draws him toward God similarly as the Earth pulls a rock downward.[28] This gravitational pull of love is the primary mover of human beings.[29] Since humans love, humans must strive to love rightly, and the proper object of love is not one another but God, who created us.[30] Bernard Roland-Gosselin highlights how Augustine understands the will to be divided in humans, meaning that humans can end up loving what is pure or impure. Love can be a force for good, but misapplied, love can guide people toward that which is impure if one loves pleasure, pride, or power more than the proper object of love, which is God.[31] Thus, the power of love compels us to seek for God, to love God, and to act out that love for God in our love for fellow human beings, and this love compels us to act even if we humans misapply it.

Love redeems for Augustine. The fact that human beings do love coupled with their need for love pushes humans to seek out love. Our very human nature leans toward God, leading us to love God.[32] The drive to love comes from God because God is love. Love is a supernatural gift from God, a gift that, like GPS coordinates, helps us seek out the giver.[33] Because love unifies—it unifies within the Trinity, unifies creation to God, and unifies amongst creation—love provides an understanding of the order of the universe and one's place within it.[34] This gravitational pull of love which orients and centers human beings enables and completes the redemption of human beings.

Love of God draws one in, but Augustine also discusses how love can lead one astray. Ideally, one would love oneself and other people because we either are just or could be just. To love something for a different reason—personal pleasure, perhaps—is an error in Augustine's view. To love fully and rightly, one must love "out of God" and "in God," both of which mean that the lover aims the love at God, a love which is then refracted back to the thing loved in or through God.[35] If one enjoys oneself or others on their own account rather than God's account, Augustine describes this as lust.[36] Unchaste love loves things without God, and such so-called love suffers from the same error as eating for pleasure: when one eats, pleasure results, but eating for pleasure (rather than for physical sustenance) substitutes a side effect—the pleasure— for the purpose.[37] To love rightly, one must aim love for friends, family, and the like toward God instead.[38]

On Augustine's analysis, a lack of rightly ordered love contributed to the initial fall of humankind from a state of grace. In *The City of God*, when discussing the Genesis 3 narrative of the expulsion of Adam and Eve from the Garden of Eden for eating the forbidden fruit, Augustine explains that Eve was the weaker member of humanity, so she was approached by Lucifer in the disguise of a snake. Adam, being less gullible, may still be tricked into following a bad example that he himself would not likely set. It was Adam's adherence to social compulsion that made Adam follow Eve's transgression, though Adam did not at the time know it was a transgression.[39] In his *The Literal Meaning of Genesis*, Augustine argues that Adam is a more 'inspirited' human than Eve is, and thus Adam's deception needs clearer explanation of how that could occur. Adam's fall is, like Solomon's, due to the "love of women dragging him into this evil" because Adam was "unwilling to cross the woman."[40] Adam was not afraid of her, but he was afraid for her. Without him, Eve might "pine away" and perish. It was out of "loving concern for their mutual friendship" that Adam ate, and in eating, Adam was condemned.[41] Love for Eve—not lust—is what led Adam to fall with her.

In this interpretation of the Genesis 3 narrative, Augustine insists that Adam is deceived in an entirely different way than Eve. It is his concern for Eve that opens the door to this deception at all. Had Adam not been her true friend, had Adam not worried that she would be helpless without him, Adam would not have fallen with her. Alas, Adam was her true friend, and Adam did worry about her self-sufficiency.[42] These concerns rated higher than Adam's scrutiny of the origin of the fruit, and thus Adam ate. Just as love can redeem, love can condemn.

ARWEN'S REDEMPTIVE LOVE AND ADAM'S DAMNING LOVE

In this twist—the redemptive and damning power of love—stand Aragorn and Arwen from Peter Jackson's films. As noted above, little tension arises from Aragorn and Arwen's romance in Tolkien's text because Aragorn is set on his quest to regain Gondor's throne by the time we meet him, with Arwen consistently supporting him through messages and items delivered through friends and relatives (*FR* II, viii; *RK* V, ii). The plot of *The Lord of the Rings* does not reveal the origins of Aragorn and Arwen's love; Aragorn's quest for the kingship is likely influenced by Elrond telling him that Arwen would not marry someone unimportant, but *The Lord of the Rings* does not hang upon the reader knowing that particular background information (*RK*, Appendix A, I, v). With Peter Jackson's films, though, the love story between Arwen and Aragorn is a source of tension throughout the films.[43] That tension manifests in Aragorn's uncertainty regarding whether he will pursue becoming—let alone become!—king of Gondor, but Jackson also spreads the uncertainty further by tying Arwen's fate to the fate of Middle-earth. In the films, the revelation of Arwen's fate propels Aragorn toward much-needed victory and kingship. In his quest, Aragorn follows Arwen out of love, but unlike Adam, he follows Arwen to salvation rather than damnation.

Arwen and Aragorn invert Augustine's approach to Adam and Eve: the man follows the woman out of love, but when he follows, he is restored to his rightful place as King rather than deposed from his place in the realm. The major components of Augustine's telling of the fall of Adam and Eve are inverted or shifted significantly in Jackson's telling of Arwen and Aragorn's romance. Eve leads to the fall of humanity through her choice to eat the forbidden fruit, and Adam's choice to eat the fruit is out of his great love for Eve rather than out of an affirmation of her decision. The Fall of humankind is, then, Eve's fault, and Adam's great failing is following the woman. Their fall is into evil—the badness is not merely potential, for their actions have resulted in a deprivation of goodness. Adam and Eve alone cannot fix their situation. In giving Adam the fruit, Eve provides Adam with his tool of damnation. Adam and Eve now must start a new age—the age of sinful humankind—and Eve herself can be saved through childbearing (Gen. 3:1; 1 Tim 2:15).

Contrast this with Aragorn and Arwen. Arwen's decision to reforge the sword and her fate becoming tied to the fate of Middle-earth fundamentally move Aragorn toward goodness instead of badness. Just as with Adam and Eve, Aragorn follows Arwen out of love for her. Jackson has included Augustine's notion of a partner following the other out of love. Unlike with Eve, Arwen's peril is not clearly depicted as a result of her decision, but Arwen is clearly shown to be the one who insists on the re-forging of Elendil's sword. Unlike with Eve, Arwen's choice brings healing rather than damnation. While both of their choices have negative personal consequences—unnecessary death—Arwen's choice makes the world a fundamentally better place. Arwen's choice itself is not one that marks her as sinful or weak minded; Jackson does not condemn Arwen's choice, for she fully recovers from her illness and brings new life through her commitment to Aragorn (Jackson's *RK*, chapter 74).[44] Eve's choice brought pain, separation, and damnation for herself and Adam, but Arwen's heals the rift between Elves and Men, albeit eucatastrophically (Gen. 3:16). Arwen provides Aragorn with the sword, which is the tool of his redemption; it is the power to command this sword that guarantees Aragorn's safe passage through the Dimholt road and allegiance of the Army of the Dead. Aragorn's crowning becomes the start of the Fourth Age—the Age of Men. It is the vision of her (possible) child that convinces Arwen to stay and fight, so, like Eve, Arwen (and possibly all of Middle-earth) is saved through childbearing.[45] The most striking difference is the function of the couple's love: Aragorn's love of Arwen leads to the best outcome for Middle-earth, and Arwen's sacrifice of her Elven immortality and eventual continuation of Aragorn's family line ensure that this 'best outcome' will persist through generations. Arwen's love for Aragorn directs him away from worse choices and toward the best choices; her love guides and possibly compels him to do what is good. Her love draws him toward right action, showing that romantic as well as platonic love is redemptive in this adaptation of Tolkien's works.

Thus, we can consider Arwen a type of Eve, yet really an Anti-Eve.[46] Arwen's fealty to Aragorn ends up driving him directly toward the exact sort of greatness needed to save all of Middle-earth. Had Arwen not acted to reforge the sword, likely all would have been lost. Even as Arwen's health faltered, Arwen did not forsake her romantic love for Aragorn but wished for his well-being (Jackson's *RK*, chapter 10, 30). Aragorn never ceased his fealty to Arwen, either, but Aragorn's actions were not led by Arwen's trust in him until he found out that, like Eve, she is likely to suffer alone if he does not act (Jackson's *RK*, chapter 30). Aragorn's love of Arwen leads Aragorn into a final decision: he will fight for the fate of Middle-earth, take up his mantle as King, and do what he can to combat the evil that corrupts her along with the rest of Middle-earth (Jackson's *RK*, chapter 30). In Jackson's portrayal of Aragorn, without Arwen as additional motivation, Aragorn would not likely throw himself into the kingly role.[47] Aragorn fights, and Aragorn wins by drawing troops out of Mordor (despite the likelihood of his own demise), easing Sam and Frodo's passage (Jackson's *RK*, chapters 60, 67). In so doing, Aragorn creates a new paradise for his beloved, a new age in a new, revitalized country. Arwen's love saves Aragorn, who saves the world.

In Jackson's telling, Arwen is no mere reward. Arwen labors as Aragorn does, albeit in different ways, and it is through Arwen's love of Aragorn and his love of her that redemption comes to Middle-earth. While Sam and Frodo's love of one another surely redeems, and Frodo's care for Gollum shows elements of redemptive love, Jackson's interpretation of Arwen and Aragorn deserve to be added to the list of characters for whom love redeems.

The gravitational pull of love between Arwen and Aragorn—one that Jackson toys with and attempts to convince the viewer that either will give up the other—pulls them together toward victory.[48] Each strives for greatness, but Aragorn does not embrace his kingly nature until Arwen needs him to. In Augustine's understanding, Adam fell because of the love he had for Eve; in Jackson's, Aragorn rose because of the love he had for Arwen.

Jackson's telling of Arwen's and Aragorn's love rises to Tolkien's *eucatastrophe* by denying "universal final defeat" and "giving a fleeting glimpse of Joy, Joy beyond the walls of the world, poignant as grief" (*OFS*, 75). Arwen faces certain death because of Mordor's evil, and Aragorn takes the Paths of the Dead to fight to save the world (and Arwen, if possible). More poignantly, Arwen acquiesces to future death in order to experience the joy of a life of love with Aragorn. Arwen's renunciation of her Elven immortality may be seen as a fall of sorts, but this fall saves Middle-earth because her love saves, leads, and supports Aragorn. As Enright argues, female characters in Tolkien invert power, showing "a virtue that in Tolkien's view is crucial to salvation—the choice of love over pride," and this type of salvation is "a message central to the novel and one that transcends all gender roles."[49] What Enright writes about Tolkien's approach to female characters applies to Jackson's interpretation of Arwen and Aragorn as well. Both select love over pride, Arwen in giving up her immortality and Aragorn in giving up his uncertainty to fully fight for the kingship of Gondor and the defeat of Mordor. For both, their love overcomes their pride, and that overcoming redeems not just themselves but all of Middle-earth.

Love redeems in Augustine and in Jackson's telling of Tolkien's tale. If Arwen is the anti-Eve, it is by *kenosis*: she empties herself of her Elven power in such a way that inspires Aragorn to fulfill his destiny (Phil 2:5–8). Love of Aragorn leads to Arwen's *kenosis*, and love of Arwen leads to Aragorn's world-saving. By helping Aragorn take up his kingly mantle, and by providing heirs for the continuation of his line, Arwen redeems Aragorn: her love guides him to be who he ought to be, to be his best. And although Arwen divests herself of her immortality, she does so out of love for Aragorn and her (potential) future children. Jackson's surprisingly Augustinian approach shows how love for Arwen saves Aragorn rather than damns him, redeeming him by drawing him toward doing what is right. All of Middle-earth is saved by the love Arwen and Aragorn share. Love "bears all things, believes all things, hopes all things, endures all things," and, in Jackson's telling of Tolkien, redeems all things (1 Cor 13:7 NRSV).

NOTES

1. I am grateful to the Augustana Research and Artist Fund for a grant supporting work on this project.

2. See also Richard L. Purtill, *J.R.R. Tolkien: Myth, Morality, and Religion* (San Francisco: Harper & Row, 1984), 77.

3. Kristin Kay Johnston, "Christian Theology as Depicted in *The Lord of the Rings* and the Harry Potter Books," *JRS* 7 (2005): 1–9; Philip E. Kaveny, "Frodo Lives but Gollum Redeems the Blood of Kings," in *Picturing Tolkien: Essays on Peter Jackson's* The Lord of the Rings *Film Trilogy*, ed. Janice M. Bogstad and Philip E. Kaveny (Jefferson, N.C.: McFarland, 2011), 183–93; Ralph C. Wood, *The Gospel According to Tolkien: Visions of the Kingdom in Middle-earth* (Louisville: Westminster John Knox, 2003), 117–55; and Matthew Dickerson, *Following Gandalf: Epic Battles and Moral Victory in* The Lord of the Rings (Grand Rapids: Brazos, 2003), 162–64.

4. Janet Brennan Croft, "Jackson's Aragorn and the American Superhero Monomyth," in Bogstad and Kaveny, *Picturing Tolkien*, 219.

5. Richard Purtill describes both Arwen and the crown as Aragorn's rewards in Tolkien's works (Purtill, *Tolkien*, 78).

6. Croft, "Jackson's Aragorn," 220; Richard C. West, "Neither the Shadow nor the Twilight: The Love Story of Aragorn and Arwen in Literature and Film," in Bogstad and Kaveny, *Picturing Tolkien*, 231–34; Kayla McKinney Wiggins, "The Art of the Story-Teller and the Person of the Hero," in *Tolkien on Film: Essays on Peter Jackson's* The Lord of the Rings, ed. Janet Brennan Croft (Altadena, CA: Mythopoeic Press, 2004), 113; Jane Chance, "Tolkien's Women (and Men): The Films and the Book," in Croft, *Tolkien on Film*, 177–91; Cathy Akers-Jordan, "Fairy Princess or Tragic Heroine? The Metamorphosis of Arwen Undómiel in Peter Jackson's *Lord of the Rings* Films," in Croft, *Tolkien on Film*, 195–211; Victoria Gaydosik, "Crimes Against the Book? The Transformation of Tolkien's Arwen from Page to Screen and the Abandonment of the Psyche Archetype," in Croft, *Tolkien on Film*, 219–26; Maureen Thum, "The 'Sub-Creation' of Galadriel, Arwen, and Éowyn: Women of Power in Tolkien's and Jackson's *Lord of the Rings*," in Croft, *Tolkien on Film*, 242–45. Plus see also John R. Holmes, "*The Lord of the Rings*," in *A Companion to J.R.R. Tolkien*, ed. Stuart D. Lee, BCLC (Malden: Wiley Blackwell, 2014), 138.

7. See Richard C. West, "'Her Choice Was Made and Her Doom Appointed': Tragedy and Divine Comedy in the Tale of Aragorn and Arwen," in *The Lord of the Rings 1954–2004: Scholarship in Honor of Richard E. Blackwelder*, ed. Wayne G. Hammond and Christina Scull (Milwaukee: Marquette University Press, 2006), 317–18.

8. Peter Jackson, commentary on *TT*, chapter 38; Gaydosik, "Crimes Against the Book?" 219.

9. Croft, "Jackson's Aragorn," 219; see also Candice Fredrick and Sam McBride, *Women Among the Inklings: Gender, C.S. Lewis, J.R.R. Tolkien, and Charles Williams*, Contributions in Women's Studies (Westport, CT: Greenwood, 2001), 110–11.

10. Croft, "Jackson's Aragorn," 219.

11. Jackson's *FR*, chapter 26; Jackson's *TT*, chapter 33; Jackson's *RK*, chapter 30; Croft, "Jackson's Aragorn," 220.

12. Croft, "Jackson's Aragorn," 220; *FR* II, viii; *RK* V, ii.

13. Anna Caughey, "The Hero's Journey," in Lee, *Companion*, 413; Ruth S. Noel, "Tolkien's Understanding and Use of Mythology to Create a Profound Effect," in *Readings on J.R.R. Tolkien*, ed. Katie de Koster, LCS (San Diego: Greenhaven Press, 2000), 139.

14. Croft, "Jackson's Aragorn," 220.

15. Nancy Enright, "Tolkien's Females and the Defining of Power," in *J.R.R. Tolkien's* The Lord of the Rings, ed. Harold Bloom, new ed., BMCI (New York: Bloom's Literary Criticism, 2008), 175–76.

16. Vanessa Phillips-Zur-Linden, "Arwen and Edward: Redemption and the Fairy Bride/Groom in the Literary Fairytale," *Mallorn* 50 (2010): 37.

17. Armand A. Maurer, *Medieval Philosophy*, 2nd ed., EGS 4 (Toronto: Pontifical Institute of Medieval Studies, 1982), 16.

18. Gerald W. Schlabach, *For the Joy Set Before Us: Augustine and Self-Denying Love* (Notre Dame: University of Notre Dame Press, 2001), 29–30; Augustine, *De doctrina christiana libri quattuor*, ed. Carl Hermann Bruder, 2nd ed. (St. Louis: Synodi Missouriensis Lutheranae, 1927), 3.10.16, 1.35.39, 1.36.40, 2.7.10, 3.10.14, 3.16.24.

19. Augustine, *De moribus ecclesiae catholicae et de moribus manichaeorum libri duo*, ed. Johannes B. Bauer, CSEL 90 (Vienna: Hoelder-Pichler-Tempsky, 1992), 1.17.31, 11.2.4; Eugène Portalié, S.J., *A Guide to the Thought of Saint Augustine* (Chicago: H. Regnery, 1960), 107–8.

20. Schlabach, *For the Joy*, 30; Augustine, *De doctrina christiana* 1.5.5; Augustine, *De Civitate Dei, Book X*, ed. Patrick G. Walsh, APCT (Oxford: Aris & Phillips, 2014), 10.3.

21. Schlabach, *For the Joy*, 36–37; Augustine, *Confessiones*, 2nd ed. (Oxford: Jacob Parker Press, 1872), 4.9.14.

22. Augustine, *Enarrationes in Psalmos 1–50, Pars 1b: Enarrationes in Psalmos 18–32*, ed. Clemens Weidmann, CSEL 93.1b (Vienna: Österreichischen Akademie der Wissenschaften, 2011), 31.5; Étienne Gilson, *The Christian Philosophy of Saint Augustine*, trans. L.E.M. Lynch (Providence: Cluny, 2020), 200.

23. Gilson, *Christian Philosophy*, 193. See Augustine, *De Civitate Dei, Books VIII & IX*, ed. P. G. Walsh (Cambridge: Aris & Phillips Classical Texts, 2013), 9.7.2.

24. Augustine, *The Trinity*, FC 45 (Washington, DC: Catholic University of America Press, 1963), 6.5.

25. Augustine, *The Trinity* 8.9.

26. Augustine, *The Trinity* 8.9.

27. Gilson, *Christian Philosophy*, 191.

28. Augustine, *Confessiones* 13.9.10.

29. Augustine, *The Trinity* 11.7.12.

30. Augustine, *Enarrationes in Psalmos* 31.2.5.

31. Bernard Roland-Gosselin, "St. Augustine's System of Morals," in *Saint Augustine: His Age, Life, and Thought*, ed. Martin Cyril D'Arcy (New York: Meridian Books, 1957), 241.

32. Roland-Gosselin, "St. Augustine's System of Morals," 233.

33. Maurer, *Medieval Philosophy*, 17; the analogy is mine.

34. Augustine, *The Trinity* 8.10.14.

35. Augustine, *The Trinity* 8.9.

36. Augustine, *De doctrina christiana* 3.10.16.

37. Augustine, *Confessiones*, 2.6.14; 10.31.38.

38. Augustine, *Confessiones*, 4.12.18.

39. Augustine, *De Civitate Dei, Books XIII & XIV*, ed. Patrick G. Walsh, C. Collard, and Isabella Christine, APCT (Liverpool: Liverpool University Press, 2017), 14.11.

40. Augustine, *Genesi Ad litteram libri duodecim: Eiusdem libri capitula, de genesi ad litteram imperfectus liber, locutionum in heptateuchum libri septem,* ed. Joseph Zycha (Vienna: Österreichischen Akademie der Wissenschaften, 2013), 9.42.58–59.

41. Augustine, *De genesi ad litteram* 9.42.59–60. Augustine remains convinced that Adam would not be able to be tricked by the serpent due to his 'inspirited' nature.

42. In context, the discussion of self-sufficiency and Eve's lack of it makes sense because this discussion occurs after an extended conversation about how Eve is a helpmeet, and thus Eve assists Adam, but Eve herself is subordinate to Adam and therefore needs his guidance. See Augustine, *De genesi ad literam* 9.5.9.

43. Peter Jackson, commentary on *TT*, chapter 38; Gaydosik, "Crimes Against the Book?" 219.

44. Jane Chance, The Lord of the Rings*: The Mythology of Power*, rev. ed. (Lexington: University Press of Kentucky, 2001), 122–23. Especially for Tolkien, Arwen and Aragorn's union holds political and familial significance. They unite the houses of Men and Elves, and Arwen provides for continuation of the lineage. See, for example, George Thomson's claim that, in the joining of Arwen and Aragorn, "fertility and the natural cycle are reasserted." See George H. Thomson, "*The Lord of the Rings*: The Novel as Traditional Romance," *WSCL* 8 (1967): 47.

45. Arwen achieves "immortality through children," which, according to Jessica Kemball-Cook, makes her Aragorn's active partner rather than a passive love interest. See Jessica Kemball-Cook, "Male Chauvinist Lions: Sex Discrimination in Tolkien and C.S. Lewis, Part 1," *Mallorn* 10 (1976): 17.

46. Donald Richmond names Arwen a mother and compares her to Mary because of the significance of Arwen's motherhood. See Donald P. Richmond, "Tolkien's Marian Vision of Middle-earth," *Mallorn* 40 (2002): 13.

47. It is difficult to assess the impact of Arwen in Aragorn's decision making about the kingship in Tolkien's narrative. However, Elrond makes it clear that he sees Aragorn as having abandoned the path to kingship (Jackson's *FR*, chapter 24).

48. See, for example, the tension Jackson tries to create between Aragorn, Arwen, and Éowyn in *TT*, chapter 33.

49. Enright, "Tolkien's Females," 173.

BIBLIOGRAPHY

Akers-Jordan, Cathy. "Fairy Princess or Tragic Heroine? The Metamorphosis of Arwen Undómiel in Peter Jackson's *The Lord of the Rings* Films." Pages 195–214 in *Tolkien on Film: Essays on Peter Jackson's the Lord of the Rings*. Edited by Janet Brennan Croft. Altadena, CA: Mythopoeic Press, 2004.

Augustine. *Confessiones*. 2nd ed. Oxford: Jacob Parker Press, 1872.

———. *De Civitate Dei, Book VIII & IX*. Edited by Patrick G. Walsh. Cambridge: Aris & Phillips Classical Texts, 2013.

———. *De Civitate Dei, Book X*. Edited by Patrick G. Walsh. Oxford: Aris & Phillips, 2014.

———. *De Civitate Dei, Books XIII & XIV*. Edited by Patrick G. Walsh, C. Collard, and Isabella Christine. Liverpool: Liverpool University Press, 2017.

———. *De doctrina christiana libri quattuor*. Edited by Carl Hermann Bruder. 2nd ed. Sancti Ludovici: Synodi Missouriensis Lutheranae, 1927.

———. *Enarrationes in Psalmos 1–50, Pars 1b, Enarrationes in Psalmos 18–32*. Edited by Clemens Weidmann. CSEL 93.1b. Vienna: Österreichischen Akademie der Wissenschaften, 2011.

———. *Genesi ad litteram libri duodecim: eiusdem libri capitula, de genesi ad litteram imperfectus liber, locutionum in heptateuchum libri septem*. Edited by Joseph Zycha. Vienna: Österreichischen Akademie der Wissenschaften, 2013.

———. *De moribus ecclesiae catholicae et de moribus manichaeorum libri duo*. Edited by Johannes B. Bauer. CSEL 90. Vienna: Hoelder-Pichler-Tempsky, 1992.

———. *The Trinity*. FC 45. Washington, DC: Catholic University of America Press, 1963.

Caughey, Anna. "The Hero's Journey." Pages 404–17 in *A Companion to J.R.R. Tolkien*. Edited by Stuart D. Lee. Malden: Wiley Blackwell, 2014.

Chance, Jane. *The Lord of the Rings: The Mythology of Power*. Rev. ed. Lexington: University Press of Kentucky, 2001.

———. "Tolkien's Women (and Men): The Films and the Book." Pages 175–94 in *Tolkien on Film: Essays on Peter Jackson's The Lord of the Rings*. Edited by Janet Brennan Croft. Altadena, CA: Mythopoeic Press, 2004.

Croft, Janet Brennan. "Jackson's Aragorn and the American Superhero Monomyth." Pages 216–226 in *Picturing Tolkien: Essays on Peter Jackson's Lord of the Rings Film Trilogy*. Edited by Janice M. Bogstad and Philip E. Kaveny. Jefferson, NC: McFarland, 2011.

Dickerson, Matthew. *Following Gandalf: Epic Battles and Moral Victory in* The Lord of the Rings. Grand Rapids: Brazos, 2003.

Enright, Nancy. "Tolkien's Females and the Defining of Power." Pages 171–86 in *J.R.R. Tolkien's* The Lord of the Rings. Edited by Harold Bloom. BMCI. New York: Bloom's Literary Criticism, 2008.

Fredrick, Candice, and Sam McBride. *Women Among the Inklings: Gender, C.S. Lewis, J.R.R. Tolkien, and Charles Williams*. Contributions in Women's Studies. Westport, CT: Greenwood, 2001.

Gaydosik, Victoria. "Crimes Against the Book? The Transformation of Tolkien's Arwen from Page to Screen and the Abandonment of the Psyche Archetype." Pages 215–30 in *Tolkien on Film: Essays on Peter Jackson's the Lord of the Rings*. Edited by Janet Brennan Croft. Altadena, CA: Mythopoeic Press, 2004.

Gilson, Étienne. *The Christian Philosophy of Saint Augustine*. Translated by L.E.M. Lynch. Providence: Cluny, 2020.

Holmes, John R. *"The Lord of the Rings."* Pages 133–45 in *A Companion to J.R.R. Tolkien*. Edited by Stuart D. Lee. BCLC. Malden: Wiley Blackwell, 2014.

Johnston, Kristin Kay. "Christian Theology as Depicted in *The Lord of the Rings* and the Harry Potter Books." *JRS* 7 (2005): 1–9.

Kaveny, Philip E. "Frodo Lives but Gollum Redeems the Blood of Kings." Pages 183–93 in *Picturing Tolkien: Essays on Peter Jackson's* The Lord of the Rings *Film Trilogy*. Edited by Janice M. Bogstad and Philip E. Kaveny. Jefferson, NC: McFarland, 2011.

Kemball-Cook, Jessica. "Male Chauvinist Lions: Sex Discrimination in Tolkien and C.S. Lewis, Part 1." *Mallorn* 10 (1976): 14–19.

Maurer, Armand A. *Medieval Philosophy*. 2nd ed. Toronto: Pontifical Institute of Medieval Studies, 1982.

McKinney Wiggins, Kayla. "The Art of the Story-Teller and the Person of the Hero." Pages 103–22 in *Tolkien on Film: Essays on Peter Jackson's* The Lord of the Rings. Edited by Janet Brennan Croft. Altadena, CA: Mythopoeic Press, 2004.

Noel, Ruth S. "Tolkien's Understanding and Use of Mythology to Create a Profound Effect." Pages 134–40 in *Readings on J.R.R. Tolkien*. Edited by Katie de Koster. San Diego: Greenhaven Press, 2000.

Phillips-Zur-Linden, Vanessa. "Arwen and Edward: Redemption and the Fairy Bride/ Groom in the Literary Fairytale." *Mallorn* 50 (2010): 37–41.

Portalié, Eugène. *A Guide to the Thought of Saint Augustine*. Chicago: H. Regnery, 1960.

Purtill, Richard L. *J.R.R. Tolkien: Myth, Morality, and Religion*. San Francisco: Harper & Row, 1984.

Richmond, Donald P. "Tolkien's Marian Vision of Middle-earth." *Mallorn* 40 (2002): 13–14.

Roland-Gosselin, Bernard. "St. Augustine's System of Morals." Pages 225–48 in *Saint Augustine: His Age, Life, and Thought*. Edited by Martin Cyril D'Arcy. New York: Meridian Books, 1957.

Schlabach, Gerald. *For the Joy Set Before Us: Augustine and Self-Denying Love*. Notre Dame: University of Notre Dame Press, 2001.

Thomson, George H. *"The Lord of the Rings*: The Novel as Traditional Romance." *WSCL* 8 (1967): 43–59. doi:10.2307/1207129.

Thum, Maureen. "The 'Sub-Creation' of Galadriel, Arwen, and Éowyn: Women of Power in Tolkien's and Jackson's *Lord of the Rings*." Pages 231–58 in *Tolkien on Film: Essays on Peter Jackson's the Lord of the Rings*. Edited by Janet Brennan Croft. Altadena, CA: Mythopoeic Press, 2004.

Tolkien, J.R.R. *The Letters of J.R.R. Tolkien*. Edited by Humphrey Carpenter. Boston: Houghton Mifflin, 2006.

———. "On Fairy Stories." Pages 27–84 in *Tolkien On Fairy-stories*. Edited by Verlyn Flieger and Douglas A. Anderson. London: HarperCollins, 2008.

West, Richard C. "Her Choice Was Made and Her Doom Appointed: Tragedy and Divine Comedy in the Tale of Aragorn and Arwen." Pages 317–30 in *The Lord of the Rings 1954–2004: Scholarship in Honor of Richard E. Blackwelder.* Edited by Wayne G. Hammond and Christina Scull. Milwaukee: Marquette University Press, 2006.

———. "Neither the Shadow nor the Twilight: The Love Story of Aragorn and Arwen in Literature and Film." Pages 227–37 in *Picturing Tolkien.* Edited by Janice M. Bogstad and Philip E. Kaveny. Jefferson, NC: McFarland, 2011.

Wood, Ralph C. *The Gospel According to Tolkien: Visions of the Kingdom in Middle-earth.* Louisville: Westminster John Knox, 2003.

Chapter 13

Spiritual Sloth and Diligence in Tolkien's Work

Martina Juričková

In almost every literary work, the main conflicts arise from the struggle between good and evil.[1] In fantasy literature, including Tolkien's works, as they are considered the epitome of the genre, this struggle is often all the more evident to the reader since good and evil are frequently embodied by specific character types—good mostly by fair races and evil by foul monsters. The foul and fair wage an eternal war on each other due to an apparently innate, and simple, moral dichotomy. That this moral distinction can seem to be so clear cut on a surface level allows certain readers to criticize Tolkien for his good characters being consistently good and his evil characters immutably evil.[2] While some scholars have tried to disprove or modulate these criticisms, most frequently using Boromir and Gollum as examples of morally ambiguous characters, it is not easy to assess the characters' morality with certainty.[3] However, one way to gauge morality can come via the identification and evaluation of the characters' virtues and vices, because virtue and vice are key theological markers of moral goodness or wickedness from a human perspective.[4]

Tolkien's work was heavily and consciously influenced by his faith, as he proudly admitted on several occasions. For example, in the famous letter to Milton Waldman, he wrote: *The Lord of the Rings* "is involved in, and explicitly contains the Christian religion," and in a letter to Father Robert Murray he added that it is "a fundamentally religious and Catholic work; unconsciously so at first, but consciously in revision" (*Letters*, 131 and 142, respectively). Of course, Middle-earth is supposed to be set in time long before the coming of Christ and is thus essentially not a Christian world, but it is a monotheistic world permeated with Christian morality, disguised as "natural theology"

(*Letters*, 165). And since vices and virtues often act as primary determinants of morality, we presume that they would play as important a role in the constitution of Middle-earth's morality as they do in modern Christian faith and practice. In line with his philosophy of sub-creation, presented in the essay "On Fairy-stories," we can expect that the characters' exercise of virtues or vices, the total sum of which indicate their moral value, also influences their attainment of the moment of eucatastrophe.[5] This hypothesis is supported by Tolkien's claim that Frodo was only granted the eucatastrophic ending of his quest thanks to his previous exercise of such virtues as pity and mercy (*Letters*, 246). Analogically, any character's exercise of virtues should complement their attainment of eucatastrophe, and, conversely, the exercise of vices should deter it or outright contribute to the fate of discatastrophe.

Because the number of virtues and vices is great and the extent of this chapter limited, we narrow its scope to but one polar pair of these moral habits. But how to pick which pair? Many Christian traditions, following the teaching of Thomas Aquinas, believe that all sins have their root in the seven capital vices, which are also the gravest of vices.[6] Recognizing the struggle between virtue and vice, good and evil, are of great significance in Tolkien's work, we will focus on the theological aspect of the pair which proves most evident in Tolkien's depiction of the vice and its opposing virtue. Subjecting Tolkien's three major Middle-earth books—*The Hobbit*, *The Lord of the Rings*, and *The Silmarillion*—to scrutiny, the most theologically relevant vice in them turns out to be sloth, the opposing virtue of which is diligence.

PHYSICAL SLOTH

Sloth is usually interpreted as physical laziness, and there can be many examples of it found in Tolkien's stories as well. It manifests itself mainly in the characters' weariness in journeying, neglect of duty, or the shirking of duty onto someone else, which almost always has dire consequences. For example, when Gondorians neglected their guard over Mordor after Sauron's first defeat, evil creatures re-inhabited the land to prepare it for the Dark Lord's return (*RK*, Appendix A). All the three aforementioned of Tolkien's books criticize the negative impact of idleness almost from the first pages and accentuate the need to take action and do so quickly. At issue is that the Free Peoples of Middle-earth usually wait for the enemies' moves and merely react to those; they only defend themselves in haste rather than proactively working to counter evil before and as it arises. It follows that good people need greater diligence and wariness in order to fight the evil more effectively. What happens when one neglects to take action when needed is best illustrated by the Shire-folk, who fail to recognize the right moment to stand against the ruffians oppressing them and as a result are tyrannized by them (*RK*, VI, viii). Because of this, and because of their overall seclusion from and ignorance of the world outside their borders, the Hobbits' actions reveal a proneness to sloth. In this, they are like another race, the Ents.

Tolkien described Hobbits as particularly liable to sloth manifested; not only in their unsophisticated pacifism and ignorance of the larger world, but especially in their general carelessness (*Letters*, 203). For example, the four Hobbit heroes in *The Lord of the Rings* come to catastrophic ends due to their overt reliance on other authorities to decide the course of their journey, disregard of these authorities' advice, and neglect to learn enough about the history or geography of the places they visit several times. The accident at the Barrow-downs or Frodo's heedless escape from Shelob's tunnel illustrate their carelessness well. In addition, the Shire-folk generally display a lot of "that's not my business" attitude when they are trying not to interfere in any-body else's problems as long as it does not concern them personally, some due to fear and others due to mere ignorance and wish not to be disturbed in their way of life. Such was their attitude also toward Lotho's foreign business with the pipe weed (*RK*, VI, viii), but his business was "not anybody's busi-ness" only until it became everyone's business and misery, when the ruffians Lotho was trading with moved into the Shire.

The Ents display the same kind of ignorance toward everything happening outside Fangorn forest until it starts destroying their forest via Saruman's Orcs. The Ents are so slothful and inert that they literally become treeish again. It is their ignorance of the Entwives' needs that drives the females away and their neglect in trying to search for them until it was too late led to their race dying out. Moreover, as Charles Nelson points out, after the disap-pearance of the Entwives, the Ents withdrew deep into the forest, wallowing in self-pity, whereby they neglected even their duty as tree shepherds and allowed for the outside evil (Saruman) to destroy the trees they were sup-posed to protect.[7]

ACEDIA

However, physical idleness is just one of the aspects of sloth. The original Christian understanding of this vice pertains rather to spiritual (in)activ-ity. The Latin name of this vice is *acedia*, and denotes a "sourness of the mind."[8] Originally the term comes from Greek ἀκηδία which had a broad scope of meaning, from "lack of care" to "exhaustion" and "apathy." It was only in the fourth century when the monk Evagrius of Pontus (345–399 CE) adopted this term for a specific temptation he and other desert hermit monks were facing and provided the first complex definition of spiritual sloth.[9] It was only in the thirteenth century when the term *acedia* was substituted by *sloth* (with the first such translation in literature written in the British Isles dating back to year 1000 and the monastic writer Aelfric), also signifying the shift in the vice's meaning toward negligence in physical activity.[10]

The Catechism of the Roman Catholic Church today defines sloth as a "form of depression due to lax ascetical practice, decreasing vigilance, carelessness of heart."[11] To this, Helen Oppenheimer's entry in *A New Dictionary of Christian Ethics* adds that it is a form of spiritual apathy, particularly to God and his law, that cuts into the receptivity of people to charity—the general "couldn't care less attitude."[12] It is characterized by indifference, negligence, hesitation to God's calling and the destiny he allocates for us, and disregard and coldness for one's neighbor and their needs.

But to understand the essence of the vice, we need to consider how Evagrius originally defined it and how its conception later evolved. In Evagrius' interpretation, *acedia* is a vice to which the ascetic and hermit monks who lived in isolation in the deserts were particularly susceptible. He defines *acedia* as the working of the "noonday" demon who instilled into the monks' hearts and minds images and desires of things more pleasurable than reading, praying, and contemplation to which they were supposed devote all their time, trying to distract them from their duties.[13] From the beginning, *acedia* was a very complex, multi-faceted vice impossible to be identified as purely spiritual or carnal vice because it affected all the human faculties—concupiscible, irascible, and rational[14]—in order to avert the monks from attaining the higher states of spiritual perfection, *apatheia* and *gnostiké*, that is "a kind of self-controlled tranquillity resulting from the satisfaction of emotions and desires" and a "true happiness through the purification and perfection of the rational soul," as Jones explains.[15] The noonday devil always appealed to the monks' greatest weaknesses based on the person's natural disposition to a host of temptations, the combination of which was directed just to one singular end—making the monk so tired and disgusted with his job that he would quit his vocation or life.[16] The vice, in Evagrius' understanding was thus a combination of the power of an external evil agent and the disposition of human nature which tended to perpetrate the devil-induced ideas.[17]

The teaching about *acedia* was brought to Western Europe by John Cassian who adapted the definition of *acedia* to the specifics of monastic life.[18] Medieval monasteries were self-sustained communities in which manual work played as important a role as praying and contemplation, so in this context the carnal aspect of *acedia* slowly started to gain prominence. Cassian defined it as a "slothful laziness stemming from 'a wearied or anxious heart'" and a sadness which "wearies the soul and keeps one from proper labor and action."[19] As Wenzler observes, all through the eleventh century *acedia* was then understood as primarily physical idleness until the emergence of Scholasticism in the twelfth century attempted to revive its spiritual significance and consolidate the teaching of the Desert Fathers with Classical Greek and Roman philosophy in order to show that the two are not mutually exclusive.[20] Thomas Aquinas, one of the greatest Scholastic thinkers two centuries later, made the definition of *acedia* applicable to the general laic Christian public.

Aquinas quotes Damascene's definition of sloth as a kind of "oppressive sorrow, which . . . so weighs upon man's mind, that he wants to do nothing," and hence "implies a certain weariness of work."[21] But unlike other sources, he supplies a reason for this spiritual weariness—it does not come out of nowhere or out of disbelief in God or out of some external temptation; instead, man is negligent to acquire spiritual goods due to them being perceived as arduous and on account of the attendant labor. It is the idea of a long "process of transformation through habituation that humans must undergo" that makes them unwilling to devote themselves to the offered spiritual good and God's love.[22] In fact, as DeYoung notes, Aquinas's sloth is "characterized by the movement of the will which is the opposite of love," particularly Christian love—charity.[23] This sorrow is a response to the feeling of oppression by a present evil or hardship and makes one resistant to God's charity toward us. As DeYoung summarizes it, God wants to give us his friendship and graces in order to change us from the sinful fallen people to new heavenly people, but as this process is tedious and hard, and also due to the natural inclination of our sinful nature to seek the easiest path, we are reluctant to undergo it and reject God's love.[24]

Towards the end of Middle Ages, the public's knowledge of *acedia* was shaped mainly through confessionals—books that initially served confessors as guides on how to conduct a good confession in their parishioners. These included scrutinous questions designed to help people examine their conscience thoroughly. As far as *acedia* was concerned, the questions targeted the recognition of its manifestation not only in the life of the clergy or the practice of religion among the layfolk, but also in every aspect of their everyday lives with respect to their social class, marital status, occupation or geographical area.[25] Thus the understanding of the vice was broadened from a mere (put very simply) "negligence in the fulfilment of spiritual duties" to the "slackening attention and man's inability to sustain concentration and to engage in one and the same activity for any prolonged period."[26] Or as Alain de Lille (1128–1202/1203) states it in his *Theologicae Regulae*: "Acedia is the torpor of the mind by which one either neglects to begin good works or grows weary in finishing them."[27]

In the Renaissance era, the influence of the Roman Catholic Church decreased in Western life due to the onset of the Protestant Reformation and the rise of humanism, and the medieval theological-moral system was largely replaced by various nontheological systems that based their moral proclamations on the analysis of human behavior and psyche. Sloth was reduced to physical laziness, weariness, inertia, or torpor, often ascribed to the imbalance of bodily humors (blood, bile, phlegm) or equated with illnesses such as podagra, paralysis, melancholy, and depression. At the best, the public became to recognize sloth as a vice when it caused "neglect in the obligation of one's *status* or profession" or a failure in the performance of one's duties.[28]

In the later centuries, even within a theological context thinkers contented themselves with summarizing or harmonizing the various historical traditions about the concept of *acedia*/sloth rather than exploring its presence and effects in modern humans' lives.[29] Ironically, in the secularized capitalistic work-driven and achievement-focused society of the third millennia, where an individual's worth is measured by how much and how hard one works, sloth is once again viewed as the greatest vice.[30] Unfortunately, devoid of its original spiritual significance.

The spiritual aspect of sloth—and its adjacent vices—manifests itself in numerous ways throughout Tolkien's work.[31] In his books, spiritual sloth usually arises from the characters' lack of longanimity and belief in Providence. Interestingly, each book takes a slightly different approach to the vice. In *The Hobbit* and *The Silmarillion*, the criticism of sloth is more implicit, with the first accentuating rather the physical aspect of sloth and the latter depicting both aspects in about equal merit. In contrast, *The Lord of the Rings* highlights its spiritual aspect more and is also the novel which explores the vice to the fullest.

Disbelief

In *The Hobbit*, spiritual sloth is mainly reflected in the dwarves' lack of belief in anything beyond the material world. While Dwarves as a race, especially in *The Silmarillion*, are reverent to Aulë, one of the semi-divine Valar, in *The Hobbit*, there is no mention of this—obviously, because this book was not originally intended to be a part of the legendarium. Nonetheless, Thorin's dwarves appear to lack belief in any kind of divine beings or Providence as such, similar to the exiled Noldor in the second half of the *Quenta Silmarillion*—though in their case, the lack of trust in the Valar and Eru is due to the fact that the Valar have forsaken them. Having to rely on their own powers, the attitudes of both Thorin's dwarves and the Noldor to conflicts or problems become more matter-of-fact, whereby in the *The Hobbit* and the later parts of *The Silmarillion*, hope gains more of a secular quality, in contrast to the *Ainulindalë* and *Valaquenta*, which represent a retelling of the Christian myth of the creation of the world. In these parts of the legendarium, hope has a more theological character, as the Valar and Eru represent angels and God. However, Tolkien's depiction of the Noldor's declining belief and hope in the Valar and Eru teaches an important theological lesson. Thinking to be forsaken by the divinities, the Noldor forsake them in return, become ignorant of the signs of Providence in their lives, and try to defeat the Satanic Melkor on their own. This is not unlike the Israelites in the Old Testament, who at various times feel abandoned by God, begin to worship foreign gods, do not listen to God's calls to return, and try to create a kingdom on their own. But the Noldor's efforts prove unsuccessful as long as they persist in pride and wrath at the Valar. They are only able to defeat the Dark Lord when they humble themselves, regret their sins, and plead for divine help. This is a great illustration of how even people in our world are incapable of defeating the demons that tempt them on their own, but need God's help and mercy to do so. And that we, like the Noldor, and Israelites, learn only when we humble ourselves before God (Jas 4:10).

Superstition

Another sign of spiritual sloth and disbelief in Providence is superstition, foregrounded mainly in *The Hobbit* and in the story of Túrin, where the concept is, in fact, the most elaborated from among all of Tolkien's stories. In *The Hobbit*, superstition is exemplified by Thorin's company's belief that having only thirteen members will bring them ill luck, and the Lake-town folk's beliefs in ancient legends and prophecies on which they rely in the hopes that someone else will come and make amends with the dragon in their stead. The Lake-town folk had little hope in themselves and hence viewed Thorin as their savior, while all the time their eventual savior, Bard, was in their midst. This not only creates a powerful moral paradox but echoes the life of Christ and complements the Christ-figure aspect of Bard's character.

In Túrin's story, the vice of superstition is, according to Tom Shippey, mainly linked to the concepts of "doom" and "fate," words people use when they cannot find a better explanation (or identify the true one) of their (mis)fortunes.[32] Theologically, belief in these concepts indicates a lack of belief in God, his immense love and mercy, as well as his sovereignty. Tolkien promotes the superstition in Túrin's story through his fatalistic approach to unlucky objects (the Dragon-helm of Dor-lómin, and the sword Anglachel), Melkor's curse, or inherited failings, but mainly name symbolism. Túrin changes his name several times in the hope to escape his fate, refusing to admit that fate does not consist in any external forces but in his own actions.

As Helen Lasseter Freeh points out, "to accept the supremacy of fate over free will is to remove responsibility for one's actions and thus the subsequent consequences of those actions."[33] By blaming his misfortunes of his fate, Túrin just tries to get rid of the feeling of guilt arising from his own poor decisions. However, his attempts to change his identity do not change who he is inside as long as he is unwilling to change his behavior dominated by pride and stubbornness (cf. Matt 23:27). The last nickname he gives himself, Turambar, "Master of Doom," sounds all the more hypocritical since he cannot even master his own vices but allows himself to be easily driven by them, which thus provides corroboration for the antithesis Nienor Níniel develops his name into: *Túrin Turambar turun ambartanent: master of doom by doom mastered* (*Silmarillion*, 223). It is his vices that make up Túrin's doom as he is overmastered by them. Moreover, his superstition deprives him of most of his joy of life, manifested in his lack of laughter, and makes him bitter—which are both signs of despair—a symptom of *acedia*.

In her essay, Freeh further discusses to what extent the outcome of Túrin's life is determined by Melkor's curse and by Túrin's own decisions. She observes that even the fictional narrator of Túrin's story ascribes his misfortunes almost solely to the effect of the curse at the beginning. However, it has to be noted that Túrin knew nothing about this curse as it was revealed only to his father Húrin while imprisoned by Melkor.[34] Thus, he could not consciously blame his ill luck on it. At most, he could only blame it on the dragon's spell—the dragon who was sent by Melkor deliberately to track Túrin down and challenge him. But even its effect was temporary and, as Freeh shows, all the disastrous happenings in Túrin's life are the consequences of the choices he makes based on his free will, usually incurred by his vices. What is perceived as fate are actually just the inevitable outcomes of a chain of wrong decisions.

Fear, Depression, and Despair

Despair typically arises from fear, which is sensible if it is felt in the presence of some evil, like the Dark Lord's (in such case, a lack of fear would be a sign of pride or daring), and can be even a positive force when it prompts one to action (fighting the evil). But if it leads to lethargy, paralysis, or abandonment of duty, it becomes vicious; a sign of sloth. Good examples of such debilitating fear are occasions when warriors, threatened by their enemies, run away from the battlefield or the scene when Frodo is attacked by the monster from the lake at Moria gate, the horror of which roots everyone to the ground except for Sam (*FR*, II, iv).

A long-term exposure to such fear can lead to the development of depression. In fact, Treloar claimed that "in contemporary language sloth looks

[like] depression, which often manifests itself as inactivity," and I would add, leans to despair.[35] The concept of depression is most explored in *The Lord of the Rings*, where its best representative, according to Treloar, is Théoden, in whom this state is incited by Saruman's lies and manipulation, distilled through Gríma, due to which Théoden loses contact with reality and, consequently, all hope. Depression, caused by a lack of hope in healing, can also apply to the state Frodo experiences when he annually falls ill on the anniversaries of his wounds, or what Faramir, Merry, and Éowyn experience after being hurt in confrontation with the Nazgûl, which they call the Black Shadow. While in the case of Men, their depression is reflected mainly in rapid physical (health) deterioration, like in Théoden's case, its harmful effects on the psyche are best evidenced in Merry's strain of thought while walking through the streets of Minas Tirith, when it seemed to him "a meaningless journey in a hateful dream, going on and on to some dim ending that memory cannot seize," (*RK*, V, xiii), which perfectly captures the essence of depression.

As for despair, Tolkien often used the word colloquially, indicating momentary loss of hope in a successful end of some activity, but not the ultimate loss of hope in Providence. Such approach to despair is dominant mainly in *The Hobbit*, where the characters never give up utterly but face their growing fear and despair with stubbornness and determination. In contrast, in *The Lord of the Rings*, the hope in the existence of Providence, as some power beyond the physical world that governs all happenings in it, is emphasized from the early pages, when Gandalf tells Frodo that chances (coincidences) do not exist and Frodo was meant to inherit the Ring just as Bilbo was meant to find it (*FR*, I, ii). In this novel, there is probably no character on the side of good who would not acknowledge Providence to some extent, though they may not be aware of it themselves, because as Gandalf notes, some call it chance or luck. It is this unconscious belief which prevents characters from giving up, but makes them fight for their survival and can even give birth to new hope along the lines "oft hope is born when all is forlorn." (*RK*, V, ix). This is best exemplified by Sam's song in the tower of Cirith Ungol (*RK*, VI, i).

Although providential power seems to permeate Middle-earth, "those who live within the design cannot always discern it."[36] Those who are unable to discern it or are imperceptive to it, cannot find a good source of hope outside it and so succumb to despair. Despair becomes vicious only when it leads to utter recoil from the joy of life and life as such. Craig Boyd, analyzing the effects of hope or its lack and regaining it in *The Leaf by Niggle*, claims that "people who despair acknowledge that the object hoped for is, in truth, a good to be pursued. Yet, [they] are committed to the belief to which [they] cannot attain because it seems too difficult."[37] In Gandalf's words, the essence of despair is "see[ing] the end beyond all doubt," (*FR*, II, ii). Seeing the end as bad and "beyond all doubt" denotes the lack of hope for a better one. Comparing Denethor's and Éowyn's attitude to their despair—the first mentioned being an epitome thereof as a person succumbing to despair—it turns out that in Tolkien's stories, death is almost an inevitable result of despair, as characters who lack hope (particularly in Providence) tend to give up on their lives and see the only resolution of their miseries in suicide. For instance, Denethor, unable to imagine not being the ruler of Gondor anymore, prefers to burn in a pyre rather than to cede his ruling power. On the contrary, Éowyn, finding new sense of life in her relationship with Faramir, is healed of her despair and stops longing for valiant death on the battlefield.

The depiction of despair in *The Silmarillion* supports this observation, particularly again in Túrin's story. While there are several instances when Túrin falls to despair following a sin he has committed (accidentally killing Beleg Cúthalion, forsaking Finduilas), which validates his despair, on other occasions it leads him to a trance-like state of depression, like when he mourns the death of Finduilas. Similar debilitating yet partially validated despair is experienced by Beren, mourning the death of Finrod. However, while Beren overcomes his despair due to the power of love, Túrin in the end, learning the truth about his relation to Nienor Níniel, succumbs to it.[38] His story is a good example of when despair, in combination with other vices such as pride and imprudence, reverts the attainment of personal eucatastrophe and leads to a catastrophe instead, in the same manner as Denethor's story.[39]

DILIGENCE

Because *acedia* is manifested in so many varied forms, theologians over the ages have not agreed on any single virtue that would stand as its contrary. Usually, they name a number of virtues that serve as the remedy of *acedia* dependent on its particular symptoms in a given individual. For example, Evagrius suggested that the best way to win over one's *acedia* is to face and withstand the temptation it provides.[40] Thus, according to him, the virtues opposed to *acedia* are endurance, perseverance, patience, and fortitude.[41] Aquinas, who understood *acedia* as a slothful sorrow of the soul, therefore contrasted it with the virtue of spiritual joy as a subspecies of charity.[42]

Since the late Middle Ages and even today the virtue most frequently listed as the antidote to sloth is busyness.[43] This, however, has to be distinguished from the excessive and inappropriate form of busyness—restlessness that is induced by the vice of *acedia*. Instead, we refer to moderate busyness, carried out in appropriate measure and out of virtuous motives. This kind of busyness is called diligence, or in a related sense, solicitude. This virtue Aquinas defines as a combination of shrewdness and alertness of mind, "in so far as a man through a certain shrewdness of mind is on the alert to do whatever has to be done."[44] In his understanding, solicitude has a rather general meaning, denoting an earnest endeavor to obtain something. Depending on its object, solicitude can be either virtuous or vicious. It is vicious when the object of the endeavor is something pertaining to the end of any of the other cardinal vices. Due to this, Aquinas does not even define it as a specific virtue. Tolkien's work represents negative forms of solicitude with all the Dark Lords' and their servants' activity, as it is aimed at the destruction and torture of their opponents.

Similar to sloth, two kinds of diligence can be recognized: spiritual and physical. In Tolkien's works, physical diligence is manifested in the characters' loyalty, helping each other—even militarily, attending to their duties, taking care of and healing wounded mates, studiousness and the responsible search for information, alertness to danger and perceptiveness to signs of good or bad omen, repairing the damage inflicted by the enemy, marching on for long periods of time until the point of utter exhaustion, and much more. But the ultimate exercises of diligence and the theologically symbolic narrative function thereof are the quests the various characters take (to destroy Smaug and the Ring, to reclaim the Silmarils). The reason is that Tolkien thought that one of the best cures for physical sloth (laziness) was journeying, for it delivers one from "the plantlike state of helpless passive sufferer" and exercises will and mobility, without which, according to him, "a rational mind becomes stultified" (*Letters*, 183).

In comparison, based on what has been said about sloth, it can be inferred that spiritual diligence regards willing execution of God's will and law with great emphasis on charity, accompanied by the cardinal virtues of prudence, temperance, fortitude, and justice. Other characteristics that pertain to spiritual diligence are focus of mind, carefulness, sincere interest in the needs of one's neighbor, helpfulness, liveliness, good-naturedness—basically any virtue that pertains to charity. It seems that the essence of diligence is perfectly encompassed in the Benedictines' motto *ora et labora* ("pray and work"). In line with that, a diligent person does not shun any hard work, physical or spiritual, but works industriously to achieve the desired ends, using virtuous means and not heeding the toil and trouble, because he or she believes in God's help.

Curiosity

One of the manifestations of negative diligence is curiosity. Curiosity is a vice opposed to the virtue of studiousness, which Aquinas defines as a moderate and duly regulated desire of knowledge which is becoming to a person.[45] It follows that curiosity is an *inordinate* desire of the knowledge of truth. This desire can be inordinate in five ways:

1. When someone desires to know something in order to misuse the knowledge to commit a sin; for example, to spread lies.
2. When the desire to learn a particular thing withdraws someone from their other duties or subjects they are obligated to learn.
3. When someone wants to learn something that is unlawful for them to learn or to learn through evil means.
4. When someone does not refer the knowledge to its due end, God.
5. When someone desires to know what is above their capacity to comprehend.[46]

Aquinas's predecessors, such as Augustine, merited the moral quality of the desire for knowledge based on the object of knowledge. This desire was considered sinful if its object turns a person's gaze, ergo their metaphysical orientation, away from God, resulting in a perverted fixation on the object, along with pride and alienation from others.[47] In Aquinas's interpretation, the evilness of the desire of knowledge does not consist so much in the object of the knowledge itself, rather in the manner and purpose of the pursuit of the knowledge, as the above-mentioned points indicate. And since studiousness is a sub-species of the cardinal virtue of temperance, curiosity is one of the sins against temperance as long as we only consider the manner and extent of the desire for knowledge. However, taking into consideration the fact that gaining some knowledge, even unbecoming knowledge, is an active process often involving a lot of hard intellectual work, we can say that curiosity represents an inordinate diligence. Especially in the case of Tolkien's stories this aspect of curiosity is emphasized as the characters who display it themselves point out how much they had to toil to gain that forbidden knowledge or what creative ways they had to design to conceal their related doings from others. Or, considered the twofold nature of *acedia*, curiosity can be also viewed as its active form, as it makes one's mind restless, distracts one from what one ought to be learning and directs his or her to other matters which are not suitable for the person to know.

The best example of such negative curiosity-inspired diligence in Tolkien's stories is the use of Palantíri. In themselves, the stones are not evil (*UT*, 405). On the contrary, being devised to provide teleconnection with distant parts of the country, they allowed Gondorian kings to monitor and govern their territories more effectively, and so contributed to their virtuous diligence. However, after Sauron gained possession of one of them and started manipulating the minds of anyone who looked into the other stones, they became vicious. Thus, Saruman's use of the Palantír turned him into Sauron's thrall and enhanced his malice, and Denethor's use of the stone led him to despair and ultimately to suicide. A partial exception to this is Pippin. On the one hand, he, like the other Palantír users, at first tries to conceal his use of the stone, but on the other hand, as Boyd observes, he is not as easily manipulated and destroyed by the knowledge gained thanks to his friends who deter him from relapse, help him confess his sin, make his knowledge public, and thus provide his salvation.[48] Nonetheless, his curiosity injures even him as he is burned by the handling of the stone and pained by Sauron's interrogation. Therefore, all these examples confirm the hypothesis that the exercise of negative diligence by both good and bad characters usually leads to discatastrophe and/or self-destruction. The only positive use of the stones is by Aragorn, who is the sole rightful owner of the Palantíri and so they must obey his will.

Interestingly, in his personal life, Tolkien seemed not to view curiosity as strictly vicious as his faith might suggest. Instead, his published correspondence reveals that he used the word in general, everyday meaning. For example, he identified curiosity as a quality "without which a rational mind becomes stultified" (*Letters*, 183). This positive outlook on curiosity made its way into *The Lord of the Rings*, too.[49] According to Boyd, it is Sam's "attentive curiosity to others," especially to the Elves, that provides the initial reason to set on the journey with Frodo.[50] Sam looks up to the Elves as creatures greater than himself, admires them, and wants to learn from them. In turn, his acquaintance with the Elves opens his eyes to a wider perspective of the quest, elevates him from his rustic ignorance and ennobles him. This is the only example in the novel when initial curiosity leads to something good and the fact that all the other showcases of curiosity have negative connotations indicates that Tolkien reconsidered his approach to this quality as early as the beginning of Book II of *The Fellowship of the Ring*, where at the Council of Elrond Boromir already displays an unhealthy curiosity about the Ring.[51] It also follows that Tolkien viewed curiosity as positive only as long as it was about something that is beneficial to a person to know, such as when he applied his linguistic curiosity to the study of words' origins—in that case it would be properly equated with Aquinas's virtue of studiousness—and he used the word *curiosity* with its general laic meaning.

Hope

Of Tolkien's novels, the amalgam of spiritual and non-spiritual diligence is most elaborated in *The Lord of the Rings*, which also most emphasizes the working of Providence in characters' lives and stresses the need to hope in it almost from the very first pages in an attempt to teach the reader that nothing good is achieved without spiritual diligence and belief in Providence (God).

Hope in general (not only in Providence) is one of the few virtues recognized as such even by the characters. The embodiment of hope, both as a living object of faith due to his Maia nature (most evident after his resurrection), and as its source via inspiring others to it, is Gandalf. As a member of the Istari, his special task is to rekindle the hope of Middle-earth's inhabitants. This is the substance of his stewardship over Middle-earth. On occasion, Gandalf still retains his function of *deus ex machina*, which was essentially his primary role in *The Hobbit*; however, in the sequel it is less often seen (for example, when he collects and brings more Rohirric warriors to the battle of Helm's Deep, thus contributing to their victory). In the *LOTR*, Tolkien writes Gandalf as a more complex and realistic character with strong theological function as the comfort he radiates parallels the comfort radiating from Jesus. Analogically to Gandalf, the embodiments of despair are the Nazgûl, who radiate fear instead.

Akin to Gandalf, Aragorn also radiates hope and courage. He bears the name *Estel*—an Elvish word for hope understood as "a trust that is not defeated by the ways of the world because it is rooted in their awareness that they are the children of the creator-god and thus will ultimately be saved, which rather recalls the virtue of faith" (*Morgoth*, 320–21).[52] Thus Aragorn's name presages his fate, with the condition that this may be fulfilled only if he follows the path of virtue and objective good. But since neither Gandalf nor Aragorn are vice-less, they cannot be viewed as direct allegories of Jesus, only as Christ figures, bearing some qualities similar to him. Their analogue in *The Hobbit* is Bard, who is always active, protective of the Lake-town people, cautious, and prudent, and therefore in sharp contrast to Thorin. Bard is a descendant of the Dale men whom even the dwarves praised for their diligence and courage in fighting the dragon Smaug at his coming, so it is unsurprising that Tolkien, relishing in putting his heroes into similar situations as their ancestors to highlight their moral contrast, brought out Bard's diligence at Smaug's second coming. Thanks to him keeping his senses, urging people to fight, giving them courage, sparking hope, and being the only one holding place when everyone else abandons the burning town (like Gandalf and Aragorn), is the victory of the Lake-men over the dragon secured. Besides helping the Lake-men survive after the attack and build the city anew, Bard and the Elvenking also show diligence in immediately setting off to settle matters with Thorin and company and not just waiting idly for their mercy. Yet they do not push it so much as to attack them and demand fair share in the treasure by force, but view battle as the last option. Thus, they maintain the image of strict but kind rulers.

The embodiment of hope as one who never abandons it is Sam. Although he mentions several times that he never really had any hope in the quest, claiming he does not need hope as long as despair can be postponed and ascribes this to his cheerful nature (*TT*, IV, iii)—in my opinion, this is exactly what hope is about; Sam has his definitions distorted—his actions prove the contrary. Even in the gravest troubles, he still thinks that everything will somehow be solved and turn to good in the end, and this belief gives him strength to endure and overcome any nascent despair most easily, as illustrated by his song in Cirith Ungol (*RK*, VI, i). At first, Sam's hope lies in the leadership, knowledge, and strength of Gandalf and Aragorn, but after separation from them, it becomes more and more rested in Providence, even though he may not be conscious of it. In fact, Sam is the character whose belief in Providence is the strongest, after Gandalf. His philosophy is: "Where there's life, there's hope," (*TT*, IV, vii) and he holds to it to the very end of their quest, when he cannot believe Gandalf would send them on a journey without the hope of return, and so still hopes he and Frodo will be saved from the ruin of Mordor (*RK*, VI, iii).[53] His hope is not rooted in any reasonable evidence, but beyond it, which indicates Providence. Further, the working of Providence in Sam is manifested in his frequent premonitions of evil, sudden thoughts that seem to come to him out of nowhere (for example, to use Frodo's phial against the Watchers and shout an Elvish chant, while he cannot speak the language at all), and likewise, his sudden urges to move on in the last stages of their journey, which he shares with Frodo, but mainly in the feeling that he has had from the beginning of the journey that he has some duty toward Frodo.

Providence

Similar premonitions and sudden thoughts are experienced also by many other characters, which again indicates their belief in Providence, which is disguised as an inner voice obviously coming from an external source. For instance, Providence is what brings all the different characters to Elrond's Council, guides Aragorn to the same spots Merry and Pippin left hints at (again motivated by Providence) during their capture by the Orcs, or draws the giant eagles to others' help (working as *deus ex machina*) several times not only in *The Lord of the Rings* but also the other two books. In *The Hobbit*, a character most perceptive to the voice of Providence is, of course, Bilbo. Contrary to the hopeless dwarves, Bilbo's sloth is less spiritual in nature, pertaining to his negligence to go on adventures, but once there, he keeps his spiritual diligence more easily. He is usually the last to sink in spirit and lose hope, which he often finds in seemingly insignificant things, such as a pipe in his pocket when lost in the goblin tunnels. Other times, he finds it in entirely different things from the dwarves, highlighting the contrast in their values. For instance, when the company is shut in the tunnel, its outer entrance barred and the inner leading to Smaug's lair, which makes the dwarves most desperate, but surprisingly Bilbo feels "a strange lightening of the heart" (*Hobbit*, XIII). A little later, when they finally get out of the Mountain and, realizing Smaug is gone, Thorin's spirits rise while Bilbo's lower due to the unresolved mystery of Smaug's whereabouts. Both these situations employ the already several-times-used pattern that Bilbo's (un)easiness is incurred by some inexplicable movement of spirit, some inner voice or will other than his own. The same power makes him nervous on Durin's Day, giving him "a queer feeling that he was waiting for something" (*Hobbit*, XI), thus making him the only one alert and observant enough at the right moment for open-ing the secret door—an eucatastrophic moment contributed to by Bilbo's diligence all throughout the story. Even though he does not fully understand or openly acknowledge it, Bilbo is the only one who exercises belief in Providence and is guided by it, just like Sam. Hence, thanks to it, he never entirely loses hope and is always spiritually diligent. Moreover, as explained in one of Tolkien's later notes (*UT*, 331), Providence has always played an important role in Bilbo's life and was the main reason why he remained "unattached." It was not for his negligence to share his comfort or desire to be independent, rich, and his own master, but because Providence appointed him a greater fate.

In comparison, in *The Silmarillion*, the power of Providence is not stressed and explored as much as in *The Lord of the Rings*, even though it is notably more apparent than in *The Hobbit*, proving that overall physical diligence pre-vails over spiritual in this book. The characters most perceptive to Providence in the form of Eru's direct will are the Valar. In their case, we cannot really speak of the working of Providence, as they had lived with Eru and par-ticipated in his creation Music, in which a different part of his mind was revealed to each of the Valar according to their specific attributes. Consulting then their individual knowledge together, they were able to comprehend the Creator more complexly. Yet while it may seem that the comprehension of his will came to them naturally, it was not always so; many parts of his designs interwoven into the Music remained unclear to them, as if in a mist, and they understood them only after repeated and thorough pondering. As for other characters in *The Silmarillion*, the closest they come to some manifestation of the working of Providence in them is through some foreknowledge. For example, it is providential foreknowledge that leads Fëanor to ponder how to preserve the light of the Two Trees imperishable, Idril to build a secret tunnel from Gondolin to save her people, and Beren to go to Doriath where he stumbles across Lúthien. But most importantly, Providence persuades Turgon to allow his daughter's marriage to a Man, which complements the final eucatastrophe as Eärendil indeed finally reaches Valinor and pleads with the Valar for help and redeems Turgon from the sin of not recognizing Tuor's coming as a sign of omen and not listening to Ulmo's warnings, which led his city, Gondolin, to destruction (*Silmarillion*, 288). In *The Lord of the Rings*, an example of providential foreknowledge can be Faramir's and Éomer's decisions to allow Aragorn's and Frodo's companies to move freely in their lands upon careful investigation and prudent evaluation of all threats and benefits, instead of blindly obeying the laws, complementing thus the final eucatastrophe. Foresight, however, is a manifestation of diligence only when applied to good uses and inciting appropriate action (such as when Aragorn's grandmother insisted on her son's Arathorn's marriage with Gilraen, foreseeing that the union was the last chance for a possible future king, or Turgon allowing the marriage of Idril and Tuor). But if the foresight does not prompt one to act for the good of the whole society, but instead leads to an attempt for its inhibition, like in Denethor's case, it is rather vicious. Denethor's main problem is that not only does he refuse to acknowledge the existence of Providence, or at least rest his hope in it, he sees it as a force that tries to supplant him and so he puts his hope solely in himself. And that, as Peter Kreeft remarks, is vicious—a sign of pride, because the object of hope should always be an external entity, whether hope is understood as a theological or nontheological virtue.[54] Moreover, this attitude of Denethor's toward Providence just adds to his despair.

Joy

Talking of despair, its opposite is joy of life. As Louis Markos observes, Tolkien put special emphasis on this virtue because the ability and willingness to accept and take joy in appropriate pleasures—and in appropriate measure, I would add—is a sign of appreciation of God's gifts and therefore a virtue. He claims that eating, drinking, or even smoking in moderation is good because it "can enhance fellowship, inspire gratitude, and draw shy people out of themselves," whereas excessive indulging in these activities separate people from their responsibilities and from each other.[55] Louis Markos bases his argument on C.S. Lewis's opinion on temperance, who defines it not as an abstinence from pleasures, but their enjoyment "in the right length and no further."[56] That means that good Christians, even if they choose to abstain from some pleasure, should not condemn those or forbid others from enjoying them. Instead, they should be able to recognize and duly appreciate their value in human life. According to Genesis, the whole of creation was given to people, and it would be sinful not to use the resources God gave for people to use, and to not take pleasure in them (Gen 1:26). Indeed, that is exactly what Satan tries to do, to kill joy of God's creation and thus destroy people's connection and love to God. And that is exactly what Sauron does too; he leaves all lands under his dominion destroyed and barren, devoid of life and hence also joy, filled with despair instead.[57] Sauron's actions are the exact opposite of what the Elves do. Unlike Sauron, the Elves fill every place with beauty, light, life, joy, and hope, and their realms in the Third Age are sanctuaries of peace, wisdom, hope, and healing, full of a combination of music, song, feasting, and meditation. The life joy that the exiled Elves display, being redeemed of their sin against the Valar, basically imitates the joy they felt in Valinor. In fact, in *The Silmarillion*, the Valinor Elves are the only ones described as always joyful, due to their proximity to the semi-divine Valar, who, in turn, find their life joy in close spiritual connection to Eru (see, for example, *Silmarillion*, 37–41). However, in *The Lord of the Rings*, the Elves' revelling in peace and joy of life in certain aspects verges on the vice of sloth, as in their egoistic attempt to conserve the joy in time, they shut themselves off from the outer world, ignorant of its fate, just like the Ents or Hobbits. They are more morally ambivalent than they seem at first sight and at least as ambivalent as the Hobbits.

As for the hobbits, they partially redeem themselves from their careless slothfulness through their cheerfulness, despair-proof nature, and joy of the simple things in life. As evidenced by Sam, and more so by Merry and Pippin, they can never have a heavy heart for long. Instead, they have unbreakable spirits thanks to which they can withstand temptation or torture by the enemy longer than other races, shake off any troubles, heal easily, and tend to joke even amidst the greatest peril, as evidenced by Merry and Pippin, who jokingly refer to their capture by the Orcs as a "little expedition," (*TT*, III, iii). Furthermore, even though they are overwhelmed by the beauty and majesty of Men and Elven cities and treasure such experience, they still retain their ability to appreciate simple things, and this ability is only refined through the lack of these things on their journey. The best example of this is Sam's joy of a ray of light, a glimpse of a star, and bit of drinkable water amidst the desolation of Mordor, which represent the fulfilment of what he was hoping for. But the best embodiment of life joy is Tom Bombadil. His joy of life is manifested by his overall bearing—the sing-song manner of speech, dancing walk, and general light-heartedness, and accentuated by his colorful attire (*FR*, I, vi). His light-heartedness is so big that it verges on sinful carelessness, of which he is therefore also an embodiment.

CONCLUSION

The remarkable contrast between how much emphasis Tolkien put on the spiritual forms of sloth and diligence in comparison to their nonspiritual forms accentuates the theological relevance of his stories. Preferring to teach his lessons through showing—through the impact of characters' moral decisions on the plot development—rather than theorizing or preaching, the theology in them is implicit, but none the less powerful. Sloth and diligence seem to be the rule-confirming exception to this as in their depiction their theological understanding is the most evident. On the spiritual level, these moral habits pertain to the belief in Providence, or a lack thereof, which is the most explicit indication of God in Tolkien's universe, apart from Eru, who, from the narrative perspective, is but a minor and mostly passive or wholly absent character in the legendarium. The existence of Providence is all the more important as resting hope in it motivates the characters to greater exertion and their hard work, complemented by the exercise of other virtues, is then rewarded by God showing them mercy in the form of a eucatastrophe. However, if the characters do not have hope in Providence, they see "the end beyond all doubt" (*FR*, II, ii), and so fall into despair and resign all effort, which, in combination with their other vices, inevitably leads them into some sort of catastrophe or death.

NOTES

1. This chapter was written with the support of projects UGA *Zobrazenie cností a neresí vo fantasy literature* ("Depicting virtues and vices in fantasy literature") and *Morálne hodnoty vo fantasy literature* ("Moral values in fantasy literature"). Parts of it were adapted from my doctoral thesis, "Vice and Virtue in J.R.R. Tolkien's Works" (PhD diss., Constantine the Philosopher University in Nitra, 2021). That said, I want to express special thanks to all the reviewers for their advice and suggestions that helped me adapt it to the current form, as well as Alan Reynolds for helping me with the references, Craig A. Boyd for providing me with copies of his articles, and Douglas Estes for providing me with several other useful resources.

2. Humphrey Carpenter, *J.R.R. Tolkien: A Biography* (London: Harper Collins, 2002), 293.

3. See, for example, Brian Rosebury, "Revenge and Moral Judgement in Tolkien," *TS* (2008): 1–20; Lynn Forest-Hill, "Boromir, Byrhtnoth, and Bayard: Finding a Language for Grief in J.R.R. Tolkien's *The Lord of the Rings*," *TS* (2008): 73–97; and Jorge J. E. Gracia, "The Quests of Sam and Gollum for the Happy Life," in *J.R.R. Tolkien*, ed. Harold Bloom, new ed., BMCV (New York: Infobase, 2008), 79–88.

4. "Virtue is a good quality of the mind, by which we live righteously, of which no one can make bad use, which God works in us, without us," (Aquinas, *ST*, II–I, q. 55, a. 3–4). Vices are the exact opposites of virtues, hence defined as habits that dispose us toward evil.

5. Which implies that artists, in exercise of their God-given creative power, should, through their work, "lead their readers to goodness by presenting them with good moral models and explaining the importance and praiseworthiness of adhering to principles of objective morality," see Martina Juričková, "Thomistic Elements in

Tolkien's Philosophy of (Sub)Creation," in *First Nitra Postgraduate Conference in English Studies: Trends and Perspectives*, ed. Judita Ondrušeková (Praha: Verbum, 2019), 94.

6. Aquinas, *ST* I–II, q. 84, a. 3.

7. Charles W. Nelson, "The Sins of Middle-earth: Tolkien's Use of Medieval Allegory," in *J.R.R. Tolkien and His Literary Resonances: Views of Middle-earth*, ed. George Clark and Daniel Timmons, CSSFF 89 (Westport: Greenwood, 2000), 90.

8. Siegfried Wenzel, *The Sin of Sloth: Acedia in Medieval Thought and Literature* (Chapel Hill: University of North Carolina Press, 1967), 54.

9. For further discussion, see Janelle Aijian, "Fleeing the Stadium: Recovering the Conceptual Unity of Evagrius' *Acedia*," *HeyJ* (2019): 1–14; Andrew Crislip, "The Sin of Sloth or the Illness of the Demons? The Demon of Acedia in Early Christian Monasticism," *HTR* 98 (2005): 143–69; Christopher Jones, "The Problem of Acedia in Eastern Orthodox Morality," *Studies in Christian Ethics* (2019): 1–16; and especially, Wenzel, *Sin of Sloth*; and Rebecca Konyndyk DeYoung, "Aquinas on the Vice of Sloth: Three Interpretive Issues," *The Thomist* 75 (2011): 43–64.

10. Wenzel, *Sin of Sloth*, 6, 89, 165.

11. *Catechism of the Catholic Church*, par. 2733.

12. Helen Oppenheimer, "Sloth," in *A New Dictionary of Christian Ethics*, ed. John MacQuarrie and James Childress (Louisville: Westminster, 1986), 590.

13. Evagrius, *Praktikos*, par. 12, in *Evagrius of Pontus*, trans. Robert E. Sinkewicz (Oxford: Oxford University Press, 2003).

14. Since humans consist of corporeal and incorporeal parts, which in this world cannot be separated from each other, spiritual activities involve some movement of the body, as DeYoung ("Aquinas," 61) points out. For example, when praying you kneel down or clasp your hands together.

15. Jones, "Problem of Acedia," 4–7. See also Sinkewicz, *Evagrius of Pontus*, 211, 244, 278.

16. Evagrius, *Praktikos*, par. 12. See also Aijian, "Fleeing the Stadium," 5, and Jones, "Problem of Acedia," 8.

17. Evagrius, *Praktikos*, par. 28. See also Wenzel, *Sin of Sloth*, 14.

18. Wenzel, *Sin of Sloth*, 22.

19. Cassian, *Institutes*, 10.I–II, in *John Cassian: The Institutes*, trans. Boniface Ramsey (New York: Paulist Press, 2000). See also Jones, "Problem of Acedia," 13.

20. Wenzel, *Sin of Sloth*, 30.

21. Aquinas, *ST* II–II, q. 35, a. 1.

22. DeYoung, "Aquinas," 62.

23. DeYoung, "Aquinas," 46.

24. Rebecca Konyndyk DeYoung, "The Vice of Sloth: Some Historical Reflections on Laziness, Effort, and Resistance to the Demands of Love," *The Other Journal* 10 (2007).

25. DeYoung, "Aquinas," 35, 32.

26. Wenzel, *Sin of Sloth*, 46.

27. Cited in Wenzel, *Sin of Sloth*, 67.

28. Wenzel, *Sin of Sloth*, 91. Compare the information in this paragraph with the same source, pages 108–9, 175, 181.

29. Wenzel, *Sin of Sloth*, 187. There is growing interest in *acedia*; for example, see Uche Anizor, *Overcoming Apathy: Gospel Hope for Those Who Struggle to Care* (Wheaton: Crossway, 2022).

30. DeYoung, "Vice of Sloth."

31. Tolkien himself presumably suffered from an active form of sloth. Boyd accentuates the parallel between Tolkien and the character of Niggle whom Tolkien devised as a kind of his mirror reflection. Both of them are always niggling away, attending to many chores other than what they should be working on, or on the other hand, just being idle. They struggle to overcome their own inertia and the distractions from the outside world (job, people around them). See Craig A. Boyd, "The Thomistic Virtue of Hope in Tolkien's *Leaf by Niggle*," *Christian Scholar's Review* 48.2 (2019): 131–45.

32. Tom Shippey, *The Road to Middle-earth* (New York: Houghton Mifflin, 2003), 261–68.

33. Helen Lasseter Freeh, "On Fate, Providence, and Free Will in *The Silmarillion*," in *Tolkien among the Moderns*, ed. Ralph C. Wood (Notre Dame: University of Notre Dame Press, 2015), 51–77.

34. It is also debatable whether it really was a curse or rather a prophecy based on the observation of Húrin and his spouse's own and their ancestors' characters.

35. John Linton Treloar, "The Middle-earth Epic and the Seven Capital Vices," *Mythlore* 16 (1989): 40.

36. Freeh, "On Fate, Providence, and Free Will," 51–77.

37. Boyd, "Thomistic Virtue," 131–45.

38. Freeh presents Beren's story as the perfect antithesis of Túrin's story. In contrast to Túrin, Beren and Lúthien, using their free will in agreement with the voice of Providence, make a series of right decisions, which saves them from the disastrous consequences. In addition, unlike Túrin who isolates himself from other people and prefers to rely only on himself, Beren and Lúthien are able to gratefully accept advice and help offered to them (either by Finrod or Huan) and are willing to even sacrifice their lives and happiness for the sake of others, thereby exercising what could be identified as the Catholic virtue of charity. See Freeh, "On Fate, Providence, and Free Will," 51–77.

39. According to Mandos' prophecy (*Lost Road*, 333), Túrin will become the one to ultimately defeat Melkor at the end of time (in a version of Middle-earth's Armageddon), which is a privilege that suggests his moral rehabilitation in Eru's eyes.

40. Evagrius, *Praktikos*, par. 28.

41. Evagrius, *Eight Thoughts*, 6.5, 6.17–18. See also Wenzel, *Sin of Sloth*, 11; and Aijian, "Fleeing the Stadium," 10.

42. Aquinas, *ST* II–II, q. 28.

43. Wenzel, *Sin of Sloth*, 89.

44. Aquinas, *ST* II–II, q. 55, a. 6.

45. Aquinas, *ST* II–II, q. 165, a. 2.

46. Aquinas, *ST* II–II, q. 167, a. 1.

47. Craig A. Boyd, "Augustine, Aquinas, and Tolkien: Three Catholic Views on *Curiositas*," *HeyJ* 62.2 (2020): 222.

48. Boyd, "Augustine, Aquinas, and Tolkien," 230.

49. Craig A. Boyd, "Nolo Heroizari: Tolkien and Aquinas on the Humble Journey of Master Samwise," *Christianity and Literature* 68.4 (2019): 605–22.

50. Boyd, "Nolo Heroizari," 605–22.

51. It may also be due to the fact that the whole story moved to darker issues, so the depiction of curiosity followed the same direction.

52. The Elves distinguish a second kind of hope, *amdir*, which is an expectation of good which, though uncertain, has some foundation in what is known, which more properly recalls the Christian understanding of hope (*Morgoth*, 320–21).

53. This concept is nicely illustrated in the scene at Cross-roads, when Sam and Frodo, seeing the flower crown on the fallen head of the king's statue, realize that evil cannot conquer forever; an idea repeated when Sam sees a star behind the shadows of Mordor—quite a eucatastrophic moment.

54. Kreeft, *Philosophy of Tolkien*, 202.

55. Louis Markos, *On the Shoulders of Hobbits: The Road to Virtue with Tolkien and Lewis* (Chicago: Moody, 2012), 79.

56. Lewis, *Mere Christianity*, 78–79.

57. Markos, *Shoulders of Hobbits*, 77–78.

BIBLIOGRAPHY

Aijian, Janelle. "Fleeing the Stadium: Recovering the Conceptual Unity of Evagrius' *Acedia*." *HeyJ* (2019): 1–14.

Anizor, Uche. *Overcoming Apathy: Gospel Hope for Those Who Struggle to Care*. Wheaton: Crossway, 2022.

Aquinas, Thomas. *Summa Theologica*. Raleigh: Hayes Barton Press, 1999.

Boyd, Craig A. "Augustine, Aquinas, and Tolkien: Three Catholic Views on *Curiositas*." *HeyJ* 62.2 (2020): 222–33.

———. "Nolo Heroizari: Tolkien and Aquinas on the Humble Journey of Master Samwise." *Christianity and Literature* 68.4 (2019): 605–22.

———. "The Thomistic Virtue of Hope in Tolkien's *Leaf by Niggle*." *Christian Scholar's Review* 48.2 (2019): 131–45.

Catholic Church. *Catechism of the Catholic Church*. Citta del Vaticano: Libreria Editrice Vaticana, 2023.

Carpenter, Humphrey. *J.R.R. Tolkien: A Biography*. London: Harper Collins, 2002.

Crislip, Andrew. "The Sin of Sloth or the Illness of the Demons? The Demon of Acedia in Early Christian Monasticism." *HTR* 98 (2005): 143–69.

DeYoung, Rebecca Konyndyk. "Aquinas on the Vice of Sloth: Three Interpretive Issues." *The Thomist* 75 (2011): 43–64.

———. "The Vice of Sloth: Some Historical Reflections on Laziness, Effort, and Resistance to the Demands of Love." *The Other Journal* 10 (2007).

Forest-Hill, Lynn. "Boromir, Byrhtnoth, and Bayard: Finding a Language for Grief in J.R.R. Tolkien's *The Lord of the Rings*." *TS* 5 (2008): 73–97.

Freeh, Helen Lasseter. "On Fate, Providence, and Free Will in *The Silmarillion*." Pages 51–77 in *Tolkien among the Moderns*. Edited by Ralph C. Wood. Notre Dame: University of Notre Dame Press, 2015.

Gracia, Jorge J.E. "The Quests of Sam and Gollum for the Happy Life." Pages 79–88 in *J.R.R. Tolkien*. Edited by Harold Bloom. New ed. BMCV. New York: Infobase. 2008.

Jones, Christopher. "The Problem of Acedia in Eastern Orthodox Morality." *Studies in Christian Ethics* (2019): 1–16.

Juričková, Martina. "Thomistic Elements in Tolkien's Philosophy of (Sub)Creation." Pages 91–98 in *First Nitra Postgraduate Conference in English Studies: Trends and Perspectives*. Edited by Judita Ondrušeková. Praha: Verbum, 2019.

———. "Faith, Hope, and Despair in Tolkien's Works." *JTR* 12.1 (2021): Article 1.

———. "Vice and Virtue in J.R.R. Tolkien's Works." Doctoral thesis. Nitra: UKF, 2021.

Kreeft, Peter. *The Philosophy of Tolkien: The Worldview Behind* The Lord of the Rings. San Francisco: Ignatius Press, 2005.

Lewis, C.S. *Mere Christianity*. London: HarperCollins, 2016.

MacQuarrie, John, and James Childress, eds. *A New Dictionary of Christian Ethics*. Louisville: Westminster, 1986.

Markos, Louis. *On the Shoulders of Hobbits: The Road to Virtue with Tolkien and Lewis*. Chicago: Moody, 2012.

Nelson, Charles W. "The Sins of Middle-earth: Tolkien's Use of Medieval Allegory." Pages 83–94 in *J.R.R. Tolkien and His Literary Resonances: Views of Middle-earth*. Edited by George Clark and Daniel Timmons. CSSFF 89. Westport: Greenwood, 2000.

Newbigin, Lesslie. *Sin and Salvation*. Philadelphia: Westminster, 1957.

Ramsey, Boniface, ed. *John Cassian: The Institutes*. New York: Paulist Press, 2000.

Rosebury, Brian. "Revenge and Moral Judgement in Tolkien." *TS* 5 (2008): 1–20.

Sinkewicz, Robert E., ed. *Evagrius of Pontus: The Greek Ascetic Corpus*. Oxford: Oxford University Press, 2003.

Shippey, Tom. *The Road to Middle-earth*. New York: Houghton Mifflin, 2003.

Tolkien, J.R.R. *The Letters of J.R.R. Tolkien*. Edited by Humphrey Carpenter. London: Allen & Unwin, 1981.

Treloar, John Linton. "The Middle-earth Epic and the Seven Capital Vices." *Mythlore* 16 (1989): 37–42.

Wenzel, Siegfried. *The Sin of Sloth: Acedia in Medieval Thought and Literature*. Chapel Hill: University of North Carolina Press, 1967.

Chapter 14

Evil and the Fall into Violence in Tolkien's Mythopoesis

John C. McDowell

It began with the forging of the Great Rings. With the appearance of a black screen comes a barely audible whisper, an Elven voice. Within moments, Galadriel, Lady of Lothlórien, provides a translation while accompanied by a solemn musical theme. "The world is changed," she utters. The prologue of Peter Jackson's filmic interpretation of John Ronald Reuel Tolkien's first book of the *Lord of the Rings* then places onto Galadriel's lips different moments from the source material (phrases used by Treebeard, tree-herder of Fangorn, and Théoden, Lord of the Mark). Without any further elaboration, the theme of change could become one of simple nostalgia. After all, "Much that once was is lost," Galadriel laments. However, as the somber voiceover continues, the story being recounted instead becomes one of fall or descent. Included here is a portentous reference to "the race of Men who, above all else, desire power," and the subsequent deception by "the Dark Lord Sauron" the Maia whose One Ring was forged "to rule them all (viz., the other rings binding 'the strength and will to govern each race')." In addition, there is an explicit reference to Sauron's power for domination as being grounded in "his cruelty, his malice, and his will to dominate all life" which were "poured into this [One] Ring." The language of fall is utilized to describe the events of the falling of the lands of Middle-earth to the power of the Ring, and the onscreen imagery depicts the brutal devastation produced by the violent invaders sent by this Dark Lord.

This framing of the mythopoesis of Middle-earth often leads commentators to speak of a "struggle between good and evil" in their analysis of the material.[1] For instance, Tolkien's Aragorn announces that "good and ill have not changed since yesteryear; nor are they one thing among Elves and Dwarves

279

and another among Men. It is a man's part to discern them" (*TT*, III, ii). Even though such concepts are far from unique to Christian theology, they do gain the attention of theological readers. Since Christians, for instance, interrogate everything that shapes living through the lens of their commitment to God's life-givingness and its rich demand to "abide in blessedness," they are committed to sustaining the kind of critical attention that weans discernment and judgment from all that contributes to creatures becoming, in Athanasius' term, "decomposed."[2] It is in this process of "intelligent participation in the order of peace" that the theological work of cultural evaluation serves to identify and overcome, wherever possible.[3]

But how does evil function in *Lord of the Rings*, and what (re)interpretative choices have Jackson's cinematic texts made?[4]

A MYTHOPOESIS OF EVIL

Evil is a notion often spoken of "lightly, promiscuously, and irresponsibly."[5] One tendency is to assume that each use shares a common conceptual grounding. Tolkien, at least, claims that he designs and redrafts his *LOTR* through his mythopoesis from within a particular moral perspective—that of a Catholic sensibility (*Letters*, 142 and 269). This identification of the particularist flavor of his work, though, should not be taken at face value, since any cultural text may exhibit a variety of influences, not merely literary but conceptual and ideological. Nonetheless, any exploration of Tolkien's mythopoesis of evil could make at least five observations from a broadly Augustinian perspective.

Without Ontological Origination

Within an Augustinian schema, evil is not ontologically original. It is not something that exists prior to, or is a product of, the creative act. However pervasive and inescapable evil may seem to be, ontologically "it cannot be as *primordial* [or *original*] as goodness," and therein it becomes "scandalous at the same time it becomes historical."[6] The early material in *The Silmarillion* envisions a primordial perfection and relational harmony in the creative ordering of all things by Eru Ilúvatar. Of no less significance is the *LOTR*'s opening with the chapter "Concerning Hobbits." As Nicholas Boyle explains, it is not the hero-warrior or the grand events that are the focus as much as "the hobbits' perspectives on them."[7] Through them Tolkien explores "ways of living" that are set in contrast to self-aggrandizing desire.[8]

In contrast, despite the reference to a fall, Jackson's interpretation neither mentions a creation scene, nor launches the *FR* with the vision of what the fall has been from. Likewise, the movies miss Tolkien's design of Sauron's origins. While there remain hints of the fragile ecological balance the goodness of life in and of itself that is destroyed by Sauron's aggression, the movie version of the *FR* rushes into a grandly scaled scene of violence between "the last alliance of Men and Elves" and the unmitigated evil of Sauron.

Without Ontological Substance

Given that evil is not primordial or created the way it is spoken of as "existing" is, of course, a theological oddity. A theological account of "existence" is properly a way of speaking of the graced reality of the creature as creature. In that regard, evil does *not exist*. It has no reality or ontology of its own, meaning it is a way of describing a quality of creaturely *acts*, even if those acts are "absurd" since they are not expressions of creatures' reality and purposefulness.[9] Consequently, the Augustinian tradition regards evil as a privation of the good, as ontological nothingness or an absence of the goodness of existence, as a negation that resists and undoes the good. Rowan Williams explains, "Evil . . . is a privation of . . . harmony with the pattern of mutuality and 'self-displacement'; which is God's own life and thus the heart of life well-lived within creation."[10]

Tolkien has a tendency of putting considerable weight on the *decision* or *choice* behind the subsequently wicked acts of the Ainur, Melkor the Morgoth, and of Sauron. This coheres with the non-beingness of evil, its uncreatedness. It is produced "out of the creatures themselves, who are created by God."[11] The depiction of the constrained disagreement and broadly cooperative parameters of life in the Shire, as opposed to the imposing of a singularizing sovereign domination of Sauron's megalomania, is stark. Tolkien can thereby render the contrast as a moral one, consequently demonstrating the disposition that leads to the kind of aggressive expansionism that Sauron engages in when he moves against neighboring territories. There is no reason for these figures' choosing evil other than an inexplicable desire for a form of existence different from that which befits the symphonic togetherness with other creatures. Tolkien's mythopoesis, then, resonates with the notion of the pure will that reflects John Milton's depiction of Satan in *Paradise Lost*. Brian Rosebury finds that for Tolkien "evil is conceived in terms of freely-chosen negation, of a willful abdication from the original state of created perfection."[12] Yet it is here that the Augustinian theologian would ask about the nature of this will when it is depicted within a *drama*, even if the dramatic narrative be mythically or fantastically stylized. There is a need for deep material reflection on how vices are *learned* since the desires of the will do not emerge from a vacuum. This is one of the many things that Augustinianism's talk of "original sin," at its best, can emphasize. For his part, Tolkien is not averse to describing Melkor's motivations as "arrogance" and "malice," and of his servant for a time Ossë taking "delight in violence" and having "rage in his wilfulness" (*Silmarillion*, 34). Some context, at least, is provided for Sauron's wickedness by linking his story to Melkor's manipulations. Elrond reveals that even Sauron was not evil in the beginning (*FR*, II, ii), and this provides the ontological context to resist a certain kind of Manichaeanism, even if it is more symbolic than dramatic. On the other hand, Tolkien tends to unpack Sauron's motivations more within the category of pure political self-interest, and those of Melkor psychologically as a sense of shame "which became secret anger," envy of the splendor of the Children of Ilúvatar, vengefulness, and a megalomaniacal desire for "the dominion of Arda" (*Silmarillion*, 18, 23). Moreover, the *RK* does temper Sauron's destructiveness by circumscribing his ambitions as being an enhancement of his area of despotic control (*RK*, V, x). It is with Melkor, in contrast, that dominion brings pure destruction: "To corrupt or destroy whatsoever arose new and fair was ever the chief desire of Morgoth" (*Silmarillion*, 170).

Jackson, however, removes Tolkien's constraints on Sauron's imperialist expansion (although Frodo's vision of people in chains under Orc mastery in the mirror of Galadriel in Lothlórien does align with Tolkien's understanding) and instead depicts him apocalyptically. Driven simply by "malice," he seeks the pure destruction of the "free peoples of Middle-earth." This entails, among other things, that Jackson has decontextualized evil by making it appear *ex nihilo*. By default, then, wickedness is located purely in Sauron's will in such a way as to render it arbitrary both in practice and ontologically. Without an ontology of the good, Jackson imperils a coherent account of evil. Instead, those who persistently act wickedly would have to be simply "monstrous" (or insane), and their wills would somehow be evil by nature since no social conditions can contextualize any appropriate description of it. Whatever one wants to say at the ontological level regarding the nothingness of evil, in a narration that has traceable causes and consequences, this evil is a *novum*, that which comes from nowhere other than the will. This account, ascribing "causality to the pursuit of the Satanic illusion, the illusion of the pursuit of evil for its own sake," theologian John Milbank considers to be deeply problematic, since even those deemed wicked couch their "defective desires" in terms of something positive.[13] One of many consequences of this is articulated by Peter Barry: "once we deny that evil people are human beings, we are more likely to respond to them in the way that we respond to non-human monsters. . . . So understood, evil people, because of their monstrosity, are best eliminated en masse, the sooner the better."[14]

The Augustinian theologian would also ask at this point about the role of the Ring and the mythic fantasy's concentration of evil on it and its appeal. Jackson's Sauron, described as "the enemy of the free peoples of Middle-earth," is depicted as having poured his *cruelty* and *malice* into the One Great Ring of Power. Malice is a vice that resonates with the notion of wickedness for wickedness' sake. That means that the One Ring is reified as *intrinsically* evil *by nature*, bearing immanent value not so much as *fetishizable* in Karl Marx's sense of the term, but as a device that provides its wearer with considerable power. As Jackson's Gandalf proclaims at the Council of Elrond, "it is altogether evil" (Jackson's *FR*, chapter 23). It becomes an effective sign of evil, and a means of its escalation whereby Sauron intensifies his control even among those who seek to wield it against him. The Ring is an object of desire, and it corrupts those who desire it, with its bearers demonstrating self-destructive addiction to it. This is, however, a particularly un-Augustinian sentiment. The notion, of course, only makes sense when the Ring functions as an amplifier of desire, a powerful means of accentuating the capacity to realize one's self-interest. After all, Tolkien's depiction, at least, owes much to Plato's recounting of the Ring of Gyges, and there it serves to display the nature of desire and unmask the conventions of the veneer of seemingly just social arrangements.[15] It is less intelligible, however, to comprehend the *LOTR*'s depiction of the Ring as itself *actively* seductive. Importantly, Gandalf admits to Pippin that "I do not wish for mastery," although he (and Galadriel) is nonetheless momentarily tempted by it (*TT*, III, x). The problem, nonetheless, is that even if the *desire* for the Ring's power is paramount on occasions, the texts can mask the way desire is *socially* configured. To connect the temptation for the Ring with the narcissism of "power" *simpliciter* is too tidy, lacking psychological nuance. Boromir, at least, gets to voice his feeling that, properly harnessed, the Ring could be used as a significant defensive weapon against the forces of Mordor. Beyond that, however, there is little sense of what motivates the desire for power: for instance, a fear of scarcity, a fear for the lack of a self that then asserts itself reactively, hedonistic decadence, the manipulations of political propaganda and nationalistic sentiment, trauma's self-protection, and so on.

The Pervasive Lure of the Ring

It is important to notice that Tolkien offsets this more voluntaristic emphasis on moral decision by the indeterminate will when wrestling with both the notion of the corrupting addictiveness of power (the Ring in particular) and the pervasiveness of distorted desires throughout the narrative. Something theologically interesting occurs in the construal of the Ring as binding the affections so that desire for the Ring reshapes what is valued and reshapes judgments under those conditions. In an astute characterization of Sméagol and of the way the Ring conditions his life, the *LOTR* exposes those who imagine that evil is that which is something others, the enemy engaged in colonial aggrandizement, do. This character, Gandalf explains, is related to Hobbit folk, but had become tragically despoiled by the desire for the Ring, and lives as "an almost subhuman human creature" living "in dreadful solitude" apart from the friendship he has with himself.[16] With him, the misshaping of desire does not lead to colonizing control, domineering sovereignty. Instead, it forces him into isolation and a life of subsistence. His pleasure is in "my precious," the Ring itself. Thus it reveals that "monstrous acts are by no means always committed by monstrous individuals."[17] In fact, Mary Midgley observes the contrary effect: "A great deal of evil is caused by quiet, respectable, unaggressive motives like sloth, fear, avarice and greed."[18] The way Tolkien deals with the Ring's impact on the likes of Sméagol, and to a degree Frodo and Bilbo, as well as the warrior Boromir, challenges the simplistic projectionist mode prevalent in what Augustinians call the Manichaean sensibility (we are good, others are wicked). Furthermore, it is evident that though they resist the lure of the Ring, there is nonetheless a moment of temptation for even Gandalf and Galadriel. Only Tom Bombadil appears to be immune on account of the innocence of his characterization (*FR*, I, vii).

Moreover, Tolkien's material on the greed of the Sackville-Baggins, Sméagol's positive transformation through the care of Frodo and its undoing with the subsequent violence against him, and the abuse of Gríma by Curunír (Saruman), among other things, can contribute to a thicker account of evil's psychology and cultural conditioning. This renders evil less particular and radical and instead more pervasive and banal. Jane Chance comments that "the difference between the isolated, safe, jolly Shire and the distant, evil Dark Power is not as marked as it might seem, for power struggles exist among the different Hobbit families in the Shire region, absurd in some cases and significant in others."[19]

The cinematic interpretation suggests some potential for complexity in the relationship between an envious and suspicious Sam and Gollum, in the latter's gradual moral growth, and in the corrupting of Frodo by the Ring. Yet many of the most interesting and subtle elements in the source text suggesting mundane causes of antagonism are largely absent. Even the ecologically destructive impact of heavy industry is predominantly reduced to the operations of the military industrial complex. The movies, in other words, condense evil into the destructive violence caused by political megalomania.

De-creative Destructiveness

Karl Barth explains that what the Christian traditions mean by evil cannot bypass the sense that it is "detrimental" to creaturely well-being.[20] It is so for those who are the victims of wicked acts and desires. Here Sauron's driving desire is dominion over others, destroying those who resist. Jackson's image of Saruman's manufacture of his war machine in the biomechanized birthing of the purely instrumentalized Uruk-hai is helpful in this regard. What wickedness is inclined to produce is further wickedness, violent desires supplying the means for conducting its violence. The impact this has on the environment is also notable. Accordingly, Jackson's Treebeard laments the destruction of the forests as fuel for Isengard's war machine.

In a telling move, Tolkien also explores the notion that this destruction involves a *self-destruction*, or "denaturalizing."[21] A good image is that used by Athanasius (ca. 296–373) when he speaks of one becoming "decomposed."[22] In the author of Middle-earth's hands, at least two moments gesture toward this. First, the nine Nazgûl, or Ringwraiths, once kings of Men, have devolved under Sauron's domination into servants of his will and, in a telling visual metaphor, their physical form has a distinctly shadowy character to it. Lisa Coutras explains that "their being is diminished as it falls under the power of evil until they 'fade' into the spirit world."[23] Tolkien implies that evil is nonbeing. Secondly, and in a scene visually realized by Jackson, Sméagol's desire for the Ring results not merely in an elongated life but in, for the viewer, a harrowing descent into an emaciated state. As Barth explains, evil is the "perverse and perverting" antithesis of all that is good, "offering only menace, damage and destruction," corruption and death.[24] Frodo is corrupted by the Ring as it grows heavier on him and his strength to resist begins to wane so that his appearance becomes one of struggling with serious illness, like that of a modern drug addiction. Accordingly, Bulgakov explains, "evil is a parasite of being; it arises in being as its sickness."[25]

Premature Attempts at Finality

At choice moments, the *LOTR* speaks of hope and hopelessness and these function as commentary on the difficulty of resisting Saruman's and Sauron's deadly advances into neighboring territories. This sensibility, swinging from hope into despair, induces a somber mood. Crucially, the way Tolkien progresses to the end of his story precludes any simplistic desire for a comforting resolution. There can be no neat and easy resolution to the damage caused by the war as if the conflict does not leave an indelible mark. The hostilities take their toll on many of the protagonists: Boromir lies dead, his father Denethor's despair leads to self-immolation, many of the Elves have departed

Middle-earth, and Frodo permanently suffers his wound. Moreover, violence and wickedness do not end. Tolkien's is not an apocalyptic depiction of the finality of the clash between good and evil. As Toby Widdicombe recognizes, "in Tolkien's view, evil can never be finally defeated. It is recursive. It takes many forms. It has to be defeated again and again."[26] *The Silmarillion*, for instance, explains that when Frodo casts the Great Ring of Power into the fires of Mount Doom (or Orodruin) "it was unmade and its evil was consumed" (*Silmarillion*, 366). In other words, it was not evil *per se* that was destroyed, but only a particular expression of it. After all, as Tolkien laments that even though the War in Europe has ended, "Wars are always lost, and The War always goes on" (*Letters*, 101). Gandalf certainly makes it clear that "the evil of Sauron cannot be wholly cured, nor made as if it had not been" (*TT*, III, viii). What Tolkien calls the *eucatastrophe*, then, refuses sentimental slippage into conventional reductions of hope-talk to a mode of consolation. While a eucatastrophic sensibility means that loss is not finally catastrophic, the melancholic description of Frodo's post-bellum struggles remains poignant.

The contrast with Jackson's more apocalyptic gesture is marked, however. It is not insignificant that his prologue to his *FR* makes the claim that with the victory of the Last Alliance there was "this one chance to destroy evil forever." Yet, as Charles Mathewes' argues, "simple visions of a progressive-eliminationist [or apocalyptic-eliminationist] response to evil's challenges are vexed by its . . . shallow understanding of human corruption, of the depths and the darkness of the human soul."[27]

THERE AND NOT BACK AGAIN: AN ORC'S TALE

Tolkien's mythography, then, can reveal an intelligible cultural imaginarium for identifying forms of wickedness, practices of evil, and depicting evil's destructive effects. The material at its best does not try to *make sense* of evil either by justifying it as part of the natural order of things. Even if evil is theologically unintelligible, according to Christopher Garbowski, "The Augustinian sense of fallen humanity . . . elevates *The Lord of the Rings* above a binary good vs. evil tale: the best characters either realize that evil is not only in the 'other' but also a potential within themselves."[28] However, theological talk of evil is talk not of some metaphysical abstraction. It remains crucial to critically identify how it is that desires are formed and malformed in histories of practice. Such a process develops what Donald MacKinnon calls a "phenomenology of moral evil."[29] Only then could theologically appropriate tactics for reforming practices emerge as the well-ordered means of resisting evil.

Generally, of course, theology does not deal with specifically discrete "theological topics," but instead has to do with a mode of reading, or discerning, or interrogating. As Robert Jenson explains, "It is the task of the Christian community to interpret every aspect of human life, and every aspect of the world in which we live that life, by the story of Jesus of Nazareth and by the promise that story makes."[30] Within such a vision, violence—as a privation of peace—disrupts the peaceableness of God so that those vivified in the renewing work of God are to witness to their call "to be nonviolent."[31] Even if "violence is not the only form that evil takes, . . . it is certainly one of the most destructive and pervasive forces of evil."[32] Tolkien does not glamorize nor valorize violent conflict for its own sake. He comments to his son Christopher that "the utter stupid waste of war, not only material but moral and spiritual, is so staggering to those who have to endure it" (*Letters*, 64). Accordingly, Christine Chism speaks of Tolkien's "responsive defiance against the war and against war-hypnotism wherever it might be found."[33]

This is far from the end of the story for the Augustinian theologian, though. In fact, there are two matters arising from Tolkien scholarship that call for reflection. After all, to Christopher, he does admit that there remains an important place for war within a broken world so that it "always was (despite the poets), and always will be (despite the propagandists) . . . and [it] will be necessary to face it in an evil world" (*Letters*, 64). What is evident in the *LOTR* is a form of limited violence designed as a resistance to the sheer destructiveness of Sauron's insatiably megalomaniacal expansionism.

Conflict in a Romantic Mode

First, there are moments in the *LOTR* when killing is trivialized. Admittedly, Tolkien's description of battle scenes is usually narratively quite condensed, in contrast to Jackson's giving them spectacular and extensive screen time. Yet, with the likes of Aragorn, the Rohirrim, Boromir, and to a lesser degree Faramir, Tolkien exhibits something of what Anna Slack calls a residual "hero-anxiety." This exhibits a fascination with heroes of a certain type. Accordingly, George Clark speaks of Tolkien's "love for . . . men of prowess and courage fighting a desperate battle for the right against seemingly overpowering odds."[34] Again, the weight of the piece, especially with its telling of the tale through the Hobbits, subverts popular hero codes. One scholar, Nancy Enright, for instance, observes that Tolkien often uses virtuous female characters to contest codes of pagan warrior-heroism since these "female characters epitomize his critique of traditional, masculine and worldly power, offering an alternative that can be summed up as the choice of love over pride, . . . and ultimately more powerful than any domination by use of force."[35] Additionally, Faramir virtuously acts with the kind of cultivated wisdom sorely lacking in both Isildur, when Ring-bearer, and later even his brother Boromir, for whom the good life is bound up with valor and strength.

Nevertheless, the *LOTR* integrates Sauron's imperialistic belligerence as the condition for the exercise of heroic action in violent resistance to it. The Ring-bearer can only be successful because of the way Sauron and his monstrous army are encountered at Pelennor Fields and the Gates of Mordor. The clash is between the survival of numerous free kingdoms in Middle-earth and the merciless megalomania of Sauron and his allies. Accordingly, the self-defensive conflict is portrayed as a virtuous action of reactive justice, in marked contrast to the atrocities committed by the designated enemy (the Nazgûl's use of torture, the Uruk-hai's terroristic destruction of women and children, and Saruman's genetically 'unnatural' technological warfare). As Frodo announces, "It is useless to meet revenge with revenge: it will heal nothing" (*RK*, VI, viii). The sense of morally righteous violence is accentuated by the way *There and Back Again: A Hobbit's Tale* enables the heroic warriors to pass into the lore of celebratory legend. Additionally, there are the consoling assurances pervading Gandalf's motivational rhetoric to Pippin of "White Shores" in Jackson's *RK*. Andrew Lynch, therefore, declares that in spite of his war-experiences,

> Tolkien principally makes the War of the Ring into a theater of heroic action in which the military prowess of groups and individuals is recognized as necessary, ennobling, and deeply effective. His war may be 'grim' and 'terrible,' but it is often valorous and lofty in style, and of the major friendly characters, only Boromir and Théoden actually die in its fighting.[36]

Lynch continues by contrasting the nostalgic mood utilized in the configuration of the violence when conducted in a more medieval or chivalrous mode of combat, as compared to the modern industrial manufacturing of war, with concomitant ecological devastation, by Isengard and Mordor.[37] Perhaps the spirit of *Beowulf* surfaces, or Alfred Lord Tennyson's inspiring rendition of heroism in those fighting for British imperialism, or the mythicizing of an apocalyptic drama of the clash between figurations of good and evil in which "winner-takes-all." There may even be in Jackson's *TT* a resonance to Hitler at Nuremburg in Saruman's captivation of his troops with the motivational power of his voice, thereby following a convention that further legitimates violent resistance in opposition to fascism. Following on from this political nod, a distinctive problem is presented with strategic appeasement. Gríma Wormtongue's counsel for neutrality to Théoden is masked as serving Isengard's interests, and the sagacious Gandalf marshals the Rohirrim for an impending war for their very survival. The problem with apocalyptic renditions such as these for the Augustinian tradition, Mathewes argues, is that while we live in history "we must not think that we are engaged in a war that we can ever, in any recognizable sense, 'win.'"[38]

The Only Good Orc Is a Dead Orc

However, if evil is to "be transformed and not simply defeated," then things get tricky with the configuration of the Orcs as utterly monstrous and therefore irredeemable.[39] During the Battle of the Hornburg (or Helm's Deep), Gimli and Legolas compete over the numbers of Orcs they slay (*TT*, III, vii). This cheapens the lives of the Isengardians. Jackson accentuates the moment for humorous effect so that the emotional weight of the enemy's slaughter is lightened. Wood appears to have missed this with his comment that

> *The Lord of the Rings* remains a remarkably unpagan book for disclosing what is dangerous in traditional heroism. . . . No pagan delight in killing one's own kind is present anywhere in Tolkien's work. Since every creature of Ilúvatar is essentially good until inveigled by evil, Tolkien has his heroes repeatedly extend mercy to defeated enemies.[40]

Wood attempts to explain that Sauron and his minions are utterly unforgivable since they are "wholly evil."[41] This, then, morally legitimates the slaying of these figures. Wood even goes so far as to proclaim that to "slay them is to experience the joy of justice."[42] It is important, therefore, to indicate a crucial theological critique of this moral sensibility. If Jesus' mission involves eschatologically restoring God's creative peace, then there is an inescapable seriousness about the question of what kind of life it is that the enemy has so that it can be so trivialized and dispensed with. After all, in a less Manichaean mood Wood says elsewhere, "Christians are commanded never to return evil for evil but always good instead."[43]

Consequently, for several commentators *LOTR* contains moments that project evil too readily onto "others," thereby finally applying to them "blame" while mitigating the capacity for substantial critical interrogation of one's own practices.[44] Lynch, for instance, claims that "Tolkien mainly treats the nature of war according to the . . . rightness and wrongness of their [sides'] overall causes."[45] Should it be the case that virtually all "the bad guys" are dehumanized, then Tolkien's texts could help to indicate the depth of cultural values of antagonism, mechanisms that generate and sustain a sense of healing that requires violent agency, and the difficulty of depicting good and evil within a mythopoeic epic narrative.[46] In other words, Tolkien can alert the reader to the possibility that "it may [well] be impossible to unlearn violence because it is inscribed in the way things are, in the very nature of the world."[47] An honest theological analysis would have to explore what Richard Slotkin calls "regeneration through violence."[48] The notion that violence is a good, a positive contribution to healing and well-being, that "violence 'saves,'" provides an alibi or justification for violent actions in certain contexts.[49] What this "powerful ideology" undermines, among other things, is the lamentability of violence. Any way of mitigating the sense of violence as a negation, as a disruptive and destructive practice, can temper the theological need for countering rather than radically transforming it.

An honest theological critique should then expose claims such as that of Hal Colebatch when he announces that "it is a tribute to the power of the whole tale" that the nature of Orcs does not seem "a problem worth considering."[50] This commentator goes as far as speaking of the Orcs as "necessary . . . enemies," while decoupling this fantasy-expressive-of-*facts* from Tolkien's "real world" attitude to the Germans. Yet, as Tolkien explains, mythopoesis is not self-referential but, on the contrary, a form of world-reflective "narrative art, story-making in its primary and most potent mode" (*OFS*, 61). Even if the material is not allegorical, it is arguably the case that Tolkien's reimagining of the narrative significance of the Ring, its relation to the rise of a dark tyrannical force, from *The Hobbit* onwards reflects the growth of National Socialism in central Europe, and the Nazi Party's celebration of the mythic dimension of Wagner's Ring-cycle. Yet, where Colebatch excuses the exterminating action on the formal grounds of a necessary element within fantasy literature, it remains important to appeal against using myth as "an intellectual smokescreen behind which more intractable issues can be concealed."[51] Yet any mythographizing of theological claims has to take shape within a drama, a narrative complete with agents. According to Patrick Curry, the Orcs "unavoidably become more individual, arguing with each other, expressing fear and revulsion of the Nazgûl, and engaging in blokey camaraderie ('the lads')." It is this "individuality," Curry concludes, that "surely makes Orcs more like the other races."[52] This generates a problem for Virginia Luling's reading. According to her, Orcs are not "in the full sense alive," so that there should arise "no objection to killing them."[53]

Tolkien admits in a distinctly un-Augustinian fashion that "Evil is largely incarnate, and . . . physical resistance to it is a major act of loyalty to God" (*Letters*, 156). Yet, at his best, the depiction of the degradations of Sméagol and Frodo under the attraction of the Ring are crucial here. Evil is not something that others are in a way that one is not. Moreover, unlike a good many of his commentators, Tolkien reveals an integrity when admitting his struggles with his depictions. For instance, as Dimitra Fimi observes, in a series of notes from the late 1950s onwards, Tolkien shifts from imagining the Orcs to be corrupted Elves "to Orcs as corrupted forms of Men or even corruptions of fallen Maia in one version" (all of which would be theologically troubling when they are treated as irredeemable).[54]

One of several thorny questions, though, is why the possibility of redemption is not extended to the enemy. No disruptive examples of Orcs or Uruk-hai exercising virtue are provided to offset the species binary. They simply lack *as a species* the virtues that demarcate and define heroism among the characters of the Fellowship (even if Boromir is more easily lured to the power of the Ring). No complex motivational history is provided to comprehend the wickedness of their desires. At one point Aragorn describes the Orcs in the service of Isengard as "not trusty servants" and as treacherously self-aggrandizing (*TT*, III, v). The dramatic and symbolic value attributed to these figures, then, produces them simply to provide dramatic threat and malignant menace, that which is "grotesque or monstrous."[55] Whether one wants to use the metaphysically loaded term *Manichaeism* of this tendency or not, and no matter how Augustinian the mythic framing appears otherwise to be (something that Jackson, for his part, has largely dispensed with anyway), there significantly remains a substantive difficulty. That is that good and evil are configured in such a way as to produce a stringent duality at a crucial point, an antagonistic ontology.

Sharin Schroeder admits that Tolkien had some trouble with his construal of monsters throughout his writing and only considerably later comes to express ethical concerns with them.[56] The bio-figuration of the Orcs follows binaristic conventions for depicting evil. Jackson visualizes this by interpreting the Orcs and their Uruk-hai genetic-modifications as "extremely monstrous," "as ugly and sadistic figures of darkness and evil."[57] In an explanation that does not theo-ethically help matters, Tolkien claims that "the Orcs are definitely stated to be corruptions of the 'human' form seen in Elves and Men. They are (or were) . . . in fact degraded and repulsive versions of the (to Europeans) least lovely Mongol-types" (*Letters*, 210). On this, Fimi argues that Tolkien occasionally "combines stereotypical ideas straight out of Victorian anthropology."[58] At another point, the mythographer reduces Orcs to automata, biomechanical forms without real life. This would certainly relieve the pressure of the residual Manichaeism, but it would do so only at the expense of denying the Orcs their status as agents.

Jackson's movies loosen some of the more careful ways in which Tolkien attempts to handle such matters, and they cast the bestial ferocity of the Orcs with a monstrous appearance to match. They even literally devour one of their own at one point (Jackson's *TT*, chapter 8). Their horrific otherness is accentuated by the contrast with the youthfully beautiful Elves and the childlike vulnerability and innocence of the key Hobbits. The disparity this provides with the sheer destructiveness of Sauron's preemptive aggression delivers a guilt-free, in fact even a righteously, cathartic violence for those who resist the Dark Lord's apocalyptic viciousness. If anything, the atrocious violence instigated by Saruman's and Sauron's advances into Rohan and Gondor respectively are the canvas on which the exercise of reactively heroic action is displayed, especially since the deaths are portrayed as noble sacrifices. It is the identifiable heroes' lives, rather than those of the disposable Orcs, that the narrational lens deems worthy of life (and grievability for their noble sacrifices when those lives are taken).

INTO THE WEST: CONCLUSION

In response to Max Müller's dismissal of mythology as a linguistic disease, Tolkien admits that "mythology is not a disease at all, though it may like all human things become diseased" (*OFS*, 41). As a result, "not all [mythologies] are beautiful or even wholesome, not at any rate the fantasies of fallen Man" (*OFS*, 42). In this way, he is critically attuned to "the impact of the National Socialist corruption of mythology," to "a parallel spectacle of world-creation gone wrong" that "can become a killing tool."[59] Tolkien's mythopoesis constructs a fantasy within which some of the destructive and dehumanizing implications of that which blights the good life of the creature are indicated and explored. In particular, through the perspective of the Hobbits, and without sentimental consolation, the *LOTR* traces the harm caused by simple self-aggrandizement when it takes form in both domination (Sauron and Saruman) and hedonistic self-indulgence (Sméagol/Gollum).

One moment is significant in this regard. When Frodo learns about the Ring in his possession, he expresses alarm and asserts that Gollum's life should not have been spared by Bilbo. Gandalf, however, counters: "It was Pity that stayed his hand. Pity, and Mercy: not to strike without need" (*FR*, I, ii). The Hobbit maintains that Gollum "at any rate he is as bad as an Orc, and just an enemy. He deserves death." Nonetheless, while unaware of any complexity of the Orcs themselves, the wizard warns: "Many that live deserve death. And some that die deserve life. Can you give it to them? Then do not be too eager to deal out death in judgement." Frodo's logic aligns with how many commentators critique Tolkien's monstrous Orcs: the only good Gollum is a dead Gollum. Pity and mercy, though, when informed by a commitment to the peaceable incarnated communicativeness of God's inexhaustible liveliness, are the very virtues that expose and repair desire when it is distorted by hate, fear, and the pride of self-concern. This sensibility is conducive to a witness most catholic: that all things flourish within the beneficent purposefulness of God's creative and recreative action.

NOTES

1. Charles A. Huttar, "Tolkien, Epic Traditions, and Golden Age Myths," in *J.R.R. Tolkien*, ed. Harold Bloom, new ed., BMCV (New York: Infobase, 2008), 4.

2. Athanasius, *On the Incarnation*, trans. John Behr (Yonkers: St Vladimir's Seminary Press, 2011), 57, 59, respectively.

3. John Webster, *The Domain of the Word: Scripture and Theological Reason* (London: Bloomsbury, 2012), 164.

4. Films are 'texts' when they are critically 'read,' and lenses when "we read *through* them"; see Kevin J. Vanhoozer, "What is Everyday Theology? How and Why Christians Should Read Culture," in *Everyday Theology: How to Read Cultural Texts and Interpret Trends*, ed. Kevin J. Vanhoozer, Charles A. Anderson, and Michael J. Sleasman, Cultural Exegesis (Grand Rapids: Baker Academic, 2007), 36.

5. Alasdair MacIntyre, foreword to *Naming Evil, Judging Evil*, ed. Ruth W. Grant (Chicago: University of Chicago Press, 2006), vii–viii.

6. Paul Ricoeur, *The Symbolism of Evil*, trans. Emerson Buchanan (New York: Harper & Row, 1967), 156, 203.

7. Nicholas Boyle, *Sacred and Secular Scriptures: A Catholic Approach to Literature* (London: Darton, Longman & Todd, 2004), 250.

8. Boyle, *Sacred and Secular Scriptures*, 258.

9. Karl Barth, *Church Dogmatics, Vol. III: The Doctrine of Creation Part 3*, trans. G. W. Bromiley and R. J. Ehrlich (Edinburgh: T&T Clark, 1960), 178.

10. Rowan Williams, *On Augustine* (London: Bloomsbury, 2016), 104.

11. Sergius Bulgakov, *The Bride of the Lamb*, trans. Boris Jakim (Grand Rapids: Eerdmans, 2002), 153.

12. Brian Rosebury, *Tolkien: A Cultural Phenomenon*, 2nd ed. (New York: Palgrave Macmillan, 2003), 35.

13. John Milbank, *Being Reconciled: Ontology and Pardon*, RO (London: Routledge, 2003), 3.

14. Peter Brian Barry, *The Fiction of Evil* (London: Routledge, 2016), 27.

15. Plato, *Resp.* 359–60.

16. Ralph C. Wood, *Literature and Theology*, Horizons in Theology (Nashville: Abingdon, 2008), 30.

17. Terry Eagleton, *On Evil* (New Haven: Yale University Press, 2010), 143.

18. Eagleton, *On Evil*, 143.

19. Jane Chance, *Tolkien, Self and Other: "This Queer Creature,"* NMA (New York: Palgrave Macmillan, 2016), 153–54.

20. Barth, *CD*, III/3: 310.

21. Karl Barth, *The Christian Life: Church Dogmatics IV.4 Lecture Fragments*, trans. George W. Bromiley (Edinburgh: T&T Clark, 1981), 213.

22. Athanasius, *Incarnation*, 59.

23. Lisa Coutras, *Tolkien's Theology of Beauty: Majesty, Splendor, and Transcendence in Middle-earth* (New York: Palgrave Macmillan, 2016), 129–30.

24. Barth, *CD*, III/3: 354, 310.

25. Bulgakov, *Bride of the Lamb*, 153.

26. Toby Widdicombe, *J.R.R. Tolkien: A Guide for the Perplexed* (London: Blooms-bury, 2020), 132.

27. Charles T. Mathewes, *Evil and the Augustinian Tradition* (Cambridge: Cambridge University Press, 2001), 231.

28. Christopher Garbowski, "Evil," in *A Companion to J.R.R. Tolkien*, ed. Stuart D. Lee, 2nd ed., BCLC (Chichester: Wiley Blackwell, 2022), 407.

29. Donald M. MacKinnon, "Subjective and Objective Conceptions of Atonement," in *Prospect for Theology: Essays in Honour of H.H. Farmer*, ed. F. G. Healey (London: James Nisbet, 1966), 176f.

30. Robert W. Jenson, *Essays in Theology of Culture* (Grand Rapids: Eerdmans, 1995), 47.

31. Jenson, *Essays*, 48.

32. L. Gregory Jones, *Embodying Forgiveness: A Theological Analysis* (Grand Rapids: Eerdmans, 1995), 82.

33. Christine Chism, "Middle-earth, the Middle Ages, and the Aryan Nation: Myth and History in World War II," in *Tolkien the Medievalist*, ed. Jane Chance, RSMRC (London: Routledge, 2003), 86.

34. Anna Slack, "Slow-Kindled Courage: A Study of Heroes in the Works of J.R.R. Tolkien," in *Tolkien and Modernity 2*, ed. Thomas Honegger and Frank Weinreich, Cormarë 10 (Zollikofen: Walking Tree, 2006), 138; and George Clark, "J.R.R. Tolkien and the True Hero," in Bloom, *Tolkien*, 49.

35. Nancy Enright, "Tolkien's Females and the Defining of Power," in *J.R.R. Tolkien's* The Lord of the Rings, ed. Harold Bloom, new ed., BMCI (New York: Infobase, 2008), 171–72, 173.

36. Andrew Lynch, "Archaism, Nostalgia, and Tennysonian War in *The Lord of the Rings*," in Bloom, *Tolkien's* The Lord of the Rings, 103.

37. Lynch, "Archaism, Nostalgia, and Tennysonian War," 113.

38. Mathewes, *Evil and the Augustinian Tradition*, 236.

39. Mathewes, *Evil and the Augustinian Tradition*, 231.

40. Ralph C. Wood, *The Gospel According to Tolkien: Visions of the Kingdom in Middle-earth* (Louisville: Westminster John Knox, 2003), 94.

41. Wood, *Gospel According to Tolkien*, 94. An increasing body of scholarship asks whether there is an ethnic portrayal of evil. Cf. Christine Chism, "Race and Ethnicity in Tolkien's Works," in *J.R.R. Tolkien Encyclopedia: Scholarship and Critical Assessment*, ed. Michael D. C. Drout (New York: Routledge, 2007), 556; Robert Stuart, *Tolkien, Race, and Racism in Middle-earth* (Cham: Palgrave Macmillan, 2022), 67–69; Cynthia Fuchs, "'Wicked, Tricksy, False': Race, Myth, and Gollum," in *From Hobbits to Hollywood: Essays on Peter Jackson's* Lord of the Rings, ed. Ernest Mathijs and Murray Pomerance, Contemporary Cinema 3 (Amsterdam: Rodopi, 2006), 249–65; Helen Young, *Race and Popular Fantasy Literature: Habits of Whiteness*, RIPL 30 (London: Routledge, 2016), 16; and Douglas Kellner, "*The Lord of the Rings* as Allegory: A Multiperspectivist Reading," in Mathijs and Pomerance, *Hobbits to Hollywood*, 17–39.

42. Wood, *Gospel According to Tolkien*, 94.

43. Wood, *Literature and Theology*, 32.

44. Wolfhart Pannenberg, *Systematic Theology*, trans. Geoffrey W. Bromiley (Grand Rapids: Eerdmans, 1991), 2:237.

45. Lynch, "Archaism, Nostalgia, and Tennysonian War," 111.

46. Boyle, *Sacred and Secular Scriptures*, 248.

47. Jones, *Embodying Forgiveness*, 77.

48. Richard Slotkin, *Regeneration Through Violence: The Mythology of the American Frontier, 1600–1860* (Middletown: Wesleyan University Press, 1973).

49. Walter Wink, *The Powers That Be: Theology for a New Millennium* (New York: Doubleday, 1998), 42. Cf. Walter Wink, *Engaging the Powers: Discernment and Resistance in a World of Domination* (Minneapolis: Fortress, 1992), 13.

50. Hal G. Colebatch, *Return of the Heroes*: The Lord of the Rings, *Star Wars, Harry Potter, and Social Conflict*, 2nd ed. (Christchurch: Cybereditions, 2003), 143–44.

51. John C. Hunter, "The Evidence of Things Not Seen: Critical Mythology and *The Lord of the Rings*," in Bloom, *Tolkien*, 143. Accordingly, Tom Shippey's reading of Tolkien as "reaching out towards universal and mythic meaning" expresses a conceptual naïveté; see Tom Shippey, *J.R.R. Tolkien: Author of the Century* (Boston: Mariner Books, 2002), 225. For a justification of the violent conflict in apocalyptic terms, see Anderson Rearick, "Why Is the Only Good Orc a Dead Orc: The Dark Face of Racism Examined in Tolkien's World." *MFS* 50 (2004): 871.

52. Patrick Curry, "The Critical Response to Tolkien's Fiction," in Lee, *Companion*, 369.

53. Virginia Luling, "Those Awful Orcs," *Amon Hen* 48 (1980): 5.

54. Dimitra Fimi, *Tolkien, Race and Cultural History: From Fairies to Hobbits* (New York: Palgrave Macmillan, 2009), 155.

55. Garbowski, "Evil," 401.

56. Sharin Schroeder, "'It's Alive!' Tolkien's Monster on the Screen," in *Picturing Tolkien: Essays on Peter Jackson's* The Lord of the Rings *Film Trilogy*, ed. Janice M. Bogstad and Philip E. Kaveny (Jefferson: McFarland, 2011), 118, 119.

57. Kellner, "Allegory," 27.

58. Fimi, *Tolkien, Race and Cultural History*, 159.

59. Chism, "Middle-earth," 86, 63, 64, respectively.

BIBLIOGRAPHY

Athanasius. *On the Incarnation*. Translated by John Behr. Yonkers: St. Vladimir's Seminary Press, 2011.

Augustine. *City of God*. Translated by Henry Bettenson. Harmondsworth: Penguin, 1972.

Barry, Peter Brian. *The Fiction of Evil*. London: Routledge, 2016.

Barth, Karl. *The Christian Life. Church Dogmatics IV.4 Lecture Fragments*. Translated by Geoffrey W. Bromiley. Edinburgh: T&T Clark, 1981.

———. *Church Dogmatics, Volume III: The Doctrine of Creation Part 3*. Translated by G. W. Bromiley and R. J. Ehrlich. Edinburgh: T&T Clark, 1960.

Boyle, Nicholas. *Sacred and Secular Scriptures: A Catholic Approach to Literature*. London: Darton, Longman & Todd, 2004.

Bulgakov, Sergius. *The Bride of the Lamb*. Translated by Boris Jakim. Grand Rapids: Eerdmans, 2002.

Carpenter, Humphrey. *J.R.R. Tolkien: A Biography*. London: Unwin, 1977.

Chance, Jane. *Lord of the Rings: The Mythology of Power*. Lexington: University Press of Kentucky, 2001.

———. *Tolkien, Self and Other: "This Queer Creature."* NMA. New York: Palgrave Macmillan, 2016.

Chism, Christine. "Middle-earth, the Middle Ages, and the Aryan Nation: Myth and History in World War II." Pages 63–92 in *Tolkien the Medievalist*. Edited by Jane Chance. RSMRC. London: Routledge, 2003.

———. "Race and Ethnicity in Tolkien's Works." Page 556 in *J.R.R. Tolkien Encyclopedia: Scholarship and Critical Assessment*. Edited by Michael D. C. Drout. New York: Routledge, 2007.

Clark, George. "J.R.R. Tolkien and the True Hero." Pages 43–57 in *J.R.R. Tolkien*. Edited by Harold Bloom. New ed. BMCV. New York: Infobase, 2008.

Colebatch, Hal G. P. *Return of the Heroes: The Lord of the Rings, Star Wars, Harry Potter, and Social Conflict*. 2nd ed. Christchurch: Cybereditions, 2003.

Coutras, Lisa. *Tolkien's Theology of Beauty: Majesty, Splendor, and Transcendence in Middle-earth*. New York: Palgrave Macmillan, 2016.

Croft, Janet Brennan. *War and the Works of J.R.R. Tolkien*. Westport: Praeger, 2004.

Curry, Patrick. "The Critical Response to Tolkien's Fiction." Pages 355–73 in *A Companion to J.R.R. Tolkien*. Edited by Stuart D. Lee. 2nd ed. Chichester: Wiley Blackwell, 2022.

Eagleton, Terry. *On Evil*. New Haven: Yale University Press, 2010.

Ellwood, Gracía Fay. "The Good Guys and the Bad Guys." *Tolkien Journal* 3.4 (1969): 9–11.

Enright, Nancy. "Tolkien's Females and the Defining of Power." Pages 171–95 in *J.R.R. Tolkien's The Lord of the Rings*. Edited by Harold Bloom. New ed. BMCI. New York: Infobase, 2008.

Fimi, Dimitra. *Tolkien, Race and Cultural History: From Fairies to Hobbits*. New York: Palgrave Macmillan, 2009.

———. "Was Tolkien Really Racist?" *The Conversation* (7 December, 2018), theconversation.com/was-tolkien-really-racist-108227.

Flieger, Verlyn. "The Orcs and the Others: Familiarity as Estrangement in *The Lord of the Rings*." Pages 205–22 in *Tolkien and Alterity*. Edited by Christopher Vaccaro and Yvette Kisor. NMA. Cham: Palgrave Macmillan, 2017.

———. *There Would Always Be a Fairy Tale: More Essays on Tolkien*. Kent: Kent State University Press, 2017.

Fuchs, Cynthia. "'Wicked, Tricksy, False': Race, Myth, and Gollum." Pages 249–65 in *From Hobbits to Hollywood: Essays on Peter Jackson's Lord of the Rings*. Edited by Ernest Mathijs and Murray Pomerance. Contemporary Cinema 3. Amsterdam: Rodopi, 2006.

Garbowski, Christopher. "Evil." Pages 399–409 in *A Companion to J.R.R. Tolkien.* Edited by Stuart D. Lee. 2nd ed. Chichester: Wiley Blackwell, 2022.

Hammond, Wayne G., and Christina Scull. *The Lord of the Rings: A Reader's Companion.* Boston: Houghton Mifflin, 2005.

Hood, Gwyneth. "Nature and Technology: Angelic and Sacrificial Strategies in Tolkien's *The Lord of the Rings.*" *Mythlore* 19.4 (1993): 6–12.

Hunter, John C. "The Evidence of Things Not Seen: Critical Mythology and *The Lord of the Rings.*" Pages 141–60 in *J.R.R. Tolkien.* Edited by Harold Bloom. New ed. BMCV. New York: Infobase, 2008.

Huttar, Charles A. "Tolkien, Epic Traditions, and Golden Age Myths." Page 3–16 in *J.R.R. Tolkien.* Edited by Harold Bloom. BMCV. New ed. New York: Infobase, 2008.

Jenson, Robert W. *Essays on Theology of Culture.* Grand Rapids: Eerdmans, 1995.

Jones, L. Gregory. *Embodying Forgiveness: A Theological Analysis.* Grand Rapids: Eerdmans, 1995.

Kellner, Douglas. "*The Lord of the Rings* as Allegory: A Multiperspectivist Reading." Pages 17–39 in *From Hobbits to Hollywood: Essays on Peter Jackson's* Lord of the Rings. Edited by Ernest Mathijs and Murray Pomerance. Contemporary Cinema 3. Amsterdam: Rodopi, 2006.

Kim, Sue. "Beyond Black and White: Race and Postmodernism in *The Lord of the Rings* Films." *MFS* 50 (2004): 875–907.

Korpua, Jyrki. *The Mythopoeic Code of Tolkien: A Christian Platonic Reading of the Legendarium.* Jefferson: McFarland, 2021.

Kozloff, Sarah. "*The Lord of the Rings* as Melodrama." Pages 155–72 in *From Hobbits to Hollywood: Essays on Peter Jackson's* Lord of the Rings. Edited by Ernest Mathijs and Murray Pomerance. Contemporary Cinema 3. Amsterdam: Rodopi, 2006.

Luling, Virginia. "Those Awful Orcs." *Amon Hen* 48 (1980): 5–6.

Lynch, Andrew. "Archaism, Nostalgia, and Tennysonian War in *The Lord of the Rings.*" Pages 101–15 in *J.R.R. Tolkien's* The Lord of the Rings. Edited by Harold Bloom. New ed. BMCI. New York: Infobase, 2008.

MacIntyre, Alasdair. Foreword to *Naming Evil, Judging Evil.* Edited by Ruth W. Grant. Chicago: University of Chicago Press, 2006.

MacKinnon, Donald M. "Subjective and Objective Conceptions of Atonement." Pages 169–82 in *Prospect for Theology: Essays in Honour of H.H. Farmer.* Edited by F.G. Healey. London: James Nisbet, 1966.

Mathewes, Charles T. *Evil and the Augustinian Tradition.* Cambridge: Cambridge University Press, 2001.

McBride, Sam. *Tolkien's Cosmology: Divine Beings and Middle-earth.* Kent: Kent State University Press, 2020.

McDowell, John C. "Much Ado about Nothing: Karl Barth's Being Unable to Do Nothing about Nothingness." *IJST* 4.3 (2002): 319–35.

McLarty, Lianne. "Masculinity, Whiteness, and Social Class in *The Lord of the Rings.*" Pages 173–88 in *From Hobbits to Hollywood: Essays on Peter Jackson's*

Lord of the Rings. Edited by Ernest Mathijs and Murray Pomerance. Contemporary Cinema 3. Amsterdam: Rodopi, 2006.

Midgley, Mary. *Wickedness: A Philosophy Essay*. London: Routledge, 1984.

Milbank, Alison. "'My Precious': Tolkien's Fetishized Ring." Pages 33–45 in The Lord of the Rings *and Philosophy: One Book to Rule Them All*. Edited by Gregory Bassham and Eric Bronson. PCP 5. Chicago: Open Court, 2003.

Milbank, John. *Being Reconciled: Ontology and Pardon*. RO. London: Routledge, 2003.

Pannenberg, Wolfhart. *Systematic Theology*. Vol. 2. Translated by Geoffrey W. Bromiley. Grand Rapids: Eerdmans, 1991.

Plato. *The Republic*. Translated by Desmond Lee. 2nd rev. ed. London: Penguin, 1987.

Rearick, Anderson. "Why Is the Only Good Orc a Dead Orc: The Dark Face of Racism Examined in Tolkien's World." *MFS* 50 (2004): 861–74.

Ricoeur, Paul. *The Symbolism of Evil*. Translated by Emerson Buchanan. New York: Harper & Row, 1967.

Risden, E. L., ed. *Tolkien's Intellectual Landscape*. Jefferson: McFarland, 2015.

Rosebury, Brian. *Tolkien: A Cultural Phenomenon*. 2nd ed. New York: Palgrave Macmillan, 2003.

Schroeder, Sharin. "'It's Alive!' Tolkien's Monster on the Screen." Pages 116–38 in *Picturing Tolkien: Essays on Peter Jackson's* The Lord of the Rings *Film Trilogy*. Edited by Janice M. Bogstad and Philip E. Kaveny. Jefferson: McFarland, 2011.

Shippey, Tom. *J.R.R. Tolkien: Author of the Century*. Boston: Mariner Books, 2002.

———. *The Road to Middle-earth*. Rev. ed. New York: Houghton Mifflin, 2003.

Simonson, Martin. "*The Lord of the Rings* in the Wake of the Great War: War, Poetry, Modernism, and Ironic Myth." Pages 153–70 in *Reconsidering Tolkien*. Edited by Thomas M. Honegger. Cormarë 8. Zollikofen: Walking Tree, 2005.

Slack, Anna. "Slow-Kindled Courage. A Study of Heroes in the Works of J.R.R. Tolkien." Pages 115–41 in *Tolkien and Modernity 2*. Edited by Thomas Honegger and Frank Weinreich. Cormarë 10. Zollikofen: Walking Tree, 2006.

Slotkin, Richard. *Regeneration Through Violence: The Mythology of the American Frontier, 1600–1860*. Middletown: Wesleyan University Press, 1973.

Stratyner, Leslie, and James R. Keller, eds. *Fantasy Fiction into Film: Essays*. Jefferson: McFarland, 2007.

Stuart, Robert. *Tolkien, Race, and Racism in Middle-earth*. Cham: Palgrave Macmillan, 2022.

Tally, Robert T. "Let Us Now Praise Famous Orcs: Simple Humanity in Tolkien's Inhuman Creatures." *Mythlore* 29.1/2 (2010): 17–28.

Vanhoozer, Kevin. "What Is Everyday Theology? How and Why Christians Should Read Culture." Pages 15–60 in *Everyday Theology: How to Read Cultural Texts and Interpret Trends*. Edited by Kevin J. Vanhoozer, Charles A. Anderson, and Michael J. Sleasman. Cultural Exegesis. Grand Rapids: Baker Academic, 2007.

Webster, John. *The Domain of the Word: Scripture and Theological Reason*. London: Bloomsbury, 2012.

Widdicombe, Toby. *J.R.R. Tolkien: A Guide for the Perplexed*. London: Bloomsbury, 2020.

Williams, Rowan. *On Augustine*. London: Bloomsbury, 2016.

Wink, Walter. *Engaging the Powers: Discernment and Resistance in a World of Domination*. Minneapolis: Fortress, 1992.

———. *The Powers That Be: Theology for a New Millennium*. New York: Doubleday, 1998.

Wood, Ralph C. *The Gospel According to Tolkien: Visions of the Kingdom in Middle-earth*. Louisville: Westminster John Knox, 2003.

———. "Tolkien's Augustinian Understanding of Good and Evil: Why *The Lord of the Rings* Is Not Manichean." Pages 85–102 in *Tree of Tales: Tolkien, Literature, and Theology*. Edited by Trevor Hart and Ivan Khovacs. Waco: Baylor University Press, 2007.

———. *Literature and Theology*. Horizons in Theology. Nashville: Abingdon, 2008.

Young, Helen. *Race and Popular Fantasy Literature: Habits of Whiteness*. RIPL 30. London: Routledge, 2016.

Chapter 15

A Far Green Country

The Eschatology of Tolkien's Middle-earth

Donald T. Williams

Ask most people for Tolkien's greatest and most original contribution to theology and they will either not understand the question or respond (very rightly) that it is his elucidation and application of the *imago Dei* in the doctrine of sub-creation.[1] Eschatology—the doctrine of last things—will probably not occur to them. They will have missed an important element of Tolkien's worldview and an important reason why their sojourns in Middle-earth help to restore their ability to live with hope in this world. For the world-shaping power of the Christian *eschaton* to bend the course of the cosmos into history, into story shaped with meaning, is reflected in the world-historical structure of Tolkien's Middle-earth in ways that are central to its unfolding and that give meaning to the lives of the children of Ilúvatar who live there or who visit via their imaginations. And thereby hangs a Tale.[2]

Eschatology is not simply a matter of filling in one's "this is the way the world ends" chart with the right combination of bangs and whimpers. It is ultimately what makes the unfolding of any world—primary or secondary—a history, that is, a story with a plot. It is, in other words, what keeps that history from exemplifying Henry Ford's infamous definition: "one damn thing after another." It is what gives it a shape, a *beginning*, a *middle*, and an *end*, and hence a meaning, a purpose—for the end is not just a stopping point but a *telos*.

We think of eschatology as concerned with the end of the story because we think we already know the beginning and we are living the middle. We need to be able to believe that there is an end that flows from that beginning through that middle in such a way that the good guys win in a manner as surprising as it is inevitable—indeed, eucatastrophic. Theological eschatology will be successful if it presents us with an ending that is faithful to the texts of the story we already have, and flows from and fulfills the meaning they promise, while exemplifying the shape of the ending hinted at by prophecy. It thereby gives us, not the ability to read the last chapter in advance, but the ability to believe that it will justify our current struggles when it happens. Its job, in other words, is to enable us to live in *hope*—hope that is warranted by God's character and consistent with his Word.

Tolkien of course was writing epic fantasy as feigned history, not theology. Nevertheless, precisely because his legendarium is presented as feigned history, its plot lines unfold in ways that hint at an *eschaton* for his secondary world, and his narrators and wise characters comment on those events in ways that highlight their significance. This allows us to develop an eschatology for Middle-earth that can cast light on the themes of biblical eschatology that Tolkien as a Christian took as giving meaning to life in the primary world. We will begin with a survey of Tolkien's own thoughts about how his story relates to the Christian story and then attempt to see what light an eschatological perspective can shed on the ages of Middle-earth.

PROLEGOMENA

The place to start in Tolkien's own understanding of what he gave us in his legendarium is his letter to Robert Murray, S. J., of 2 December 1952:

> *The Lord of the Rings* is of course a fundamentally religious and Catholic work; unconsciously so at first, but consciously in the revision. That is why I have not put in, or have cut out, practically all references to anything like 'religion,' to cults or practices, in the imaginary world. For the religious element is absorbed into the story and the symbolism. (*Letters*, 142)

He adds in the unsent draft of a letter to Peter Hastings of September 1954, "I would claim (if I did not think it presumptuous in one so ill instructed) to have as one object the elucidation of truth, and the encouragement of good morals in this real world, by the ancient device of exemplifying them in unfamiliar embodiments, that may tend to 'bring them home'" (*Letters*, 153). These statements about his fiction are consistent with his view of the purpose of his life as expressed to Camilla Unwin on 20 May 1969: "The chief purpose of life, for any one of us, is to increase according to our capacity the knowledge of God by all the means we have, and to be moved by it to praise and thanks" (*Letters*, 310).

What exactly are the claims that Tolkien advances? Tolkien's secondary world is not superficially or accidentally, but purposefully and fundamentally, Christian in its basic worldview. It was not started as an attempt to teach Christian doctrine ("unconsciously at first"), but when Tolkien became aware of how profoundly his most basic beliefs were reflected in the design and plot of his imaginary world, he took deliberate steps to strengthen them and bring them out ("consciously in the revision"). His works are not allegories (*Letters*, 34; cf. *FR*, Foreword), and they are not even as explicitly symbolic of Christian truths as, for example, C.S. Lewis's Narnia books. As Tolkien expressed it in the unsent draft of a letter to Michael Straight in January or February of 1956, "Though one may be in this reminded of the Gospels, it is not really the same thing at all. The incarnation of God is an infinitely greater thing than anything I would dare to write" (*Letters*, 181). But one can indeed be "reminded" of the Gospels and other Scriptural passages and motifs because the "religious element" is "absorbed into the story."

The Christian worldview in other words is present, not in specific parallels like Lewis's Stone Table standing for the atonement, but as deeply embedded in the ontological structure of the imaginary world and in large patterns that underly the plot. Peter Kreeft summarizes it well: "The main way *The Lord of the Rings* is religious is in its form, its structure" (i.e., in its worldview, its plot, and its characters).[3] He elaborates,

> Tolkien's heroes are crypto-Christians. They do not know, believe, mention, wonder about, or allegorize Christian doctrine. But they exemplify exactly what life would be like if the Christian claims are true, especially its central paradox about immortality through death and resurrection of the self, self-realization through self-sacrifice.[4]

Matthew Dickerson confirms this perspective. Why are the references to God "so vague and veiled? . . . It is not, according to Tolkien, because the work is not Christian, but because the work is so *thoroughly* Christian."[5]

This view of things might seem to be pretty clear sailing, but some Tolkien scholars have challenged it. Claudio Testi, for example, rejects a "fundamentally" Christian view in favor of a "Catholic" synthesis of Christian and pagan elements.[6] But he is forced into this complexity by refusing to count anything other than explicitly allegorical references to Christian doctrine as "Christian." Tolkien's language in the letter to Murray is much easier to understand if one thinks in terms of worldview rather than doctrine. Murray himself wrote to a student in 1980 that "Tolkien was a very complex and depressed man and my own opinion of his imaginative creation is that it projects his very depressed view of the universe at least as much as it reflects his Catholic faith," and concluded that "there is a case to be made about Tolkien the Catholic, but I simply could not support an interpretation which made this the key to everything."[7] Verlyn Flieger agrees, noting that in 1966 Tolkien told interviewer Harry Resnick that *The Lord of the Rings* was "not a christian [sic] myth anyhow,"[8] concluding that

> only in the most general sense can *The Silmarillion* be characterized as Christian, and in no sense at all can *The Lord of the Rings* be given so defini-tive a label. That both works are informed with the spirit of Christianity is clear. However, the seeker after explicit Christian reference . . . will find little in either book to get a grip on.[9]

What are we to make of this? Flieger thinks in general that Tolkien's "con-tradictions" are the key to understanding him.[10] I would argue that a writer's statements should be taken as consistent if they can be read that way with-out distortion. In letters written to different people at different times and in different contexts, it is easy to find statements that can be made to look inconsistent. But "not a Christian myth" might easily be nothing more than a denial that Tolkien's tales contain anything as explicit as the symbolism in Lewis's Narnia stories.[11] They could still be "fundamentally" Christian, that is, "informed with the spirit of Christianity" in more than a merely general way. And Murray's opinion about Tolkien's "depressed" personality and its impact on the work is just that: an opinion. It needs to be set beside Clyde S. Kilby's opinion, after working closely with Tolkien helping him try to get *The Silmarillion* in order, that "my experience with Tolkien made it clear to me that he was a devout Christian and very sure of a larger fulfillment beyond the grave."[12]

In the final analysis, the stories themselves must tell us how fundamentally biblical their worldview is. But we have been given no reason not to look at them in the light of Tolkien's own statement that they reflect his Catholic beliefs and no reason not to expect to find those beliefs embedded deeply in the texture of Middle-earth as a created world. To those stories themselves we must now turn.

TIME AND *TELOS*

In Middle-earth as in the Bible, the end is present in the beginning. Genesis begins with what was likely a truly radical idea: "In the beginning, God cre-ated the heavens and the earth" (Gen 1:1). It was radical because it takes the typical cosmogony of Ancient Near Eastern polytheism and stands it on its head. Unlike the biblical version, creation stories told by Israel's neighbors typically begin with some variation of a primordial mixing of matter and gods. In the Babylonian creation stories, for example, Apsû and Tiâmat are beings who represent the primordial fresh-water and salt-water seas.[13] From their sexual union was born the gods. Because nature is older and more primal than the gods, the gods must perforce be limited in knowledge and power; they are immortal and more powerful than mortal men, but they are trapped inside the circles of the world. It is the cyclical nature of nature, not the will of the gods, that is ultimately determinative.

Every year Marduk the sun-god overcomes Tiâmat as the spring floods recede from the plain so that fertility and new life are assured.[14] The reversal of the polytheistic pattern in Genesis changes everything. Now a singular God is the being that was there in the beginning. Instead of the primordial seas, Apsû and Tiâmat, being the source of the gods, now *God* creates Apsû and Tiâmat, as it were; they are therefore subject to his decrees. As existing before the natural world rather than being a product of it, the God of Genesis is not just immortal but eternal.[15] Homer's version of the cosmos is symbolized by the shield of Achilles, a circle bordered by the river Oceanus in which the City of War cycles endlessly around to the City of Peace and back again.[16] The God of Genesis was not born into time; rather time is his creation. Unlike the pagan gods, Yahweh is omnipresent, omniscient, and omnipotent—all these attributes being logically entailed in his relationship to time and the world as given in that first sentence.[17]

The contrasts between Genesis and the *Enuma Elish* and Homer's *Iliad* are given for illustrative purposes, as there are cyclical elements in the Hebrews' treatments of time and linear elements in those of their neighbors. People do not move on from their starting points in a completely consistent manner. Yet the creation story of Genesis gives a *basis* for time with a definitive beginning and a definitive end that the other stories lack; that this basis is not unrelated to the eschatological nature of the Christian view of history; and that Tolkien's imaginary world has a creation story that functions in a similar manner.

What is the result? Time with an ending, *telos*-driven time, now becomes a possibility in the biblical world, realized in the *protoevangelium* (Gen. 3:15). There is a plan to deal with the fall of Adam and Eve in the promise of a future seed who would come to crush the serpent's head. The fall is not going to be the final word; the world is not always going to be in the state created by the fall in a futile round of repetition as experienced by Tiâmat or as depicted on Achilles' shield. Fall and redemption are not an endless cycle endlessly repeated but singular events, one of which leads to the other. A *history* that is moving on purpose therefore begins from this moment of the fall, guided to its conclusion by a God who is able to do so. The creation story of Genesis has an opening sentence capable of generating this kind of history. We have to follow the history of Israel to its fulfillment to see the form it will take, but by the end of that narrative, messiah, atonement, sabbath rest, and indeed eucatastrophe, can be seen as already contained in the particular kind of creation we started with. For Tolkien the Christian, this simply was the "moving story" by which "Man the story-teller would have to be redeemed" (*Letters*, 89).

Middle-earth follows a similar pattern. In the beginning is Ilúvatar, the One, who creates the Ainur and sings to them a theme of music which they elaborate into a majestic symphony. But Melkor departs from the theme to create discord, occasioning a war in heaven of opposing musics. Then Ilúvatar introduces a Second and Third Theme which dovetail the rebellious notes of Melkor back into the score, causing the symphony to end in a grand resolution in spite of the efforts of Melkor and his followers to wrest it to their discordant will:

> Then Ilúvatar spoke, and he said, "Mighty are the Ainur, and mightiest among them is Melkor; but that he may know, and all the Ainur, that I am Ilúvatar, those things that ye have sung, I will show them forth, that ye may see what ye have done. And thou, Melkor, shalt see that no theme may be played that hath not its uttermost source in me, nor can any alter the music in my despite. For he that attempteth this shall prove but mine instrument in the devising of things more wonderful, which he himself hath not imagined." (*Silmarillion*, 17)

The Music then becomes the history of the world, in which the Second and Third Themes and the Final Chord are destined to be played out. The Valar and their servants the Maiar are those Ainur who enter into that history to help guide it to its destined conclusion. They each know perfectly only their own contributions to the Music, and there are secrets that Ilúvatar has kept reserved only for himself, but their presence at the original performance gives them prophetic insight into the unfolding. And therefore they know, because they were there, that, whatever Melkor-Morgoth and his servant Sauron may do, the Final Chord is coming and that therefore their labors are not in vain (*Silmarillion*, 16–18).

Ilúvatar then is no nature god. He is the creator of the Ainur, who are the creators under him of nature and are the stewards of its time and the guardians of its history. Middle-earth is therefore a theistic world with a *telos* element in its timeline, guided, as in Genesis, toward a redemptive conclusion, because it has a God whose transcendence gives him the capacity to fulfill such a role. It is because Ilúvatar is Ilúvatar that the Final Chord is coming and will be the ultimate triumph of good (*Silmarillion*, 16–18).

Tolkien's choice of metaphor is brilliant and deliberate. Western common-practice music—the kind of music Tolkien would have assumed— is a quintessentially linear art form. Without time signature and tempo, it is not music, just a solitary and meaningless tone. Thus, Tolkien does not indeed simply repeat the "Christian myth," but he captures its essence in an original myth of equally profound significance. Traditional-practice music, which may deal with discord but only on the way to a final cadence and resolution set up by the very nature of its scale, is then an essentially eschatological art form.[18] And therefore the Middle-earth which has music as its origin is an essentially eschatological world whose end is embryonically present in its beginning.[19]

Life in Arda Marred

The Great Music lies in what is for the Children of Ilúvatar in Middle-earth a mythological past. The Final Chord awaits them in a future that might, for all they know, be equally remote. But their present receives its peculiar quality from its position between those two anchor points. In the Second, Third, or Fourth Age, time as experienced by Elves or Men has one thing in common: It is the experience of life in Arda marred.

The peculiar mix of good and evil that is Arda, the peculiar mix of joy and sorrow that is life in Arda, arise not from the nature of the world's substance or from the interactions of matter and spirit within it, but from its history. Arda is good because it comes from the Music of Ilúvatar; it is corrupted because of the deeds of Melkor (who becomes known as Morgoth). The destruction of the Trees; the seduction of Fëanor; the lies sown in Morgoth's hatred of Ilúvatar, envy of the Valar, and contempt for Elves and Men; the torture and twisting of Elves into Orcs: These are not conditions that always existed—inherent in the nature of things—but evils wrought by a rebel. The Free Peoples are not trying to restore some mysterious balance between the forces of darkness and light but to defeat an Enemy.[20] If they understand their position in the larger story that gives meaning to life in Arda, they can continue the struggle with both realism and hope.

The realism lies in the understanding that the world *has* been marred. It is not as it was meant to be. That is why "as surely as the Valar began a labour, so Melkor would undo it or corrupt it," and also why "their labour was not all in vain" (*Silmarillion*, 22). In a foretaste of the final victory, Melkor is banished from the world, but the evil he has done remains behind, still augmented by his servants: "Yet the lies that Melkor, the mighty and accursed, Morgoth Bauglir, The Power of Terror and of Hate, sowed in the hearts of Elves and Men are a seed that does not die and cannot be destroyed; and ever and anon it sprouts anew, and will bear dark fruit even unto the latest days" (*Silmarillion*, 255). That seed will sprout anew *unto* the latest days. But, as the very use of such a phrase implies, not after them.

The hope lies in the understanding that if Middle-earth has not always been as it is, it does not always have to remain in its fallen state. The evil of Melkor will only be *finally* overcome in the Final Chord, and not until then, but it *will* be overcome then. Therefore, the sacrifices made in the struggle against him now are not in vain, even if mortals will not live to see their final fruition. The Final Chord is Ilúvatar's act, but even in the meantime he has not abandoned Middle-earth. He continues to work in it through his servants the Valar and the Maiar and through the faithful among Elves and Men. If Bilbo was "meant" to find the Ring, and not by its maker, there must be someone at work, and in the light of the *Ainulindalë*, that someone is Ilúvatar (*FR*, I, ii).

Meanwhile, those movements of the symphony when Melkor's discordant notes are braying can be very dark. Unlike the Valar, the Children of Ilúvatar were not present for the original Music and may not have a clear understanding of how it finishes. They may be able to see no farther than the words with which *The Silmarillion* concludes:

> Here ends the SILMARILLION. If it has passed from the high and the beautiful to darkness and ruin, that was of old the fate of Arda Marred; and if any change shall come and the Marring be amended, Manwë and Varda may know; but they have not revealed it, and it is not declared in the dooms of Mandos. (*Silmarillion*, 255)

The Children of Ilúvatar in the Second and Third Ages must therefore walk "by faith and not by sight" (2 Cor 5:7), dependent on the wisdom of a figure like Gandalf to bring them hope. But they are not left as wholly in the dark as the ending of *The Silmarillion* implies. As Ulmo says to Tuor, "In the armour of Fate (as the Children of Earth name it) there is ever a rift, and in the walls of Doom a breach, until the full-making, which we call the End. So it shall be while I endure, a secret voice that gainsayeth, and a light where darkness was decreed" (*UT*, 29). There is then a full-making, an end of sorrows hinted at, and those faithful to Ilúvatar are not utterly abandoned as they wait for it. The "Second Prophecy of Mandos," which was not included in the published *Silmarillion*, elaborates on that "full-making," speaking of a final victory of Good over Evil which even more resembles the one in the Christian Apocalypse.[21] Whether explicit or general, the basic framework and its significance is the same.

To understand the eschatological framework provided by the Final Chord is to gain insight into the wisdom of a character like Gandalf. It is what enables him to fulfill the mission of the Istari, to provide hope to the Free Peoples in their struggles against Sauron. To be a Maia who is a servant of the Secret Fire is to have access to a secret about the future that transforms one's vision of the present. To know that Ilúvatar's commitment to resolution at the end of the symphony has already found an expression in the past that anchors the future is to be set free to take risks that would otherwise seem doubtful. What makes Gandalf think that sending thirteen Dwarves and a Hobbit against a dragon has any chance of leading to anything other than disaster? What makes him think that sending a pair of tom-fool Halflings alone into Mordor with the Ring could possibly be anything other than the ultimate folly it seems to Denethor? Gandalf sings his own notes to the Music with knowledge of and anticipation of the cadence that is coming. As a Maia, he has, as it were, read the score and was present at the dress rehearsal.

Three beliefs then are intimately tied together for Gandalf and any who come to share his perspective: belief in the Final Chord, belief in Ilúvatar, and belief that we are not alone in our struggles against the darkness. If there is a Final Chord, there must be a composer, and if we can believe with confidence that it will be played at the end of history, there must be a conductor. If the Final Chord is to be guaranteed at the end by its presence in the beginning, then someone must guarantee it. In the case of Ilúvatar and Middle-earth, the conductor who composed it is still on the podium and still involved in the progress of the symphony. In this way three theological concepts, eschatology, theology proper, and Providence, all mutually entail one another, so that the presence of any one motif in the narrative invokes the other two, and the complex of the whole is the foundation of hope. (Motif? One is tempted to say *doctrine*; but while that word is appropriate for us readers, it may be too much for the characters.)

This complex of meaning is seen in many ways. It lies behind Cirion saying to Eorl that "I believe that the words of my oath, which I had not forethought ere I spoke them, were not put into my mouth in vain. We will part then in hope" (*UT*, 307). It allows Gildor to say to Frodo that "in this meeting there may be more than chance" (*FR*, I, iii). It explains Elrond's perspective that the Council was

> called, I say, though I have not called you to me, strangers from distant lands. You are come and are here met, in this very nick of time, by chance as it may seem. Yet it is not so. Believe rather that it is so ordered that we, who sit here, and no others, must now find counsel for the perils of the world. (*FR*, II, ii)

It is invoked in the myriad moments when the concept of chance comes up and a character or the narrator adds, "if chance you call it." And it may attain its highest expression in Gandalf's explanation to Frodo that "behind that there was something else at work, beyond any design of the Ring-maker. I can put it no plainer than by saying that Bilbo was *meant* to find the Ring, and *not* by its maker. In which case you also were *meant* to have it. And that may be an encouraging thought" (*FR*, I, ii).

Why is this an encouraging thought? Because if Bilbo was *meant* to find the Ring, there had to be someone to mean it, that is, to intend it. And this someone's intending, if it is to overrule the plans of the Ring Maker, must come from someone greater and more powerful than Sauron. This passage, only the vaguest of hints before the publication of the *Ainulindalë* in *The Silmarillion*, leaps into brilliant clarity in the light of the bigger picture thus provided. From this we see Tolkien intends that the directional intention for Middle-earth (eschatology), the existence and nature of Ilúvatar (his understanding of God's nature, i.e., theology proper), and Ilúvatar's continuing involvement behind the scenes to bring about the conditions necessary to fulfil his intentions (Providence) all mutually entail one another, so that the presence of any one in the narrative invokes the other two, and the complex of the whole is the foundation of hope. And that is an encouraging thought indeed.[22]

Life in Arda marred then is most intelligently and faithfully lived in the light of a realism that would lead to despair were it not for hope. Those who lose sight of the grounding of that hope—Saruman, Denethor, almost Théoden—fall into despair and become tools of evil. Those faithful to the ideals of the West who are most exemplary—Faramir, Aragorn, Frodo—remain so precisely by understanding and attending to that grounding.

It is no accident that Faramir, the most faithful of all the men of Gondor to its original ideals, inhabits the one place in the story of the Ring where we get a glimpse of a formal worship of Ilúvatar that is otherwise kept carefully in the background.[23] The breaking into the story of Númenórean worship at this particular point has to be significant: In a moment of silence before meat in Henneth Annûn, Faramir and his men "look toward Númenor that was, and beyond to Elvenhome that is, and to that which is beyond Elvenhome and will ever be" (*TT*, IV, v). It would seem that this "wizard's pupil" has profited from his instruction in Ilúvatarian theology. His rootedness in that which "will ever be," that is, in eternity as the backdrop which gives meaning to time and guarantees its proper unfolding, is the foundation of his integrity. Like Gandalf he can afford to make sacrifices and take risks because he believes that the changes in time, including the great one that will be the resolving Final Chord, depend on something that is bigger than he is and that is dependable because it is unchanging.

In "The Tale of Aragorn and Arwen," Aragorn too grounds his faithfulness in something larger than the provincial little slice of time available to the direct vision of even a long-lived mortal like himself. Trying to explain to Arwen his costly faithfulness at the end of his life, he roots their lives in more than just the present moment: "Let us not be overthrown at the final test, who of old renounced the Shadow and the Ring. In sorrow we must go, but not in despair. Behold! We are not bound forever to the circles of the world, and beyond them is more than memory. Farewell!" (*RK*, Appendix A, I, v). Arwen has given up the immortality of the Elves *within* the circles of the world for her marriage to Aragorn and now finds the Doom of Men hard to bear. Aragorn asks her to find a new hope by looking outside those circles.

What does he mean? He is certainly rejecting the lie that Morgoth told Húrin: "Beyond the Circles of the World there is nothing" (*UT*, 67). Metaphysically, beyond the circles of the world lie two realms we know of: the void into which Morgoth was thrust and the realm of Ilúvatar. Temporally, the circles of the world imply the cycles of finite time as mortals know it, at the end of which is the Final Chord which gives those cycles a beginning to end, *telos* element and thus includes the hope of a meaning-ful future existence for the Children of Ilúvatar. There are no details—only hints—"more than memory"—but that is all Aragorn needs. As with Faramir, Aragorn gives the people of Middle-earth an eschatological vision in which the meaning of life in time is found in its relation to eternity, and this rela-tionship is one they can trust to be the source of ultimate goodness for them because of the eternal character of Ilúvatar.

As the Ring-bearer, Frodo is at a place where all the spiritual forces of Middle-earth intersect and where all the themes of Tolkien's legend come into focus. Carrying the Ring shows Frodo things about evil, including its under-lying spiritual character and his own weakness, that most mortals never have to face directly. It strips away, not his idealism, but his pride and his illusions. His psychological and spiritual wounds from his quest are deep. Sometimes the loss of the Ring seems to leave him empty: "It is gone forever, and now all is dark and empty" (*RK*, VI, ix). But usually, he is able to be philosophical about his sufferings: "I have been too deeply hurt, Sam. I tried to save the Shire, and it has been saved, but not for me. It must often be so, Sam, when things are in danger: someone has to lose them, give them up, so that others may keep them" (*RK*, VI, ix).

Frodo thus sees more quickly and clearly the truth that must eventually confront all mortals: that Middle-earth is for them a good gift but only an inn, not their final home. That is why, unlike Sam, he cannot find healing in the Shire and in only a few years has to avail himself of the blessing of Arwen: "If your hurts grieve you still and the memory of your burden is heavy, then you may pass into the West, until all your wounds and weariness are healed" (*RK*, VI, vi).

Frodo does not yet leave the circles of the world; a mortal has to die to do that. But the far green country he finds is the true West, which in Tolkien's cosmology is that part of Middle-earth most in harmony with the Valar and nearest to Ilúvatar, and hence a place where Frodo may find peace and pre-pare himself for that final journey. And so Frodo's life, like the whole story of

Middle-earth, ends on a note of hope that points beyond itself to that greater destination: "And then it seemed to him that as in his dream in the house of Bombadil, the grey rain-curtain turned all to silver glass and was rolled back, and he beheld white shores and beyond them a far green country under a swift sunrise" (*RK*, VI, ix).

Middle-earth then has a single eschatological framework that applies differently to Elves and to mortals. Elves were made for immortality within the circles of the world, while Men must find theirs beyond them. That is why the chief characteristic distinguishing Men from Elves is their "seeking else-whither" (*UT*, 225). For both, the Final Chord of the Great Music lets them live in hope that the transcendent might and character of Ilúvatar guarantees a denouement to the story that is fulfilling for the faithful. And it is a good thing too, because the marring of Arda by Morgoth and those who follow him is not trivial but deep-rooted and devastating, such that faithfulness in Middle-earth needs all the encouragement it can get. Indeed, nothing less than the encouraging thoughts that come from Gandalf's wisdom could provide it.

CONCLUSION

Tolkien does not give us explicit analogs to elements of Christian eschatology the way Lewis does in *The Last Battle*, with its AntiChrist (the unwitting Puzzle), False Prophet (Shift), Beast (Tash), and Battle of Armageddon.[24] Instead, he creates a world with a more subtle form of eschatological thought, a thought that is similar to our own eschatological expectations that we derive from the Bible. Akin to our own world as seen through the lens of Scripture, Middle-earth has a teleological history that flows from the mind of its Creator as an intelligible story. This history is guaranteed by the character and the Providential action of that Creator so as to give it meaning and provide grounds of hope for the finite creatures who live in it if they are willing to walk by faith and not by sight (2 Cor 5:7). To understand one's place in that history is to gain the confidence that one's struggles against the dark are not wholly in vain.

Reading biblical prophecy and apocalypse gives its readers a great number of details to assimilate into their theology. Unfortunately, it is common for these details to cause readers to miss one of the most important eschatological messages. Reimagining our own eschatology in light of the story of Middle-earth can help us avoid that mistake—it can remind us of the way in which eschatology, as it flows from the nature of Ilúvatar and how he expresses himself in Middle-earth through Providence, can give us greater meaning and hope for our own vision of theology. And that may be an encouraging thought indeed.

NOTES

1. I have written extensively about that myself in *Mere Humanity: G.K. Chesterton, C.S. Lewis, and J.R.R. Tolkien on the Human Condition*, 2nd ed. (Chillicothe, OH: DeWard, 2018), 55–84; and *An Encouraging Thought: The Christian Worldview in the Writings of J.R.R. Tolkien* (Cambridge, OH: Christian Publishing House, 2018), 38–54.

2. Eschatology in Tolkien has received relatively little direct attention over the years, though some scholars have broached the topic, such as Wood (implicitly under the rubric of "consummation") and Whittingham (explicitly and substantively in chapter 6). See Ralph C. Wood, *The Gospel According to Tolkien: Visions of the Kingdom in Middle-earth* (Louisville: Westminster John Knox, 2003), 156–65; and Elizabeth A. Whittingham, *The Evolution of Tolkien's Mythology: A Study of the History of Middle-earth* (London: MacFarland, 2007), 170–91.

3. Peter J. Kreeft, *The Philosophy of Tolkien: The Worldview Behind* The Lord of the Rings (San Francisco: Ignatius, 2005), 68.

4. Kreeft, *Philosophy*, 99.

5. Matthew Dickerson, *Following Gandalf: Epic Battles and Moral Victory in* The Lord of the Rings (Grand Rapids: Brazos, 2003), 218.

6. Claudio Antonio Testi, *Pagan Saints in Middle-earth*, Cormarë 38 (Zurich: Walking Tree, 2018), 72.

7. Quoted in Verlyn Flieger, "The Arch and the Keystone" *Mythlore* 38:1 (2019): 15.

8. Flieger, "Arch," 10. Originally from Henry Resnick, "An Interview with Tolkien [March 2, 1966]," *Niekas* 18 (1967). The text of the interview can be found on Bradley Birzer's website at https://bradbirzer.com/2015/07/12/henry-resnick-interviews -tolkien-1966.

9. Verlyn Flieger, *Splintered Light: Logos and Language in Tolkien's World*, rev. ed. (Kent, OH: Kent State University Press, 2002), xx.

10. Flieger, "Arch," 7.

11. Even in emphasizing the supposed contradictions that define Tolkien, Flieger admits that this is a probable solution to the supposed contradiction, even if she ultimately rejects it; see Flieger, "Arch," 10.

12. Clyde S. Kilby, *Tolkien and* The Silmarillion (Wheaton: Harold Shaw, 1976), 82.

13. "Apsû was the primeval sweet-water ocean, and Tiāmat the salt-water ocean"; see Alexander Heidel, *The Babylonian Genesis: The Story of Creation*, 2nd ed. (Chicago: University of Chicago Press, 1951), 3.

14. *Enuma Elish*, Tablet VII:132–4, in Heidel, *Babylonian Genesis*, 59, cf. 17.

15. See for example Gen 21:33, where Abraham distinguishes Yahweh as "the Everlasting God" (*ēl 'ôlām*), and Ps 90:2, where God lives "from everlasting to everlasting" (*ûmē'ôlām 'ad-'ôlām*) (NASB). Keil and Delitzsch comment on the Psalm: "The Lord was God before the world was—that is the first assertion of vs. 2; His divine existence reaches out of the unlimited past into the unlimited future—this is the second"; see C. F. Keil and F. Delitzsch, *Commentary on the Old Testament* (Peabody: Hendrickson, 1996), 5:50–51. DeClaisse-Walford, Jacobson, and Tanner

confirm that "the opening verses tell of the eternity of God"; see *The Book of Psalms*, NICOT (Grand Rapids: Eerdmans, 2014), 693.

16. Homer, *Il.* 18.

17. "The fact that God never began to exist can be concluded from the fact that God created all things"; see Wayne Grudem, *Systematic Theology: An Introduction to Biblical Doctrine* (Grand Rapids: Zondervan, 1994), 169; cf., Millard Erickson, *Christian Theology* (Grand Rapids: Baker, 1998), 297.

18. Famous composer and conductor Leonard Bernstein put it this way: Musical "rightness" is "the feeling that whatever note succeeds the last is the only possible note that can rightly happen at that instant." It is "the power to make you feel at the finish: *Something is right in the world. There is something that checks throughout, that follows its own law consistently, something we can trust, that will never let us down*"; in his *The Joy of Music* (New York: Simon and Schuster, 1959), 28–29.

19. For more on Tolkien's use of the music metaphor, see Jane Chance, *Tolkien's Art: A Mythology for England*, rev. ed. (Lexington: University Press of Kentucky, 2001); and Robert A. Collins, "'Ainulindalë': Tolkien's Commitment to an Aesthetic Cosmology," *JFA* 11 (2000): 257–65.

20. See Michael J. Kruger, "The Battle of Worldviews: Dualism and Theism in Tolkien and Lewis," *Canon Fodder*, 18 Sept 2012, https://www.michaeljkruger.com/the-battle-of-worldviews-dualism-and-theism-in-tolkien-and-lewis/.

21. The canonicity of the "Second Prophecy of Mandos" is disputed, but its existence is consistent with and reinforces the indisputably canonical material we have cited; see Flieger, *Splintered Light*, 160–61; cf. Tolkien's letter to Milton Waldman, *Letters*, 149.

22. See Williams, *Encouraging Thought*, esp. 19–23, 28–32, for further explication of these ideas. For other significant discussions of the eschatology of Middle-earth, see Wood, *Gospel According to Tolkien*, 56–65 and Whittingham, *Evolution of Tolkien's Mythology*, 170–91. Wood supplements our focus here on general eschatology (concerned with the fate of the world) with a discussion of personal eschatology (concerned with the fate of individuals). Whittingham confirms the perspectives offered here with her own account of how "belief in Eru's ultimate goodness, which will bring good out of evil by renewing his creation, brings hope to elves and men" (191).

23. This is of course the Faramir of the books, who would not snare an orc with a falsehood and would not pick the Enemy's Ring up if he found it lying in the road. Peter Jackson's movie Faramir is not recognizable as the same person.

24. C.S. Lewis, *The Last Battle* (New York: Macmillan, 1956).

BIBLIOGRAPHY

Bernstein, Leonard. *The Joy of Music*. New York: Simon and Schuster, 1959.

DeClaisse-Walford, Nancy, Rolf A. Jacobsen, and Beth Laneel Tanner. *The Book of Psalms*. NICOT. Grand Rapids: Eerdmans, 2014.

Chance, Jane. *Tolkien's Art: A Mythology for England*. Rev. ed. Lexington: University Press of Kentucky, 2001.

Collins, Robert A. "'Ainulindalë': Tolkien's Commitment to an Aesthetic Cosmology." *JFA* 11 (2000): 257–65.

Dickerson, Matthew. *Following Gandalf: Epic Battles and Moral Victory in* The Lord of the Rings. Grand Rapids: Brazos, 2003.

Erickson, Millard J. *Christian Theology*. 2nd ed. Grand Rapids: Baker, 1998.

Flieger, Verlyn. "The Arch and the Keystone." *Mythlore* 38:1 (2019): 5–17.

———. *Splintered Light: Logos and Language in Tolkien's World*. Rev. ed. Kent, OH: Kent State University Press, 2002.

Grudem, Wayne. *Systematic Theology: An Introduction to Biblical Doctrine*. Grand Rapids: Zondervan, 1994.

Heidel, Alexander. *The Babylonian Genesis: The Story of Creation*. Chicago: University of Chicago Press, 1951.

Keil, C. F., and F. Delitzsch. *Commentary on the Old Testament*. 10 vols. Peabody: Hendrickson, 1996.

Kilby, Clyde S. *Tolkien and* The Silmarillion. Wheaton: Harold Shaw, 1976.

Kreeft, Peter J. *The Philosophy of Tolkien: The Worldview Behind* The Lord of the Rings. San Francisco: Ignatius, 2005.

Kruger, Michael J. "The Battle of Worldviews: Dualism and Theism in Tolkien and Lewis." *Canon Fodder*. Sept. 18, 2012. https://www.michaeljkruger.com/the-battle-of-worldviews-dualism-and-theism-in-tolkien-and-lewis.

Lewis, C.S. *The Last Battle*. New York: Macmillan, 1956.

Testi, Claudio A. *Pagan Saints in Middle-earth*. Cormarë 38. Zurich: Walking Tree, 2018.

Tolkien, J.R.R. *The Letters of J.R.R. Tolkien*. Edited by Humphrey Carpenter. Boston: Houghton Mifflin, 1981.

Whittingham, Elizabeth A. *The Evolution of Tolkien's Mythology: A Study of the History of Middle-earth*. CESFF 7. Jefferson, NC: MacFarland, 2008.

Williams, Donald T. *An Encouraging Thought: The Christian Worldview in the Writings of J.R.R. Tolkien*. Cambridge, OH: Christian Publishing House, 2018.

———. *Mere Humanity: G.K. Chesterton, C.S. Lewis, and J.R.R. Tolkien on the Human Condition*. 2nd ed. Chillicothe, OH: DeWard, 2018.

Wood, Ralph C. *The Gospel According to Tolkien: Visions of the Kingdom in Middle-earth*. Louisville: Westminster John Knox, 2003.

Ancient Literature Index

317

Modern Author Index

Subject Index

Page references for figures and tables are italicized.

327

About the Editor and Contributors

Douglas Estes (PhD, University of Nottingham) is associate professor of religion at New College of Florida. Douglas has written or edited twelve books including *The Tree of Life* (Brill, 2020) and published more than fifty essays and articles in journals such as *Journal of Theological Studies* and *Catholic Biblical Quarterly*. He most recently edited *Theology and Tolkien: Practical Theology* (Lexington/Fortress, 2023).

João Fernando O. Barboza (BA, Adventist University of São Paulo) graduated in theology and English and literature.

Bradley K. Broadhead (PhD, McMaster Divinity College) is pastor of Oyen Evangelical Missionary Church in Alberta, Canada. Bradley is the author of *Jazz and Christian Freedom: Improvising against the Grain of the Contemporary West* (Pickwick, 2018), along with a few articles on theology and music. As a trombonist, he has played in a wide variety of ensembles and has taught low brass for over a decade.

Devin Brown (PhD, University of South Carolina) is professor of English at Asbury University. He is the author of eleven books, including *Discussing Mere Christianity* (Zondervan, 2015), *The Christian World of* The Hobbit (Abingdon, 2012), and recent biographies of C.S. Lewis and J.R.R. Tolkien. He wrote the script for and appears in the documentary *C.S. Lewis: Why He Matters Today*. In 2008 he served as Scholar-in-Residence at The Kilns, Lewis's home in Oxford.

Lisa Coutras (PhD, King's College London) is a theologian and scholar specializing in the intersection of theology, philosophy, and literature. Coutras is known for her book, *Tolkien's Theology of Beauty: Majesty, Splendor, and Transcendence in Middle-earth* (Palgrave MacMillan, 2016). She currently teaches theology as adjunct faculty at Houston Christian University. She also serves as adjunct faculty at West Virginia University in the Department of Behavioral Medicine & Psychiatry, contributing to new interdisciplinary research on the intersection of addiction psychiatry and the writings of Tolkien.

Austin M. Freeman (PhD, Trinity Evangelical Divinity School) is the chair of apologetics at Houston Christian University and author of *Tolkien Dogmatics* (Lexham). He has several chapters on Tolkien in the peer-reviewed *Cormarë* series (Walking Tree) and has been published in the *Journal of Inklings Studies*. He is the editor of *Theology and H.P. Lovecraft* and co-editor of *Theology, Fantasy, & Imagination* (both in the Theology & Pop Culture series).

Martina Juričková (PhD, Constantine the Philosopher University in Nitra) is a postdoc assistant in the field of English studies at the same university. She focuses on literature and particularly on the work of Tolkien. Martina has published four articles in local academic journals, her most significant publications being "'What Punishments of God Are Not Gifts?' The Meaning of Suffering in Tolkien's Life and Work" (*Ars Aeterna*, 2018) and "Death— The Gift of God to Man: Exploring the Understanding of Death in Tolkien's Legendarium" (*Religion and the Arts*, 2023).

John C. McDowell (PhD, University of Cambridge) is the Dean of College at Yarra Theological Union in the University of Divinity, and full professor of philosophy, theology, and ethics. Prior to his time as the institution's director of research, he was the Morpeth Chair of Theology & Religion at the University of Newcastle, NSW; and the Meldrum Lecturer in Systematic Theology at the University of Edinburgh. He has authored several books and over seventy articles and book chapters in theology, philosophy and ethics, including the studies in popular culture: *The Politics of Big Fantasy: Studies in Cultural Suspicion* (McFarland, 2014); *The Ideology of Identity Politics in George Lucas* (McFarland, 2016); and *The Gospel According to Star Wars: Faith, Hope and the Force*, 2nd ed. (Westminster John Knox, 2017). He has contributed to a number of volumes on theology & pop culture: *Theology and Star Wars*, *René Girard and Pop Culture*, *Theology and Batman*, *Theology and Spider-Man*, and *Theology and the DC Universe*, as well as *Marvelling Religion*.

Alison Milbank (PhD, University of Lancaster) is professor of theology and literature at the University of Nottingham, where she teaches on many aspects of religion and culture, and Canon Theologian at Southwell Minster. She is the author of *Chesterton and Tolkien as Theologians: The Fantasy of* *the Real* (Bloomsbury, 2007) and several essays on Tolkien. Her most recent monograph is *God and the Gothic: Religion, Romance, and Reality in the English Literary Tradition* (Oxford University Press, 2018) and she is currently working on divine immanence and nature in the wake of the scientific revolution.

Allan M. de Novaes (PhD, Pontifical Catholic University of São Paulo) is associate professor at the School of Theology at the Adventist University of São Paulo (Brazil). He has contributed to volumes in the Theology, Religion & Pop Culture series: *Theology and Spider-Man* and *Theology and Protest Music*. His most recent work in English is the chapter "Entertainment" for *The Handbook on Religion and Communication* (Wiley Blackwell, 2023).

Jeremy M. Rios (PhD, University of St. Andrews) is an ordained minister and independent scholar whose research focuses on theological anthropology in Dietrich Bonhoeffer and Charles Williams. He also writes about spiritual formation, family systems theory, martyrdom, and questions pertaining to the collective-person. He blogs at jmichaelrios.wordpress.com, and has written or co-authored five books. Jeremy is married, has four children, and loves cooking, reading, films, and great conversation.

Adam B. Shaeffer (PhD, Durham University) rarely had time for books until he discovered the fantasy novels on his dad's shelf at age 12; the rest is history. His primary research interests revolve around the interplay between theology and literature, attending to fiction's power to narrate theological insights in and through the thoughts and lives of imagined people and places. His poetry and fiction have appeared in *Jabberwocky*, *Resident Aliens*, and *This Mutant Life*.

Beth M. Stovell (PhD, McMaster Divinity College) is professor of Old Testament and chair of General Theological Studies at Ambrose University in Calgary, AB, Canada. Beth has authored and edited several books including *The Book of the Twelve* (co-authored with David Fuller, Cascade, 2022), *Theodicy and Hope in the Book of the Twelve* (co-edited with George Athas, Daniel Timmer, and Colin Toffelmire, T&T Clark Bloomsbury, 2021), *Making Sense of Motherhood* (Wipf and Stock, 2016), *Mapping Metaphorical Discourse in the Fourth Gospel* (Brill, 2012), and *Biblical Hermeneutics: Five Views* (co-edited with Stanley E. Porter, InterVarsity, 2012). She is the series editor for the Apollos Old Testament Commentary series and on the editorial board for *Didaktikos* and the DNI (Dictionary of Nature Imagery) Supplement series.

Julie Loveland Swanstrom (PhD, Purdue University) is associate professor of philosophy and religion at Augustana University in Sioux Falls, South Dakota. In her works, she explores odd causal cases, modern medievalisms, and philosophical and theological connections in science fiction and fantasy. Julie has published in journals including the *American Catholic Philosophical Quarterly*, *Teaching Philosophy*, and the *American Association of Philosophers Studies in Pedagogy* as well as several international journals.

Milton L. Torres (PhD, University of Texas at Austin) is a graduate professor at the School of Theology at the Adventist University of São Paulo (Brazil). His most recent book in Portuguese is titled *Students and Disciples* (CRV, 2021), an analysis of the relationship between sophists and their disciples in the literary movement known as the Second Sophistic. He is currently researching what he deems Homeric imagery in the book of Revelation.

Charlie Trimm (PhD, Wheaton College) is associate professor of Old Testament at Biola University and a director of Every Voice: A Center for Kingdom Diversity in Christian Theological Education. Charlie is the author of *Understanding Old Testament Theology* (co-authored with Brittany Kim), *The Destruction of the Canaanites*, and *Fighting for the King and the Gods: A Survey of Warfare in the Ancient Near East*. His research interests include warfare and violence in the ancient Near East, Exodus, Old Testament ethics and theology, and the work of J.R.R. Tolkien.

Donald T. Williams (PhD, University of Georgia) is professor emeritus of Toccoa Falls College. A border dweller, he stays permanently camped out on the borders between theology and literature, serious scholarship and pastoral ministry, Narnia and Middle-earth. A past president of the International Society of Christian Apologetics who is known as an Inklings scholar and a Christian Apologist, he is the author of fourteen books, including *Deeper Magic: The Theology behind the Writings of C.S. Lewis* (Square Halo Books, 2016), *"An Encouraging Thought": The Christian Worldview in the Writings of J.R.R. Tolkien* (Christian Publishing House, 2018), and *Answers from Aslan: The Enduring Apologetics of C.S. Lewis* (DeWard, 2023).